INDUSTRIAL RELATIONS RESEARCH

ASSOCIATION SERIES

Collective Bargaining in the Private Sector

EDITED BY

Paul F. Clark, John T. Delaney, and Ann C. Frost

COLLECTIVE BARGAINING IN THE PRIVATE SECTOR. Copyright © 2002 by the
Industrial Relations Research Association. Printed in the United States of America. No
part of this book may be used without written permission, except in the case of brief quo-
tations embodied in critical articles or reviews.

First Edition

ISBN 0–913447–84–6

Price: $29.95

INDUSTRIAL RELATIONS RESEARCH ASSOCIATION SERIES:
Proceedings of the Annual Meeting
Annual Research Volume
Membership Directory (published every fourth year)
IRRA Newsletter (published quarterly)
Perspectives on Work (published biannually)

Inquiries and other communications regarding membership, meetings, publications, and
general affairs of the Association, as well as notice of address changes should be addressed
to the IRRA National Office.

INDUSTRIAL RELATIONS RESEARCH ASSOCIATION
University of Illinois at Urbana-Champaign
121 Labor and Industrial Relations Building
504 E. Armory Avenue
Champaign, IL 61820 USA
Phone: 217/333-0072 • Fax: 217/265-5130
Email: irra@uiuc.edu • Website: www.irra.uiuc.edu

CONTENTS

Private-Sector Collective Bargaining: Is This the End or a New Beginning?

Paul F. Clark
Pennsylvania State University

John T. Delaney
Michigan State University

Ann C. Frost
University of Western Ontario

Collective bargaining in U.S. private-sector industries is under siege. The unrelenting intrusion of global markets into corporate boardrooms and the general antipathy toward unions by managers have contributed to a substantial decline in union density since the 1950s. The inability of unions to organize new private-sector members, the rigid postwar legal framework regulating private-sector collective bargaining, and the passage of free trade agreements now threaten to make collective bargaining an anachronism. More importantly, because it has not been able to adjust to the new realities facing private-sector business, observers are beginning to ask whether the American system of collective bargaining is suited to satisfying the needs of workers and employers today.

This volume examines collective bargaining patterns in eight major industries in an effort to determine how the parties have responded to this challenging environment. While we make no claim that the sectors studied or experiences cited reflect the situation perfectly, we believe that the contributors offer an accurate view of the problems facing private-sector collective bargaining in the United States.

Background—Collective Bargaining Today

Over the past quarter century, the Industrial Relations Research Association (IRRA) has published three volumes of case studies examining collective bargaining in North American industries. Gerald Somers published the first volume in 1980 and Paula Voos the second in 1994. With private-sector union density having fallen to 9 percent in 2002, the contributors to this volume chronicle a very different set of experiences from the contributors to the previous volumes.

Jack Barbash's assessment of the state of collective bargaining in the book by Somers, for example, emphasized the importance of power in collective bargaining (1980:587–88). At issue was how power should be exercised and how closely it should be regulated by government. This was an important consideration in the late 1970s because unions had consolidated considerable bargaining power in numerous industries during the first three-quarters of the century. This power presented a significant challenge to management and to government and allowed unions to play a strong role in determining societal outcomes.

By the early 1990s, power was still an important issue in bargaining, but observers no longer characterized labor and management as equals. Contributors to the volume by Voos, instead, expressed concern about management's increasing dominance of labor relations. It was feared that firms were using their power to impose their will on unions and workers. For this reason, the role played by U.S. labor law was seen as a decisive factor. As Voos noted, "If we want to foster cooperative joint efforts—and our public policy interest in promoting high-wage, high-productivity outcomes suggests that we should—it will be necessary to change both the economic terrain and the laws that govern organizing and collective bargaining" (1994:19).

In recent years, the balance of power has continued to shift toward management's favor. With no change in U.S. labor relations law and policy in sight, the outlook for unions is generally worse than it was a decade ago. While the decline of North American unions is not the focus of this volume, that stark reality is the context within which the chapters that follow are set.

In some of the industries examined in this volume, circumstances have changed so greatly in recent years that the very future of collective bargaining is in question. Most notably, the trucking and newspaper industries may be nearing the end of the bargaining road. The dramatic decline of bargaining in trucking is illustrated by the assessments of the authors of the 1980, 1994, and 2002 IRRA volume chapters on that industry. Writing in 1980, Barbash summed up the state of collective bargaining in the trucking industry as one of "weak employers confronting a powerful union" (1980:562). In his chapter on the same industry for the 1994 IRRA volume, Mike Belzer suggested that the situation was almost desperate for the Teamsters union. And in his chapter for this volume, Belzer reports that things have gotten worse. A confluence of forces threatens to eliminate the unionized portion of the trucking industry. According to Belzer, only a temporary delay of the implementation of the North American Free Trade Agreement (NAFTA) trucking provisions has given breathing room to unionized truckers. The delay may end soon. Ironically, if Belzer is correct, that will mean that Jim Hoffa will oversee the decline of the union built and made famous by his father. While emerging trends are less dire in some industries, unions in most sectors face a difficult future in the collective bargaining arena.

American unions face several critical challenges at the start of the twenty-first century. Perhaps the most significant challenge is bargaining in an environment of steadily decreasing union density. Over the past decade, the percentage of private-sector employees represented by a union has declined from about 13 percent to 9 percent. Similarly, representation rates in manufacturing industries declined from 21 percent in 1992 to less than 16 percent in 2001. As union density declines, so does union bargaining power. And as union bargaining power diminishes, so do the outcomes of bargaining for union members. For example, the union/nonunion wage differential has been affected by changes in union representation rates. Historically, union workers have earned about 15 percent more than nonunion workers in the same industry. In a 1997 National Compensation Study survey, the Bureau of Labor Statistics reported that the overall union/nonunion wage differential was 4.3 percent. Notably, the same survey indicated that the union/nonunion wage differential for blue collar workers was almost 38 percent. The results suggest that unions have been able to secure substantially higher compensation for employees with lower skill levels but not for higher skilled or service sector employees. This pattern, in turn, likely encourages employers to fight unionization efforts among lower-paid workers and discourages employees in high skill jobs and growing segments of the economy from joining unions. This one–two punch, in turn, reinforces the decline in union density.

Even in the auto industry, as Harry Katz, John Paul MacDuffie, and Frits Pil explain, declining unionization among parts suppliers has contributed to a reduction in wages in that segment of the industry. More telling is the fact that the United Auto Workers (UAW) has had very little success in organizing employees in firms outside of the Big Three (General Motors, Ford, and DaimlerChrysler). As the market share of those other firms grows and auto companies seek to expand modular production (which would shift some work from the automobile manufacturers to parts makers), the bargaining power of the UAW is diminished.

The chapters that follow suggest several trends and developments in collective bargaining. Some are continuations of long-standing patterns (e.g., auto assembly). Others appear to be new developments and are difficult to interpret (e.g., telecommunications). Some trends are ominous, such as the situation in trucking, though they may be a necessary precursor to the reinvention of the labor movement. Clearly, there are few instances in the private sector where collective bargaining proceeds today as it has for the past few decades. Following, we discuss some of the issues to consider when assessing the chapters.

Collective bargaining patterns and results vary considerably across the industries included in this volume. This, of course, is not a new finding. Workers in the auto industry, for example, continue to benefit from strong bargaining gains, while truckers and newspaper workers have generally seen their outcomes erode. There is also evidence of variation within industries. For example, airline pilots have negotiated generous outcome packages at a time when flight attendants and customer service employees have made less progress. Unionized drivers working for United Parcel Service (UPS) have negotiated solid bargaining gains, while other unionized truck drivers have been much less fortunate. Similarly, the wage structure in some professional sports (e.g., basketball) has been altered to reduce the initial salary for rookies. In general, these variations are a function of bargaining power. Differentials in bargaining power exist among certain occupations because of employee skill levels, the presence of solidarity, or some other unique attribute.

A second phenomenon seen in many of the industries discussed in the volume is the inability of unions, with some exceptions, to prevail in traditional job actions against employers. This factor is a manifestation of bargaining power and has likely reduced employers' fear of strikes. Moreover, the reduction of strike activity has created an environment in which the general public and perhaps some union members have little conception of what a strike is or does. As Howard Stanger's description of the situation in the newspaper industry attests, without a credible strike threat, unions have difficulty winning significant improvements in compensation, benefits, and working conditions. In such cases, the benefits of joining a union are not obvious. Where union–management cooperation has been beneficial to firms, as in the telecommunications industry, unions have secured better outcomes than competitive marketplaces would otherwise allow. But it seems clear that many employers prefer a nonunion environment to one in which there is union–mangement cooperation.

A third finding that can be drawn from the chapters that follow is that collective bargaining generally plays a far less significant role in society today than in the past. Collective bargaining outcomes and events are in the news less often today than perhaps at any other time since the 1940s. For unions, "out of sight, out of mind" could come to be "out of mind, out of existence." Unfortunately, another part of this trend is that the occasional news story about union corruption, violence, or ineffectiveness is not offset by positive stories about the benefits of unions or the gains to society that result from bargaining.

Fourth, a fundamental cause of the labor movement's ineffectiveness in the collective bargaining arena is its inability to organize new workers. Despite a significant shift of resources into organizing over the past decade, unions have not been able to recruit enough new members to stem the overall decline in membership. And some of the areas in which the labor movement has had success may have limited upside potential. For example, the unionization of graduate assistants at U.S. universities will likely provide little of the secondary benefits that resulted from organizing the automobile industry seventy years ago.

At the same time, some external developments suggest that we are in a new era and that historical bargaining patterns (and their implied trends) may no longer apply. Collective bargaining has potentially been altered by international terrorism, changing workforce conditions and worker expectations, outmoded labor laws, and the imbalance created when unions organize on a national basis and markets operate globally.

September 11 and Terrorism

Just as the general global environment changed on September 11, 2001, the threat of terrorism has raised new issues in many industries, including airlines, hospitality, trucking, and professional sports. The new environment could change the role and status of unions. Security concerns could be a critical issue in bargaining involving airline employees. As Nancy Brown Johnson suggests, those concerns have created interest in training programs focusing on such issues as self-defense, assessing passengers more closely, providing weapons to pilots, the screening of passengers and employees, and the incorporation of new background checks for airline employees. Union leadership in these areas could garner member and public support. Union interest, investment, and experience in training have historically been strong. Such leadership could help airline unions gain widespread public support, which would aid the union movement generally, and increase air passenger traffic. In particular, efforts to address some of the less popular security procedures adopted by airlines at the behest of the U.S. government could increase the support for unions among the traveling public.

One consequence of the September 11 attacks was a dramatic drop in demand for travel-related facilities and services. The hospitality industry was especially hard hit. As Jeffrey Waddoups and Vincent Eade indicate, members of the Hotel Employees and Restaurant Employees International Union (HERE) suffered approximately 11 percent (88,000 out of 800,000) of the layoffs occurring in the United States as a result of the attacks. While there are signs that the travel industry is recovering, the economic impact on hotel and hospitality workers has been significant. Moreover, the decline in attendance is likely to affect bargaining in unionized hospitality establishments into the foreseeable future. Prior to the terrorist attacks in the fall of 2001, the labor movement had been buoyed by its success in the hospitality industry. As one of its few significant success stories in recent years, the sector provided some glimmer of optimism to organized labor. The future of collective bargaining in the industry was inalterably changed on September 11.

As Belzer reports, security has also become a great concern in the trucking industry. Issues ranging from the issuance of permits to transport hazardous waste to granting Mexican drivers full access to U.S. highways have come under increasing scrutiny. These concerns could aid organized truckers enormously if they further delay the implementation of NAFTA provisions on trucking. The involvement of the union movement in efforts to oversee security concerns in trucking could also generate public, management, and government support.

The sports industry has similarly been affected by security concerns, albeit to a lesser extent. Attendance at sporting events could be impacted by the more stringent security measures that are being introduced in venues across the country. If attendance falls, revenues will fall as well. Clearly, this would have implications for bargaining in this high-profile industry.

Joint union–management initiatives regarding security could have a positive impact on union growth generally. As virtually every workplace receives mail, the anthrax incidents that followed September 11 are potentially relevant to all workers. Union efforts in this area, both individually and jointly with management, could be seen by workers and the public as a sign that organized labor can play an important role in the workplace. In light of September 11, few industries can ignore the possibility of terrorism. Bargaining over security-related concerns could provide unions with an opportunity to be seen in a positive light by both employees and the public. While it is not possible to predict the long-term effect of the September 11 attacks on U.S. employers or unions, clearly the ramifications of the events of that day are widespread and significant.

Changing Working Conditions

Technological change has long played an important role in union–employer relations. In recent years change has touched virtually every industry and has created a situation in which workers need to acquire new skills. Simultaneously, as markets have placed increasing pressure on firms to operate efficiently, the demand for skills has intensified among lower-level employees. This situation is apparent in the health care industry. Hospitals and health care facilities have increased the proportion of lower-skilled (and lower-paid) employees in their workplaces in an effort to cut costs. Health care workers have also experienced another common workplace phenomenon—the intensification of the pace of work in an effort to increase productivity. This is leading to widespread dissatisfaction in health care and is creating one of the more promising situations for union organizing.

In some industries, employers have used technological change to reduce the extent of unionization. As Jeffrey Keefe and Rosemary Batt indicate, unionized workers in the telecommunications industry tend to be concentrated in the wireline segment of the industry. This segment is growing more slowly than other segments and relies on older technologies that are quickly being replaced. Given that workers need to possess increasingly sophisticated skills to meet employers' expectations, unions may discover an opportunity for organizing and bargaining in the rising pace of work that is apparent in many industries. At the same time, global competition has intensified the nature of work in many workplaces. Union efforts to lessen the intensity of work, accordingly, could create a situation in which a firm is unable to survive. Put differently, union efforts to change situations in firms will not alter the market pressure to compete. This could increase the outsourcing of union jobs to nonunion locations in the United States and other nations. Accordingly, union efforts to address the implementation of use of new technologies will become increasingly important in future bargaining.

The Changing Workforce and Workers' Expectations

Ironically, although increases in the intensity of work should cultivate employees' interest in unions, it is not clear that this inevitably leads workers to desire representation. Richard Freeman and Joel Rogers (1999), in a widely cited book, reported that almost all of the union members in their study and about one-third of the nonmembers were interested in maintaining or acquiring some form of union representation (pp. 68–70). At the same time, survey respondents generally indicated that they preferred some form of representation that worked cooperatively with employers (p. 5) and that "existing institutions—from unions to EI [employee involvement] committees to government regulations—are either insufficiently available to them or do not go far enough to provide the workplace voice they want" (p. 154). Workers today want to participate at work. This finding has supported speculation that declining union density is due to a variety of constraints, such as antiquated labor laws or unfair tactics by employers.

There is another explanation. Although the sentiments expressed by workers in the Freeman and Rogers survey would seem to open the door for unionization, organized labor's traditional approaches may not be desired by today's employees. To the extent that unions are seen as opposing employers, they may be viewed as a suboptimal solution to the problem of employee voice. Employees may want representation—just not by a traditional union. It is also worth considering that employees may not desire traditional collective bargaining over wages, hours, and other terms and conditions of employment. They may wish input into the design of products, the selection of supervisors, or the processes used to produce a product or provide a service. If this is the case, collective bargaining, as currently practiced, will not provide the outcomes employees seek. The dearth of research in this area means that we do not know what employees really want from their cooperative interaction with their employers. Until we know more, it is unwise to assume they want a traditional bargaining approach or relationship.

The Outdated Nature of Prevailing U.S. Labor Law

As we have noted, U.S. labor law has been criticized for many years as being unfriendly to unions. Unions, as well as many independent observers, have argued that the National Labor Relations Board (NLRB) and U.S. courts regularly rule in favor of employers, nonunion workers who do not seek union representation, and conservative groups (e.g., National Right-to-Work Committee). In recent years, it has been argued that the politicization of workplace relations has prevented even minor changes in the existing system of laws covering employee–employer interactions. As Thomas Kochan has forcefully argued, it is time to create a new social contract—one that aligns today's workforce with the institutions and regulations that govern it (Kochan 2000). Kochan's concern is based on the growing problems arising from the incongruity between many Depression era laws and the reality of today's occupational structures, global marketplace, and changing employee preferences. Considerable evidence exists to suggest that there are aspects of U.S. labor law that create significant problems for unions. First, these laws cover an increasingly smaller proportion of the potential workforce. As exclusions grow, the power of traditional collective bargaining declines. Paul Clark provides an excellent example of this phenomenon in his discussion of recent U.S. Supreme Court decisions that address the issue of whether registered nurses are employees covered by the National Labor Relations Act (NLRA) or managers who are excluded. The underlying issue is the fact that the occupational composition of the workforce has changed dramatically since the NLRA was enacted. Because of the increase in managerial and professional work; the decline in manual, craftsman, and other laborer positions; and the increase in managerial duties for all sorts of employees, more employees have been excluded from coverage by the Act. The result is that the NLRA has become relevant to fewer and fewer workers over time (Sockell 1989).

Exclusion occurs because the workers are seen by labor tribunals as managers, independent contractors, or supervisors. The recent cases involving nurses suggest the courts may be moving in this direction regarding that profession. As most nurses direct the work of other health care employees, courts are increasingly defining them as managers who are excluded from coverage by the NLRA. Among other reasons, the inclination of courts to move in this direction is critically important because of the growing use of employee teams by employers. These teams are often given some say in decisions that the courts view as managerial in nature. Accordingly, it is inevitable that future interpretations of the NLRA will exclude more occupations from coverage. This will make it difficult for a greater number of employees to organize and bargain using traditional approaches.

Second, under the NLRA the scope of bargaining traditionally has not extended beyond wages, hours, and other terms and conditions of employment. This often excludes issues that are becoming increasingly important to employees, unions, and employers. Essentially, the existing scope of bargaining permits the establishment of an economic arrangement between employers and unions. Internal union affairs are left to unions alone to regulate, and employers have a virtual monopoly on decisions involving the business and where it should go in the future. At a time when the nature of jobs has changed and employees often have broader responsibilities, the existing scope of bargaining is increasingly out of step with employees' desires. This likely reduces employees' interest in traditional union representation.

Whereas many researchers have focused in recent years on legal impediments to unions in organizing campaigns, we believe the declining scope of coverage under the NLRA and the narrow scope of bargaining are equally significant problems. Even if the labor movement were able to win changes in the law that might make it easier to organize new workers, it is likely that, over time, the economy would render any such changes irrelevant. The structure of the economy is changing in ways that will accelerate the exclusions previously mentioned. And the narrow scope of bargaining creates a situation in which collective bargaining provides few benefits for employers and increasingly ignores issues of concern to workers. These factors will likely create pressures in all industries that do not favor union representation. For example, Stanger notes the problems that have arisen for newspaper unions attempting to address the growth of digital publications. Existing union rivalries, approaches, and conventions have worked to impede organizational success.

Interestingly, unions have engaged in few efforts to organize outside of the NLRA, and researchers have offered little advice on the likely success of such operations. Although this possibility seems to be viewed as a no-win situation, it may soon be one of the few avenues open to unions interested in representing workers. The current situation makes it likely that some organizing and bargaining efforts outside of the scope and protection of the NLRA are inevitable in coming years. Success in such efforts may allow unions to revitalize themselves and improve their image in society.

Structural Dilemmas—National Unions in a Global Marketplace

Unions were successful in the past, in part, because they were able to "take wages out of competition." When all competing employers paid the same union wage scales, employers needed to compete on other bases. Today, in a global marketplace, it is increasingly impossible for U.S. unions to take wages out of competition. Firms regularly transfer operations to other countries in order to lower costs and improve economic results. This illustrates a dilemma faced by the world's labor movement. Firms are increasingly organized on a global basis, while unions are organized on a national or local one. This makes it more difficult for unions to deal effectively with competitive decisions made by businesses. Moreover, global business organization ensures that labor laws favorable to unions in a particular country will likely come under pressure over time as businesses respond to the perceived disadvantage of such laws and relocate operations to other nations.

In several of the chapters, contributors mention the increasing efforts of unions to consolidate in an effort to better compete with employers. Until union movements coordinate their efforts more effectively on a global basis, employers will retain an advantage. As there are many factors standing in the way of such consolidation, it is difficult to be optimistic about the future of organized labor. To the extent that unions coordinate efforts, however, it may be possible for national unions to gain occasional victories in negotiations with employers.

Conclusions

Overall, the state of collective bargaining in the U.S. private sector in 2002 is mixed. In several industries, bargaining appears to be on the decline. In only a few does it appear that bargaining has the potential to play a greater role in the future than it has in the past. In virtually all of the industries studied, collective bargaining is going through a period of change.

The plight of collective bargaining is directly tied to labor's inability to organize new workers. With few exceptions, union organizing efforts have not offset yearly membership losses due to plant closings, layoffs, and retirements. And while some observers contend that workers would join unions if there were fewer risks associated with doing so (e.g., Freeman and Rogers 1999), a good case can also be made that there is little clamor for bargaining from the people who could benefit most from it. Power remains a central theme in any analysis of collective bargaining in the U.S. private sector. If unions cannot organize more effectively in the future than they have in the recent past, union power will continue to erode.

Although the trends have been negative for many unions, considerable variation exists in the prevailing strength of bargaining across U.S. private-sector industries. In particular, unions representing employees in occupations that have strong bargaining power by virtue of their special skills and are thus difficult to replace (e.g., pilots, star athletes, etc.) continue to negotiate favorable outcomes. Bargaining unit members in other occupations, however, face increasingly difficult times in their efforts to secure gains.

In industries that have maintained union density in core jobs (e.g., autos, telecommunications), some bargaining power remains. The main challenge to unions, however, differs across those sectors of the economy. In the auto industry, the UAW must organize new competitors (often foreign transplants that locate in parts of the United States that have been traditionally unsympathetic to unions). The union must also work with Big Three employers to increase their market share. Such cooperation will create a difficult dilemma for the union, as it will face pressure from members to steer the gains of cooperation to members rather than managers or shareholders. Unless enough of the gains go to the firms, corporate investment in unionized plants will likely decline. If the UAW is not able to walk this thin line effectively, the UAW's future may be dimmer than it otherwise might be. This issue will be especially salient in the next several years as Japanese firms seek to gain increased market share in segments of the industry that have driven profits for the Big Three (e.g., SUVs and large pickup trucks).

In telecommunications, the challenge is to ensure that firms allow unionized workers to participate in growing segments of the market, such as wireless communications and Internet protocol communications, rather than assigning such work to nonunion employees. While unions in this industry will also face pressure from both employers and employees, they will be required to lobby in concert with firms for regulatory actions that help the industry. As unions have long been active politically, joint efforts with employers in this arena could lead to enhanced options for unionized telecommunications employees.

The specific challenges in other industries differ, though unions uniformly must find a way to enroll new members and to gain public support. Depending on the circumstances facing specific unions, the trend may be toward productivity bargaining or de-unionization. At the margin, however, unions in every industry face significant pressure to change. Minor adjustments have not made organized labor stronger in recent years. When John Sweeney swept into power at the AFL-CIO, there was hope that an increased emphasis on organizing would help the labor movement grow. Investments in this area, however, have not produced the kinds of results necessary to change labor's fortunes. Simultaneously, campaign finance reform legislation threatens to weaken unions' political power. The current state of the labor movement raises the issue of whether the product unions are offering to potential members is an attractive one. The context provided across the chapters suggests some insight into the ways that different unions have sought to make their product more attractive. Attention to this concern may signal the industries that have a union presence a decade from now. At a minimum, the variation in union approaches across industries offers promise that some potential solutions will emerge. The critical nature of the predicament faced by some unions may be the impetus necessary for change and revival. If this is the case, the trucking and newspaper industries merit watching. Pressure from several sources puts in doubt the future of bargaining in those sectors. How unions in these two industries respond will provide a clue as to the labor movement's future. That future is tied inextricably to the rise of talented new union leaders—ones who are ready to jettison practices, and even tradition, if necessary to create a revival.

Many forces influencing collective bargaining are outside the control of unions. For example, recent court decisions mean that bargaining may be negated for many employees who have a possible managerial component in their normal duties. Depending on how courts view team-based arrangements in industries such as the hospitality sector, it is possible that recent union gains could be short-lived. In the past, national boundaries posed severe restraints on organized labor. Today, unions have likely reached a point where international combinations present one of the few opportunities to revitalize the labor movement. The political situation in the United States likely will continue to diminish the power of the union movement in the foreseeable future. And if a significant number of union leaders continue to be unwilling or unable to break with the past, mechanisms other than collective bargaining may arise to aid the interests of workers.

Does collective bargaining have a future in the American private sector? We invite readers to draw their own conclusions about this critical question as they read about the experiences of the eight major industries examined in this volume.

References

Barbash, Jack. 1980. "Collective Bargaining: Contemporary American Experience—A Commentary." In Gerald G. Somers, ed., *Collective Bargaining: Contemporary American Experience*. Madison, WI: Industrial Relations Research Association, pp. 553–88.

Freeman, Richard B., and Joel Rogers. 1999. *What Workers Want*. Ithaca, NY: ILR Press.

Kochan, Thomas A. 2000. "Building a New Social Contract at Work: A Call to Action." *Perspectives on Work*, Vol. 4, no. 1, pp. 3–12.

Sockell, Donna. 1989. "The Future of Labor Law: A Mismatch Between Statutory Interpretation and Industrial Reality." *Boston College Law Review*, Vol. 30 (July), pp. 987–1026.

Somers, Gerald G. (ed.). 1980. *Collective Bargaining: Contemporary American Experience*. Madison, WI: Industrial Relations Research Association.

Voos, Paula. 1994. "An Economic Perspective on Contemporary Trends in Collective Bargaining." In Paula Voos, ed., *Contemporary Collective Bargaining in the Private Sector*. Madison, WI: Industrial Relations Research Association, pp. 1–23.

Voos, Paula (ed.). 1994. *Contemporary Collective Bargaining in the Private Sector*. Madison, WI: Industrial Relations Research Association.

CHAPTER 1

Airlines: Can Collective Bargaining Weather the Storm?

NANCY BROWN JOHNSON
University of Kentucky

Airline industrial relations exists inexorably intertwined with the regulatory environment. The airline industry grew and developed under the Civil Aeronautics Board's (CAB) tight rein on market controls of pricing and routes. Airline unions, sensitive to the labor advantages of these regulatory controls, leveraged these protections to insulate their wages and working conditions from market vagaries and to make inroads into organizing a significant portion of the labor market. The Airline Deregulation Act of 1978 lifted the route and pricing restrictions that the CAB had firmly placed on the airlines for more than forty years and plunged the airlines into the competitive foray that continues unabated at the onset of the twenty-first century.

As the airlines began to face deregulatory reality of competition and the resulting pressure on cost containment during the early 1980s, airline management put pressure on labor to provide the airlines with financial relief necessary for the airlines to survive. This period was extremely tumultuous, as many airlines were in an extremely precarious financial position. Reducing labor costs appeared to be the strategy of choice for many carriers in the drive to maintain a competitive position in the industry if not for mere survival. Thus, airline industrial relations during this period and well into the 1990s remained strained at best.

Despite the carrier pressure on airline labor in the deregulatory era, there is compelling evidence that the airline industry remains one of the strongholds of traditional industrial relations. The industry arguably is the most unionized in the country. High-performance work practices and other managerial innovations are rare. Traditional adversarial relations continue to be the norm. However, although adversarial, airline labor–management relations occur within a subtext of consultation that may obscure the degree of participation that truly exists.

At the onset of economic deregulation, many commonly believed that regulation led to increased union power. Thus, they surmised that deregulation would lead to an erosion of union effectiveness. Nonetheless, air transport continues to be the most highly organized industry in the private sector, with union density estimated to be at 39.5 percent in the late deregulatory period between 1983 and 1997 (Hirsch and Macpherson 2000). This is down somewhat from the regulatory period, in which representation rates reached almost 50 percent (Hirsch and Macpherson 2000). In contrast, by 1995, unions represented about 37.5 percent of the public sector and slightly over 17 percent of construction and manufacturing workers (Masters 1997).

Hendricks, Feuille, and Szerszen (1980) presciently observed that the industry's institutional characteristics that arose under regulation would likely remain relatively intact in the deregulatory environment. Part of the institutional environment that has persevered is the continued existence of regulations that do not deal with economic controls. Button (1991) points out that the term "deregulation" is a misnomer, as regulations continue to endure and influence the industry. He suggests that the British term "regulatory reform" more aptly describes the dynamic regulatory environment than does "deregulation." Although safety and other regulations affect airline labor, the Railway Labor Act arguably has the greatest continuing regulatory effect on airline industrial relations. This law, and to a great extent its interpretation, has remained constant and continues to play a significant role in influencing the institutional environment.

This is not to say that the competitive landscape has left the climate of industrial relations and its effects on individual workers unscathed. Mergers, bankruptcies, and failures have played a significant role in individual workers' lives. Yet, after more than twenty years, deregulatory pressure on airline industrial relations may not be as great as once anticipated. However, a new chapter in airline industrial relations may be written in the aftermath of the September 11, 2001, attacks on the World Trade Center and the Pentagon. These events have dramatically shaken the industry and may have as much, if not greater, effect on airline industrial relations in the short run than did deregulation.

The Legal Environment

Despite the change in regulation in the product market, industrial relations continues to fall under the jurisdiction of the Railway Labor Act (RLA) of 1926. The RLA was amended in 1936 to include the airlines, based on lobbying by the Air Line Pilots Association. The RLA differs from the National Labor Relations Act (NLRA) in both spirit and scope. Unlike the contentious environment under which the NLRA was enacted, management and labor in the railroads jointly drafted the RLA. The overriding emphasis of the legislation was, and continues to be, the avoidance of service disruption through the promotion of industrial peace (Eischen 1976; Northrup 1990; Wilner 1990). At the time of enactment, a rail industry strike could have devastated the entire country. The RLA differs from the NLRA with respect to the scope of its jurisdiction and remedies for violation of the law. First, with respect to scope, the RLA is charged with dealing with four major types of disputes: representation, statutory, minor, and major disputes. Representation disputes deal with the selection and certification of an exclusive bargaining representative. Statutory disputes, typically under the jurisdiction of the courts, result from a statutory requirement under the RLA but no administrative process to handle the obligation. Disputes involving interference with the employee's right to self-organization typically fall under the statutory provisions. Unlike the NLRB, the National Mediation Board (NMB) has no authority to adjudicate such factors, leaving these matters entirely up to the courts.

Minor disputes are typically grievances over the interpretation of the agreement, and major disputes are over the formation or modification of a contract. The distinction between minor and major disputes affords a continuing source of contention between management and labor under the RLA, stemming from the dissimilar procedural requirements for each. Minor disputes legally result in binding arbitration, while major disputes have an extensive resolution process. Under the RLA, contracts do not expire; they simply become amenable, which further obscures the line between contract interpretation and modification.

Because of the lack of a definitive contract expiration date, one criticism of the RLA is that negotiations can continue ad infinitum. Upon entering negotiations, the parties submit an intent to change the contract to the NMB. If the parties have not reached an agreement once negotiations proceed, they can request mediation through the NMB. Should mediation fail to reach agreement and agreement does not appear forthcoming, the NMB proffers arbitration on the remaining issues. The parties may reject arbitration beginning after a thirty-day cooling-off period. After expiration of the thirty days, either side may engage in self-help, leaving the union free to strike or engage in other concerted activity and the carrier able to impose its last best offer, temporarily cease operations, or engage in other self-help activity. The president of the United States can institute a presidential emergency board (PEB) to intervene in the dispute if he deems that a dispute will substantially interrupt interstate commerce. If a PEB is created, the parties must refrain from self-help for an additional sixty days to give the board thirty days to issue its report and the parties another thirty days to reach an agreement. The board is essentially a fact-finding board that makes settlement recommendations. If no agreement is reached during the sixty days, either side may engage in self-help.

The dispute resolution process contributes to extended negotiations under which the parties must adhere contractually to the status quo. Some view this procedure as unduly cumbersome and extensively drawn out (Bartholomew 2000; Northrup 1990). Others argue that the process, although extensive, clearly meets the primary objective of the RLA: the avoidance of service disruption, while allowing both sides to fashion their own agreement (Stone 1990). Thus, there seems little disagreement that the negotiation process under the RLA is lengthy; however, whether or not the extensive process is a curse or a blessing remains open to question.

RLA Representation Elections

The NMB also conducts representation elections and certifies the exclusive bargaining agent. The board establishes bargaining units on a craft or class basis across an entire airline. Crafts are typically defined very narrowly, leading to a number of units and unions at a single carrier. However, unions must organize across all locations of a carrier. This carrier-wide basis was designed to prevent a carrier from being shut down from a strike at a single location and to avoid service disruption from union rivalry across locales (Northrup 1990). The NMB typically conducts elections by mail using a ballot that does not contain a "no union" option. Unions must obtain the majority of the workers in a unit voting for representation.

The RLA differs from the NLRA with respect to elections in that the law does not explicitly contain unfair labor practices. The NMB is largely charged with administering the process; however, employees, unions, and carriers enforce the RLA largely through lawsuits (Morris 1998). Violation of the law may result in criminal penalties for interference with the right to organize or remain unorganized, employees' right to bargain collectively, and the right of the majority to select his or her craft or class (Leslie 1995). However, Morris (1998) points out that criminal charges are almost never used under the RLA.

The NMB is limited in its response to violations of "laboratory conditions." They typically order rerun elections. In the case of egregious election interference, the board will order that the election be conducted with a "Laker" or a "Key" ballot. The Laker ballot is simply a ballot that has the option to vote for or against union certification, with the majority of those voting being decisive. In a Key ballot election, the NMB certifies the union unless the majority votes against representation. Hence, anyone who does not vote is voting for the union. Both ballots are considered a lower hurdle to union success than the traditional ballot. The Key ballot is reserved for those carriers with the most egregious election interference (Northrup 1990).

Despite the lack of remedies, Morris (1998) suggests that labor can obtain quick injunctive relief in the case of terminations for union activity. He argues that swift injunctive relief, under the RLA, effectively deters carriers from this type of termination, which has become commonplace under the NLRA. He contrasts the speed of this form of injunctive relief with the provisions under the NLRA, which may take up to three years to find an employer guilty of discrimination for union activity. Morris (1998) found only fifteen published court decisions and four federal cases where the courts considered injunctive relief under the RLA for an employee terminated for union activity between 1970 and 1985. Only fourteen of the forty-eight employees involved in these cases were reinstated. Despite the rarity of these cases, Morris (1998) argues that the threat and speed of injunctive reinstatement contribute to the infrequency of terminations for union activity under the RLA, resulting in a more level playing field between labor and management in representation disputes.

The Future of the RLA

The RLA clearly has its opponents (Bartholomew 2000; Northrup 1990), who contend that the law contributes to endless negotiations, fragmented bargaining with a multitude of unions, and a structure that fails to flexibly adapt to the changing product environment. Others contend that the joint labor–management foundation, under which the RLA was crafted, continues to this day (Airline Industry Labor–Management Committee 1996; Commission on the Future of Worker–Management Relations 1994; Stone 1990). The Dunlop Commission, in its meetings with labor and management of the air and rail industries in the mid-1990s, found agreement that the general spirit of the law, the avoidance of strikes and major disruptions, had been met (Commission on the Future of Worker–Management Relations 1994). A joint airline labor–management committee further reinforced support for the law in a follow-up report to the Dunlop Commission. They stated decisively that the RLA should not be legislatively altered. The report concluded, "While each side could develop a 'wish list' of legislative enactments that might further their own parochial interests, both have concluded that the potential for disruption far outweighs the marginal gain that any legislative refinements might provide" (Airline Industry Labor–Management Committee 1996:ii). Further, although the committee raised some concerns regarding the administrative efficiency of the NMB, they did strongly support the NMB retaining jurisdiction for the administration of the RLA. In part, this recommendation stemmed from the fact that to transfer some of the NMB's responsibilities to other government agencies would require legislatively tampering with the RLA. They recommended that the NMB continue its initiatives to improve efficiency in serving its constituents (Airline Industry Labor–Management Committee 1996).

The Workers and Their Unions

Because the airline industry is organized by carrier and craft, a number of different unions represent the workers in the industry, as Table 1 illustrates. Unions within the airlines tend to have a fairly narrow scope. Although a few unions dominate the industry, small and independent unions factor significantly into the labor environment. Historically, coordinated bargaining across crafts within a carrier or across carriers has not occurred. These unions traditionally operate independently and tend to work together mainly under extensive threats (Walsh 1994).

Pilots

Pilots began organizing efforts in the late 1920s (Katz, Zanar, and Dominitz 1999). These organizing efforts paid off in 1931, when David Behncke founded the Air Line Pilots Association (ALPA) and began as its first president. The incentive to organize stemmed from management pushing pilots to fly in unsafe conditions, including bad weather (Hopkins 1982). The practice of emphasizing productivity over safety resulted in relatively high mortality rates for pilots. At this point, most pilots were engaged in flying mail under contracts with the U.S. Post Office. By 1932, 70 percent of all major airlines were members of ALPA, and by the mid-1930s almost 100 percent had joined the union (Cohen 1990).

Pilots were also actively involved in wage issues. In 1932 they struck Century Airlines in response to a 40 percent wage cut (Cohen 1990). Although strikebreakers were hired, the airline was quickly sold to American Airlines. ALPA listed the names of the strikebreakers in the first issue of the *Air Line Pilot*, the union's publication, and its efforts to penalize strikebreakers were so effective that it was reported that a

TABLE 1

Major Unions of the Major Carriers in the Airline Industry

Airline	Pilots	Flight attendants	Mechanics	Passenger service
Alaska	ALPA	AFA	AMFA	IAM
America West	ALPA	AFA	IBT	Nonunion
American	APA	APFA	TWU	Nonunion
Continental	IACP (merging with ALPA)	UFA	IBT	Nonunion
Delta	ALPA	Nonunion	Nonunion	Nonunion
DHL Airways	ALPA	NA	IBT	NA
Federal Express	FEDEX Pilots	NA	Nonunion	NA
Northwest	ALPA	IBT	AMFA	IAM
Southwest	SWPA	TWU	IBT	IAM
Trans World	ALPA	IAM	IAM	IAM
United	ALPA	AFA	IAM	IAM
United Parcel Service	ALPA	NA	IBT	NA
US Airways	ALPA	AFA	IAM	CWA

Note: NA = Not applicable.
AFA—Association of Flight Attendants
ALPA—Air Line Pilots Association
AMFA—Aircraft Mechanics Fraternal Association
APA—Allied Pilots Association
APFA—Association of Professional Flight Attendants
CWA—Communications Workers of America
FEDEX Pilots—FedEx Independent Pilots
IAC—Independent Association of Continental Pilots
IAM—International Association of Machinists and Aerospace Workers
IBT—International Brotherhood of Teamsters
SWPA—Southwest Pilots Association
TWU—Transport Workers Union
UFA—Union of Flight Attendants

strikebreaker would have to go to South America to find work. Cohen (1990) describes this strike as a victory in terms of enhancement of union solidarity and strength, even though the striking pilots lost their jobs.

Almost from its inception, ALPA was active politically (Kahn 1976; Katz, Zanar, and Dominitz 1999): For six years following the Century Airlines strike, the pilots made no attempt at collective bargaining but rather focused their efforts on achieving their objectives through legislation. Franklin Delano Roosevelt had canceled the postal contracts because of exposed fraud between the airlines and the postal officials. Although most pilots criticized this action, Behncke publicly supported it and, at the same time, requested federal safety protection for pilots. The Air Mail Act of 1934 included provisions to fix maximum hours and minimum pay. Behncke also went on to lobby and obtain coverage for the airline industry under the RLA. Although his first attempt failed in 1932, he was successful in 1936 (Kahn 1976). Finally, pilots also effectively lobbied to obtain a National Labor Board (NLB) decision that made their pay a function of base pay, flight pay, and mileage pay formally incorporated into the Civil Aeronautics Act of 1938. Organization of mechanics began in 1937 and most had contracts by 1944 (Kahn 1976). The flight attendants' union was founded in 1945. They affiliated with ALPA in 1949 and split off from them in 1973.

ALPA continues as the dominant pilots' union. By 2001, ALPA had more than 59,000 members at forty-nine U.S. and Canadian carriers (ALPA–TWA 2001). ALPA represents pilots exclusively and currently represents nine of the thirteen pilot groups among the major carriers; they are in the process of merging with the independent union that represents the Continental pilots. Organized by carrier into master executive councils, each council conducts negotiations and governs affairs related to that airline. The union continues to play a leading role in the industry in terms of bargaining, politics, and regulatory matters (Walsh 1994). However, independent unions continue to represent pilots at American, Federal Express, and Southwest.

Airline pilots clearly have a strategic skill position in the airlines. The airlines cannot operate without them, and investment in training is extensive, making replacement during a strike virtually impossible. The majority of airline pilots have a college degree, and many have graduate or law degrees; they also must have a minimum of 1,500 hours flying experience and instrument and nighttime ratings. To acquire flying hours, most pilots desiring careers in the passenger airlines begin their careers as flight instructors. They then advance to a regional carrier and then make a move to the majors. Airline pilots are predominantly white males; only 3.7, 1.9, and 4.3 percent of pilots are women, blacks, and Hispanics, respectively (Bureau of Labor Statistics 2000). Pilots represent approximately 6.5 percent of total industry employment (Bureau of Labor Statistics 1999). Hirsch and Macpherson (2000) report union density for pilots between 1983 and 1997 to be 58.7 percent, on average.

Pilots' wages are among the highest in the nation; however, given their extremely steep wage profiles, they start relatively low and advance to progressively higher wages. Because of the heavy human capital investment, carriers use steep wage progressions to reduce turnover by making it costly to leave. Median pay for pilots in 1999 was $107,990 annually (Bureau of Labor Statistics 1999). However, pilots at the 10th,

25th, and 75th percentiles of annual wages were earning $35,340; $53,100; and $145,600, respectively, demonstrating wide pay variability (Bureau of Labor Statistics 1999). First-year starting pay can be as low as $17,000 annually at the regional carriers and $25,000 at the majors. Captains at the majors in 1998 earned an average $161,052 but only $80,823 at the nationals (AIR Inc. 1998), thus putting regional airline pilots in the lower tier of the wage structure.

Flight Attendants

Although flight attendants are a relatively unskilled occupation, many have some college education. Most carriers train flight attendants over a period of four to seven weeks prior to employing them (Bureau of Labor Statistics 1999). Flight attendants are about 80 percent female, 12 percent black, and 8 percent Hispanic (Bureau of Labor Statistics 2001). Flight attendants have relatively steep pay scales, with median annual earnings at $37,800 in 1988. In 1998, they started as low as $13,700 per year and could progress to $50,000 annually as a senior flight attendant at a major airline (Bureau of Labor Statistics 1999, 2000). Many are employed part-time. Walsh (1988) states that many carriers view flight attendants as expendable and encourage their turnover. However, this philosophy runs counter to a pay system with relatively steep seniority ladders. Hirsch and Macpherson (2000) report union density for flight attendants between 1983 and 1997 to be 72.8 percent, making them the most unionized craft in the airline industry.

Table 1 indicates that no single union is the clear choice of flight attendants. Of the ten major passenger carriers, the Association of Flight Attendants (AFA) represents workers at four of the airlines; two are represented by independent unions; and the International Brotherhood of Teamsters (IBT), the International Association of Machinists and Aerospace Workers (IAM), and the Transportation Workers Union (TWU) represent the remaining flight attendants. The AFA is the major flight attendants' union, representing more than 49,000 flight attendants at twenty-seven airlines (AFA 2001a).

Delta Airlines is the only major carrier without a flight attendant union, despite the AFA's repeated attempts to organize them. Delta established a Flight Attendant Forum in 1996 that is composed of locally elected representatives who address issues of work rules, per diem compensation, and process improvement (Cone 2000). The forum operates in direct consultation with the board of directors. Although this form of nonunion representation would represent an 8(a)(2) violation under the NLRA, it is legal under the RLA unless it takes place during an ongoing union election (Kaufman and Taras 2000). Cone (2000) perceives that the forum represents an effective voice of the nonunion workers within Delta. If the majority of flight attendants share this perception, it could serve to effectively deter formal unionization.

Mechanics

Aircraft mechanics is a skilled trade with a minimum of 1,900 hours of training over the course of two to three years. Unlike pilots and flight attendants, mechanics have job opportunities for employment outside the airline industry. Approximately two thirds of all aircraft mechanics work in the airline industry. The remainder are employed by the government or aircraft manufacturers (Bureau of Labor Statistics 1999). As with the pilots, the majority of mechanics are white males; only 6.1 percent are female, 8.3 percent are black, and 9.0 percent are Hispanic. Unionization for mechanics is lower than that of pilots and flight attendants, at 46.7 percent on average between 1983 and 1997 (Hirsch and Macpherson 2000).

The fact that mechanics can work outside the industry is reflected in their representation. In contrast to pilots and flight attendants whose unions generally only represent airline workers, mechanics have unions that have membership drawn from a variety of industries. With five of the thirteen major carriers, the IBT has the greatest number of bargaining units among the larger carriers. The IAM and the Aircraft Mechanics Fraternal Association (AMFA) represent workers at three of the major carriers each. This is a shift from the early 1980s, when the IAM represented workers at seven of the eleven major airlines. Some of the shift arose from both the failure and absorption of some airlines. However, mechanics at some airlines changed union representatives. For example, the IAM lost representation status when Continental Airlines filed bankruptcy during the 1980s to abrogate its labor agreements. The IBT was certified to represent the Continental mechanics in 1997. Recently, the AMFA has made inroads in organizing aircraft mechanics. In 1998 and 1999 the AMFA displaced the IAM as the representative of the airline mechanics at Alaska Airlines and Northwest Airlines, respectively. The AMFA organizes on the basis that it is a craft union exclusively in the airline industry, making it better suited to address the needs of its constituents.

Summary

The airline industry has extremely fragmented and dynamic representation (Cappelli 1985; Walsh 1994). Not only do a variety of unions represent workers in the airline industry, it is not unusual for the unions to play a representational form of musical chairs. Other than ALPA, no union has a clearly dominant presence in the industry. Even with respect to pilots, four (and soon to be three) of the major carriers have independent union representation. Flight attendants and mechanics have no clear representative of choice. At one time, the majority of mechanics were represented by the IAM. However, as of 2001, the IAM's presence among the major carriers has diminished and that of the AMFA and the IBT appears to have increased.

The Airline Industry

History of Regulation

The industry arose and evolved in a heavily regulated climate. The early carriers focused on obtaining contracts with the U.S. Post Office in the 1920s. These early mail contracts tended to avoid route competition and focused on expanding the nation's route structure (Pickrell 1991). In an interim period, the early mail contracts were transferred to unregulated private operators. However, this led to the proliferation of contradictory state laws and contributed to the desire for federal law. The Air Commerce Act of 1926 gave the Department of Commerce regulatory authority over the industry. Most of its early efforts focused on safety. Economic regulation began in the late 1930s, with the establishment of the Civil Aeronautics Authority in 1938, which later became the Civil Aeronautics Board (CAB).

The CAB exercised complete economic control over the industry in terms of entry, exit, pricing, and routes. After initially granting route authority to the existing sixteen trunk carriers, the CAB consistently turned down petitions for new service. The CAB consideration of existing carriers' expansion of new routes focused on granting the routes to weaker carriers to balance the relative competitive strength among the existing trunk carriers. The main concession the CAB granted to new carriers in the 1950s was to allow local service carriers to begin providing service to smaller communities (Pickrell 1991). Over time, these carriers expanded and provided jet service over regional networks. The CAB set fares based on distance traveled and forbade discounted fares. This left the carriers to compete almost exclusively on service.

By the mid-1970s, there were rumblings among Congress, the academic community, and several renegade airlines that the rigidity of the CAB restrictions was problematic. The economists argued that the regulations artificially restricted competition, leading to higher prices. At the same time, Southwest Airlines and Texas International created a natural experiment testing this theory by operating exclusively within the boundaries of Texas. As intrastate carriers, they were unconstrained by federal regulation and began competing on price and efficiency. As such, they provided the concrete justification for deregulatory efforts. Informally, deregulation began with the CAB administratively loosening restrictions in 1975 for charter carriers and allowing American Airlines to offer discounted fares. The Airline Deregulation Act of 1978 formally eliminated the CAB's authority over fares and routes and phased out the CAB entirely by 1984.

Airline Economics and Deregulatory Effects

Several features inherent to the airline industry make it somewhat unique. First, the industry is not a single market. Rather, the industry represents the sum of city pairs, each representing a market. Thus, competition is determined by the nature of direct opposition on these routes more than the number of competitors within the industry. As Alfred Kahn (1988), the father of airline deregulation, observed, deregulation established that route structures, not economies of scale, were the driving factor of carrier cost differences. Second, these route structures theoretically are somewhat flexible due to the mobility of capital—aircraft—that can be relatively easily deployed to other locales. However, the existing infrastructure constrains this flexibility in that airport gate access and air traffic control capacity are limited and continue to be regulated to some degree. Finally, the perishability of the product does not allow carriers to inventory their services.

Competition

Increased Industry Concentration. A major concern of deregulatory opponents was that it would lead to destructive competition, leading to increased industry concentration of a few dominant carriers controlling the market. Empirical evidence suggests that this has not been the case (Morrison and Winston 1995). However, recent mergers, such as the one between American Airlines and TWA, raise the specter that the industry is continuing to become increasingly condensed.

In general, evidence exists that suggests that airline competition is alive and well. There are more carriers at the onset of the twenty-first century than existed at the time of deregulation. Table 2 lists the larger certificated carriers for 1978 and 1999 (those carriers holding certificates to operate commercially from the Department of Transportation). Majors, nationals, and regionals are the largest carriers, based on total revenue. Although the number of major carriers has decreased from fourteen to thirteen, the number of nationals has grown from eleven to thirty-two. Overall, there were thirty-two certificated carriers in 1972 and eighty-nine by the mid-1990s. Thus, the vast majority of growth is with smaller start-up carriers. However, these carriers are also more apt to fail.

Historically, most airlines are dissolved through mergers or the direct sale of part of the airline operations and not because of complete closure of operations. The recent rise in merger activity raises concern of increasing consolidation within the industry. The industry has always been relatively concentrated. Cohen (1990) reports that in 1931 the four largest carriers flew 53 percent of the total miles flown. By 1983, these same largest four carriers' market share fell to 45 percent. However, by 1999 it rose to 64 percent. Of the fifty-eight carriers that began operations between 1978 and 1990, only America West is still operating, although its present financial condition remains somewhat precarious (Morrison and Winston 2000). Despite this record of failure, new carriers continue to enter the market but at significant peril. Although a federal judge in 2001 threw out an antitrust case alleging American Airlines used predatory pricing to force three small start-ups from the market, only one of the three start-ups has survived (Wilkey and MacCartney 2001). At the same time, a number of existing major carriers are or are attempting to combine. In the spring of 2001, the Justice Department approved a merger between American Airlines and TWA but quelled a merger between US Air and United in the following summer because of its anticompetitive effects. Thus, there is some reason to believe that the increased consolidation could reduce competition in some markets. Research evidence supports this concern in providing evidence that fare increases stem from increased market shares of dominant carriers (Kim and Singal 1993).

These mergers pose interesting issues for labor and have led to a diverse set of responses by the unions. ALPA, for example, endorsed the merger of American and TWA (ALPA–TWA Master Executive Council 2001) but expressed concerns regarding the US Airways and United merger (ALPA 2000). Note that the Justice Department approved the TWA–American merger but not the US Airways–United merger. Further, ALPA has obtained contractual language to approve or disapprove of code-sharing alliances and to negotiate over mergers (ALPA 1998).

Once mergers are approved, the question of representation remains. This falls under the jurisdiction of the RLA. The policy of the board is to first determine whether the merger truly constitutes a single transportation

TABLE 2

Number of Employees at Larger Certificated Carriers, 1978 and 1999

1978		1999	
Carrier	Employment	Carrier	Employment
Majors		*Majors*	
American	38,115	Alaska	8,962
Braniff	13,399	America West	11,162
Continental	15,328	American	86,277
Delta	34,674	Continental	38,730
Eastern	38,556	Delta	70,640
Flying Tiger	6,824	DHL Airways	8,537
Northwest	10,443	Federal Express	118,947
Pan American	35,267	Northwest	49,999
Piedmont	3,892	Southwest	26,938
Republic	12,633	Trans World	20,259
Trans World	36,540	United	92,216
United	53,831	United Parcel Service	4,858
US Airways	8,745	US Airways	39,852
Western	10,559	**Total majors**	**577,377**
Total majors	**318,806**		
		Nationals	
Nationals		Air Transport	602
Airlift	957	Air Wisconsin	1,770
Alaska	1,222	Airtran Airlines	3,529
Aloha	1,119	Aloha	1,995
Capital	732	American Eagle	6,991
Frontier	5,076	American International	468
Hawaiian	1,669	American Trans Air	5,881
Ozark	3,809	Arrow	373
Transamerica	1,773	Atlantic Southeast	2,640
Wien		Atlas Air	630
World	1,234	Challenge	764
Zantop	1,065	Continental Express	3,146
Total nationals	**18,656**	Continental Micronesia	1,398
		Emery	3,282
		Evergreen	550
		Executive	975
		Frontier	1,468
		Hawaiian	2,766
		Horizon Air	3,372
		Kitty Hawk	196
		Mesaba	2,719
		Midway	667
		Midwest Express	2,261
		Polar	422
		Reno Air	1,186
		Ryan	976
		Spirit	1,395
		Sun Country	1,177
		Tower	852
		Trans States	2,210
		US Airways Shuttle	398
		World	645
		Total nationals	**57,704**

Source: Air Transport Association.

system (requiring an integration of the separate bargaining units into a single unit) and then to determine which union will represent the consolidated carriers if two unions had representation rights at the former carriers. The board does not determine that a single transportation system exists until the operational merger occurs (*American Airlines/Reno Air*, 26 NMB No. 85, 1999). Once the board makes this determination, it must then determine which union will represent employees in the new system. When there is a disparity in size of the existing bargaining units, the NMB will certify the union representing the largest group of employees without an election (*Continental Airlines/Continental Express*, 20 NMB 326, 1993). The NMB will hold runoff elections between the existing unions when combining bargaining units of relatively equal size.

Competition on Routes. Another measure of competitive activity is the amount of competition on a specific route. Morrison and Winston (2000) found a general increase in competitive activity from 1977 to 1999, in that the average number of carriers per route has increased from 1.7 to 2.2. However, their research also found that the nature of competition varies, based on whether an airport has hub status, as hubs tend to create a virtual monopoly for the dominant carrier in that market. Another controlling factor in determining the extent of competition is the mere presence of Southwest Airlines in the market. This airline has virtually defined low fares and has strived to keep fares low in every market where it has a presence.

Southwest Airlines has become such a key factor in airline price competition that Morrison and Winston (2000) accounted for them separately. These authors found that the premium fares attributed to hubs may not be so much a hub premium as a non-Southwest Airlines market premium. What is interesting to consider is that Southwest has achieved price leadership not through a low-wage nonunion strategy but rather what Gittell, Nordenflycht, and Kochan (forthcoming) term the "high road of employee relations." At Southwest, the major employee groups are unionized, and wages are usually found to be at or above market.

Overall, most analysts have found that the airline fares have declined significantly from the regulatory era (Morrison and Winston 1995, 2000; Pickrell 1991). However, price discrimination appears to be a significant concern for a few. Morrison and Winston (1995) estimate that those with more inelastic demand (e.g., business travelers) represent about 14 percent of the market and pay roughly twice what they likely would have paid under regulation.

The industry has grown significantly since deregulation. Table 3 lists industry performance data by year from 1970 to 1999. The revenue passenger miles (RPMs), the amount of miles flown by paying customers, have increased almost five times since 1970. The capacity of the system has also increased by over three times, as measured by available seat miles (ASMs).

TABLE 3
Airline Industry Performance Measures

Year	System RPMs (in millions)	System ASMs (in millions)	System load factor (%)	Operating profit ($000)	Net profit ($000)
1970	131,710	265,120	49.7	43,031	(200,503)
1971	135,658	279,823	48.5	328,475	28,007
1972	152,406	287,411	53.0	584,470	214,851
1973	161,957	310,597	52.1	585,266	226,693
1974	162,919	297,006	54.9	725,740	321,641
1975	162,810	303,006	53.7	127,879	(84,204)
1976	178,988	322,822	55.4	721,933	563,354
1977	193,219	345,566	55.9	908,040	752,536
1978	226,781	368,751	61.5	1,364,863	1,196,537
1979	262,023	416,126	63.0	199,055	346,845
1980	255,192	432,535	59.0	(221,615)	17,414
1981	248,888	424,897	58.6	(454,770)	(300,826)
1982	259,644	440,119	59.0	(733,435)	(915,814)
1983	281,829	464,538	60.7	310,410	(188,051)
1984	305,116	515,323	59.2	2,151,511	824,668
1985	336,403	547,788	61.4	1,426,264	862,715
1986	366,546	607,436	60.3	1,323,101	(234,909)
1987	404,471	648,721	62.3	2,468,889	593,398
1988	423,302	676,802	62.5	3,436,503	1,685,599
1989	432,714	684,376	63.2	1,811,267	127,902
1990	457,926	733,375	62.4	(1,912,335)	(3,921,002)
1991	447,955	715,199	62.6	(1,784,741)	(1,940,157)
1992	478,554	752,772	63.6	(2,444,460)	(4,791,284)
1993	489,648	771,641	63.5	1,438,172	(2,135,626)
1994	519,382	784,331	66.2	2,713,455	(344,115)
1995	540,656	807,078	67.0	5,859,518	2,313,591
1996	578,663	835,071	69.3	6,209,069	2,803,915
1997	605,574	860,803	70.3	8,586,794	5,167,657
1998	618,086	874,090	70.7	9,327,810	4,903,203
1999	651,597	917,849	71.0	8,403,305	5,360,252

Source: Air Transport Association.
RPMs—revenue passenger miles
ASMs—available seat miles

Despite this growth, the profitability of the industry has varied widely and is never large. The industry was in significant financial peril in the early deregulatory period and again in the early 1990s. At the beginning of the 1990s, Southwest was the only major airline making money. The Gulf War, the recession of the early 1990s, increases in fuel prices, and the overcapacity of the industry were problems driving the lack of profitability (Rosen 1995). The industry clearly is cyclically sensitive, and the economic conditions of 2001 (high fuel costs and a declining economy) clearly suggest that airlines may quickly be placed in the financial peril that they faced at the beginning of the 1990s. However, Morrison and Winston's (1995) estimates found that factors under management control (load factors, longer lengths of haul, and greater route densities) primarily determine carriers' long-term financial success.

Air travelers continually lament the decline of airline service. In the days of regulation, because the CAB controlled prices and routes, carriers only had service as a basis of competition. Thus, flights operated at less than half full (load factor) and were complete with amenities. Under deregulation, load factors have risen on average to over 70 percent, as shown in Table 3. Thus, many flights are full or approaching capacity. Some argue that service declines as a function of the number of people on a flight. Meal service has been cut dramatically, as it adds another level of costs. Customer complaints of lost baggage, sitting on the runway for hours, and missed connections have increased to the point where airlines have been forced to voluntarily adopt "passengers' bills of rights" or risk Congress imposing them. Delays stemming from a lack of infrastructure at landing facilities and airports and an antiquated air traffic control system have become common. Nonetheless, service has increased if you take into account flight frequency.

Future Challenges

Within the domestic market, the greatest challenge is keeping the infrastructure growing at the same rate as the industry. Most economists agree that a crumbling infrastructure supporting air transportation provides a significant barrier to free and open competition (Kahn 2000; Morrison 2000). In particular, an inadequate and outmoded air traffic control system and aging airports foster crowding and congestion. Further, the unavailability and expense of gate access at hubs further restrict competition and serve to drive up prices. Thus, the lack of infrastructure tends to limit the capacity of the system and hinders competition, in that only a limited number of carriers can obtain sufficient economies of scale to serve a particular market.

There is a trend toward increased industry globalization (Oum, Park, and Zhang 1996). Historically, each country, according to the Paris

Convention of 1919, has complete sovereignty over its airspace (Woerth 1995). The United States has continually argued for "open skies" agreements that would negate the Paris Convention and allow carriers free and open access to all airports. However, open skies arguments have not prevailed, leaving each country to negotiate bilateral agreements to gain access and landing rights. Because governments are slow to negotiate these bilateral agreements, carriers use global alliances to gain access to foreign locales and circumvent governments. These alliances have almost doubled, from 280 in 1994 to 502 in 1998, and typically entail jointly engaging in sales and marketing, passenger and cargo service, mutual insurance, frequent flyer programs, and ground operations and maintenance (Hanlon 1999). By the end of the 1990s, these alliances have expanded with the formation of multilateral agreements among a set of carriers. Three major alliances include Oneworld, Star, and Wings. Oneworld, for example, includes British Airways, American, Cathay Pacific, and Qantas and has 15 percent of the world airline business (Hanlon 1999). Some predict that transnational airlines may exist in the near future (Hanlon 1999). However, significant legal and political constraints provide momentous barriers to the implementation of transnational airlines.

Unions worry that carriers will use these alliances to whipsaw their various unions. Thus, ALPA and the Allied Pilots Association have begun to devise alliances that parallel those of the carriers. These alliances meet regularly to coordinate union strategy and develop scope limitations. The IFALPA, the international pilots association, facilitates the discussion to address international issues that affect pilot health and safety. An example of cooperative action across carriers was a memo requesting mutual assistance of ALPA members by the Czech Air Line Pilots Association invoking the mutual assistance policies of the IFALPA, including a ban on extra flights or capacity, a recruitment ban, and assistance for pilots stranded away from their home base (ALPA 2001a). Nonetheless, these global alliances pose thorny issues for labor because they must surmount myriad labor laws, institutional practices, and cultures.

Summary

The airline industry has undergone considerable changes since deregulation. First, the industry has grown significantly, in that there exist more airlines with more flights carrying more passengers than ever before. Next, carriers have restructured routes to form hub-and-spoke systems. Due to infrastructure constraints, this reorganization tends to leave hubs with a single airline with more or less monopolistic control over the hub market. After the wave of new entrants in the 1980s, the industry appears to be in the process of consolidating both through mergers and code-sharing alliances, raising fears of increased prices in the long term.

Overall, deregulation appears to have lowered fares but more so for the customer with elastic demand, served by a nonhub market, with Southwest Airlines as a competitor. The business traveler with inelastic demand most likely pays more than he or she would have under regulation. Consistent profitability has been elusive for all but Southwest due to the cyclical nature of the airline business, making it difficult to accurately forecast demand for capacity. However, the boom of the late 1990s moved many airlines from the brink of failure to operating in the black. Overall, there is some evidence that profits have increased moderately following deregulation but with considerable variability and cyclical sensitivity.

Bargaining Outcomes

Wages

Perhaps the most significant feature of the airline industry bargaining context is the fragmentation of both representation and the subsequent bargaining process. Mark Kahn summed up the essence of bargaining in the airline industry in 1976:

> Given the fact that most airlines deal with four to six major bargaining units in collective bargaining, that the bargaining is on a single-carrier basis, that the bargaining process under the Railway Labor Act (as we shall see) is often a protracted one, and that jurisdictional and representation disputes are not uncommon, it is understandable that the airline industry is rarely free of significant union-management issues and potential work stoppages. (Kahn 1976:109)

This statement still represents the status of airline collective bargaining at the beginning of the twenty-first century. Because representation is determined on a carrier and craft basis, it encourages bargaining fragmentation. Decentralization is the norm. The structure of ALPA and the AFA, which organizes locals on a carrier basis, further reinforces the parochialism of the airline bargaining structure (Walsh 1994). Industrywide attempts at bargaining have always failed (Kahn 1980). However, regulation served to reinforce a form of pattern bargaining (Cappelli 1985). Because the CAB reduced price competition by setting fares on a cost-plus basis, management had little incentive to obtain price cost advantages. Thus, some economists argue that the regulatory environment created an incentive for labor to extract rents and that deregulation would lead to a relative decline in wage levels reflecting the new competitive landscape. However, early evidence was that these wage-level reductions were not found (Card 1986, 1989; Johnson 1991; Hendricks 1994). This led some to speculate that regulatory rents either were never achieved or that union strength in the deregulatory environment continued the extraction of rents (Card 1989).

More recent studies, however, have begun to find significant declines in airline workers' wages (Hirsch and Macpherson 2000; Card 1998; Crémieux 1996). Overall, Card's (1998) research revealed a relatively modest decay in earnings on the order of 10 percent since 1978. Hirsch and Macpherson (2000) report few real changes in earnings between 1973 and 1984 but a decrease of about 10 percent by the late 1980s and 5 percent during the period 1996 to 1997. However, these results vary by craft. All three of these studies concluded that mechanics' earnings have not fallen significantly in the deregulatory period. They also agree that flight attendants have experienced the largest declines, but the magnitude of those estimates varies by study. Crémieux (1996) found that flight attendants' earnings plummeted by 39 percent in the deregulatory period. However, Card's (1998) estimates of flight attendants' wage declines tempered Crémieux's (1996) in that they were between 11 and 18 percent. Reported drops in pilots' earnings generally fell between the mechanics' and flight attendants'. Card (1998) estimated pilot's wages declined between 3 and 11 percent, whereas Crémieux's (1996) results once again suggested slightly larger declines, ranging between 12 and 22 percent.

Card (1998) and Hirsch and Macpherson (2000) also examined earnings dispersion. Cappelli (1985) argued that regulation enforced a form of pattern bargaining, but the early regulatory environment led carriers to develop unique business strategies requiring differential labor relations responses. Johnson, Sambharya, and Bobko (1989) empirically supported this contention in their findings of a relationship between wage outcomes and the business strategies of the carriers. Thus, it was expected that earnings variation across carriers would increase in the deregulatory period. Card (1998) estimated that earnings varied among carriers up to 10 to 30 percent for flight attendants and 40 percent for pilots in the deregulatory period. Hirsch and Macpherson (2000) also found that dispersion increased significantly in the early phases of deregulation.

Even though recent research suggests evidence of airline earnings declines, airline workers have fared well relative to workers in the trucking industry, where wages fell quickly to competitive levels. Union density represents one possible explanation for the difference, as it remains high in the airline industry but fell precipitously after trucking deregulation. Although Hirsch and Macpherson (2000) maintain that unions have played a key role in the maintenance of rents for airline workers, Card (1998) suggests that the relative parity of wage declines among highly organized groups such as pilots and nonunion occupations such as managers and clerical workers indicates that the rents appeared to arise from alternative sources. Both studies provide evidence that the high skill levels partially explain the relatively high wage levels of airline workers.

With respect to airline wage trends, the relatively slow adjustment to deregulation remains curious. Several possible explanations exist. First, the wage decreases of the late 1980s and early 1990s did not directly result from deregulation but rather were a response to the dismal economic performance of the carriers in this time frame. Hirsch and Macpherson (2000) report that the airline union differential in the mid-1980s reached as high as .25 but dropped to .15 in the early 1990s. However, they found it rebounded to 1980s levels in the 1996 to 1997 period. This suggests that airline unions merely responded to the carriers' ability to pay at that time and that the declines in wages experienced beginning in the 1980s were not a permanent adjustment in regulatory rent structures but a temporary response to economic conditions. This interpretation is supported by Nay's (1991) research that found that ability to pay was a key factor in determining concessions.

A second explanation is that the form of concessions granted in the 1980s did not effectively reduce short-run wage levels. Two-tier wage scales were a prevalent concession of the 1980s (Cappelli 1987; Walsh 1988). Since the lower two-tier wage scales only apply to newly hired employees, their effectiveness in reducing labor costs is based on continued hiring of new employees. Walsh (1988) proposed that the proliferation of two-tier agreements in the airline industry was largely a symbolic maneuver to signal the changing labor relations environment. Thomas, Officer, and Johnson (1995) empirically supported Walsh's (1988) view in that they found that the stock market only responded favorably to the announcement of wage cuts and not to two-tier plans.

Nay (1991) also found that profitability had little to do with the negotiation of two-tier wage plans but instead related to wage cuts and freezes. Presently, two-tier wage plans have been almost totally eliminated from airline labor agreements.

Another explanation for the relative slow adjustment of airline wages to deregulation is that the declining wage levels may have partially resulted from the continued trend toward double-breasted operations between the feeders and the majors. Feeder wages are considerably lower than the majors and thus create wage disparity. This is highlighted in two recent labor disputes. The threatened American Airlines pilots' strike of 1997 was based on the carrier's desire to increase the number of regional jets flown under the American Eagle name by lower-cost pilots. Similarly, the 2001 Comair strike was based on the disparity between pilot pay at Comair and Delta, its parent company. Delta reportedly offered Comair pilots the highest wages among regional carriers. The pilots rejected this offer based on their desire for wages comparable to Delta pilots. The demand for comparable wages has been precipitated in part by the changing fleet of regional carriers, which has moved to phase out turboprops and add smaller jets that seat up to 100 passengers. Thus, the differences between the equipment flown by the regionals and the majors are becoming smaller.

Finally, the shift in the structure of employment may also provide a partial explanation for the gradual decline in earnings. As Table 4 illustrates, in 1980 part-time workers accounted for only 4 percent of employment among the major carriers, but the percentage rose to 18 percent in 2000. However, the ground employees of Federal Express are counted as airline employees and likely overstate the part-time estimate. If Federal Express is not included in the calculations, 12 percent of the employees at the majors are part-time workers. Nonetheless, carriers such as Continental and Delta have clearly increased the percentage of workers that are part-time over the twenty-year period. Thus, by shifting work from full-time to part-time workers, the carriers may be effectively reducing labor costs.

Recent Critical Issues

Some airline unions have agreed to employee ownership in exchange for wage concessions. The most notable example of employee ownership is at United Airlines. Under the plan initiated in 1994, employees held nearly 55 percent of United stock (pilots, 46 percent; machinists, 37 percent; and management and salaried employees, 16 percent; flight

TABLE 4
Airline Part-Time Workers

Airline	1980				Airline	2000			
	Full-time	Part-time	Total	Percentage part-time		Full-time	Part-time	Total	Percentage part-time
American	36,091	1,562	37,653	0.04	Alaska	9,112	1,221	10,333	0.12
Braniff	12,092	11	12,103	0.00	America West	10,992	2,809	13,801	0.20
Continental	13,286	790	14,076	0.06	American	86,663	14,536	101,199	0.14
Delta	36,081	1,027	37,108	0.03	American Eagle	8,189	1,235	9,424	0.13
Eastern	39,875	2,422	42,297	0.06	American Trans Air	7,018	953	7,971	0.12
Flying Tiger	6,655	629	7,284	0.09	Continental	36,156	9,788	45,944	0.21
Northwest	12,728	20	12,748	0.00	Delta	66,758	13,632	80,390	0.17
Pan American	31,914	345	32,259	0.01	Federal Express	93,073	53,371	146,444	0.36
Piedmont	4,641	632	5,273	0.12	Northwest	50,341	3,548	53,889	0.07
Republic	14,622	26	14,648	0.00	Southwest	28,860	828	29,688	0.03
Trans World	31,900	1,379	33,279	0.04	Trans World	18,835	1,301	20,136	0.06
United	46,910	2,723	49,633	0.05	United	90,398	11,416	101,814	0.11
US Airways	10,194	185	10,379	0.02	United Parcel	5,231	197	5,428	0.04
Western	9,721	512	10,233	0.05	US Airways	41,708	4,125	45,833	0.09
Total majors	**306,710**	**12,263**	**318,973**	**0.04**	**Total majors**	**553,334**	**118,960**	**672,294**	**0.18**

Source: Office of Airline Information, Bureau of Transportation.

attendants refused participation) (*Risk Management* 2001). Early in the ownership process, results were encouraging, as workers assisted United management in improving operations and cutting costs. Despite ownership, however, machinists threatened to strike and pilots engaged in a slowdown in the summer of 2000. Although workers had cut costs and the profitability of the airline had improved, workers did not receive corresponding increases in wages (*Risk Management* 2001). Northwest also negotiated ESOP provisions in 1993. Not unlike United, a pilots' strike ensued in 1998, and a PEB ended a mechanics' strike in the spring of 2001. Gittell, Nordenflycht, and Kochan (forthcoming) conclude that ESOP provisions do not alone lead to positive labor relations or outcomes for the carriers.

The most recent set of negotiations have tended to focus on labor attempting to reclaim the concessions given up during the late 1980s and early 1990s. As the airlines' performance increased during the late 1990s, unions began to focus on achieving wage gains. Given the historically marginal performance of the airlines, this is not altogether surprising. Although unions still retain an interest in obtaining seats on the board, wages appear a top priority. The 2001 settlement between Delta and ALPA resulted in Delta pilots obtaining the highest wages in the industry, but, in exchange, the union gave up its voting seat on the board.

The relationship between the feeder regional carriers and the majors provides a thorny issue for labor. In many cases, the feeder airlines are owned entirely by a major carrier. Yet, because of the RLA's emphasis on the craft and carrier basis of organization, they negotiate separately with potentially different unions. This structure may be eroding pilot bargaining power. Pilots, by virtue of their ability to shut down an airline and the inability of the carrier to stockpile inventories, typically have significant bargaining power. However, as the Comair strike illustrates, much of Comair's business during the strike was shifted to Delta and to other feeder carriers that are part of the "Delta Connection." Thus, the ability of the union to impose financial costs on the carrier was mitigated by the ability of the carrier to shift work to its parent company and other subsidiaries.

Innovative Work Practices

Some have argued that the airlines are ripe for new, innovative work practices (Womack and Jones 1996). Gittell, Nordenflycht, and Kochan (forthcoming) surmise that three basic labor relations approaches exist in the deregulated airline industry: union avoidance and low wages, motivated and committed employees through ownership and employee voice, and traditional collective bargaining. The first approach, pioneered by Frank Lorenzo at Continental Airlines in the 1980s, has largely failed. With the exception of Delta, most major carriers are largely unionized. Although Delta remains essentially nonunion, it has some of the highest wages in the airline industry. Thus, most carriers have continued to operate under the third traditional labor relations approach with perhaps a governance twist. As Gittell, Nordenflycht, and Kochan (forthcoming) found, most carriers that have used governance strategies—Western, Eastern, Northwest, TWA, and United—have adopted ESOPs in concessionary bargaining. Further, only the plans at Northwest and United continue to exist. As these authors note, the provisions do not appear to substitute for sustained improvement in labor–management goodwill or productivity and service. These researchers cite only Southwest and the "new" Continental as examples of airlines with a committed workforce that emanates from labor and management trust. Where Southwest created this culture from its inception, Gordon Bethune has apparently turned Continental around, from a low-wage, nonunion carrier to a high-commitment carrier, through incentives, extensive communication, and management commitment (Bethune 1998).

Eaton (1996) suggests that some of the inherent problems of a quality approach apply to the airline industry. He contends that increased load factors logistically make it difficult to provide quality service. The high volume of customers and the subsequent crowding simply reduce service almost by definition. Finally, he notes that customer orientation often fades in the face of recessionary pressures. Because of the expense of these practices, Eaton (1996) suggests that carriers abandon them when faced with financial strain. The work of Gittell, Nordenflycht, and Kochan (forthcoming) supports Eaton's (1996) predictions. They found that shared governance is associated with reduced service failure and increased productivity, but it is also associated with reduced return on assets.

On the other hand, Stone (1990) makes a strong case that the RLA itself encourages participation. She contends that the status quo provisions of the RLA, which require that the contractual provisions of the labor agreement continue for up to thirty to sixty days following impasse or PEB appointment, facilitate union participation in the strategic direction of the company. She cites evidence that carriers have been prevented, without union consent, from moving operations or transferring work following impasse because of status quo provisions. Employers can be enjoined from making such changes. Thus, she contends that RLA unions can play an active role in influencing the strategic direction of the carrier.

In contrast to Stone (1990), Northrup (1990:513) contends that the provisions of the RLA are outmoded and "saddle the industry with mistakes of an older, declining past." He believes that the RLA promotes the drawing out of collective bargaining indefinitely, making it unresponsive to the changes demanded by deregulation. Thus, he believes that the RLA promotes traditional collective bargaining.

Work Stoppages

There have been relatively few work stoppages from the 1990s to the present. As shown in Table 5, over this period there have been only eight strikes involving American carriers, and, of these, only the Eastern strike was prolonged. That strike spanned more than a year and ended with the carrier's failure. The Comair pilots' strike, which lasted eighty-one days, is the only recent strike to exceed fifteen days. By contrast, the decade of the 1980s had more strikes of longer duration. The Continental and Eastern strikes were by far the most bitter, and both involved carriers under the auspices of Frank Lorenzo, who exemplified antiunion animus. Lorenzo filed bankruptcy at Continental to abrogate the labor agreements and bought Eastern Airlines with the apparent objective of dismantling it. However, even factoring out strikes with these two carriers, strikes of the 1980s were about two times as frequent and of longer duration than the strikes during the 1990s.

During the 1980s, many carriers were attempting to obtain concessions even if they were financially sound (Walsh 1988). During the early 1990s, the carriers were also negotiating concessions. However, it was abundantly clear during this period that the airlines would not survive without concessions and that the carriers could not afford strikes. Also during the 1990s, airline unions began experimenting with other forms of protest.

The AFA has created a form of strike that it has trademarked. The form of protest is known as Create Havoc Around Our System™ (CHAOS), a combined strategy of public information and targeted work actions using random, unannounced strikes. The strikes may occur on a single flight, a type of aircraft, or systemwide for a week. The AFA began using this form of protest in its 1993 strike against Alaska Airlines. Although illegal under the NLRA, intermittent strikes are not prohibited by the RLA (*Pan American World Airways, Inc. v. International Brotherhood of Teamsters, etc.* 894 F.2d 36 [2d Circ. 1990] and *Association of Flight*

TABLE 5

Strikes in the Airline Industry

Strike began	Strike ended	Union	Carrier	Duration (days)	Comments
3/26/01	6/14/01	ALPA	Comair	81	
3/12/01	3/12/01	AMFA	Northwest	0	PEB appointed
8/29/98	9/12/98	ALPA	Northwest	15	
12/20/97	12/20/97	ALPA	Skyway	89 minutes	
2/15/97	2/15/97	APA	American	24 minutes	PEB appointed
11/18/93	11/22/93	APFA	American	5	
10/5/92	10/8/92	IAM	US Airways	4	
3/4/89	1/17/91	IAM	Eastern	684	
3/7/86	5/18/86	IFFA	Trans World	72	
5/17/85	6/14/85	ALPA	United	29	
3/4/85	6/3/85	IAM	Alaska	92	
2/28/85	3/27/85	TWU	Pan American	28	
2/7/85	2/7/85	IAM (agents)	Ozark	1	
8/15/84	8/15/84	TWU	Pan American	1	
10/1/83	4/17/85	UFA	Continental	565	Continental filed bankruptcy
10/1/83	9/15/85	ALPA	Continental	716	Continental filed bankruptcy
8/13/83	4/17/85	IAM	Continental	614	Continental filed bankruptcy
5/22/82	6/25/82	IAM	Northwest	35	
12/5/80	12/21/80	UFA	Continental	17	
9/25/80	11/16/80	SFCA (pilots)	Pacific Southwest	53	
5/6/80	6/12/80	AMFA	Ozark	38	
4/13/80	8/18/80	IAM	Altair	127	
1/13/80	2/1/80	IAM (mechanics)	Southwest	20	

Source: National Mediation Board.
IFFA—Independent Federation of Flight Attendants
SFCA—Southwest Flight Crew Association

Attendants v. Alaska Airlines 847 F. Supp. 832, 1993). Thus, the AFA continues to actively use CHAOS campaigns.

The Allied Pilots Association attempted a sick-out in a dispute with American Airlines over the purchase of and merger with Reno Air. The dispute, concerning the merging of the American Airlines and Reno Air seniority list, was considered a "minor dispute" under the RLA, making it unlawful for the pilots to engage in self-help. The pilots continued the sick-out in violation of a temporary restraining order and were fined $45.5 million dollars in compensatory damages. The appeals court in the spring of 2001 affirmed the lower court's award of the compensatory damages (*American Airlines, Inc. v. Allied Pilots Association*, 228 F. 3d 574, 2000 U.S. App.). Similarly, in 2000, the pilots at Delta Airlines began systematically refusing to work overtime during a time when the carrier and the union were in active negotiations. The court issued an injunction against ALPA to prevent it from encouraging its members to engage in overtime refusals (*Delta Airlines, Inc. v. Air Line Pilots Association*, International, Civil Action File No. 1:00-CV-3207-WBH, 2001). Thus, the recent RLA case law suggests that once the parties are released to engage in self-help, the form of that self-help is relatively unconstrained. However, prior to being released, the courts do not condone concerted activity.

In the airlines, PEBs have been rare events. For the thirty years following 1966, there were no PEBs in the airline industry. In the late 1990s, two PEBs have been created, suggesting an increased willingness to appoint them. In 1997, President Clinton created an emergency board to handle the dispute between American Airlines and its pilots, represented by the independent union of the Allied Pilots Association. President Bush also appointed a board for the 2001 dispute between Northwest Airlines and the AMFA. Clinton waited until the pilots at American Airlines walked off the job before appointing the PEB. However, Bush appointed the board prior to the formal strike declaration. In both cases, the parties resolved their differences before the sixty-day expiration of the board, when they would have been again free to use self-help.

One theory for the recent willingness to rely on the PEB is that the dominance of a single carrier over a hub has contributed to a single airline strike, significantly affecting regional traffic. Others contend that the parties desired the PEB as a face-saving device, and thus it was supported by the participants. Nonetheless, some have suggested that the appointment of a PEB tends to drive the parties farther apart than would be the case if impasse had resulted in a strike (Northrup 1990; Wilner 1990). However, many believed that if Delta and its pilots had not reached agreement in the 2001 negotiations, Bush would have appointed a PEB to avert a strike. Nonetheless, the parties did reach agreement prior to the time when the parties could have engaged in self-help and a PEB could have been appointed.

Organizing

Table 6 contains the NMB election data for the airlines between 1972 and 1999. These data show that on average the NMB conducted fifty elections per year in the airline industry and that unions won about 45 percent of these elections. However, the number of elections varies over time. In the regulatory period, the number of union elections averaged about fifty per year, with a win rate of 48 percent. This number rose to almost sixty-five per year in the early deregulatory period, but the win rate fell to 39 percent. Most likely, the increase in elections but decrease in success reflects the entrance of the new nonunion carriers. However, the number of elections dropped in the late deregulatory period to forty-five elections per year, but the success rate increased to almost regulatory levels.

TABLE 6
Union Elections in the Airlines

Year	Airline elections	Unions certified	Percentage certified
1972	42	24	0.57
1973	45	17	0.38
1974	42	14	0.33
1975	44	22	0.50
1976	56	31	0.55
1977	68	37	0.54
1978	54	25	0.46
1979	59	24	0.41
1980	95	35	0.37
1981	70	21	0.30
1982	54	22	0.41
1983	59	29	0.49
1984	51	20	0.39
1985	43	17	0.40
1986	43	17	0.40
1987	54	24	0.44
1988	49	27	0.55
1989	40	18	0.45
1990	32	15	0.47
1991	29	17	0.59
1992	38	9	0.24
1993	43	17	0.40
1994	51	18	0.35
1995	43	24	0.56
1996	43	24	0.56
1997	46	27	0.59
1998	64	31	0.48
1999	55	29	0.53
Average	50.43	22.68	0.45
1972–1978	50.14	24.29	0.48
1979–1984	64.67	25.17	0.39
1985–1999	44.87	20.93	0.47

Source: National Mediation Board annual reports.

Although union-organizing activity under the NLRA has dropped by more than one half, unions in the airline industry continue to engage in active organizing. In the 1970s and 1980s, the NLRB held more than 7,000 elections in a year, on average. This number dropped to slightly more than 3,000 by 1994 (Masters 1997), although over this time, the union win rate in NLRB elections remains relatively stable at 49 percent. The number of airline union elections have dropped by slightly more than 10 percent, with an almost constant win rate, from the regulatory to the late deregulatory period.

Taken together, the NMB and NLRB data suggest that, although airline unions are slightly less successful in winning elections, their election activity continues at a relatively high level. However, Table 6 refers to all airline union elections. Johnson and Hoobler (2001) report data exclusively for pilots, flight attendants, and mechanics, which have win rates of 61 percent and 63 percent for the regulatory and deregulatory periods, respectively. Thus, airline unions that attempt unionizing other crafts, such as fleet and passenger service workers, tend to have lower win rates. Further, some evidence suggests that the airlines have taken a harder line in organizing these crafts. Two examples of airlines' aggressive antiunion tactics provided by Katz, Zanar, and Dominitz (1999) were the passenger service campaigns of the Communications Workers of America (CWA) at American Airlines and US Airways, where the CWA did win bargaining rights at US Airways but not at American.

Unique to the airlines is the high number of multi-union elections. Where, under the NLRA, multi-union elections represent about 4.2 percent of the total number of elections (Sandver and Ready 1998), under the NLRA they represent nearly 52 percent for pilots, mechanics, and flight attendants (Johnson and Hoobler 2001). Studies of the NLRA elections show that multi-union elections have a much higher success rate. Dworkin and Fain (1989) argue that units with strong union sentiment attract multiple unions. If this argument is correct, then the multi-union election is merely symbolic of the strength of the pilots, flight attendants, and mechanics whose win rates do exceed those of the industry average and of the NLRB elections.

Over the past three years, most of the larger elections at the major carriers have involved clerical workers, passenger service employees, or fleet service employees. These employees have not been previously represented. The major union victories were the IAM and CWA winning representation rights for passenger service employees at United and US Air, respectively. Additionally, fleet service workers were also successfully organized by the TWU at America West. On the other hand, unions were unsuccessful at organizing passenger service employees at American and America West, fleet service employees at Delta, and clerical workers at United and US Airways. Thus, organizing support services appears more difficult for unions than for the traditional airline crafts.

Conclusion

A great deal of uncertainty faced airline labor during the early deregulatory period when airlines struggled to find a successful formula for operating competitively. What emerged was a network industry with a system of regional carriers that fed the hub-and-spoke system of the majors. The hub-and-spoke network expanded internationally through code-sharing and global alliances.

Part of the uncertainty faced by each carrier was played out through experiments with alternative formulations for successful industrial relations policies and practices. Because of the fragmentation of airline collective bargaining, there was little formal coordination in bargaining, leaving each carrier and its unions to develop its own industrial relations scheme (Cappelli 1985, 1987; Walsh 1994). However, many carriers apparently negotiated concessions in the late 1980s simply to demonstrate that they could and less out of economic necessity (Thomas, Officer, and Johnson 1995; Walsh 1988). Many concessions were in the form of two-tier wage scales, which limited the carriers' ability to affect labor costs and potentially created significant equity concerns among employees.

The decade of the 1990s began dismally for the airline industry. Eastern and Pan Am, old stalwart trunk carriers, failed. Profitability for virtually all carriers, except Southwest, appeared elusive. Problems of overcapacity and high fuel prices plagued the industry. However, by the middle of the decade, airlines began to cruise along with the economic boom of the 1990s and turned red ink to black.

The decade of the 1990s began a return to relatively conventional industrial relations. After the experiments with two-tier wage scales of the 1980s, many airlines demonstrated the need for genuine wage relief in the early 1990s. Thus, unions negotiated direct wage cuts and labor cost concessions in exchange for profit sharing and governance, in hopes of facilitating carriers' survival. Evidence suggests that these concessions did contribute to significant wage declines for airline workers during the 1990s. However, the question remains how much of the decrease was a response to deregulation and how much was a response to the economic peril of the airlines. By the end of the decade, when the carriers were beginning to demonstrate financial gains, unions began seeking a share of the success through wage gains and decreased interest in governance. Experimentation with participative management and other "high-performance work practices" has been limited to only a couple of carriers. Thus, it appears that airline unions were returning to a more traditional form of adversarial industrial relations.

Perhaps the return to conventional industrial relations is not surprising. Unionization continues to be high and organization continues. The RLA has been a constant institutional factor from the inception of airline industrial relations. Although it has its critics, the industry actors support the core of its framework. Most agree that it clearly avoids service disruption but at the price of long, drawn-out negotiations. Disagreement occurs over the value of this trade-off.

As we begin the millennium, the industry seems to be in the throes of the consolidation process, predicted by many at the advent of deregulation. Explicitly, this consolidation is taking shape in the form of mergers, such as American and TWA, or extensive marketing agreements, such as those between Northwest and Continental. Consolidation is also taking shape, though, through an almost virtual vertical integration of code-sharing alliances at both ends, regionally and globally.

Industry consolidation through mergers likely disrupts the economic lives of individual workers and their unions. A variety of unions represent workers, and there is always some jockeying for which unions will ultimately gain bargaining rights and the resulting seniority provisions. However, mergers may enhance union power, as unions may be in a better position to take wages out of competition should they begin to work together. On the other hand, the network structure of regionals and international alliances enhances management's bargaining power to shift work during a strike, ultimately reducing labor's power.

Thus, the future of airline industrial relations remains somewhat unpredictable. Labor, thus far, has weathered deregulation surprisingly well despite the turbulence. Unionization continues to be relatively high, and wages did not decline significantly until the late 1990s. Further, there is some evidence that relative wages were on the upswing in the late 1990s. However, the industry continues to have increased variability in wages and working conditions, and recent attempts to level out the variability have been met with mixed results. Probably more disconcerting for labor is that the structure of the industry is such that the variability will likely continue and provide management the opportunity to whipsaw labor. The fragmentation of labor is likely to exacerbate the situation. Thus, the changes in the industry will likely require that labor unions begin to work together to attempt to remove wages as a source of competition, or else the declines they have suffered so far are likely to increase further.

The Aftermath

The terrorist attacks on the World Trade Center and the Pentagon of September 11, 2001, will unequivocally shape the future of the airline industry, its workers, and its representatives. Although this chapter was essentially completed in early September 2001, one month following these events, it seems a bit anachronistic. On the other hand, a mere month makes it difficult to write with foresight or perspective on the long-term implications for airline workers. Yet, for an industry where financial turbulence is virtually standard operating procedure, a mere month has yielded a swift and profound short-term financial reaction to the events. The resulting economic reverberations seem not unlike the response to deregulation that evolved over years, not days. Consequently, I will briefly review the major events of the month following the September 11, 2001, attacks and discuss their implications for the future of airline industrial relations.

The attacks led to an unprecedented grounding of the air system by the president for over two days. Resumption of service was gradual as airports struggled with heightened security requirements and decreased service demand resulting mainly from fear of future attacks. Already stressed from a downturn in the economy, these actions contributed to pushing the already uncertain financial position of the airlines into a dive. As airlines have no way to inventory product, downtime and any subsequent decrease in demand create unrecoverable losses. Congress explicitly recognized this fact by enacting the Air Transportation Safety and System Stabilization Act on September 22, 2001. The act provides funds to compensate carriers for direct losses due to the federal ground stop order, not to exceed $10 billion. It also amends transportation laws to authorize the Secretary of Transportation to provide insurance for either American or foreign-flag carriers operating in the United States, reimbursement to air carriers for increased insurance costs resulting from the events of September 11, and compensation for victims of the attack and their families.

Despite congressional relief, the airlines continue to face extreme financial vulnerability on several fronts. The most obvious is the decreased

demand for service for customers with elastic demand, based on continued security concerns. Additionally, the events of September 11 also
strained the already taxed economy, converting the business traveler,
who was once considered to have relatively inelastic demand, to one
whose demand has become relatively elastic. As a result of the recession,
businesses have substituted nonessential travel with alternatives such as
online interactive meetings to reduce expenses. At the same time, airline
capacity is relatively high and difficult to adjust in the short run. Looking
for relief on other fronts, the airlines have cut their payrolls by more
than 100,000 employees, representing at least a 15 percent cut. Table 7
shows the announced layoffs by carrier, as of October 2001.

TABLE 7
Airline Layoffs, September–October 2001

Company	Employees laid off
UAL Corp.	20,000
AMR Corp.	20,000
Continental	12,000
Delta	12,000
US Airways Group	11,000
Northwest	10,000
America West	2,000
Midway Air[a]	1,700
American Trans Air	1,500
Atlas Air	1,000
Mesa Air Group	700
Midwest Express	450
Frontier Airlines	440
Total	92,790

Source: Association of Flight Attendants
<http://www.nmb.gov/publicinfo/alstrikes.html>. [10/09/01].
[a]Filed for bankruptcy.

Security remains a top priority for the industry. In addition to the obvious goal of self-preservation, airlines and their unions have long recognized
that airline safety and the viability of the industry are inescapably connected. Thus, ALPA and the AFA have been active in pursuing enhanced
airline security in the aftermath. In testimony before the Senate committee
on Commerce, Science, and Transportation on September 20, 2001,
Captain Duane Woerth, president of ALPA, requested such safety enhancements as stronger cockpit doors; arming the cockpit crew members

with stun guns; federal air marshals; enhanced identification systems for airline employees; discrete switches for flight attendants to notify the cockpit of problems in the cabin; security and background checks on all airline employees; and a revision of the "Common Strategy" used by the FAA, law enforcement, airlines, and pilots during hijackings to include provisions for suicidal hijackers (ALPA 2001b). Patricia Friend, president of AFA, testified before the U.S. House of Representatives Aviation Subcommittee in general support for the pilots' calls for enhanced security (with the exception of opposing the arming of pilots) but additionally asked for enhanced training for flight attendants to deal with hijackers (AFA 2001b). An Aviation Security Bill passed the Senate on October 11, 2001, but has stalled in the House of Representatives over the provisions to include a financial package to assist laid-off airline workers and whether the government should take over control of airline security.

As noted throughout this chapter, airlines have been plagued with financial problems throughout the deregulatory era. Even before the September 11 attacks, the downturn in the economy was once again threatening many airlines' balance sheets. After the attacks, virtually no airline has been left unscathed, and most continue to face potentially devastating economic hardship that is unlikely to mitigate in the near future. Even Southwest Airlines, which has historically had the most solid financial position of any airline in the deregulatory period, has announced cutbacks. With time, security concerns will likely become less salient to passengers, who will return to the air either because of a lack of further attacks or of the belief that life must go on. However, the recession may delay their return until it is economically viable. In the interim, this is likely to mean concessionary bargaining for airline workers to attempt to protect remaining jobs. In recognition of this fact, the AFA voluntarily offered to reopen negotiations and offer contract concessions with American Airlines shortly after the attacks, in the explicit recognition of the precarious financial future of the airline. Whether or not these concessions will be large enough to help the industry, let alone the carriers operating at the margin, remains uncertain. In the past, there was a faint cry for re-regulation that could become louder if the viability of the industry hangs in the balance. The early regulators were concerned that without regulation the industry would advance toward destructive competition. Industry competition has been intense, but no one could have anticipated the destruction that took place on September 11.

Acknowledgments

This chapter is dedicated to the airline employees who lost their lives in the terrorist attacks of September 11, 2001. I would like to thank James Armshaw, of the National Mediation Board; Robert DeLucia and Derick Deck, of Air Conference; Seth Rosen, of the Air Line Pilots Association; Stephen Sleigh, of the International Association of Machinists and Aerospace Workers; and Paul Jarley, for providing valuable information and insights.

References

AFA. 2001a. "About AFA." <http://www.flightattendant-afa.org/aboutafa.htm>. [April 11, 2001].
_____. 2001b. "Flight Attendants Testify Before Congress on Aircraft Security Issues." <http://www.flightattendant-afa.org/pr092501congress.htm>. [October 14, 2001].
AIR Inc. 1998. U.S. Airlines Salary Survey and Career Earnings Comparison. Atlanta: Air Inc.
Airline Industry Labor–Management Committee. 1996. Report of the Airline Industry Labor–Management Committee to the National Mediation Board. Washington, DC: Airline Industry Labor–Management Committee.
ALPA. 1998. "United Airlines Pilot Leaders to Study Feasibility of Code-Sharing Alliance between United, Delta." <http://www.alpa.org/internet/download.html?file=News/1998News/NR98019.htm>. [April 30, 1998].
_____. 2000. "United Airlines Pilots Express Strong Concerns over the Proposed Merger of United and US Air." <http://www.alpa.org/internet/download.html?file=News/2001News/NR00038.htm>. [May 24, 2000].
_____. 2001a. "Request for Mutual Assistance by Czech Air Line Pilots Association." <http://www.alpa.org/internet/airlinenews/ifalpa/ma_8-29-01.html>. [August 29, 2001].
_____. 2001b. "Statement of Captain Duane Woerth, President of the Air Line Pilots Association, International, from testimony on Aviation Security before the Committee on Commerce, Science, and Transportation, U.S. Senate, September 20, 2001." <http://www.alpa.org/internet/tm/tm092001.htm>. [October 12, 2001].
ALPA–TWA Master Executive Council. 2001. "The Acquisition of TWA by American Airlines." <http://www.alpa.org/internet/tm/tm20101.htm>. [February 1, 2001].
Bartholomew, Bradley C. 2000. "Viewpoint: Remove Airlines from the Railway Labor Act." Aviation Week and Space Technology, September 11, p. 98.
Bethune, Gordon. 1998. From Worst to First. New York: John Wiley & Sons.
Bureau of Labor Statistics. 1999. "National Occupational Employment and Wage Estimates: 53-2011 Airline Pilots, Copilots, and Flight Engineers." <http://www.bls.gov/oes/2000/oes532011.htm>.
_____. 2000. "Occupational Employment, Training, and Earnings." <http://stats.bls.gov.oep/noeted/emprprt.asp>. [April 13, 2001].

_____. 2001. *Employment and Earnings*. Washington, DC: GPO.

Button, Kenneth. 1991. "Introduction." In Kenneth Button, ed., *Airline Deregulation*. New York: New York University Press, pp. 1–4.

Cappelli, Peter. 1985. "Competitive Pressures and Labor Relations in the Airline Industry." *Industrial Relations*, Vol. 24, no. 3 (Fall), pp. 316–318.

_____. 1987. "Airlines." In David B. Lipsky and Clifford B. Donn, eds., *Collective Bargaining in American Industry*. Lexington, MA: Lexington Books, pp. 135–86.

Card, David. 1986. "The Impact of Deregulation on the Employment and Wages of Airline Mechanics." *Industrial and Labor Relations Review*, Vol. 39, no. 4 (July), pp. 527–38.

_____. 1989. "Deregulation and Labor Earnings in the Airline Industry." Princeton University Industrial Relations Section Working Paper No. 247 (January).

_____. 1998. "Deregulation and Labor Earnings in the Airline Industry." In James Peoples, ed., *Regulatory Reform and Labor Markets*. Boston: Kluwer, pp. 183–229.

Cohen, Issac. 1990. "Political Climate and Two Airline Strikes: Century Air in 1932 and Continental Airlines in 1983–1985." *Industrial and Labor Relations Review*, Vol. 43, no. 2 (January), pp. 308–23.

Commission on the Future of Worker–Management Relations. 1994. Fact Finding Report. Washington, DC: U.S. Department of Labor and U.S. Department of Commerce.

Cone, Cathy. 2000. "Delta Personnel Board Council." In Bruce Kaufman and Daphne Gottlieb Taras, eds., *Nonunion Employee Representation: History, Contemporary Practice, and Policy*. Armonk, NY: M.E. Sharpe, pp. 469–73.

Crémieux, Pierre-Yves. 1996. "The Effect of Deregulation on Employee Earnings: Pilots, Flight Attendants, and Mechanics, 1959–1992." *Industrial and Labor Relations Review*, Vol. 49, no. 2 (January), pp. 223–42.

Dworkin, James B., and James R. Fain. 1989. "Success in Multiple Union Elections: Exclusive Jurisdiction vs. Competition." *Journal of Labor Research*, Vol. X, no. 1 (Winter), pp. 91–101.

Eaton, Jack. 1996. *Globalization and Human Resource Management in the Airline Industry*. Aldershot, Great Britain: Avebury Aviation.

Eischen, Dana E. 1976. "Representation Disputes and Their Resolution in the Railroad and Airline Industries." In Charles M. Rehmus, ed., *The Railway Labor Act at Fifty*. Washington, DC: National Mediation Board, pp. 23–70.

Gittell, Jody Hoffer, Andrew von Nordenflycht, and Thomas A. Kochan. Forthcoming. "Mutual Gains or Zero Sum? An Initial Exploration of Employee Stakeholder Orientation in the Airline Industry." *Proceedings of the Fifty-Third Annual Meetings* (New Orleans, January 4–7, 2001). Madison, WI: Industrial Relations Research Association.

Hanlon, Pat. 1999. *Global Airlines*. Oxford: Butterworth Heinemann.

Hendricks, Wallace. 1994. "Deregulation and Labor Earnings." *Journal of Labor Research*, Vol. 15, no. 3 (Summer), pp. 207–34.

Hendricks, Wallace, Peter Feuille, and Carol Szerszen. 1980. "Regulation, Deregulation, and Collective Bargaining in the Airlines." *Industrial and Labor Relations Review*, Vol. 34, no. 1 (October), pp. 67–81.

Hirsch, Barry T., and David A. Macpherson. 2000. "Earnings, Rents, and Competition in the Airline Labor Market." *Journal of Labor Economics*, Vol. 18, no. 1 (January), pp. 125–55.

Hopkins, George E. 1982. *Flying the Line: The First Half-Century of the Airline Pilots Association*. Washington, DC: ALPA.

Johnson, Nancy Brown. 1991. "Airline Workers Earnings and Union Expenditures Under Deregulation." *Industrial and Labor Relations Review*, Vol. 45, no. 1 (October), pp. 154–65.

Johnson, Nancy Brown, and Jenny Hoobler. 2001. "Airline Union Density: An Account of Relative Prosperity." Unpublished paper, University of Kentucky.

Johnson, Nancy Brown, Rakesh Sambharya, and Philip Bobko. 1989. "Deregulation, Business Strategy, and Wages in the Airline Industry." *Industrial Relations*, Vol. 28, no. 3 (Fall), pp. 419–30.

Kahn, Alfred E. 1988. "Surprises of Airline Deregulation." *American Economic Review*, Vol. 78, no. 2 (May), pp. 316–22.

———. 2000. "Airline Competition." Testimony before the Subcommittee on Antitrust of the United States Senate Committee on the Judiciary (May 2, 2000).

Kahn, Mark L. 1976. "Labor–Management Relations in the Airline Industry." In Charles M. Rehmus, ed., *The Railway Labor Act at Fifty*. Washington, DC: National Mediation Board, pp. 97–128.

———. 1980. "Airlines." In Gerald G. Somers, ed., *Collective Bargaining: Contemporary American Experience*. Madison, WI: Industrial Relations Research Association, pp. 325–72.

Katz, Daniel M., Louise P. Zanar, and Erica J. Dominitz. 1999. "A Commentary on Professor Morris's Comparison of Discrimination for Union Activity Under the NLRA and RLA." *Employee Rights and Employment Policy Journal*, Vol. 3, no. 2, pp. 305–48.

Kaufman, Bruce, and Daphne Gottlieb Taras. 2000. "Note from the Editors." In Bruce Kaufman and Daphne Gottlieb Taras, eds., *Nonunion Employee Representation: History, Contemporary Practice, and Policy*. Armonk, NY: M.E. Sharpe, p. 473.

Kim, Han E., and Vijay Singal. 1993. "Mergers and Market Power: Evidence from the Airline Industry." *American Economic Review*, Vol. 83, no. 3 (June), pp. 549–69.

Leslie, Douglas L. 1995. *The Railway Labor Act*. Washington, DC: BNA.

Masters, Marick F. 1997. *Unions at the Crossroads*. Westport, CT: Quorum.

Morris, Charles J. 1998. "A Tale of Two Statutes: Discrimination for Union Activity under the NLRA and the RLA." *Employee Rights and Employment Policy Journal*, Vol. 2, no. 2, pp. 317–60.

Morrison, Steven A. 2000. "Statement of Steven A. Morrison, Professor of Economics at Northeastern University." FDCH Congressional Testimony, May 2, 2000.

Morrison, Steven A., and Clifford Winston. 1995. *The Evolution of the Airline Industry*. Washington, DC: Brookings.

———. 2000. "The Remaining Role for Government Policy in the Deregulated Airline Industry." In Sam Peltzman and Clifford Winston, eds., *Deregulation of Network Industries*. Washington, DC: AEI-Brookings Center for Regulatory Studies, pp. 1–40.

Nay, Leslie. 1991. "Determinants of Concession Bargaining in the Airlines." *Industrial and Labor Relations Review*, Vol. 44, no. 2 (January), pp. 307–23.

Northrup, Herbert P. 1990. "The Railway Labor Act: Time for Repeal?" *Harvard Journal of Law and Public Policy*, Vol. 13, no. 2 (Spring), pp. 441–515.

Oum, Tae Hoon, Jong-Hun Park, and Anming Zhang. 1996. "The Effects of Airline Codesharing Agreements on Firm Conduct and International Air Fares." *Journal of Transport Economics*, Vol. 20, no. 2 (May), pp. 187–202.

Pickrell, Donald. 1991. "The Regulation and Deregulation of U.S. Airlines." In Kenneth Button, ed., *Airline Deregulation*. New York: New York University Press, pp. 5–47.

Risk Management. 2001. "United Airlines ESOP Woes." *Risk Management*, Vol. 48, no. 6 (June), p. 9.

Rosen, Seth. 1995. "Corporate Restructuring: A Labor Perspective." In Peter Cappelli, ed., *Airline Labor Relations in the Global Era*. Ithaca, NY: ILR Press, pp. 21–41.

Sandver, Marcus Hart, and Kathryn J. Ready. 1998. "Trends in and Determinants of Outcomes in Multi-Union Certification Elections." *Journal of Labor Research*, Vol. XIX, no. 1 (Winter), pp. 165–72.

Stone, Katherine Van Wezel. 1990. "Labor Relations on the Airlines: The Railway Labor Act in the Era of Deregulation." *Stanford Law Review*, Vol. 42, no. 4 (April), pp. 1485–547.

Thomas, Steven L., Dennis Officer, and Nancy Brown Johnson. 1995. "The Capital Market Response to Wage Negotiations in the Airlines." *Industrial Relations*, Vol. 34, no. 2 (April), pp. 203–17.

Walsh, David J. 1988. "Accounting for the Proliferation of Two-Tier Wage Settlements in the U.S. Airline Industry, 1983–1986." *Industrial and Labor Relations Review*, Vol. 42, no. 1 (October), pp. 50–62.

———. 1994. *On Different Planes*. Ithaca, NY: ILR Press.

Wilkey, John R., and Scott MacCartney. 2001. "American Airlines Wins a Victory as Judge Dismisses Antitrust Case." *Wall Street Journal*, April 30, p. A3.

Wilner, Frank. 1990. *The Railway Labor Act and the Dilemma of Labor Relations*. Omaha, NE: Simmons-Boardman Books, Inc.

Woerth, Duane E. 1995. "International Aviation." In Peter Cappelli, ed., *Airline Labor Relations in the Global Era*. Ithaca, NY: ILR Press, pp. 41–53.

Womack, James, and Daniel Jones. 1996. *Lean Thinking*. New York: Simon & Schuster.

CHAPTER 2

Autos: Continuity and Change in Collective Bargaining

HARRY C. KATZ
Cornell University

JOHN PAUL MACDUFFIE
University of Pennsylvania

FRITS K. PIL
University of Pittsburgh

Introduction

The auto industry historically has played a prominent role in American collective bargaining, introducing many now common features: multi-year contracts, with cost-of-living adjustment escalators and built-in annual real wage increases; supplementary unemployment benefits; "thirty and out" pensions;[1] quality of working life programs; and pattern bargaining. From the early 1980s on, automotive labor relations was again in the forefront in taking actions to modify this long-established model, under pressure from both foreign and domestic competitors and from new production methods often linked to team working and related innovative human resource practices.

Labor and management in the auto industry faced a combination of long-term structural factors and periodic sharp cyclical downturns. These pressures led to increased diversity and decentralization in collective bargaining outcomes, at both company and plant levels; widespread experimentation with new work designs and human resource practices at the workplace; and debate within both union and management ranks about the best way to deal with these changes. Japanese and German companies also became owners or co-owners (along with American company partners) of assembly plants and auto companies in the United States. The fact that virtually all of the assembly plants that were solely owned by Japanese or German companies operated without a union introduced the threat of nonunion operations to what had been one of the few remaining fully unionized sectors in the American economy. Another new twist to the structure of the U.S. auto industry was provided through the merger of German-based Daimler-Benz and the Chrysler Corporation (to form DaimlerChrysler).

Modifications of the industry's collective bargaining model in the 1980s included "concessionary" contracts that replaced traditional bargaining formulas with company-specific profit-sharing plans and work rule changes; extensive new income and job security programs to cope with industry restructuring; joint labor–management efforts around training and quality; and new work structures at the shop-floor level, such as teams combined with very few job classifications. Even though these pressures continued to loom in the background, in the 1990s the U.S. auto industry benefited from the effects of a sustained macroeconomic boom and the enhanced competitiveness of domestic products, particularly in the light truck and sport utility vehicle (SUV) segments. This cyclical rebound led to solid employment growth in the auto sector and strong compensation gains, particularly at the auto assembly firms. Then in 2001, in the next spin of the cyclical wheel, serious financial problems emerged in the auto industry and particularly at Ford Motor and DaimlerChrysler, threatening the gains won by the domestic industry and the UAW during the 1990s.

In this chapter, we first review the industry's distinctive and often innovative history of labor–management relations. In the next section, we describe the primary parties involved in U.S. automotive labor relations: the unions and the companies. Subsequent sections focus on the competitive and technological environment affecting the bargaining context for the U.S. automotive industry; the structure of collective bargaining; new developments in collective bargaining from 1979 to the present, highlighting the past ten years; and the future challenges confronting the industry.

The Parties

The Unions

The United Automobile Workers (UAW) is the primary union representing employees in the auto industry.[2] The International Union of Electrical Workers (IUE), which recently affiliated with the Communications Workers of America, also represents some hourly workers in the assembly firms (primarily in the electrical products plants of these firms). By the late 1940s the UAW had organized all hourly workers in the companies that assembled cars and trucks.[3] Until 1985, the UAW was an international union, as it included Canadian autoworkers. In 1985, the Canadian autoworkers voted to secede, and a separation agreement was negotiated between the U.S. and Canadian parts of the UAW to form the Canadian Auto Workers.

The UAW is a large and fairly centralized union. The internal structure of the union includes departments organized along company lines in the auto industry and an agricultural implements department. National union staff coordinate bargaining within each department and also assist in the implementation of benefits, employee assistance, health and safety, and quality of working life programs.

The central figure in the union over the postwar period was Walter Reuther, who along with his brothers was active in the union's sit-down strikes and organizing efforts in the 1930s. Reuther served as president of the UAW from 1947 until his death in 1970. During his tenure, Reuther led a coalition (the "administrative caucus") that dominated the national affairs of the union, and, while he was alive, Reuther's influence and imagination encouraged an innovative spirit within auto bargaining (Stieber 1962). Under Reuther's guidance, the UAW also was very active in national and local politics and a strong supporter of the Democratic Party.

Yet, even with the dominance of the Reuther coalition, the UAW historically has had strong democratic traditions that appeared in the 1980s and 1990s in the debates occurring within the UAW between the "New Directions Movement" and the "Administrative Caucus." In 1996, the UAW, United Steel Workers (USW), and International Association of Machinists (IAM) announced plans to merge by 2001. Merger talks, however, stalled (with IAM pulling out of the process) over disagreements concerning how union officials would be selected (elections versus appointment) and other matters (Bureau of National Affairs 2000).

The UAW continues to be organized in three primary departments aligned with the main domestic companies, even following Chrysler's merger with Daimler-Benz. This merger has also given the UAW president a seat on the board of the German corporation. Supplier firms, recently spun off from the Big Three (Delphi from GM and Visteon from Ford), are still covered by the UAW department for the parent company.

The Companies

The American assembly companies are commonly referred to as the "Big Three": General Motors (GM), Ford, and Chrysler. We will continue to use this term for consistency over the time covered and for simplicity, even though the creation of DaimlerChrysler means that "Big Two-and-a-Half" would be more appropriate. The Big Three produce a number of car and truck parts, and they assemble these parts into final vehicles, although the extent to which these assemblers are "vertically integrated" (use parts produced in their own plants) varies. Overall, the trend across all the assemblers is toward much more disintegration (i.e., many fewer parts procured from fully owned suppliers). The Big Three are completely unionized, and their national (companywide) collective bargaining agreements cover the companies' final assembly and parts plants. In addition, the Saturn Corporation, a subsidiary of GM, operates a sizable unionized auto assembly complex in Spring Hill, Tennessee, covered under a separate contract that differs substantially from the national GM agreement; a second Saturn plant, in Delaware, also operates under a distinctive contract but one much closer to the national norm than to the original Spring Hill contract. Table 1 contains basic information about these companies.

TABLE 1
U.S. Automotive Companies: North American Assembly Operations

Company	U.S. assembly plants	Assembly plants Canada	Mexico	1999 vehicle production	2000 vehicle production
GM	26	3	2	5,416,315	5,187,101
Ford	19	3	3	4,355,940	4,388,668
Chrysler	10	3	3	2,834,539	2,567,720

Source: Automotive News Market Data Book (2000, 2001).

There are also a number of assembly plants with Japanese and German ownership, referred to in the industry and in this paper as the "transplants." Table 2 contains summary information on these plants. Three of the transplants acquired union status by virtue of their joint-venture arrangements with U.S. companies: NUMMI (GM–Toyota), Diamond Star (Chrysler–Mitsubishi), and Auto Alliance (Ford–Mazda). These arrangements have been somewhat fluid; they have been altered at two of these plants since they opened. Two German transplants started production in the 1990s—BMW in Spartanburg, North Carolina, in 1994, and Mercedes-Benz in Vance, Alabama, in 1997. Overall, transplant production increased from just over 2 million in 1990 to 3.2 million in 1999. More transplant capacity will come online in the next few years, primarily from the Japanese automakers, with plant locations primarily in the Deep South (Alabama and Mississippi).

TABLE 2

Japanese and German Automobile Assembly Plants (Transplants) Based in the United States and Canada

Company	Company ownership	Plant location	Production start-up	Output 1990	Output 1999	Output 2000
Auto Alliance International	Ford 50% Mazda 50%	Flat Rock, MI	1987	189,906	165,143	107,431
BMW Mfg. Corp.	BMW 100%	Spartanburg, NC	1994	0	2,412	38,665
Honda of America Mfg.	Honda 100%	East Liberty, OH	1989	406,352	685,900	225,723
Honda of America Mfg.	Honda 100%	Marysville, OH	1982	370,979	448,283	451,367
Mitsubishi Motor Mfg.	Mitsubishi 100%	Normal, IL	1988	142,190	159,702	221,975
Mercedes-Benz U.S.	Daimler-Benz 100%	Vance, AL	1997	0	77,696	80,005
New United Motor Mfg., Inc.	GM 50% Toyota 50%	Fremont, CA	1984	205,287	156,395	344,076
Nissan Motor Mfg. USA	Nissan 100%	Smyrna, TN	1983	235,248	324,645	377,275
Subaru–Isuzu Auto, Inc.	Fuji Hvy. Ind. 50% Isuzu 50%	Lafayette, IN	1989	46,348	192,200	208,676
Toyota Motor Mfg. (IN)	Toyota 100%	Princeton, IN	1998	0	NA	129,724
Toyota Motor Mfg. (KY)	Toyota 100%	Georgetown, KY	1988	211,265	369,526	123,553
CAMI Inc.	GM 50% Suzuki 50%	Ingersoll, Ontario	1989	105,860	112,314	107,651
Honda Canada Mfg.	Honda 100%	Alliston, Ontario	1986	104,572	274,908	326,823
Toyota Motor Mfg. (Canada)	Toyota 100%	Cambridge, Ontario	1988	60,804	211,082	183,739
Volvo Canada, Inc.	Volvo 100%	Halifax, Nova Scotia	1963	8,062	NA	NA

Sources: Ward's Automotive Yearbook (various years); *Automotive News Market Data Book* (various years).

Although the UAW has launched various organizing drives in unorganized transplants in recent years, none of these drives have come close to being successful. The UAW, for example, tried to unionize Nissan workers in 1997 and then tried again in 2001 but soundly lost both representation elections (receiving only 32 percent of the vote in the most recent election) (Bureau of National Affairs 2001b). Despite these losses, UAW efforts to organize the transplants continue, most recently at Honda.

The Bargaining Context

The Competitive Environment

From 1946 until 1979, the auto industry in the United States was on a prosperous growth path, even in the face of the industry's periodic sharp cyclical swings. Over these years domestic production of cars and trucks increased from 5 to 13 million vehicles. This economic environment was conducive to steady improvements and general stability in labor relations. Three environmental factors were critical: growth in domestic auto sales, a low level of imported vehicle sales, and a high degree of unionization. Yet, in the early 1980s, a labor and management that had grown accustomed to long-run growth in total vehicle sales and profits were confronted by a number of fundamental changes in the auto market.

One important aspect of the change was an increase in international competition in the form of increased vehicle imports. The level of imports increased steadily during the 1960s and 1970s, from a postwar low of 5 percent in 1955, surged during the 1980s, and then declined in the 1990s (see Table 3) as Japanese and German companies increased their North American production capacity. The market share of these foreign automakers, based on sales of both imported and locally manufactured products, has increased steadily during this period, to the point where Toyota may soon surpass DaimlerChrysler as the third-largest seller of passenger vehicles in the United States.

In the early 1980s American automakers also confronted sizable declines in sales, induced by a sluggish American economy. From 1979 to 1982 employment in the auto industry (SIC 371) declined by 29.4 percent (from 990,400 to 699,300). Ford and Chrysler were hardest hit during this downturn. Then in the mid-1980s auto sales began to rebound strongly, and employment in the industry and the financial status of the auto assemblers markedly improved.

When a sluggish economy returned in the early 1990s, it had dramatic effects on both employment and profits among the Big Three. By 1991, auto industry employment was down to 789,000; most of this drop

TABLE 3

U.S. New Vehicle Sales of American Automakers, Japanese Transplants,
Japanese Imports, and Total Imports, 1991–1999
(Numbers in thousands of units)

Year	American automakers		Japanese transplants		Japanese imports		Total imports		American automakers (all motor vehicles)
	Sales	% of total sales	Sales	% of total sales	Sales	% of total sales	Sales	% of total sales	Production
1991	8,672	69	1,312	10	1,862	15	2,566	20	7,182
1992	9,279	71	1,438	11	1,698	13	2,336	18	7,864
1993	10,246	73	1,644	12	1,578	11	2,153	15	8,852
1994	10,997	73	1,920	13	1,597	11	2,147	14	9,874
1995	10,761	73	2,031	14	1,337	9	1,908	13	9,406
1996	10,580	72	2,311	16	1,127	8	1,714	12	9,177
1997	10,716	72	2,303	15	1,271	8	1,937	13	9,485
1998	10,636	70	2,419	16	1,309	9	2,037	13	9,217
1999	11,253	69	2,586	16	1,500	9	2,493	15	10,208

Sources: Sales—*Ward's Automotive Yearbook* (various years); Production—*Automotive News Market Data Book* (various years).
Note: For purposes of this table, the term "American automakers" denotes General Motors, Ford, and Chrysler.

reflected job losses for the Big Three because the transplants continued to bring new capacity online. GM was hit particularly hard in this period and announced plans to cut blue collar employment by 80,000 and close a number of plants.

Then beginning in 1993, profits rebounded strongly at the Big Three, with Chrysler performing particularly favorably. Along with this sales and profit rebound, employment also rebounded, although not as strongly, as the auto companies made extensive use of overtime (particularly at Ford and Chrysler) and benefited from productivity improvements. Industry (SIC 371) employment finally exceeded its previous peak (990,400 in 1979) when it rose to 995,300 in 1998. Much of the surge in sales, profits, and employment was tied to phenomenal growth in the light truck and SUV segments, where the Big Three faced less competition from Japanese and German competitors.

Cyclical factors once again came to the fore in the spring of 2000 when auto sales began to slump due to a recession and the bursting of the dot.com bubble. Auto industry employment began to slide, falling to

906,600 as of November 2001. These conditions starkly revealed the overcapacity situation for the auto assemblers, both in North America and worldwide; estimates of excess global capacity ranged from 20 to 30 percent. Even during the boom years of the 1990s, this overcapacity existed, although it was masked by the fact that the most profitable assembly plants (those building trucks and SUVs) were working considerable overtime, while plants building older sedan models were operating considerably under capacity.

While Ford and Chrysler had performed better than GM in the 1990s boom period, this pattern reversed over the next few years. Chrysler's financial troubles were already emerging at the time of the Daimler–Chrysler merger and accelerated as difficulties with post-merger integration led to a large-scale departure of Chrysler executives. Chrysler's financial situation hit its nadir in early 2001, and in February 2001, DaimlerChrysler announced plans to cut its workforce by 20 percent over the next three years (this would amount to 12,300 hourly workers). While savings resulting from the Chrysler–Daimler-Benz merger were expected to grow to some $3 billion per year, instead, the company lost $583 million in 2001.

As of early 2002, speculation surfaced in the press as to whether DaimlerChrysler would reverse the merger by selling off Chrysler, given that expected synergies and economies had not appeared in the merged company. Whether Chrysler could survive again as an independent company is not clear; if this sell-off occurred, the assets might simply be divided between GM and Ford. Other non-U.S. automakers might be interested as well (e.g., Volkswagen, Hyundai, and Renault, all of which have expanded global sales aggressively [for Renault, through its purchase of a controlling interest in Nissan]), but none have any production capacity in the United States. However, Daimler-Benz may also face pressure from its board (which under German codetermination is made up of nearly 50 percent employee representatives) to devote considerable resources to the revival of Chrysler.

Ford's troubles came to the fore in late 2001, and the company lost $5.4 billion in 2001, including restructuring charges (Ford had earned a profit of $3.47 billion in 2000). While heavily influenced by the crisis with Firestone tires, Ford's problems also seemed to be related to its effort in the late 1990s to expand into consumer services, which took attention away from the core manufacturing business. Ford announced a turnaround plan on January 11, 2002, that would eliminate more than 20,000 jobs in its North American operations, close four North American plants, and discontinue four slow-selling vehicles. The plant closings will occur after the company's current contract with the UAW expires in September 2003 (Bureau of National Affairs 2002). The plan was labeled as "back to basics" and will include the sell-off of most consumer services firms acquired in recent years.

GM has returned to profitability during this time, reversing a long period of market share decline dating back to the late 1970s. GM has also led the industry in using low-interest financing arrangements to boost sales in the post-September 11 period, a successful marketing strategy that may well shorten the length of the current downturn. Nevertheless, GM too is closing some of its older and less flexible assembly plants in both Canada and the United States. At the same time, GM has just completed construction of two new assembly plants, the first Big Three investment in new production capacity in the United States since the Saturn plant in 1989; both are located near older GM plants—in Lansing, Michigan, and Lordstown, Ohio—that will be closed once the new plants are fully operational.

Thus across the Big Three, the current cyclical downturn is creating pressure to close down older plant capacity, even as competitive pressures create incentives to build or buy (through retrofitting some older plants) capacity that is more flexible and can produce lower volumes of multiple products from multiple platforms in a cost-effective way.

Also significant for collective bargaining in recent years has been the formation of more extensive linkages between the assembler companies and their parts suppliers. Most assemblers dramatically reduced the number of their parts suppliers and initiated longer-term contracts with a select group of suppliers that remained. Recently, both Ford and GM spun off their internal parts plants into separate companies, Visteon and Delphi, respectively. Other first-tier suppliers have also grown through merger and acquisition, forming (along with the Big Three spin-offs) a new class of "mega-supplier" capable of designing, building, and handling the complex logistics for major modules or subsystems of the vehicle. The mega-suppliers are primarily nonunion, with some exceptions, although the UAW is devoting considerable organizing resources to change this. The collective bargaining implications of these spin-offs and the emergence of the mega-suppliers are discussed later in this chapter.

Partially as a result of the spin-off of supplier divisions, but also as a result of a strong trend in the direction of outsourcing, employment at supplier plants has increased dramatically since the 1980s, at the expense of employment at vehicle assembly plants (see Table 4). While auto parts employment grew 60 percent from 1980 to 2000, over the same period employment fell 3 percent at auto assembly plants. Interestingly, this shift in employment has not been accompanied by a commensurate increase in wages for production workers at auto parts plants. The figures in Table 4 reveal that the auto assemblers' wage was 15 percent higher than the wage of auto parts workers in 1980, but by 2000 assemblers were making 31 percent more than workers in the auto parts sector. The pressure on wages from the nonunion parts sector, which is now larger than the unionized sector, is the primary reason behind this differential.

TABLE 4

Employment and Wages in U.S. Motor Vehicle Assembly and Parts Sectors, 1980–2000

Year	Assembly employment	Assembly wage (hourly $)	Parts employment	Parts wage (hourly $)
1980	252,800	10.80	268,800	9.40
1981	251,900	12.29	283,700	10.38
1982	220,700	13.01	247,900	10.91
1983	252,900	13.36	265,700	11.61
1984	289,500	14.12	309,700	12.16
1985	307,300	14.81	314,900	12.69
1986	296,500	14.99	310,200	12.71
1987	286,400	15.33	316,300	12.69
1988	265,500	16.09	327,800	13.11
1989	259,500	16.51	332,400	13.26
1990	237,800	17.26	315,200	13.22
1991	229,300	18.34	315,200	13.62
1992	228,900	18.32	333,000	14.22
1993	229,900	19.44	345,000	14.74
1994	245,700	20.71	383,300	15.56
1995	267,900	20.57	414,600	16.18
1996	265,800	21.06	424,400	16.46
1997	268,100	21.63	435,400	16.60
1998	250,700	21.81	430,800	16.48
1999	249,400	21.73	432,900	16.98
2000	244,400	22.91	431,300	17.41

The assembly data refer to SIC 3714, while the parts data refer to SIC 3711.
The data are from various issues of *Employment & Earnings*, U.S. Department of Labor, Bureau of Labor Statistics.

Plant-Level Performance Differentials

In the face of heightened competition, the Big Three and the UAW made substantial changes in their industrial relations practices from the early 1980s on. An important force for change was the perception that Japanese-owned plants, both in Japan and in the United States, had substantial productivity and quality advantages over the typical Big Three plant because of their use of lean production, a system developed by Toyota and used to varying degrees by all Japanese companies.

Lean production is described as combining a different way of thinking about production goals (quality and productivity as mutually attainable, not a trade-off) with new production methods aimed at boosting efficiency. This occurs through the elimination of waste (reducing buffers through just-in-time inventory systems and "building in" rather than "inspecting in" quality) and human resource practices aimed at motivating workers and developing their skills (work teams, job rotation, problem-solving groups, increased worker training, performance-based bonus pay, and reduction of status barriers) (Womack, Jones, and Roos 1990). Underpinning the entire system is the idea of "kaizen," or continuous improvement in production processes and in productivity and quality outcomes. According to this model, buffer reduction reveals production problems and creates the pressure to solve them. Then, if workers are sufficiently skilled and motivated, they will respond with extensive participation in the improvement process.

The perception of lean production as the source of Japanese competitive advantage represented an important shift away from Japan-specific explanatory factors such as lower wage rates, longer working hours, cooperative enterprise unions, lifetime employment, and cultural traits (e.g., a strong work ethic and a group orientation conducive to teamwork). These culturally-based explanations for the Japanese performance advantage were undermined by the performance of the Japanese transplants in the 1980s. Data from MIT's international assembly plant study indicated that the transplants, using American workers, engineers, managers, and (at some plants) union officials, achieved performance results, in terms of both productivity and quality, that matched or surpassed most American plants (Krafcik and MacDuffie 1989; Pil and MacDuffie 1999).[4]

Furthermore, the source of the transplants' performance advantage appeared to be their implementation of lean production methods very similar to those used in plants in Japan (Shimada and MacDuffie 1987; Florida and Kenney 1993). However, these practices have been adapted to the U.S. context (Pil and MacDuffie 1999).

This view of lean production has been challenged on two points. Some researchers question whether lean production is indeed a distinctive paradigm with performance advantages, pointing to industry and company-level statistics on inventory levels and financial performance that show only modest variation across U.S. and Japanese companies (Williams et al. 1994). According to these researchers, any Japanese or transplant cost advantages are due to lower wages in the various tiers of the supply system.[5] Other accounts of the transplants develop a broader critique of "lean production" as relying on "sweating" workers through a faster work pace, rigid job standardization, intensive peer pressure for higher work effort within teams, and continual stress from the lack of buffers and from "kaizen" efforts to remove work content from jobs (Parker and Slaughter 1988; Babson 1995).

Recent Comparative Productivity, Quality, and Work Practice Data

On the performance front, North American plants have exerted tremendous efforts to increase efficiency over the past decade. Our research, based on round three of the international assembly plant study, suggests that the average North American plant now requires less than seventeen hours to build a standard vehicle (see MacDuffie and Pil 1995, for methodology). While this still lags behind the less than thirteen hours it takes the Japanese producers, the U.S. productivity increase represents a tremendous improvement from the twenty-two hours it took on average to assemble vehicles in U.S. plants in 1994.

Most of these labor productivity improvements have come via significant efforts to improve product design, streamline production layout, and optimize production tasks and throughput. There has been little increase in the use of high-involvement work practices. As can be seen in Table 5, in recent years more plants use teams. However, in the plants that have teams, their average use has dropped from 49 percent to 25 percent. Similarly, there has been little increase in job rotation, with most plants reporting that workers are capable of rotating but rarely do. Suggestions programs continue to be sparsely used, and less than a third of suggestions received from workers are actually implemented.

TABLE 5
U.S.-Owned Plants in North America

	1994	2000
% of plants that have teams	35.0	46.0
% of workers in teams, for plants with teams	49.0	25.0
Job rotation	1.6	1.8
Suggestions per employee	.3	.2
% of suggestions implemented	42.0	31.0

Source: F. Pil and J. P. MacDuffie, unpublished data; International Motor Vehicle Program International Assembly Plant Survey—24 plants in 2000, 26 plants in 1994.

While North American plants have improved remarkably on the labor productivity front, the lack of high-involvement work systems has hurt them on the quality front. Looking at major quality items originating in the assembly plant (based on J. D. Power surveys), defects have fallen sharply, from sixty-nine defects per 100 vehicles to forty-five defects. However, the Big Three plants in North America are still far behind the performance levels of Japanese and European producers, who are currently attaining rates of thirty to thirty-five defects per 100 vehicles.

Overall, the data show that, while the idea of lean production as a new production paradigm capable of superior performance has taken hold strongly among corporate management at the U.S. companies, the implementation of lean production at U.S. plants has been relatively slow and varies for different aspects of this system. Most quickly adopted have been lean production policies on the reduction of buffers. The pace of implementation of new human resource practices has been slower, particularly in the cases where new work structures such as teams are being implemented at existing plants. The area in which U.S. companies have followed the lean production model least is with regard to product variety and manufacturing flexibility.

One of the key performance criteria that companies will have to deal with in years ahead is organizational flexibility with respect to production volumes. As more content shifts out of assembly factories and as efforts continue to increase the tie between the customer and manufacturing, flexibility in terms of production volumes will become increasingly important. Vehicle sales vary dramatically during the course of the year, and the current solution of maintaining between one and two months of inventory in the marketplace is under increasing cost pressure, as well as competitive pressure, as customers seek more customized products.

While increased incentives and other tools can be used to even out customer demand during the course of the year, another avenue is to increase manufacturing flexibility (Holweg and Pil 2001). Currently, plants face very high fixed costs, and per-unit costs increase dramatically as production volumes drop. Indeed, it costs the average North American plant 84 percent of full capacity costs to run at half-capacity production levels for a week. While it is slightly cheaper to produce at half capacity for a one-year period, this still costs almost 77 percent of full capacity costs. Labor represents an important source of rigidity, and layoffs seem to be the primary solution. This is true, even for some of the transplants.

There are very few provisions in place, either at transplants or at the Big Three, to alter labor levels more flexibly in response to shifts in demand. During the auto sales boom of the 1990s, that was not a big issue, as plants were often running close to full capacity. However, if the recent decline in auto demand accelerates, this could become an important issue.

Various experiments in production flexibility are under way overseas. These include the banking of hours in periods when labor demand is low, which can be used at a later date without incurring overtime. The models in vogue in Europe at the moment typically limit the number of hours that can be banked or withdrawn in any one period, specify the length of time that banked hours can be held, and provide an agreed on overtime payment if no work-hour reductions follow a period of overtime. BMW in Germany, for example, goes a step further and has a pool of temporary workers who are shifted between factories as demand for products shifts across its vehicle lines. BMW is paid by a temporary agency to train a pool of workers and guarantees these workers a five-year contract but can use them across any of its production facilities. If at some point BMW has no need for the workers, it pays a subsidy to the temporary agency to find employment for the workers at other firms.

In contrast, the Big Three auto companies, like other large U.S. manufacturing firms, have very little flexibility in altering their labor usage during the course of the year (short of lay-offs). Most of management's efforts are centered on increasing capacity utilization rather than managing reductions in demand. The most common approach is to run plants for three shifts or use three crews of workers to run two shifts six or seven days a week. These issues warrant attention, as production (and labor relations) flexibility may emerge as a key source of international comparative advantage (or disadvantage) in the years ahead.

Mergers and Coproduction

Consolidation among the auto assembly companies, including mergers and coproduction agreements, became a strong trend around the globe in the late 1990s. Ford—already the owner of Jaguar and Aston Martin and with a controlling equity share of Mazda—bought Volvo and Land Rover. GM purchased the 50 percent of Saab that it did not already own; increased its equity stake in Isuzu, Suzuki, and Fiat; and is likely to purchase Korean firm Daewoo as the latter emerges from bankruptcy. In Europe, French-based Renault purchased a controlling equity stake in Nissan and Samsung, and German-based Volkswagen bought Bentley, with BMW claiming the Rolls-Royce brand. In Korea, Hyundai took over Kia and became by far the dominant firm in both domestic and export sales.

From the U.S. standpoint, the largest change in ownership in the auto sector, as noted previously, is the merger of Chrysler with Daimler-Benz. Initially billed as a merger of equals, it quickly became clear that it was more a takeover of Chrysler by Daimler-Benz, as one by one, senior Chrysler executives were forced out. Daimler-Benz also increased their stake in Mitsubishi, leaving Honda and Toyota as the only two fully independent Japanese automakers. Even Honda and Toyota, while asserting their independence, became more intertwined with the fate of other firms, with Honda beginning to sell engines to GM and Toyota embarking on a joint-venture plant and product in Europe with Peugeot. All of these firms remained unionized throughout the period of consolidation. But the fact that a smaller number of global firms remain at the start of the automotive industry's second century means that the industrial relations policies of those firms will have even more impact than in the past.

The Structure of Collective Bargaining

Pattern Bargaining

Prior to 1979, the U.S. auto bargaining structure involved very strong pattern following within and across the auto companies. From the early 1980s on, however, the degree of pattern following has declined across the Big Three, and cross-company variation has increased with the entry of Japanese transplants.

In the traditional bargaining structure that prevailed at the Big Three, compensation is set by national company-specific and multiyear (from 1955 to 1999, they were three-year) agreements. Some work rules such as overtime administration, employee transfer rights, and seniority guidelines are also set in the national contracts. Local unions, in turn, negotiate plant-level agreements, which supplement the national agreements. The local agreements define work rules such as the form of the seniority ladder, job characteristics, job bidding and transfer rights, health and safety standards, production standards, and an array of other rules, which guide shop-floor production. The local agreements do not regulate either wages or fringe benefits, which are set in the national contract. Some indirect influences on wage determination do occur at the plant level, in the definition and modification of job classifications provided through the local agreements.

Local bargaining over work rules allows for the expression of local preferences and some adjustment to local conditions. In this system the grievance procedure, with binding third-party arbitration, serves as the end point of contract administration, although disputes concerning production standards, new job rates, and health and safety issues are not resolved through recourse to arbitration.

The influence of the agreements reached in the auto assembly firms has traditionally extended out to the auto supplier sector and beyond. The UAW, for example, has used the auto assembly agreements as a pattern setter in their negotiations in the agricultural implements industry. Other unions, especially those linked to auto production, such as the rubber industry, also looked to the contracts in the auto assembly firms as pattern setters. From the early 1950s until the late 1970s, the extent of interindustry pattern following varied somewhat over time, but generally there was a high degree of pattern following. In the 1980s, the pattern-leading role of the Big Three settlements declined (Budd 1992).

The Bargaining Process: Wage Rules and Fringe Benefit Determination

From 1948 until 1980, formulaic mechanisms were used to set wage levels in collective bargaining agreements in the Big Three.[6] The formulaic wage-setting mechanisms traditionally included in the contracts were an annual improvement factor (AIF) that after the mid-1960s amounted to 3 percent per year and a cost-of-living adjustment (COLA) escalator that often provided full or close to full cost-of-living protection.

The importance of these formulaic mechanisms was that they provided continuity in wage determination across time and across the assembly companies at any given time. The continuity across time was provided by the fact that, except for minor adjustments, the formula mechanisms rigidly set wages from 1948 until 1979 among the Big Three companies.[7] Continuity across the industry was provided by intercompany pattern following and by the fact that, in the plants covered by the company agreements, the national contract wage was not modified in local bargaining.

Along with increases in real hourly earnings, autoworkers received steady improvements in their fringe benefit package. A number of these fringe benefit advances such as supplementary unemployment benefits, "thirty and out" pensions, and paid personal holidays were innovations that eventually spread to the auto supplier firms and to a number of other industries. Over the postwar period, fringe benefits became a larger share of total worker compensation.

Job Control Unionism

At both national and shop-floor levels, the labor relations system in the Big Three traditionally relied on contractually defined procedures to regulate disagreements between labor and management. The contractual regulation of these procedures was heavily focused on "job control."[8] Wages were explicitly tied to jobs and not to worker characteristics. In addition, much of the detail within the contract concerned the specification of an elaborate job classification system, with much attention paid to the exact requirements of each job and to seniority rights that were tied to a job ladder guiding promotions, transfers, and layoffs (Piore 1982).

From the late 1940s until the late 1970s, the application of wage rules and job control unionism produced steadily rising real compensation to autoworkers and long-term growth in auto employment and production. With limited import penetration in auto sales, this was a bargaining process where the geographic bounds of union organization closely matched the relevant product market. The consistency the bargaining process had with the economic environment was one of the primary factors contributing to the system's attractiveness to both labor and management. Important political functions for labor and management also were served by the stability and continuity in the auto negotiation processes.

Developments in Collective Bargaining From the Early 1980s On

Wages

As import share rose in the 1980s and economic recession took hold, the absolute power of labor and management at the Big Three auto companies declined, and the contracts negotiated in the early 1980s reflected this power decline. In addition, the relative bargaining power of the UAW was weakened by factors such as the rise in imports, the ease by which the companies could move production offshore, and the erosion of strike leverage due to excessive production capacity. In collective bargaining at the Big Three, the wage rules traditionally used to set wage levels were modified significantly, first as part of efforts to avoid bankruptcy at Chrysler in 1979 and 1980. In agreements reached at the Big Three after 1979, the traditional formulaic wage rules were replaced by lump sum increases, periodic base pay increases, and profit sharing.[9] With respect to fringe benefits, the agreements reached at the Big Three after 1979 included a number of concessions.

By the mid-1990s, however, the UAW had regained substantial bargaining power relative to the Big Three, and this gain was reflected in favorable contract terms. The 1993–1996 Big Three–UAW contracts provided a 3 percent base pay increase in the first year and 3 percent lump sum pay increases in the second and third years of the contracts. The contracts also ensured the continuing of the company-based profit sharing programs. The 1999–2003 Big Three–UAW contracts were even more favorable, as they provided a return to the traditional 3 percent base pay increases, along with COLA payments (and profit sharing) in each of four years. The lengthening of the contract to four years (from the traditional three-year contract duration) apparently provided attractive stability and predictability to both the union and management. The 1999–2003 contracts also include a $1,350 up-front lump sum payment, as well as improved income and employment security provisions, as described below.

Table 6 reports the hourly wages (including COLA payments) received by auto assemblers at GM from 1980 to 2000.[10] The figures show the limited growth in real earnings received by auto assemblers over the 1980s and early 1990s, as a result of the abandonment of the regular 3 percent per year AIF wage increases. From 1980 to 2000 the real wage of Big Three autoworkers grew by 8.8 percent, and nearly all of this increase occurred from 1995 to 2000 (6.2 percent). Yet, given the declines in real earnings suffered by many other American workers, autoworkers' hourly wages rose sizably, relative to other production workers over this period, as shown in column C of Table 6. Total hourly labor costs at GM in 1999 were $50.51, given the extensive pay and costly fringe benefits provided to autoworkers.[11]

The introduction of profit sharing received much attention in the press, particularly in light of the traditional pattern-setting role auto assemblers have played in American collective bargaining. The payouts of the profit sharing plans adopted by the Big Three from 1983 on have varied substantially, in large part due to differences in the financial performance of the companies (see Table 7). The profit sharing payouts between 1983 and 2000 at GM, Ford, and Chrysler, respectively, totaled $6,916; $47,545; and $45,025. The variation in profit sharing payouts received by workers across companies was the source of some controversy within the workforce and the UAW.

Income and Employment Security Programs

The contracts at the Big Three after 1979 also included a number of new income and job security programs, programs that were induced by

TABLE 6

Auto Assembler Hourly Wages at General Motors, 1980–2000

Year	Column A Auto hourly wage	Column B Auto real hourly wage	Column C Ratio of auto to average production worker hourly wage
1980	9.77	11.86	1.47
1985	13.15	12.22	1.53
1990	15.69	12.00	1.57
1995	18.52	12.15	1.62
1996	18.89	12.04	1.60
1997	19.39	12.08	1.58
1998	20.24	12.42	1.58
1999	21.10	12.67	1.59
2000	22.21	12.90	1.68

Column A is the hourly base wage (including COLA payments) received by assemblers at General Motors. The information is from an unpublished series of the UAW.

Column B is the hourly wage reported in column A divided by the consumer price index, as reported by the Bureau of Labor Statistics, *Monthly Labor Review*, various issues (1982–1984 = 100).

Column C is the hourly auto assembler wage reported in column A divided by the average hourly earnings of production or nonsupervisory workers on private nonfarm payrolls, as reported in the Bureau of Labor Statistics, *Monthly Labor Review*, various issues.

the layoffs and plant closings occurring at the Big Three. These programs included "guaranteed income stream benefits"; joint national employee development and training programs at each company funded by company contributions; and "jobs bank" programs protecting workers displaced by nonmarket- (i.e., nonsales) related causes.[12] A worker's seniority heavily influenced the level and duration of benefits he or she received in these programs, although the specific benefit criteria varied across the programs.

Big Three contracts in the 1990s provided extensive additions to the income security package. A significant new element in these contracts was the provision that workers could not be laid off for more than thirty-six weeks *whatever the cause*. The contracts also included guaranteed employment levels at each Big Three plant. The companies agreed to replace workers at rates that depend on whether a plant is above or below its employment target and due to the cause of any employment declines. The basic guarantee is that for every two workers who leave due to attrition, one new worker is to be hired.

TABLE 7

Big Three Average Worker Profit Sharing, 1983–2000

Year	Ford ($)	GM ($)	Chrysler ($)
1983	402	605	0
1984	1,993	515	0
1985	1,262	329	0
1986	2,177	0	0[a]
1987	3,762	0	0[a]
1988	2,874	242	725
1989	1,025	50	0
1990	0	0	0
1991	0	0	0
1992	0	0	425
1993	1,350	0	4,300
1994	4,000	550	8,000
1995	1,700	800	3,200
1996	1,800	300	7,900
1997	4,400	750	4,600
1998	6,100	200	7,400
1999	8,000	1,775	8,100
2000	6,700	800	375
Total	47,545	6,916	45,025

Sources: Unpublished table prepared by the UAW Research Department, February 8, 1995, and various news stories in the Daily Labor Report, Bureau of National Affairs.
[a] Chrysler workers received a $500 contractual payment, not tied to profits.

A key factor that looms in the background, influencing the workings of the employment guarantees and the companies' efforts to improve productivity, is the fact that the workforces at all of the Big Three companies have substantial seniority, as there has been only limited new hiring among these firms since 1979. At GM, for example, as of January 1, 2001, 23 percent of the workforce had thirty or more years of seniority, while 49 percent had between twenty and thirty years' seniority (only 9 percent of workers had less than ten years' seniority).[13] This means that a substantial number of workers will retire from GM (and the other auto companies) over the next ten years.

GM has already greatly reduced its workforce in recent years through retirements and other forms of attrition. The GM workforce (including Delphi) went from 247,000 to 168,000, from January 1994 to January 2000. Over the same period, GM's sales of cars and trucks in the United States declined only slightly, from 5,041,615 in 1994 to 4,453,167 in 2000 (Ward's Automotive Yearbook 2001). The sizable decline in GM employment in part reflects productivity improvements and the out-sourcing of production to domestic and foreign suppliers and assem-blers. Meanwhile GM's market share of U.S. car and truck sales declined, from 32.7 percent in 1994 to 27.8 percent in 2000.

Fearing even further erosion of its employment base and bargaining power, the UAW pushed for further income and employment protections in its 1999–2003 collective bargaining agreements with the Big Three, with substantial success. New funds were added and, most notably, the agreements expanded the scope of the plant-closing moratorium letter.[14] The new letter provides that each of the companies will not close, nor partially or wholly sell, spin off, consolidate, or otherwise dispose of any plant or business unit during the life of the contract. This letter was added to the DaimlerChrysler contract at the UAW's insistence after the UAW targeted DaimlerChrysler to set the pattern for 1999 contract bar-gaining. DaimlerChrysler apparently accepted the moratorium condi-tions in part because, as of 1999, the company's plants were generally running extensive overtime and the company's bargainers expected that GM's and Ford's eventual acceptance of pattern-following terms (at the urgings of the UAW) would disadvantage GM and Ford relatively more than DaimlerChrysler. This strategy backfired on DaimlerChrysler when, after its sales sharply turned down in 2000 and 2001, the company was unable to make use of plant closings due to the moratorium letter (a similar problem emerged at Ford in late 2001). In this way, the UAW took advantage of its bargaining power and the rivalries that existed across the Big Three companies.

It is interesting to note that the existence of very costly income and employment security programs at the Big Three did not completely set-tle employment security issues. For example, in the summer of 1998, a costly strike occurred at two GM plants in Flint, Michigan. More than 12,000 UAW members walked off the job, and within days twelve of GM's assembly plants had to shut down for lack of parts. With extensive rhetoric in both directions, it took through the middle of July for the strike to enter arbitration and settle. Ultimately, the fifty-four-day strike cost GM $2 billion.

GM was not the only automaker hit by labor disputes over outsourc-ing issues. Chrysler for example, faced a major walkout at its Warren, Michigan, engine plant in 1997. This dispute lasted twenty-nine days and resulted in Chrysler losing the production of 89,000 trucks. Then in early 2002, questions surfaced regarding how Ford would implement its announced cutbacks, given the plant-closing moratoriums and related language that appear in the company's collective bargaining agreement with the UAW.

The Increase in Diversity and Decentralization

The pay concessions and the move to contingent compensation schemes that tied wages to company performance increased the variation in employment conditions across the auto assembly companies. In addition, sizable pay variation was created through the addition of the unionized transplants and the Saturn subsidiary, each of which had a separate agreement with the UAW, and through wage and benefit policies at the nonunion transplants.[15] Sizable variation also now appears in the work practices used in unionized auto assembly plants, as a result of the fact that work rules and work organization have been modified in different ways and at a varied pace across auto assembly plants. The threat of increased employment loss due to either increased foreign sourcing of vehicles, plant closings due to excess capacity, or the outsourcing of certain operations all created pressures to lower costs and improve product quality. Ultimately, the pressure for increased interplant work rule divergence came from the same source, as the pressure for intercompany pay variation and the fear that even greater losses in employment would result if previous policies were maintained. Companies often used investment decisions as explicit leverage for these changes, a strategy unions perceived as whipsawing (i.e., forcing plants to compete against each other through concessions).

The traditional work system in assembly plants involved numerous job classifications, a very heavy and highly structured role for seniority rights in job assignments (transfers, promotions, shift preferences, etc.), and a clear separation in the responsibilities of workers and managerial employees. The joint team-based approach, in contrast, provides greater and broader responsibilities to the blue collar workforce, in many instances involving workers in production and, in some cases, even basic business decisions. The core of this approach is the work team, typically led by an hourly team coordinator. As teams spread, the number of supervisors has been reduced, and the role of the remaining supervisors shifted to a coaching and facilitating role (although discipline did remain a key function of supervision).

The pace at which the team-based approach is spreading varies across the Big Three. GM has experimented most extensively with this approach by initially using nonunion "Southern strategy" plants as a testing ground for the concept. In the early 1980s GM started spreading the team approach in its northern assembly plants, and then in the late 1980s GM management often made the use of a team approach a necessary precondition for the survival of what were then often redundant facilities. Ford and Chrysler were more gradual in their implementation of the team-based approach, in part because neither was building new assembly plants in the 1980s and 1990s and thus did not have the opportunity to experiment in greenfield sites and in part because the GM experience of introducing teams in existing (brownfield) plants did not always work out well (Katz, Kochan, and Keefe 1987).

Yet, from the early 1990s on, even at a number of Ford and Chrysler assembly plants, management was pressuring the union and workforce to move to a team-based approach. Both Ford and Chrysler management began pushing what they referred to as "modern operating agreements" (MOAs), which included teams, reduced job classifications, and weakened seniority rights. MOAs were often negotiated at a time when corporate decisions were being made about investment in a new product or new technology for a given plant; some were only approved under a threat that the plant would be closed. The provisions of MOAs were negotiated centrally by the company and the UAW and then approved locally, creating some tensions between the national and local unions. Yet despite these varied and often difficult founding conditions, evidence from the Chrysler MOA plants suggests that the majority of workers became quite positive about these work reforms as they gained experience in work teams. Ultimately, the actual experience of working under the MOA work reforms was more important in shaping worker responses than the forcing strategy used during implementation to overcome the barrier of workers' negative preconceptions (Hunter, MacDuffie, and Doucet 2002).

Substantial variation is now widespread in how teams and other features of this approach are actually being implemented. In team plants, for example, there is wide variety in the procedures used to select team leaders and the role that hourly team members exert in that selection process. Along with the variation produced by team systems, there is wide variation appearing across assembly plants in the role that workers play in business decisions. The existence of teamwork organization is part of a deepening of worker involvement in business decisions. Yet in many other ways and not directly linked to teams per se, there is wide variety appearing in the role that workers and union officials are playing in plant operations, and in broad terms the lines are blurring between the roles that workers and managers exercise in the production process.

This blurring occurs, for example, when workers serve on a task force to solve a specific production problem, and when workers become part of joint committees on such issues as insourcing, quality, or scrap reduction that are now typically key parts of each plant's administrative structure. In some Big Three assembly plants, union officers now meet regularly with plant managers as business issues or crises arise; in some cases this participation extends to involvement in the preparation of a plant's long-term business plans.

The most extensive participatory labor–management relationship in the auto industry (and perhaps the most extensive anywhere) occurs at the Saturn Corporation (Rubinstein and Kochan 2001). As early as 1982, GM undertook an extensive study of the small-car segment and concluded that it needed to undertake a substantively new approach to its products and manufacturing model, as well as its labor relations, if it was going to be competitive. GM and the UAW decided to explore the issue in a joint effort, ultimately resulting in the creation of the Saturn Corporation in 1987 and the opening of the Saturn plant in Spring Hill, Tennessee. Billed as "A different kind of company, a different kind of car," Saturn has served as the test bed for a number of new innovations, ranging from its "no haggle" pricing, to its space-frame product technology, to process technology such as its lost-foam engine casting process (Pil and Rubinstein 1998).

Most intriguing, however, is Saturn's innovative labor–management relationship. Centered on a consensus decision-making process, it includes a partnering arrangement whereby the UAW has not just been involved in supplier selection and dealer approval but also in the day-to-day management of Saturn operations. Every supervisor (called a "module adviser") has a union counterpart. The union also has a partnership role in other managerial areas, including sales, finance, and engineering. Workers perform a variety of job tasks in their work area and also perform some of the planning and control tasks traditionally carried out by supervisors. At the top level of Saturn is a "strategic advisory committee" that engages in long-range business planning and includes the president of the UAW local union.

There are two extremely novel aspects of shop-floor industrial relations at Saturn. For one thing, seniority plays a limited role in matters such as job assignments, job bidding, overtime, and shift assignments, as these matters are settled informally by the work units (i.e., by workers themselves). Perhaps most revolutionary is the presence of union and management "partners" who co-manage decisions within the Saturn complex.

Although the union does not have a formal place on the GM board of directors, which makes the ultimate decisions concerning Saturn's investments, products, and pricing, the strong role played by UAW partners at Saturn gives the union a level of involvement in decision making that is unparalleled in contemporary American industrial relations.

Ten years since the start of production, Saturn can point to many successes, including the often imitated success of its no haggle policy in selling vehicles, its early insight that it is important to build vehicles to customer demand, and consistently superior ratings on its product quality. The union–management relationship is still going strong but has had its share of challenges, the most prominent occurring in 1998 when the union issued a strike notice centered on the long-term viability of Saturn's product line based at Spring Hill. This was followed shortly thereafter by the defeat of Mike Bennett, who had been president of the Saturn UAW local since Saturn's inception and had helped develop the cooperative agreement over the past decade. Bennett was defeated by Robert "Jeep" Williams, who at one point advocated abandoning the flexibility of Saturn's 32-page agreement in favor of the 640-page national UAW contract in force at all other GM factories in the United States (Bradsher 1999). While Williams did not call for the replacement of the contract in the 1999 election, his platform did include a push to adopt work rules common at other GM factories and to eliminate the link between pay and plant productivity.

The conservative stance of the national offices of the UAW toward Saturn is mirrored on the GM management side. In 1994, Saturn was folded into GM's small-car group. That decision, coupled with GM's recent move to increase its stake in Suzuki and Isuzu, as well as its new investments in Fiat and Daewoo, suggests that Saturn has not been the key to GM's long-term success, as Roger Smith (then CEO of GM) had predicted at Saturn's creation. Indeed, it is Saturn's innovative approach to creating a different kind of dealership atmosphere for purchasing its vehicles that is proving to be its most lasting legacy. The fact that GM did not invest in new products for Saturn during the 1990s, while trying to reverse its declining market share and improve its cost structure, eventually hurt sales and Saturn's image with consumers. This may have limited severely the potential for the innovative Saturn labor–management relationship and collective bargaining contract to diffuse throughout GM and the industry.

Despite the general pattern of diversity and decentralization, new corporate-level initiatives to standardize the production system across plants around the world may have a more centralizing effect. The trend differs from a past in which production systems varied widely across facilities, depending on past history, product line, vintage of technology, nature of labor relations, and the inclinations of current managers and union officials. One factor, as previously noted, is the influence of lean production, which most auto companies have seized on as their model for manufacturing. But a more universal impulse derives from the high level of complexity and volatility affecting many modern manufacturing operations and therefore the goal has become reducing process variance while also establishing a clear basis for evaluating the impact of changes in production methods. Standardization becomes an important step in both internal learning processes and in the transfer of learning across settings.

The most prominent examples of this trend can be found at Ford and Chrysler. Following their MOA initiatives, which were carried out jointly with the UAW but only affected a small number of assembly plants, by the late 1990s both companies chose to promote a common production system throughout all of their North American plants. Modeled closely on the Toyota approach, these were called the Ford Production System and the Chrysler Operating System. A replication strategy has also been attemped by GM, with new plants in China, Poland, Argentina, and Brazil all modeled on their successful implementation of lean production at Eisenach in the former East Germany.

Mercedes-Benz has been much influenced by the success of its new plant in the United States, which was set up from the start to operate under lean production, and its managers now speak of implementing a common production system, modeled on Toyota, which will be applied in its German factories as well. This approach may conceivably be extended worldwide throughout DaimlerChrysler.

Whether or not these efforts at standardization will be successful is difficult to predict; the historical record suggests that such efforts often fail to achieve anything more than partial diffusion. This trend is also directly counter to the pattern of diversity and decentralization observed for industrial relations and collective bargaining. But it is worth noting that a logic now exists for automakers to undertake careful efforts to coordinate production globally, particularly for products built on common platforms, and that efforts to transfer knowledge across plants are far more extensive and sophisticated than in the past. This logic could certainly affect corporate strategies for industrial relations in such areas as work organization, pay and benefits, and dispute resolution. Union responses could thus have a more determinant effect on whether the standardization of production systems is, even partially, achieved.

The Boundaries of the "Internal" and "Independent" Auto Parts Sector

Variation in employment relations has increased in the auto parts sector, generally in a manner similar to developments in the assembly sector. At the same time, a number of factors differ in these two sectors, in part due to differences in the timing and intensity of nonunion employment growth. Before they were split off into separate companies, the "internal" parts operations of GM, Ford, and Chrysler had been the largest producers in the auto parts industry.

Prior to the spin-off of Delphi and Visteon, Big Three company negotiators frequently complained about the competitive pressures confronting the internal parts plants and expressed the desire to create separate lower-tier pay rates for the internal parts operations. The UAW successfully resisted these demands, but the union was less successful in constraining the outsourcing of parts production and the negotiation of work rule concessions. In line with the Big Three–UAW bargaining structure, there were separate local (often plant) agreements at the internal parts operations, and from the early 1980s on there were major concessions negotiated in the work practices at the internal parts plants.

To improve their ability to sell auto parts to a range of customers and for bargaining leverage vis-à-vis the UAW, in May 1999, GM formally spun off its parts subsidiary, Delphi Automotive Systems, against the objections of the UAW.[16] The formal terms of the spin-off initially provided that Delphi workers were covered under the same terms of the GM–UAW national agreement. Then in 1999 a separate Delphi–UAW national contract was negotiated. The 1999–2003 Delphi–UAW agreement closely mirrors the GM–UAW agreement for the 45,000 workers at Delphi's U.S. plants and provides that wages, layoff benefits, pensions, health care, and other benefits all be on par with the GM–UAW national contract. The Delphi contract also includes a mirror card check union recognition clause that is important to the UAW, given the fact that some of Delphi's plants are nonunion and the possibility of future acquisition by Delphi of nonunion operations.

Interestingly, the UAW negotiated even more favorable terms with Ford in the Visteon Corporation's 1999 contract that governed the 2000 Visteon spin-off. The 1999 Ford–UAW contract provides lifetime coverage under Ford–UAW contracts for the 23,500 hourly employees of Visteon (these employees will actually continue to be formally paid by Ford). New Visteon workers, like Delphi workers, are guaranteed coverage for eight years under contracts that mirror the terms of the Ford national agreement. Consistent with the better relationship that has long existed between Ford and the UAW as compared to GM and the union, Ford did not formally spin off Visteon until after having negotiated this new contract with the UAW.

Declining Unionization of Independent Auto Suppliers

Since the growth of nonunion competition has become such a significant factor in the independent auto parts sector, it is worth examining how nonunion growth has occurred. The "independent" (non–Big Three) parts companies, which produce auto parts but do not assemble those parts into final vehicles, were heavily, although never completely, organized with a lag behind the unionization of the Big Three. The percentage of the supplier plants with a majority of their workers covered by a collective bargaining agreement rose from 50 to 55 percent in 1940 to 95 percent in 1957, and unionization then produced a substantial rise in the earnings of organized workers.[17]

Union coverage in the independent parts plants, however, fell substantially from the mid-1970s on (Katz and Darbishire 2000:43–44). The fall in unionization has been a major cause of the decline in the earnings of workers in the independent parts firms relative to the earnings of workers in auto assembly plants. Relative earnings declines occurred earlier, and have been much greater, in small firms. These earnings declines are probably linked to the fact that unionization declines were particularly large in small auto supplier firms.

The push for concessions at the independent parts firms from the early 1980s on was exacerbated by the fact that independent parts firms faced all the pressures that were impinging on the auto assemblers, yet lacked the financial resources of the assemblers and faced more low-wage domestic nonunion competition. Even in the face of a set of common pressures, substantial diversity emerged in the employment relations strategies pursued by independent parts firms. This diversity was influenced by business and union strategies and the degree to which new investments, or the lack thereof, gave management an interest in work reorganization and bargaining leverage.

Modular Production

The boundary between the auto assemblers and the auto parts producers will shift even further if modular production spreads. Modularity became a popular concept in the late 1990s, as auto assembly firms realized that increasingly large chunks of new vehicles could be pre-assembled by suppliers. Pressure toward modular assembly for the Big Three was most pronounced in the small-vehicle lines, where profitability has been lacking. This is different from Japanese auto assembly firms, for example, that view modularity as a means to reduce the length of the main assembly line in order to shift complexity to subsidiary lines and as a tool to permit pretesting of key subsystems. In contrast to their American counterparts, most Japanese auto assembly firms do not feel a strong need to have the modules integrated out of house. In the United States, our interviews suggest that modularity and outsourcing are often thought of as mutually interchangeable concepts.

The UAW opposes modularity because of its link to outsourcing to potentially nonunion suppliers (GM's euphemism for outsourcing is telling: "Co-design modularity"). It is instructive to examine GM's Yellowstone project to understand the UAW's concerns. In 1999, GM announced plans for a major new-vehicle program aimed at enhancing profitability in its small-vehicle segment. Mark Hogan, then vice president of the small-car division, announced plans for two or three new assembly plants, as well as changes at some existing plants, including Saturn and CAMI, the GM–Suzuki joint-venture plant in Cambridge, Ontario. These plants would be designed based on GM's experience with its Blue Macaw plant in Brazil.

Two of the new plants were intended to replace existing plants in Lansing, Michigan, and Lordstown, Ohio, and GM actually had a site picked out for each. A key feature of the new plants was that they would be co-located with a large number of outside suppliers that would supply fifteen modules directly to final assembly from nearby supplier parks. However, this raised significant concern with the UAW, which viewed it as a ploy to reduce assembly jobs. In early 1999, UAW president Yokich likened modular assembly to outsourcing saying, "It's just another way to destroy good-paying jobs and benefits . . ." and threatened to deal with it during negotiations (Ward's 1999:35). Hogan replied to this claim by stating that retirements, rather than layoffs, would be used to reduce the workforce, and suppliers exploring participating in the projects said GM indicated it wanted the supplier facilities to accept the UAW (Winter and Green 1999). However, with contract negotiations starting in the spring of 1999, UAW pressure soon forced GM to downplay the new initiatives. Ultimately, the Yellowstone name, tainted by its links to outsourcing of UAW labor, was dropped. However, GM continues to explore the idea of increasing the external supply of modular components and has been experimenting with it at its Opel facilities in Europe.

The trend toward modularity seems likely to continue, although with more focus on the potential gains from giving design responsibility to suppliers rather than on the potential savings in labor costs from having suppliers (many nonunion) take on tasks traditionally done in assembly plants. Automakers have multiple incentives to give a larger share of value-added activities such as design to suppliers, and suppliers also have incentives to build up their capabilities to take on those activities. (Sako and Warburton 1999). In the United States and Europe, suppliers are pursuing this goal through merger and acquisition, partly so they can compete for module contracts with Delphi and Visteon, which already have more in-house design capability. In Japan, greater emphasis is placed on horizontal collaboration across suppliers that remain as separate firms (Takeishi and Fujimoto 2001), although Toyota recently revealed its intent to control these collaborative design processes indirectly by taking an increased equity stake in the key suppliers.

There are inherent limits to modularity in automotive product architecture. Unlike personal computers or many other consumer electronics products, there are no industry-level agreements on what constitutes a module and no industry standards for the common interface that allows modules to be easily connected. Along a product architecture dimension from modular to integral, automobiles are fundamentally more integral than information technology and electronic products, and indeed automakers have an incentive to continue differentiating vehicles rather than allowing them to be assembled from commoditized modules. Thus the competitive dynamics associated with truly modular designs based on clear industry standards (which have led most information technology firms to outsource all production to contract manufacturers) are unlikely to appear in the automotive industry (Fixson and Sako 2002), despite the appeal of this notion in the popular press.

New Organizing

The UAW also has been seriously challenged by the decline occurring in the percentage of the auto workforce that is organized. The decline has been particularly steep in the independent auto parts sector, but the increasing share of nonunion (transplant) auto assembly plants is also emerging as a key threat to the union's strength. Spurred by the increased push for organizing occurring within other national unions in the United States, a shift encouraged by the election of John Sweeney to the presidency of the AFL-CIO in 1995, the UAW has begun to more aggressively organize within and outside the auto sector in recent years.

In 1999, the UAW restructured its internal organizing hierarchy, adding a new vice president for organizing, former Region 1 head Bob King, and increased the amount of money spent on organizing. The UAW has used card check and election neutrality provisions to assist its organizing activities. GM and Ford, for example, agreed to accept card check recognition within their operations and those of any subsidiaries. These provisions are particularly important in Delphi and Visteon, as some of these plants are unorganized and the number of unorganized plants may grow in the future due to acquisitions of unorganized facilities. Notably, Chrysler did not agree to the UAW's request for card check recognition in 1999 contract bargaining, a particularly important issue for the UAW, given its ongoing efforts to organize the Alabama assembly plant originally built by Daimler-Benz and now a part of DaimlerChrysler.

Some of the UAW's increased organizing activity is focused on campaigns to organize workers outside the auto sector (led by Elizabeth Dunn, the vice president of the UAW in charge of its technical office and professional department). The UAW, for example, has been aggressively conducting organizing drives among university graduate teaching assistants and in the health care sector. An important victory came in March 2001 when the UAW led the successful unionization of teaching assistants at New York University, the first private-sector university to recognize such a union (Bureau of National Affairs 2001a). The UAW also gained members when the National Writers Guild and the Graphic Arts Guild each voted to affiliate with the union (Bureau of National Affairs 1999).

A Look to the Future

The events of the 1990s confirm that a key determinant of the future course of auto labor relations will be the strength of the U.S. economy, given the heavy influence the business cycle exerts on auto sales and labor's bargaining power. It also remains to be seen how well and how quickly DaimlerChrysler and Ford recover from their recent financial difficulties and the extent of any further international mergers and consolidation. Experience suggests that consolidation exerts mixed effects on labor's bargaining power. Consolidation reduces labor's power by enhancing outsourcing opportunities and providing whipsaw advantages to ever larger corporate behemoths. Yet consolidation potentially benefits labor through the generation of oligopoly-based economic rents.

A number of long-term structural challenges also confront the UAW and its members (and obviously auto management, as well, given the interactive nature of labor relations). A particularly critical issue is whether the UAW (or other unions) will find a way to reverse the sizable growth in nonunion employment occurring in both auto parts and auto assembly operations. As this chapter describes, although the Big Three remain fully organized, the auto sector is increasingly unorganized. The UAW and other unions have had only limited success organizing in the independent parts sector, even as they increasingly relied on state-of-the-art organizing techniques. In the assembly sector, the abject failure experienced in recent UAW organizing at the transplants is foreboding.

Union strength is also waning in the auto sector due to the heightened opportunities assembly and parts companies have to outsource production, especially since so much of any outsourced work tends to go to nonunion (and low-wage) domestic or international sites. While the UAW has benefited from the fact that just-in-time and other lean production methods have produced pressure for production concentration and hence the absence of long-predicted U.S. de-industrialization in this sector, the fact or threat of outsourcing continues to weaken the union. The bargaining process and collective bargaining outcomes at Delphi and Visteon, once the current carryover provisions have expired, will provide a telling indicator of whether the UAW is able to reverse the negative impact of this trend.

Another potential point of leverage for the UAW is the current industry trends toward supplier parks, which co-locate suppliers of large subassemblies near the assembly plants they support. These supplier parks are already common in Europe, where suppliers are much more likely to be unionized than in the United States. Ford has established the first such park in the United States near its Chicago assembly plant. The UAW is aiming to create the most favorable conditions possible for union coverage of that entire site, partly by encouraging the selection of already unionized suppliers and partly by pressuring for union recognition (or at least neutrality agreements) for any nonunion supplier joining the park. Some anecdotal evidence exists that large pay and benefit differentials at a supplier park, both among suppliers and with the assembly plant, are very difficult to sustain because the geographic proximity facilitates easy comparison and can give rise to strong perceptions of inequity. Thus there is a natural pull toward some homogenization of pay and benefits at such sites, making the UAW strategy more tenable. If successful, this approach could give the UAW limited inroads at suppliers that have been resolutely nonunion in the past.

This chapter reports on the substantial shrinkage occurring in the employment at the Big Three companies and the associated aging of these companies' workforces. Given that the Big Three are the high payers and pattern setters in the auto industry, these developments do not bode well for the future bargaining power of the UAW. The current contracts at the Big Three force the companies to hire one new worker for every two that retire, but in the face of the incredibly high seniority found among current Big Three employees, attrition may lead to further large-scale employment declines at these companies to the point at which their pattern-setting role dissipates even further.

Intensified international competitive and technological imperatives continue to put pressure on auto companies around the globe to achieve greater flexibility within their production systems. U.S. auto companies, and particularly the Big Three, have been relatively sluggish to introduce internal flexibility through changes in work practices, especially when compared to the recent changes occurring in Europe and the long-standing advantages held by Japanese companies. The 1990s confirmed, and probably reinforced, the strategy of U.S. companies to rely on a "full-capacity" business strategy, as profits were made only when the companies operated at or near full capacity. This strategy focuses on a traditional mass production approach and avoids the internal reorganizations and shifts in labor practices dealing with work organization, working time, and other matters associated with more flexible forms of production. As a result, the U.S. auto companies are relatively sensitive to economic volatility, as compared to their competitors in Europe, Japan, and elsewhere. In this way, the volatility of future auto demand may prove to be as critical to corporate success as will the level of auto demand. Whether this vulnerability plagues the U.S. companies and autoworkers in the future obviously will depend on the course of future world and U.S. economic developments.

Whatever the course of economic developments, it is clear that there will be much to be learned from the auto industry. While the influence of the Big Three and the UAW may decline, the auto sector remains a sizable employer and a source of revealing information concerning the evolution of production practices and industrial relations.

Notes

[1] Thirty and out pensions provide that a worker can retire and receive pension benefits after thirty years of service, no matter what his or her age.

[2] For an analysis of the internal political operation of the UAW, see Stieber (1962).

[3] For lively accounts of the early history of the UAW, see Reuther (1976) and Howe and Widick (1949). An interesting account of the UAW during World War II is provided in Lichtenstein (1982).

[4] This research used a methodology for productivity that adjusts for differences in vertical integration, product size, option content, and absenteeism to ensure comparability across plants. Quality data are derived from J. D. Power's Initial Quality Survey, adjusted to include only those defects that the assembly plant has some control over.

[5] Williams et al. (1994) claim that performance differentials observed in the MIT assembly plant study are not valid because such plant-level comparisons cannot be made accurately. However, their own case rests on shaky empirical evidence, including national industry data that include car and truck producers, as well as suppliers, and company data that are unadjusted for vertical integration, among other problems.

[6] The history of wage setting in the U.S. auto industry is discussed in more detail in Katz (1985).

[7] A chronology of postwar bargaining in the U.S. auto industry is in Bureau of National Affairs (various years) and U.S. Department of Labor (1969).

[8] Job control unionism is not synonymous with business unionism. The latter refers to the political philosophy of the labor movement. There are labor movements such as the Japanese that could be characterized as business unionist but not job control oriented.

[9] See Katz (1985 and 1988) for descriptions of early and mid-1980s bargaining.

[10] Assembler hourly wages at Ford were nearly identical to those at GM, while earnings at Chrysler were lower in the early and mid-1980s due to the special concessions described. Skilled trades workers (such as tool-and-die makers and electricians) generally earn hourly wages that are approximately 20 percent higher than the wages of auto assemblers.

[11] This figure is from an internal GM source.

[12] These and other job and income security programs are described more fully in Katz (1985 and 1988).

[13] The UAW-represented workforce at GM on January 1, 2001, totaled 122,547.

[14] The maximum layoff spell was extended to forty-two weeks, in view of the lengthening of the contracts to four years.

[15] The transplants, both union and nonunion, typically pay wages that are close to Big Three levels. However, the transplants have pension, medical care, and other fringe benefits that differ substantially from the benefits provided at the Big Three (the transplants often provide lower benefits) and from one another, often based on local labor market conditions.

[16] Chrysler had reduced its vertical integration with much less fanfare in the early 1980s during its brush with bankruptcy.

[17] Mean earnings in the supplier firms relative to earnings in assembly firms rose from 87.5 percent to 95.3 percent from 1940 to 1957 (Katz 1988).

References

Automotive News Market Data Book. 2000. Detroit: Crain Communications.
———. 2001. Detroit: Crain Communications.
Babson, Steve, ed. 1995. *Lean Work: Empowerment and Exploitation in the Global Auto Industry.* Detroit: Wayne State University Press.
Bradsher, Keith. 1999. "Saturn Plant's Union Leaders Are Voted Out," *New York Times,* February 26, p. 1 (Late edition, East Coast).
Budd, John W. 1992. "The Determinants and Extent of UAW Pattern Bargaining." *Industrial and Labor Relations Review,* Vol. 45, no. 3 (April), pp. 523–39.
Bureau of National Affairs. 1999. "UAW Drawing New Members From Outside Manufacturing Industries," *Daily Labor Report,* August 18, p. C-8.
———. 2000. "Failed Bid for Mega-Industrial Union Linked to Differences Among Three Parties," *Daily Labor Report,* September 14, p. C-1.
———. 2001a. "NYU Agrees to Recognize, Bargain With UAW For Graduate Teaching Assistants," *Daily Labor Report,* March 5, p. AA-1.
———. 2001b. "Workers at Nissan Plant Overwhelmingly Reject Union Representation," *Daily Labor Report,* October 5, p. AA-1.
———. 2002. "Ford to Close Five Plants in Coming Years in Effort to Boost Profits, Reduce Capacity," *Daily Labor Report,* January 14, p. A-11.
———. Various years. *Collective Bargaining Negotiations and Contracts: Wage Patterns.* Washington, DC.
Fixson, Sebastian, and Mari Sako. 2002. "Modularity in Product Architecture: Will the Auto Industry Follow the Computer Industry?" Working paper, International Motor Vehicle Program, MIT.
Florida, Richard, and Martin Kenney. 1993. *Beyond Mass Production: The Japanese System and Its Transfer to the U.S.* New York: Oxford University Press.
Holweg, Matthias, and Frits K. Pil. 2001. "Successful Build-to-Order Strategies Start with the Customer." *Sloan Management Review,* Vol. 43, no. 1 (Fall), pp. 74–83.
Howe, Irving, and B. J. Widick. 1949. *The UAW and Walter Reuther.* New York: Random House.
Hunter, Larry W., John Paul MacDuffie, and Lorna Doucet. 2002. "What Makes Teams Take? Employee Reactions to Work Reorganization." *Industrial and Labor Relations Review,* Vol. 55, no. 3 (April), pp. 448–72.
Katz, Harry C. 1985. *Shifting Gears: Changing Labor Relations in the U.S. Automobile Industry.* Cambridge, MA: MIT Press.
———. 1988. "Automobiles," in D. Lipsky and C. Donn, eds., *Collective Bargaining in American Industry.* Lexington, MA: D.C. Heath, pp. 13–54.
Katz, Harry C., and Owen Darbishire. 2000. *Converging Divergences: Worldwide Changes in Employment Systems.* Ithaca: Cornell University Press.
Katz, Harry C., Thomas A. Kochan, and Jeffrey H. Keefe. 1987. "Industrial Relations Performance and Productivity in the U.S. Automobile Industry." *Brookings Papers on Economic Activity,* No. 3, Special Issue on Microeconomics, pp. 685–715.
Krafcik, John F., and J. P. MacDuffie. 1989. "Explaining High Performance Manufacturing: The International Assembly Plant Study," Working paper, International Motor Vehicle Program, MIT.
Lichtenstein, Nelson. 1982. *Labor's War at Home.* London: Cambridge University Press.

MacDuffie, John Paul, and Frits K. Pil. 1995. "The International Assembly Plant Study: Philosophical and Methodological Issues," in S. Babson, ed., *Lean Work.* Detroit: Wayne State University Press, pp. 181–96.

Parker, Mike, and Jane Slaughter. 1988. *Choosing Sides: Unions and the Team Concept.* Boston: South End Press.

Pil, Frits K., and John Paul MacDuffie. 1999. "What Makes Transplants Thrive: Managing the Transfer of 'Best Practice' at Japanese Auto Plants in North America." *Journal of World Business,* Vol. 34, no. 4 (Winter), pp. 372–91.

Pil, Frits K., and Saul Rubinstein. 1998. "Saturn: A Different Kind of Company?" in R. Boyer et al., eds., *Between Imitation and Innovation.* London: Oxford University Press, pp. 361–73.

Piore, Michael J. 1982. "American Labor and the Industrial Crisis." *Challenge* 25 (March–April), pp. 5–11.

Reuther, Victor G. 1976. *The Brothers Reuther and the Story of the UAW: A Memoir.* Boston: Houghton Mifflin.

Rubinstein, Saul, and Thomas Kochan. 2001. *Learning from Saturn: Possibilities for Corporate Governance and Employee Relations.* Ithaca: ILR Press.

Sako, Mari, and Max Warburton. 1999. "Modularization Project: Report from the European Research Team," Working paper, International Motor Vehicle Program, MIT.

Shimada, Haruo, and John Paul MacDuffie. 1987. "Industrial Relations and 'Humanware': Japanese Investments in Automobile Manufacturing in the United States," Working paper, Sloan School of Management, MIT.

Stieber, Jack. 1962. *Governing the UAW.* New York: Wiley.

Takeishi, Akira, and Takahiro Fujimoto. 2001. "Modularization in the Auto Industry: Interlinked Multiple Hierarchies of Product, Production, and Supplier Systems," Working paper, International Motor Vehicle Program, MIT.

U.S. Department of Labor. 1969. Wage Chronology—General Motors Corporation, 1939–68. Bulletin 1532, Bureau of Labor Statistics. Washington, DC: GPO.

Ward's. 1999. "GM Plans New Sigma Plant." *Ward's Auto World,* 35(5), p. 35.

Ward's Automotive Yearbook. 2001. Southfield, MI: Ward's Communications, 63rd ed., p. 248.

Williams et al. 1994. *Cars, Analysis, History, Cases.* Providence, RI: Berghahn Books.

Winter, Drew, and Jeff Green. 1999. "Modularity: The Hottest Topic." *Ward's Automotive Yearbook.* Southfield, MI: Ward's Communications, pp. 54–55.

Womack, James P., Dan Jones, and Dan Roos. 1990. *The Machine That Changed the World.* New York: Rawson Associates.

CHAPTER 3

Health Care: A Growing Role for Collective Bargaining

PAUL F. CLARK
Pennsylvania State University

Introduction

The United States health care industry is a large and growing segment of the American economy. In 2000, national health expenditures in the United States totaled 1.3 trillion dollars (Carter 2002). By 2008, this figure is expected to increase to nearly 2 trillion dollars. The industry is one of the leading employers in the United States, with roughly 6.04 million people working in health-related professional and technical positions. Administrative support, maintenance and service, and ancillary jobs push this number to more than 9 million employees (Healthcare Financing Administration 2001; Bureau of Labor Statistics [BLS] 2001a).

The U.S. health care industry is also an industry in crisis. At the heart of this crisis are rising health care costs, declining government spending, increasing pressures on public and private budgets, changing demographics, and accelerating scientific and technological advances. These issues have resulted in significant changes in the structure, organization, financing, and delivery of health care. Most of these changes are the result of the introduction of managed care and the growth of health maintenance organizations (HMOs) (Wunderlich, Sloan, and Davis 1996).

In many respects, managed care and its manifestations have adversely impacted health care employees, resulting in increased unionization. Collective bargaining in the health care industry, particularly for professional employees in the private sector, is at a relatively early stage of development, compared to many other industries in the United States. However, it is fast becoming an important part of our health care

91

system, and the evidence suggests great potential for the growth of collective bargaining in this industry in the years ahead. This chapter will examine the parties, the practices, and the challenges involved in collective bargaining in the U.S. private-sector health care industry.[1] Particular attention will be given to the two largest segments of the industry—hospitals and long-term care (nursing homes, rehabilitation facilities, etc.)—and to the relationship between employers and those employees most responsible for providing patient care, registered nurses (RNs) and physicians. As managed care influences every aspect of health care today, the impact of this phenomenon on the employment relationship will serve as the framework for this discussion.

The Health Care Industry

The two most significant sectors of the U.S. health care industry, in terms of expenditures and numbers of patients and employees, are the acute care hospital sector (including medical centers and clinics) and the long-term care/nursing home sector.[2]

Hospitals

The private hospital sector of the U.S. health care industry is made up of two major types of acute care facilities.[3] The majority of hospitals are not-for-profit community hospitals; the remainder are privately owned, for-profit hospitals.[4] As Table 1 indicates, in 1999 there were 3,012 not-for-profit community hospitals and 747 for-profit hospitals (American Hospital Association [AHA] 2001).

Not-for-profit community hospitals are defined as hospitals that reinvest any leftover moneys rather than distributing such funds to persons or groups. These hospitals are usually built and financed by citizens' or religious groups, with money for constructing facilities coming from individuals, charities, the sale of tax-exempt bonds, and local and state government grants. Most have between 100 and 300 beds, with urban hospitals often having considerably more and rural hospitals sometimes having as few as 25 to 50. Traditionally, such hospitals serve a limited geographic area and are administered by a board of directors composed of citizens from that area (Raffel and Raffel 1997).

For-profit hospitals constitute the second type of hospital. These hospitals are usually owned by corporations and each year distribute profits to their shareholders. In 1999, there were 747 for-profit hospitals in the United States. Most of these operate in four states: California, Florida, Tennessee, and Texas (Raffel and Raffel 1997). Many are part of national chains, the largest of which are HCA (with 200 hospitals and 170,000 employees) and Tenet (with 114 hospitals and 111,000 employees) (Federation of American Hospitals 2002). Because of mergers and closings, the total number of private hospitals has fallen in recent years from 3,844 in 1995 to 3,797 in 1997 to 3,759 in 1999 (AHA 2001). At the same time, the hospital sector has seen the growth of hospital "systems" and "networks." According to the AHA, a multihospital system "is two or more hospitals owned, leased, sponsored, or contract managed by a central organization" (AHA 2001). A single, freestanding hospital may be categorized as a system if it owns or leases nonhospital pre-acute or postacute health care organizations (clinics, rehabilitation facilities, or nursing homes). The AHA defines a network as "a group of hospitals, physicians, other providers, insurers and/or community agencies that work together to coordinate and deliver a broad spectrum of services to their community" (AHA 2001:198). Based on these definitions, network participation does not preclude system affiliation, nor does system affiliation preclude network participation. Of the 3,759 private hospitals registered with the AHA in 1999, 2,238 were affiliated with a system and 1,310 were part of a network (AHA 2001). This represents an increase from 1995 when 1,990 such hospitals were system affiliated and 1,178 were associated with a network (see Table 1).

TABLE 1

Nonpublic Community Hospitals and Long-Term Care Facilities[a]
in the United States, 1985–1999

	1985	1990	1995	1999
Total nonpublic community hospitals	3,349	3,940	3,844	3,759
Not-for-profit hospitals	2,544	3,191	3,092	3,012
For-profit hospitals	805	749	752	747
Community hospitals in a system	NA	NA	1,990	2,238
Community hospitals in a network	NA	NA	1,178	1,310
Total nonpublic long-term care facilities	18,100	NA	15,300	15,917
Not-for-profit facilities	3,800	NA	4,300	4,818
For-profit facilities	14,300	NA	11,000	11,099

Sources: AHA (1988, 1992, 1998, 2001); Strahan (1987, 1997); and Gabrel (2000).
[a] Includes nursing homes.

Long-Term Care/Nursing Homes

As of 1997, there were 15,800 private long-term care facilities in the United States with 1,186,900 residents. The majority of these facilities are traditional nursing homes that care for the elderly; however, the number also includes Alzheimers, AIDs, hospice, and other special care facilities. The average number of beds per facility is 107. Thirteen percent of these facilities are hospital based; the remainder are separate facilities. Seventy-two percent are for-profit operations and 28 percent are not for profit (Gabrel 2000).

The growth of large corporate chains is even more prevalent in long-term care than it is among acute care hospitals. Fifty-two percent of all long-term facilities are part of a health care chain; the remaining 48 percent are owned and operated individually. Among the largest chains are Beverly Enterprises (559 facilities in 29 states), Mariner (360 facilities in 32 states), Vencor/Kindred (312 facilities in 31 states), and Manor Care (298 facilities in 32 states) (American Health Care Association [AHCA] 2001).

In 1997, the private long-term care/nursing home sector employed 1.3 million employees, including 128,800 RNs (Gabrel 2000). The demographics of the United States indicate that more people are living longer and that the elderly population (that group most needing long-term care/nursing home services) is growing. In 1994, approximately one in eight Americans was sixty-five or older. By 2030, one in five Americans will have reached this age. This suggests significant growth in the long-term care/nursing home sector. Estimates are that 2.33 million employees, including 328,000 RNs, will be working in this sector by 2005 (see Table 2) (AHCA 2001; Gabrel 2000).

TABLE 2

Employees in Nonpublic Community Hospitals and
Long-Term Care Facilities[a] in the United States, 1985–1999

	1985	1990	1995	1999
Total nonpublic community hospitals	2,436,590	2,806,004	3,044,376	3,223,501
Not-for-profit hospitals	2,215,771	2,533,362	2,701,594	2,861,968
For-profit hospitals	220,819	272,642	342,782	361,533
Total nonpublic long-term care facilities	1,044,100	NA	1,206,100	966,500
Not-for-profit facilities	310,800	NA	383,100	308,800
For-profit facilities	733,300	NA	823,000	657,700

Sources: AHA (1988, 1992, 1998, 2001); Strahan (1987, 1997); and Gabrel (2000).
[a] Includes nursing homes.

The Industry in Transition

The U.S. health care system, as previously described, is in the midst of a period of transition and transformation. Central to these changes is the increasing cost of health care and the rapidly evolving ways in which health care services are delivered and financed. The reforms that have been introduced in the course of this transformation have had a tremendous impact on employees in this industry and have led to widespread dissatisfaction among the health care workforce.

Health care expenditures have risen significantly in the United States over the last decade. Between 1990 and 2000 total spending on health care rose from $696 billion to $1.3 trillion. Over this period, health care expenditures per capita grew 69 percent, while the nation's population increased by only 10 percent (HCFA 2001). The growth in health care spending is the result of a confluence of complex factors, including accelerating scientific and technological developments; changing demographics; and declining government spending, which has put increasing pressures on the budgets of public and private health care institutions.

One of the most significant factors contributing to the increased cost of health care is the development and expanded use of technologically advanced equipment and procedures for diagnosis and treatment. Magnetic resonance imaging, coronary bypass surgery, and organ transplantation, for example, have become relatively common in the United States, much more so than in virtually any other country in the world (Raffel and Raffel 1997).

The aging of the U.S. population is another significant factor. The elderly are much more likely to suffer from chronic illnesses and their complications than their younger counterparts. Consequently, they have more frequent and longer hospital stays and higher surgical rates. In addition, the elderly are treated more aggressively in the U.S. health care system than in many other countries, resulting in longer life expectancies. As life expectancies have increased, so has the need for long-term care. These factors have pushed, and will continue to push, the costs of health care in the United States rapidly upward (Raffel and Raffel 1997).

Increasing pressures on the budgets of public and private health care institutions have their origins in the enactment of Medicare and Medicaid in 1965. These programs spurred a rapid growth in the demand for, and the use of, health care services. One of the results was an unprecedented increase in the cost of care and the share of the nation's resources that it consumed. Between 1970 and 1980, the inflation rate for health care was double the overall Consumer Price Index (CPI). This spurred the drive for new approaches to the delivery and financing of health care (Wunderlich, Sloan, and Davis 1996).

Hospitals

In the 1950s and 1960s, hospital care in the United States was delivered on a "fee-for-service" basis. Patients receiving treatment in hospitals either paid for these services "out of pocket" or submitted their bills to an insurance company that paid them in full or in part. However, as costs rose, the main providers of health insurance—employers and insurance companies—began to look for new, cost-effective approaches to providing care (Knight 1998). The promarket policies of the Reagan administration created a favorable climate in the 1980s, in which these approaches could flourish (Budrys 1997). The system that developed to address these issues is called managed care.

Managed Care. The last two decades have seen managed care and managed care organizations like HMOs come to dominate the health care system in the United States. Managed care is a market-based approach to the delivery of health care services that includes a number of cost-control strategies such as prepayment arrangements and preadmission authorizations. HMOs and preferred provider organizations (PPOs) have served as the primary vehicles for delivering managed care.

By the 1990s, HMOs and managed care were increasingly penetrating the health care market. Between 1985 and 2000, HMO enrollment rose from 20 million to 81 million members (Managed Care Online 2001). This growth significantly influenced the structure of the industry and the manner in which health care services were delivered. The consolidation of hospitals and health care systems through closings and mergers and the reorganization of work within these facilities were two of the products of market-driven health care reforms (Wunderlich, Sloan, and Davis 1996).

The widespread closings and mergers were efforts to take advantage of economies of scale and strengthen providers' positions in the health care marketplace. Between 1980 and 1993, the AHA reported the closures of 675 community hospitals. The AHA also reported 215 mergers involving 445 hospitals or health care systems between 1980 and 1992. While this trend peaked in 1994 when 650 hospitals (constituting 10 percent of the market) were involved in mergers or acquisitions, merger activity has continued through the present, with nearly 300 hospitals involved in such transactions in 1998 (Lutz 1994; Wunderlich, Sloan, and Davis 1996; Levin Associates 1999).

Hospital closures reduce the number of excess hospital beds and lead to cost savings by permitting the remaining hospitals to spread costs over a wider patient base. Mergers are pursued to either eliminate competitors or to expand services (Wunderlich, Sloan, and Davis 1996). Ultimately, cost containment is the driving force behind market-driven reforms such as closures and mergers.

Impact on Physicians. Physicians have been affected in significant ways by market-based health care reform. Most of the complaints of physicians center on the perception that reform has heavily "tipped the balance of power" (Mangan 1999:A-14) toward the hospitals, health care systems, and HMOs/insurers and away from the practitioners. In many cases, this has resulted in longer hours, lower reimbursements, work speedups, and, perhaps most significantly, interference with patient care (Mangan 1999).

The impact of health care reform has been felt by physicians in virtually all types of practices. Physicians employed by hospitals and health systems have been particularly affected. The mergers and consolidations that have resulted from reform, along with the difficulty of maintaining a private practice, have increased the number of physicians working directly for hospitals and health systems. Between 1983 and 1997, the percentage of doctors who practiced as employees increased from 24 to 43 percent (Cochrane 1999).

These physicians were among the first to feel the effects of the financial pressures experienced by hospitals in recent years. These pressures have manifested themselves in service cutbacks, reductions in pay, and changes in contract terms. Physicians have been pushed to reduce the time they spend with each patient and to increase their patient contact hours (Vandermeer 1999).

Managed care guidelines have also greatly impacted the way these physicians treat patients. The implementation of Diagnosis-Related Groups (DRGs) in the 1980s set fairly rigid standards for hospital physicians to follow regarding the length of a hospital stay for a given medical problem. Physicians are often forced to get the approval of an HMO or insurance company representative before going forward with a test or procedure. This has resulted in tremendous frustration among doctors accustomed to making patient care decisions without interference or oversight. One gynecologist expressed his anger this way, "Some clerk who is completely nonmedical and never knows the patient will get on the computer and deny me the procedure. In the glory days, you were able to practice medicine without interference from people with no education telling you what medicines to use and whether or not you can operate on a patient" (Groves 2000:1).

Medical interns and residents also have been affected by health care reform. Since they are undertaking a required training program and since their future success depends on a positive evaluation by supervising physicians, interns and residents have very little power within the health care hierarchy. Traditionally, interns and residents have worked very long hours for very low pay. As hospitals have been squeezed financially, they in turn have squeezed their most vulnerable employees, interns and residents, sometimes reducing pay, increasing hours (100 to 120 hours a week is not unusual), and, in the face of cutbacks, compelling them to do the work of nurses and aides (Committee of Interns and Residents/Service Employees International Union [CIR/SEIU] 2001b).

Physicians in private practice have also been significantly affected by health care reform. To have a financially viable practice today, self-employed physicians must usually contract with one or more managed care plans (e.g., HMOs and PPOs). In fact, the proportion of physicians with managed care contracts of one kind or another increased from 61 percent in 1990 to 88 percent in 1996 (Knight 1998).

Self-employed physicians, whether in solo, partnership, or group practices, are vulnerable to the economic leverage of health plans. They complain that HMOs and insurance companies use this advantage to impose low reimbursement rates, onerous paperwork requirements, and unreasonable patient care restrictions on them (Carlson 1999).

Impact on Nurses. Because personnel costs make up the largest single expense in hospital budgets and nursing personnel represent the largest single group within most hospitals' personnel budgets, RNs are one of the groups most affected by manifestations of health care reform (Kangas, Kee, and McKee-Waddle 1999). A 1997 study by Armstrong-Stassen et al. found that being involved in a merger had a negative impact on hospital nurses' perception of their work environment. Specifically, nurses in hospitals that had undergone a merger reported a heightened fear of job loss and reduced satisfaction with their nursing careers.

The restructuring of work is another means by which hospitals and health care systems have sought savings. A study by Corey-Lisle et al. (1999) found that the restructuring of nurses' jobs has taken a number of forms. Nurses' jobs have been affected, both directly and indirectly, by the widespread downsizing of hospital staffs. As the number of nurses has been reduced, the remaining nurses have been required to take care of more patients. Also, because managed care calls for hospitals to admit only "the sickest patients for the shortest possible stays" (Sochalski and Aiken 1999:1), RNs have reported that patient "acuity" (how sick a patient is) has risen. Accordingly, the patients under the care of nurses are more seriously ill and require greater attention. The result is significantly increased workloads for nurses (Sochalski and Aiken 1999). Downsizing of the nurse workforce has been accompanied by an expanded use of unlicensed assistive personnel (aides, technicians, orderlies, etc.) in hospitals. They are increasingly being asked to do work formerly performed by RNs. RNs, in turn, are being asked to supervise these workers. Where this has occurred, it has fundamentally changed the work of nurses from direct patient care at the bedside to indirect supervision of care (Preuss 1999). Nurses report that the loss of direct contact has reduced the satisfaction they receive from their work and increased the stress they feel on the job (Corey-Lisle et al. 1999).

In addition, in an effort to achieve greater workforce flexibility, hospitals have de-emphasized nurse specialization. Rather than having designated nurses acquire significant experience and expertise by regularly working in specialized areas like intensive care or neonatal units, RNs are being increasingly rotated or "floated" to areas of need. Nurses argue that asking them to work in unfamiliar patient care areas increases stress and decreases the quality of patient care (Corey-Lisle et al. 1999).

A recent study by Clark et al. (2001) found that restructuring also has a negative effect on nurses' perception of the climate for patient care in their hospitals. In this study, nurses who experienced job restructuring judged their ability to provide quality patient care more negatively than nurses who had not experienced this manifestation of health care reform.

These conclusions are further supported by a 2001 survey of RNs by the American Nurses Association (ANA), a professional organization of RNs, which concluded that nurses perceive a deterioration in their working conditions and a decline in the quality of nursing care. Thirty-eight percent of the respondents in this study reported that they have felt "exhausted and discouraged" on leaving work. Thirty-four percent say they have felt "discouraged and saddened by what they could not provide their patients." And twenty-nine percent feel they are "powerless to effect change." Seventy-five percent of the nurses surveyed conclude that the quality of nursing care has declined (ANA 2001a).

These studies suggest that for many nurses "hospitals have become lousy places to work" (Jaklevic and Lovern 2000:46). This has been cited as one of the reasons for a nurse shortage that began in the late 1990s and is expected to continue into the first decade of the new century. One study projects a 400,000 nurse shortage by 2021 (American Federation of Teachers [AFT] 2001a; Collins 2001).

Long-Term Care/Nursing Homes

Over the past decade, changes in the long-term care/nursing home sector have been as dramatic and traumatic as in the hospital sector. In 2001, five of the seven largest nursing home chains were in bankruptcy under Chapter 11, including Mariner, which lost $1.78 billion in 1999, and Vencor/Kindred, which lost $692 million the same year. These financial difficulties can, in part, be traced to changes in the Medicare system that occurred in the late 1990s (SEIU 2001a).

Funding. Funding for long-term care comes from three sources. In 1998, Medicaid, a jointly funded federal–state program that is administered by the individual states, accounted for 68 percent of long-term care/nursing home reimbursements. Medicare also helps pay for long-term care; however, Congress has placed restrictions on the use of Medicare funds for this purpose so that in 1998 these funds accounted for only 8 percent of revenues in this sector. Patients themselves or patients' private insurance accounted for 23 percent of total reimbursements (AHCA 2001).

The Medicare restrictions have made Medicaid payments the critical variable in funding long-term care. Inadequate Medicare funding has caused a financial crisis in the long-term care/nursing home sector (Saphir 2000; SEIU 2001a). These difficulties have impacted the work experiences of employees in that sector. Among the problems faced by these workers are very low pay, short staffing, exceptionally high rates of injury and illness, and a lack of training opportunities.

Impact on Employees. The median hourly wage for a certified nurse assistant in California nursing homes was $7.12 in 1997. SEIU claims that wages are so low that "many caregivers and their families are eligible for food stamps, public housing, and free school lunches" (SEIU 1997a:iii). The union further claims that nursing home wages often leave families below the federal poverty line (SEIU 1997a). Exacerbating the low-wage problem is the fact that most nursing home workers do not get health or retirement benefits. According to the Current Population Survey, 52 percent of employees working in nursing homes do not receive health insurance from their employer, forcing them to rely on their spouse's insurance, Medicaid, or go without medical care (Economic Policy Institute [EPI] 1997).

Short staffing is also a significant problem across the long-term care/nursing home sector (Pear 2002). In 2001, forty-one states reported that facilities in this sector were unable to hire the staff they needed ("Acceptable Nursing Home Care" 2000). One factor responsible for short staffing in this sector is a relatively high rate of turnover. A number of studies conducted in recent years found turnover rates for RNs in nursing facilities to range from 28 to 59 percent, while the rate for RNs in acute care hospitals ranged from 12 to 23 percent (Decker and Dollard 2001). The turnover rate for certified nurse assistants in 1998 was reportedly more than 93 percent, one of the highest such rates for any U.S. occupation (AHCA 1999).

Much of this problem can be attributed to changes in Medicaid and to the inroads managed care is making in the long-term care/nursing home sector. Because of these factors, patients are being released from hospitals "quicker and sicker." Many of these patients go directly to long-term care/nursing home facilities. This means that the acuity levels of patients at nursing homes are increasing, making the jobs of already short-staffed caregivers even more demanding and stressful (SEIU 1998).

Employees in long-term care/nursing home facilities also face significant safety and health problems. Nursing home workers have the highest rate of occupational illness and injury among the twenty fastest-growing industries in the United States. Illness and injury rates in this sector grew 57 percent between 1984 and 1995, surpassing rates in such dangerous industries as mining, construction, and trucking. SEIU contends that many of these injuries are linked to understaffing, a conclusion supported by the National Academy of Sciences Institute of Medicine (SEIU 1997b).

In sum, very low pay and poor benefits, short staffing, and exceptionally high rates of injury and illness are all present in the long-term care/nursing home sector. Unions as well as government and consumer groups have all decried the negative effect these problems have on patient care. Unattractive employment conditions and the inability to give adequate care have resulted in growing interest in union representation among employees in the long-term care/nursing home sector.

Health Care Unions

In recent years, the health care industry has seen a steady and significant increase in union activity. The increase has been particularly notable among nurses and, to a lesser extent, among physicians. Union member density for health care workers (the percentage of the workforce holding union membership) in 2000 was 13.5 percent. This figure includes RNs; LPNs; lab technicians and technologists; medical scientists;

and respiratory, occupational, and physical therapists, in both the private and public sectors and in both hospitals and long-term care facilities (it does not include physicians). This was the same level of union density as the overall workforce and suggests that unions have established a significant presence among health care professionals (AFT 2001b).

Union member density for RNs in 2000 was 16.9 percent, a 1.5 percent increase over the 1995 level of 15.4 percent. Nurses were one of only two health care professions having union density rates above the national average for that year (occupational therapists at 20.8 percent were the other group). This level of density means that of the 2.1 million nurses in the U.S. workforce, roughly 355,000 belong to unions (AFT 2001b).

In addition to having one of the highest levels of union member density among health care workers, RNs in recent years have also had one of the highest levels of coverage density (the percentage of nurses covered by a collective bargaining agreement). For all industries, this figure was 14.9 percent in 2000. The coverage density for nurses that year was 19.1 percent, up .6 percent from five years earlier. Again, only occupational therapists, at 24.7 percent, had a higher coverage density (AFT 2001b).

Union density levels for physicians are significantly lower than for nurses. Of the more than 700,000 physicians in this country, 6 percent, or approximately 40,000, are estimated to belong to unions (Greenhouse 1999; Thompson 2000).[5]

Another important indicator of union activity is National Labor Relations Board (NLRB) elections. Recent years have seen a significant increase in such elections among health care workers. Between 1995 and 1999, the number of NLRB elections in this industry rose almost 78 percent, from 291 to 517 (see Table 3).[6] This occurred at a time when elections for all industries increased less than 9 percent (AFT 2001b).

Unions representing health care workers were also more successful at winning NLRB elections than were their counterparts in most other industries. In 1997, for example, unions won 63 percent of elections involving health care employees, compared to a win rate of 50 percent for all unions (AFT 2001b). For elections involving only hospital workers that year, the number was slightly higher, at 64 percent (Deshpande 2000). The win rate for RNs in 1997 was higher still, with 67 percent of organizing drives involving nurses resulting in union representation. The win rate for RN elections represented a 10 percent increase from 1987 (ANA 1998). Similar data are not available for elections among physicians.

TABLE 3
NLRB Representation Elections, 1990–1999

	Number of elections		Percentage change from previous year		Percentage won by unions	
Year	Health care	All industries	Health care	All industries	Health care	All industries
1990	367	3,623	—	—	56.7	49.5
1991	342	3,179	-6.8	-12.3	52.3	46.9
1992	299	2,993	-12.5	-5.9	54.5	49.9
1993	324	3,055	8.4	2.1	58.3	50.4
1994	356	3,079	9.9	0.8	61.2	48.6
1995	291	2,911	-18.3	-5.5	53.6	50.4
1996	370	2,792	27.1	-4.1	55.4	47.3
1997	407	3,075	10.0	10.1	63.4	50.4
1998	486	3,339	19.4	8.6	61.7	56.0
1999	517	3,162	6.4	-5.3	64.4	53.0

Source: NLRB annual reports (1990–1999).

Numerous unions represent workers in the U.S. health care industry. This appears to be a function of at least two factors. First, a large segment of the health care workforce only became eligible to organize in the last twenty-five years, after many national and international unions were already well established. Thus, there was less reason for the formation of entirely new health care unions to organize these workers. Second, during this period, many existing unions suffered significant, and sometimes substantial losses, of members. Not surprisingly, many of these unions saw health care as fertile ground for organizing. There are few industries in the United States that are growing at the rate experienced by the health care industry. And, unlike many of the industries that have long been a focus of the American labor movement, health care facilities cannot flee to low-wage regions of the country or to even lower-wage nations abroad. This has made health care attractive to a wide range of unions, including those with little or no previous connection to the industry.

The unions that organize health care workers in the United States represent all three of the major types of unions found in the American labor movement—craft, industrial, and general labor organizations.[7]

The union with the largest number of members working in health care is the Service Employees International Union (SEIU). SEIU has a long history of organizing health care employees, particularly in public and private nursing homes and public-sector hospitals. Organizing private-sector hospitals was a natural extension of SEIU's involvement in this sector.

SEIU not only has the most members working in health care generally (approximately 650,000), it also is as close to an industrial health care union as exists in the United States today. SEIU's ranks include significant numbers of workers in virtually all professional and nonprofessional job classifications (it does not represent hospital security guards). Recently it won the largest organizing election ever held in the health care industry, when a unit of 75,000 home health care workers in Los Angeles County voted to be represented by an SEIU affiliate (Cleeland 1999).[8]

SEIU's claim to be the preeminent health care union was bolstered by two other relatively recent events. In 1998, it added 120,000 health care workers to its membership, when 1199, National Health and Human Services Union in New York City, affiliated with SEIU (Amber 1999c). And in 1999 it brought three organizations together to form the nation's largest physicians' union, the National Doctors Alliance (NDA). The NDA was formed through a merger of the Doctors Council, the Committee of Interns and Residents (CIR), and the Union of Salaried Physicians and Dentists (USPD). It had 15,000 members at the time of its formation and is formally affiliated with SEIU. Most of its physician members work in hospitals (Tschida 1999).

SEIU can also claim the largest nurse membership of any American union. Through its Nurse Alliance, SEIU represents 110,000 nurses in a variety of settings.

A second significant union of health care workers is the United American Nurses (UAN). The UAN is the collective bargaining arm of the ANA.[9] With 96,000 members, the UAN is second only to the SEIU in the number of RNs organized. If the SEIU represents an industrial approach to health care unionism, the UAN represents the other end of the spectrum, a craft union that only organizes RNs. The UAN is actually a federation of the twenty-seven ANA state organizations that engage in collective bargaining.[10] It was created in 1999 to assist the state bodies with organizing and bargaining (Amber 1999a). The UAN affiliated with the AFL-CIO in 2001 (ANA 2001b).

A third union with a sizable health care membership is the United Food and Commercial Workers (UFCW). The UFCW has nearly 1.4 million members, 100,000 of whom work in the health care field. Of these 100,000, approximately 12,500 are RNs; the remainder are LPNs and aides, medical technicians, and clerical and maintenance personnel. UFCW members work in both hospitals and nursing homes. It has ten locals representing workers at Kaiser Permanente, the nation's largest unionized health care provider (UFCW 2002).

The American Federation of Teachers (AFT) also organizes health care workers. AFT Healthcare has approximately 60,000 members, 25,000 of whom are nurses. Its membership also includes 12,500 physicians. The AFT originally became involved in health care through its representation of school nurses, but now the majority of its members work in hospitals (AFT 2002).

Another union that focuses largely on organizing nurses is the California Nurses Association (CNA). The CNA is an independent union that was once affiliated with the ANA. In 1995, the CNA withdrew from the ANA because of its desire to pursue a more militant course of action in representing RNs. In just the past few years, the CNA has doubled its membership to 35,000 through aggressive organizing and the absorption of smaller union groups. In 2001, the Massachusetts Nurses Association voted to leave the ANA and join the CNA. Further evidence that the CNA is becoming a force beyond California is its recent alliance with the 700,000-member United Steelworkers. Under the name of the Healthcare Workers Alliance, the two unions will attempt to organize workers by targeting health care chains or geographic regions rather than on a hospital-by-hospital basis (Amber 2001; CNA 2001).

A relatively new organization modeled on the craft union approach to labor representation is Physicians for Responsible Negotiation (PRN). The PRN is the union arm of the American Medical Association (AMA). It was formed in 1999 despite the vocal opposition of a minority of AMA members who viewed unionization as inconsistent with the values and ethics of the profession. The PRN represents employed physicians as well as medical residents and interns (physicians in training programs). Its members pledge not to strike. To date, the PRN is still small, with roughly 200 members. It is not affiliated with the AFL-CIO or any other union (Poznick 2001; PRN/AMA 2001).

In addition to these unions, a number of other labor organizations organize health care workers, although their health care memberships at this point are not as substantial as the unions just described. The health care memberships of these unions also make up a relatively small proportion of the union's total membership. Among such unions are the United Auto Workers (UAW), the Office and Professional Employees International Union (OPEIU), the Teamsters, the Operating Engineers, the Laborers, the Communications Workers of America (CWA), and the United Steelworkers of America (USWA) (see Table 4).

The American Federation of State, County, and Municipal Employees (AFSCME) also has a substantial number of health care members,

TABLE 4

Health Care Employee Membership in Selected U.S. Unions, 2001

Union health care divisions	Number of physicians	Number of RNs	Total health care members	Total members (2001)
Service Employees International Union (SEIU)			650,000	1,500,000
National Doctors Alliance	15,000	0		
Nurse Alliance	0	110,000		
American Federation of Teachers (AFT)			60,000	681,000
Healthcare Division	12,500	25,000		
Office and Professional Employees International Union (OPEIU)	NA	1,840	NA	123,000
United American Nurses (UAN)	0	96,000	96,000	96,000
United Food and Commercial Workers (UFCW)	0	10,000	75,000	1,400,000
Operating Engineers International Union (OEIU)	0	4,000	NA	400,000
Physicians for Responsible Negotiation (PRN)	200	0	200	200
California Nurses Association (CNA)	0	37,000	37,000	37,000
American Federation of State, County, and Municipal Employees (AFSCME)			360,000	1,300,000
United Nurses of America	0	50,000[a]		
Union of American Physicians and Dentists	5,000	0		
United Steelworkers of America (USWA)	0	NA	17,000	667,000

Sources: Individual union websites and union publications.
[a] Includes LPNs.

although almost all of them work in the public sector. The American Federation of Government Employees also organizes health care workers in government facilities, although their membership is drawn almost exclusively from the ranks of federal employees.

The Legal Framework

Hospitals

Like most other private-sector workers in the United States, employees of private hospitals were first given the right to form unions, bargain collectively, and strike with the passage of the National Labor Relations

Act (NLRA) in 1935. Although there is a record of at least one hospital's employees organizing as early as 1936, there was little union activity among hospital workers for the first twelve years of the existence of the Act. In 1947, employees of not-for-profit hospitals (virtually all private hospitals at that time) were dropped from coverage by the Taft-Hartley Amendments to the NLRA. This action was based on the belief of Congress that health services were essential to the public's welfare, that they provided eleemosynary, or charitable, services, and that unionization could result in the disruption of those services (U.S. Congress 1947). With the exception of eight states that passed legislation that granted some or all private, not-for-profit hospital employees some collective bargaining rights during this period, most employees in this sector did not have a right to union representation (Metzger and Pointer 1972).[11]

Although for-profit hospitals were rare during the several decades following the passage of the Act, these employees were not excluded by the 1947 amendment. However, the NLRB did not exert jurisdiction over those hospitals until 1967 (NLRB 1967). In 1974, twenty-seven years after it excluded nonprofit hospitals, Congress deleted this exemption and once again brought these employees under the aegis of the Act through the passage of Public Law 93-360 (AHA 1976).

Public Law 93-360 amended the NLRA by extending coverage to nonprofit hospitals. The passage of the amendment raised additional questions about which employees were eligible to form bargaining units and which were excluded from coverage under the Act. The eligibility of physicians has proved to be a particularly difficult issue to resolve. Only in the past few years has the Board made definitive rulings on physician eligibility.

Physicians. Physicians generally fall into one of three categories in terms of their employment status. They are either employed by hospitals or health care systems, serving internships or residencies in hospitals, or self-employed. Physicians working directly for hospitals or health care systems are considered employees for purposes of the Act and can organize and bargain collectively under the law's protection.[12] Employed physicians who meet the NLRA's definition of manager or supervisor, however, are excluded from coverage, as are managers and supervisors in all industries.

Although health care employers have long argued that all employed physicians are managers or supervisors, the Board has generally rejected this argument and has applied its own narrow definition. Until 2001 this resulted in only a small portion of employed physicians being designated as ineligible to be part of the physician bargaining unit (Keating 1991). However, in 2001 the Supreme Court rejected the NLRB's definition of a supervisor in a health care setting by a 5–4 vote in its *Kentucky River* decision (U.S. Supreme Court 2001). The ruling actually addressed the status of RNs in a long-term care psychiatric facility. However, the decision could lead to a broadening of the definition of supervisor to include physicians who have even nominal oversight of other health care workers. While the NLRB will continue to make determinations regarding supervisory status on a case-by-case basis, *Kentucky River* will make it easier for the Board to exclude physicians from bargaining units, should they be so inclined. If the Board moves in this direction it would be a significant setback for physicians' unions (Alberts 2001; Newman 2001).

Medical interns and residents, often referred to as house staff, constitute the second major category of physicians. Interns and residents are doctors who have already received a medical degree but are serving a supervised period of clinical training.[13] These physicians are typically employed by hospitals or medical centers.

As far back as the 1960s, some interns and residents working for public hospitals successfully formed bargaining units. However, in a series of cases handed down after the 1974 amendment, the NLRB ruled that house staff in private facilities were primarily students, not employees, and therefore were not eligible to form unions or engage in collective bargaining (Keating 1991). In 1999, the NLRB reversed itself and extended the protection of the NLRA to interns and residents at private hospitals, reasoning that, although ". . . residents are students . . . , they are also employees who conform to the NLRA definition of an employee in every way. . . ." (NLRB 1999a).

The third category of physicians includes those who work in solo or group practices. In the past, such doctors have been considered self-employed, as their practices are essentially small businesses that treat and bill patients without the involvement of a third party. However, as these physicians have increasingly signed agreements with HMOs and other managed care organizations, they have become less and less independent. Physicians treating patients insured by these groups have been forced to reorganize the way they practice to conform with restrictions imposed by the HMOs, including getting preapproval for surgery and for referrals to specialists. They must also adhere to fee schedules determined by the insurance companies. For this reason some physicians have challenged the notion that they are self-employed or independent contractors under the definition given in the NLRA.

In 1999, the NLRB, in *AmeriHealth HMO v. UFCW, Local 56* (NLRB 1999b), considered the case of 650 primary care and specialty physicians in both solo and group practices who petitioned the Board to be represented by a union. The physicians claimed that they were de facto employees of the HMO under the NLRA's definition because they have provider contracts that give the organization control over the physicians' incomes, patient care activities, and working conditions. The NLRB rejected this argument on the grounds that the "common law agency test" indicates that the physicians were independent contractors rather than employees under the definitions of the Act. Specifically, the Board argued that "the physicians exert substantial control over how they provide their services, retain economic separateness from [the HMO], practice and advertise in their own names, perform their work at their own facilities without supervision from [the HMO], and have wide entrepreneurial discretion that affects the profitability of their practices" (Amber 1999b:1).

A second hurdle that self-employed physicians must overcome if they wish to engage in collective negotiation is the long-standing rule that nonsalaried physicians are covered by U.S. antitrust law. This ruling makes it illegal for them to band together in any way to bargain with health plans. There is legislation currently under consideration at both the federal and state levels to change this ruling.[14]

Nurses. In addition to the disputed collective bargaining rights of physicians, there has also been controversy about the rights of RNs working in private hospitals to engage in bargaining. Because RNs sometimes exercise independent professional judgment in directing less-skilled workers (such as LPNs and aides), hospitals have sought to have them categorized as supervisors under the NLRA. Generally, the Board has ruled that staff nurses are protected by the Act and that head nurses and shift supervisors are not. However, the *Kentucky River* decision (U.S. Supreme Court 2001) specifically ruled that nurses could be considered supervisors if they "direct others in dispensing medicine, serve as the highest ranking employee in a building, address staff shortages, and move employees among units as needed" (Bellandi 2001:8), at least in the context of a long-term, psychiatric hospital. As is the case with physicians, the impact of this ruling will depend on how the NLRB and the lower courts interpret and apply the high court's decision. To date, attempts to apply this ruling to acute care hospitals have not been successful.

Other Employees. Generally, other patient care employees (LPNs, aides, laboratory technicians, radiation technologists, pharmacists, and physical and occupational therapists) and nonpatient care employees (food service, maintenance, housekeeping, and security workers) in private hospitals have been considered to be covered by the Act and to have the right to be represented by a union for the purposes of collective bargaining. However, because hospital employees range widely in training, skills, responsibilities, and compensation, the passage of the 1974 amendment to the NLRA was quickly followed by questions about the most appropriate bargaining units for hospital employees. After years of contentious litigation between hospitals (who wanted large, or even facilitywide, units) and health care unions (who generally wanted smaller units), the Supreme Court decided the issue in 1991 by affirming the NLRB's ruling in *American Hospital Association v. NLRB* (U.S. Supreme Court 1991).

In its decision, the NLRB ruled that there are eight appropriate bargaining units for acute care hospitals. The Board divided professional employees into three units—physicians, registered nurses, and other professional employees (e.g., pharmacists and medical technologists). Five units were designated for nonprofessionals. These units consist of technical employees (e.g., LPNs, laboratory technicians), skilled maintenance workers, business office clericals, all other nonprofessional and service employees, and security guards (see Figure 1) (U.S. Supreme Court 1991).

FIGURE 1

NLRB (Nonpublic) Hospital Bargaining Units

Professional employees
  1. Physicians
  2. Registered nurses
  3. Other professional employees (e.g., pharmacists, medical technologists, etc.)

Nonprofessional employees
  4. Technical employees (e.g., LPNs, laboratory technicians, etc.)
  5. Skilled maintenance workers
  6. Business office clericals
  7. All other nonprofessional and service employees
  8. Security guards

Source: U.S. Supreme Court (1991).

In addition to regulating the process by which employees form unions, the NLRA provides the legal framework under which collective bargaining takes place once a union has been certified. It also provides a process unique to the health care industry to help unions and employers resolve bargaining impasses. The additional steps the parties must go through before embarking on a work stoppage were designed to minimize such disruptions in the industry (Miller 1980).

Unions must provide health care institutions, as well as the Federal Mediation and Conciliation Service (FMCS), with ten days' written notice before striking or picketing. They also are required to submit their dispute to mediation by the FMCS before initiating a work stoppage. And, if the FMCS believes a strike or lockout will "substantially interrupt" the provision of health care to a community, it can order a board of inquiry (BOI). A BOI is a fact-finding process. The fact-finder considers the issues and writes a nonbinding report that includes a recommendation for settlement. If one or both parties refuse to follow the fact-finder's recommendations, the report is made public. This often puts pressure on the parties to settle. If no agreement is reached, the parties can proceed to a work stoppage (Miller 1980).

Long-Term Care/Nursing Homes

Employees of private-sector nursing homes and for-profit, long-term care hospitals have been covered by the NLRA since its passage in 1935. Employees of nonprofit, long-term care hospitals, while originally covered by the Act, were excluded in 1947 by the Taft-Hartley Amendments. In 1974, coverage was once again extended to these employees (Feldacker 2000).

Long-term care facilities generally have a less complicated bargaining unit configuration than do acute care hospitals. This is due to the fact that nursing homes, rehabilitation facilities, and other long-term care facilities generally have fewer categories of employees than hospitals. For example, it is somewhat unusual for rehabilitation facilities to employ physicians and very unusual for nursing homes to do so. There often are a small number of RNs working in such settings, some of whom usually assume the responsibilities of supervisors, while others may work in a nonsupervisory capacity. In terms of patient care, the bulk of the workforce consists of a number of LPNs working with a greater number of certified nurse assistants. The rest of the workforce is typically made up of service workers performing dietary, housekeeping, and laundry functions; maintenance employees; and security personnel.

For this reason the Board does not extend the eight-unit rule it uses for acute care hospitals to most long-term care facilities. The most common bargaining unit in these facilities consists of nonsupervisory, nonsecurity employees, both patient care and nonpatient care, in one unit.

Such a unit would be more diverse than a typical acute care hospital bargaining unit. It could, for instance, include RNs, LPNs, and nurse assistants, as well as maintenance, dietary, and housekeeping personnel. As in other workplaces, employees who serve as guards and perform only security functions in long-term care facilities must have their own bargaining unit.

While hospitals oppose the unionization of their employees with varying degrees of aggressiveness, long-term care facilities and nursing homes generally appear to be more aggressive in their efforts to remain nonunion. For example, one of the largest operators of such facilities in the United States, Beverly Enterprises, has long been known for "the consistency and intensity of their union avoidance efforts" (Bronfenbrenner 1997). In 2001, the U.S. Supreme Court refused to overturn an NLRB decision to impose a companywide order on Beverly barring intimidation of workers seeking to join a union. The Board's investigation found that the nursing home chain was guilty of 240 unfair labor practice violations at fifty-four facilities in eighteen states and that the policies behind the violations emanated from the highest levels of the corporation ("Beverly Bid Futile to Get Labor Order Rescinded" 2001). While Beverly's response to the efforts of its employees to organize may not be representative of the industry, it is notable, given its position as a leader in the nursing home/long-term care field.

Bargaining Structure

Traditionally, collective bargaining in the U.S. health care industry occurs on a decentralized basis. This approach to bargaining is generally consistent with the bargaining structures found in many U.S. industries. At its most decentralized level, bargaining occurs between an employer and a single bargaining unit. Where a single employer has separate bargaining units of employees working in a number of separate facilities, the bargaining units might band together to bargain one common contract for all of those workplaces. This "companywide" bargaining structure is more centralized than single-employer, single-unit bargaining. An even more centralized approach occurs where the employers in an industry come together to bargain one contract with the multiple bargaining units that represent all the employees of all the employers in a geographic region or nationally. This "multi-employer" approach to bargaining represents a highly centralized structure.

In the past, bargaining in the health care industry generally has taken place between a single employer and a single group of employees who have formed a bargaining unit. This has been true of both the hospital and long-term care/nursing home sectors. However, relatively recent trends toward forming systems and networks in the hospital sector and toward corporatization in the long-term care/nursing home sector have, in some instances, led to more centralized companywide bargaining.

Hospitals

Bargaining between hospitals and their employees still most often occurs at the facility level. Usually, this involves one or more units of hospital workers bargaining with the same hospital/employer. Sometimes multiple units in the same facility will band together to engage in coordinated bargaining; sometimes the units will bargain separately with the common employer.

Although less common, companywide bargaining takes place between a single employer and bargaining units working in dispersed locations for that employer. This might occur, for instance, where a health care system or network owns multiple hospitals, either in a single region or nationally. This was the case in 2000 when Kaiser Permanente and twenty-five local unions negotiated a companywide contract (Amber 2000; Cleeland and Bernstein 2000).

Kaiser Permanente is the largest U.S. not-for-profit HMO. It has twenty-nine medical centers across the country. In April 2000, twenty-five locals of eight different international unions (SEIU, AFSCME, OPEIU, UFCW, USWA, AFT, the International Federation of Professional and Technical Unions, and the Kaiser Permanente Nurse Anesthetists Association) agreed to jointly negotiate thirty-three contracts, covering 64,000 nurses, clerks, housekeepers, and cafeteria workers with Kaiser Permanente. In September 2000, the parties signed a five-year national collective bargaining agreement for these units. The language from this agreement was incorporated into the thirty-three local agreements (Amber 2000; Cleeland and Bernstein 2000). Highlights from this historic contract are outlined in Figure 2.

An example of single-employer, multi-unit bargaining on a smaller scale is the agreement the CNA signed in March 1998 with Mercy Healthcare Sacramento. The agreement covered 1,700 RNs at five Sacramento-area hospitals owned by Mercy Healthcare (CNA 1998). Unlike the Kaiser Permanente negotiations, these nurses were all represented by the same union.

Multi-employer bargaining is another approach to negotiations that, while still not prevalent, is becoming more common in health care.

FIGURE 2

Selected Provisions
National Agreement
Kaiser Permanente and the Coalition of Kaiser Permanente Unions, AFL-CIO
October 1, 2000

Compensation	4–6 percent across-the-board annual wage increases
	Bonuses for meeting goals regarding patient satisfaction and reduction of medical errors
Staffing	After appropriate partnership training and education, joint partnership staffing teams will be involved in determining, within allocated organizational resources, how departments will be staffed. Staffing teams will annually recommend a staffing design plan that encompasses mutually acceptable numbers, mix, and qualifications of staff in each work unit.
Job security	Kaiser pledges to maximize employment security by exerting every effort to prevent displacement through attrition, retraining, and other means. In addition, Kaiser pledges that no one will lose his or her job as a result of partnership programs.
Neutrality	Kaiser pledges to remain neutral during any unionization attempts to grant union representation whenever a majority of employees express clearly and unambiguously the wish to be represented by a signatory union.
Work–life balance	The Labor–Management Regional Teams should provide leadership on work–life balance issues. They should develop operational policies, oversee implementation of work–life balance programs, and coordinate ongoing training and communication about life balance in three areas: health promotion, employee assistance, and referral services.
Issue resolution and corrective action	The parties are committed to resolving workplace concerns quickly and by those most directly involved. To that end, the issue resolution procedure will have two components: a system for raising and quickly resolving workplace issues using interest-based problem solving by those directly involved with the issue and a method of resolving performance and behavior issues in a nonpunitive fashion, in which employee supervisor and union representatives work together to identify the problem and craft the solution.
Safety and health	Health and safety teams, integrated as partnership teams, will assist in prioritizing and implementing funding, determining accountability, and developing measurements, and may assist in or oversee the implementation of consistent health and safety and prevention programs.

Source: AFT website (2002)
<www.aft.org/healthcare/contractlanguage/nationalagreement2000.pdf>.

Multi-employer bargaining "tends to evolve in urban areas and in association with homogeneity of hospitals, when a union has achieved substantial organization of the hospital employees in a given area, where bargaining histories are similar, and where employee unions or associations are able to exert significant bargaining power" (Miller 1980:412). Where unions are powerful enough to "whipsaw" individual employers against one another, multi-employer bargaining can become the employers' "countersaw" to union power (Miller 1980). Multi-employer bargaining can involve a significant number of hospitals. One example of this approach involves the League of Voluntary Hospitals in New York City and SEIU/1199 (Herzfield 1998). The most recent contract between this employer group and the union was reached in June 1998 and covers 40,000 employees in thirty-five private New York City hospitals. The contract covers a wide range of employees, including nurse aides and attendants; laundry, housekeeping, and dietary workers; building and custodial staff; X-ray and laboratory technicians; and various professionals, such as social workers, therapists, and pharmacists (Herzfield 1998).

The pattern set in the June 1998 agreement was subsequently used as a basis for contracts with other hospitals in the New York City area. In December 1998, six additional League of Voluntary Hospitals members signed an agreement with SEIU/1199, covering an additional 4,500 employees (Bureau of National Affairs [BNA] 1998). In February 1999, the League and SEIU/1199 concluded an agreement covering 4,300 more RNs in eight hospitals. The terms were based on the June contract between the parties (Herzfield 1999). This "pattern bargaining" usually occurs where there are "orbits of coercive comparison" (Miller 1980: 413) across hospitals. The result is that the New York City hospital sector becomes "one interconnected bargaining unit" (Miller 1980:413).

Another example of multi-employer bargaining is the agreement reached in 2001 between the Minnesota Hospital and Health Care Partnership and the Minnesota Nurses Association (MNA). The Partnership represents thirteen hospitals, and the MNA negotiates on behalf of 9,000 RNs in the Minneapolis–St. Paul metro area. (Lerner 2001a). Once the settlement was reached, MNA then used that settlement as a pattern for bargaining across the state, effectively forcing nonurban Minnesota hospitals to match the pay standards established in the state's largest urban area (Calkins 2002).

Physicians have shown little interest in bargaining in conjunction with other health care employees, and physician organizing is not yet so widespread that physicians in multiple locations can band together to engage in multi-unit bargaining. Thus, physician bargaining tends to be very decentralized, occurring in most cases on a single-unit basis.

Long-Term Care/Nursing Homes

Because of the significant presence of corporate chains in the long-term care/nursing home sector, the potential for centralized bargaining is greater in this sector than in the hospital sector. In reality, many different bargaining structures are in place in the long-term care sector, ranging from individual facility bargaining to statewide coordinated bargaining. Certainly, in the 48 percent of facilities that are independently owned, many of which are small, bargaining tends to occur on a facility-by-facility basis. In some states, however, employer associations bring together nursing home owners to bargain as a group.

This is the case in Connecticut where the Connecticut Association of Healthcare Facilities represents approximately fifty facilities in bargaining with SEIU/1199 ("Nursing Home Strike" 2001). While many of the larger chains operate in numerous states, companywide bargaining rarely occurs in this sector. In some instances, a company will bargain a contract for its facilities in a region or a state. The result, however, is not a master agreement but contracts for individual facilities that have a significant amount of common language.

The growing corporatization of long-term care has led to an increase in multi-unit bargaining with nursing home chains. For example, in 2001, three SEIU locals banded together to bargain a contract with the Beverly Corporation on behalf of 1,500 workers from nineteen nursing homes across Pennsylvania. The ability to negotiate with, and potentially strike, all Beverly homes in a geographic region gives the union significantly greater bargaining power than if it separately negotiated nineteen agreements (SEIU/1199 2001a). If unions like SEIU continue to be successful in organizing chain-owned facilities, they will likely attempt to centralize bargaining across companies to the greatest degree possible.

Bargaining Issues, Impasses, and Outcomes

Hospitals

Physicians. Collective bargaining for physicians is a relatively new phenomenon in the private sector. Of the three categories of physicians mentioned earlier—employees of hospitals or health care systems, interns and residents, and self-employed—unions representing interns and residents have the most significant track record in bargaining, although most of the contracts they have signed have been with public hospitals. This is not surprising, given the disputed status of physicians as supervisors.

Since the 1999 NLRB decision extending the right to bargain to interns and residents in the private sector, there has been a significant amount of organizing activity. However, there has been only one contract signed between a union representing these employees and a private hospital. In May 2001, the CIR/SEIU negotiated a contract with Brookdale Hospital in Brooklyn. The contract covered interns, residents, and some physicians and included the first salary increase in five years, increased meal allowances, parking discounts, and premium pay for chief residents (CIR/SEIU 2001a).

In the future, house staff unions will probably focus increasingly on working conditions, such as hours worked, time on call, and staffing levels. These are issues that have commonly been the focus of CIR/SEIU's contracts with hospitals in the public sector (CIR/SEIU 2001c). Patient care issues are also likely to be on the agenda. One somewhat novel issue that has been a part of some CIR/SEIU settlements with public hospitals and that could be on the table in the private sector is patient care funds. Patient care funds are union-negotiated, employer-financed funds used to purchase services and equipment that the house staff deem essential to patient care (CIR/SEIU 2001d).

Like other employees, nonintern/resident physicians are interested in higher incomes, better benefits, shorter hours, and reasonable workloads. Gaining greater control over decision making related to patient care, however, also appears to be at the top of their bargaining priorities. Physicians want more input into administrative decisions that affect patient care. And they want greater authority to make patient care decisions without consulting with, or being limited by, nonphysician representatives of HMOs and insurance companies. Their unions contend that these issues are necessary prerequisites to improving patient care. These issues are also likely to be more prominent in bargaining between nonintern/resident physicians and hospitals than they are in house staff negotiations, as these physicians are not in training and have greater expectations about their role in the patient care process.

Clearly, physicians' unions are attempting to broaden the scope of bargaining beyond the traditional wages, benefits, and working conditions. Their members see bargaining as a means to gain a greater voice in how medicine is practiced in the facilities in which they work. As in other industries, health care employers have resisted this incursion into traditional management prerogatives. However, it seems clear that, for unions to garner and keep the support of physicians, they will need to pursue this broader bargaining agenda.

Like their counterparts in hospitals, self-employed physicians are also interested in gaining greater control over the economic and patient care aspects of their practices. As was suggested earlier, these physicians are considered self-employed contractors and are prevented by federal antitrust law from having unions negotiate with providers on their behalf. Physician unions can, however, assist their members in forming independent practice associations (IPAs), and those unions can negotiate with providers on behalf of those IPAs (Carlson 1999).

Where forming an IPA is not practical, unions may function as a "third party messenger" and assist their members in the negotiations with the provider. In this situation the union does not bargain on behalf of its members/physicians but rather compiles data on the usual and customary charges for medical procedures, on maximum Medicare rates, and on reimbursement rates from major payers in a given market. The union can communicate contract offers from providers to its members and relay its members' acceptance, rejection, or counteroffers. Ultimately, however, the member/physician must make an independent decision whether to accept or reject a provider's offer (Carlson 1999).

Ultimately, negotiations by private-sector physicians are still a relatively new phenomenon, and the parties are relatively inexperienced. One area where this inexperience might be particularly problematic is in the resolution of bargaining disputes. In most private-sector impasses, strikes and lockouts or the potential for them play a role in breaking deadlocks. However, as both the NDA/SEIU and the PRN/ AMA have pledged not to strike and as lockouts by hospitals seem equally improbable, it remains unclear how disputes between these parties will be resolved (NDA/SEIU 2001; PRN/AMA 2001).

Nurses. The shortage of RNs has greatly improved the bargaining position of nurses' unions since 2000. Prior to this shortage, RNs' wages had stagnated for some time. In the 1990s, real median weekly earnings for the workforce as a whole increased by 6.8 percent, while earnings for RNs fell by .7 percent (BLS 2001b). However, as a result of the heightened competition for nurses that began at the end of the decade, nurses' wages have been growing steadily. From 1999 to 2000, median weekly wages for RNs increased 1.8 percent, while the earnings for the general workforce rose 1.4 percent.

In 1998, various studies placed the mean hourly wage for RNs working in hospitals at between $19.83 and $21.12 (Buck Consultants 1998; BLS 1998). In the early 2000s, however, unions representing nurses saw their bargaining power increase significantly. In 2001, for example, SEIU negotiated a 22 percent salary increase over three years for RNs working for two California hospitals (SEIU 2001b). In that same year, the MNA settled a contract with ten Minneapolis–St. Paul area hospitals for a 20 to 21 percent pay increase over three years that will push the pay range for hospital RNs with a bachelor's degree in that city to $23.09 to $34.63 per hour in 2003, depending on years of service (Wascoe 2001, Calkins 2002). Many nurses' contracts bargained in 2001 included an 8 percent increase at a time when the average union contract contained a 3.7 percent pay raise ("Data on Bargaining" 2002).

RNs have also been making steady progress in the area of employee benefits. This is particularly significant, given the fact that benefits have traditionally made up a smaller percentage of the payroll in health care than in other nonmanufacturing industries. In 2000, for example, health care employers spent only 1.5 percent of their payroll on pensions. In that same year, employers in other nonmanufacturing industries spent 6.8 percent of their payroll on pensions (AFT 2001b).[15] The difference in benefits is often linked to the high percentage of women in the health care industry.

Compensation and benefits are important to all employees. However, as discussed earlier, there is evidence suggesting that changes in patient care and working conditions brought about by managed care initiatives are at least as important as are economic issues to nurses working in the hospital sector. Nurses have long sought to influence the patient care process through collective bargaining (Miller 1980). However, as nurse dissatisfaction over short staffing, mandatory overtime, and floating practices has grown, and as turnover in the nursing profession has continued to rise, patient care issues have come to the forefront of hospital–nurse bargaining (Clark et al. 2001; ANA 2001a).

Like managers in most industries, hospital administrators have generally tried to limit the scope of bargaining with unions to traditional issues and have been reluctant to allow unions to participate in patient care decision making, on the basis that this falls under the heading of management's rights and responsibilities. However, today, under intense pressure from nurses' unions, hospitals are being forced to gradually open up the patient care process to greater employee involvement (Miller 1980; Bronder 2001).

Of all the patient care issues, staffing is perhaps the issue of primary concern to hospital RNs. All of the unions representing nurses have fought for language that minimizes or prevents understaffing in hospitals. The most typical provisions involve the formation of labor–management committees to monitor staffing levels and make staffing recommendations. The ability of unions involved in these committees to affect staffing-level decisions often depends on the authority these committees are given. In their weakest form, the committees are only advisory; where they are empowered to determine nurse–patient ratios, they can play a significant role.

Language in a contract between the Allina Health System in Minnesota and the MNA may go farther than any other contract to date in giving nurses greater control over the staffing problem. The Allina–MNA contract forces hospital administration to turn away new patients from a seriously understaffed unit if RNs believe the unit is not adequately staffed (Lerner 2001b).

Another approach to understaffing involves submitting disputes between the union and the hospital over staffing levels directly to a neutral outside nursing expert whose decision is binding on management. SEIU has negotiated such an approach in at least one contract (SEIU 2001b).

An additional staffing-related issue in dispute in most nurse–hospital negotiations is mandatory overtime. Hospitals argue that the nurse shortage forces them to utilize mandatory overtime. Unions contend that, whatever the reason, working twelve- or sixteen-hour shifts is not only disruptive to a nurse's private life (and contributes to the high nurse turnover rate) but also places patients in danger. Fatigued nurses are much more likely to make medication errors, miss important patient symptoms, or give incorrect treatment (Owley 2001). Nurses' unions have been successful in eliminating forced overtime in some of their contracts. Where this is not possible, they have tried to restrict the number of overtime hours nurses are forced to work. Another approach has been to bargain provisions that discourage the use of overtime by increasing the cost to employers. One SEIU/1199 contract in Wisconsin, for instance, calls for the hospital to pay nurses a $12.20 per hour premium, in addition to time-and-one-half per hour, for working a double shift (SEIU 2001b).

Two of the direct impacts of managed care have been the restructuring of nurses' jobs and hospital mergers. Restructuring and mergers have affected RNs and patient care in negative ways. The UAN has attempted to address these issues by negotiating contract language that restricts the employers' ability to restructure nurses' jobs. It also has bargained for the creation of mutual gains committees to oversee and approve any restructuring activities and for language that protects its employment contracts if the hospital is merged, sold, or changes management (ANA 2001c). Other nurses' unions have taken similar steps.

Managed care and staff shortages have also caused hospitals to "float" nurses from department to department to meet pressing needs. Nurses are very concerned about this practice, as they are sometimes moved to areas in which they have little or no experience (e.g., a medical/surgical nurse being moved to intensive care or obstetrics). They believe this reduces the quality of patient care and may even place patients in danger. Nurses are also concerned about the stress and potential liability that accompanies such moves. Again, most nurses' unions try to bargain contract language that limits this practice.

One specific approach being employed to deal with this problem is the creation of "clusters" of jobs that are very similar so that nurses can move easily across jobs within the clusters. Unions then try to win language forbidding employers from moving nurses from one cluster to another.

Another issue increasingly being addressed in collective bargaining agreements is the employer/hospital's role in representation elections at other facilities it operates. These neutrality provisions limit what employers can do in response to future organizing drives. For example, the CNA negotiated a contract with the Catholic Healthcare West (CHW) system that prohibits CHW from conducting captive-audience or one-on-one meetings with its employees. It also allows the union to choose whether the NLRB or some other neutral third party will supervise an election at nonunion CHW facilities.

An agreement by SEIU/1199 and the Healthcare Alliance of New York goes even further. In this contract the Alliance agreed to remain neutral if the union mounted an organizing drive at one of its nonunion hospitals. The contract places significant restrictions on what the employer can do and say in response to the union's organizing efforts at the facility in question. The Alliance also agreed to card check recognition, meaning the union could be certified if it obtains recognition cards from a majority of nurses, without having to go through an election. Such language makes it much easier for a union to obtain representation rights ("SEIU Locals Bargain Neutrality" 2001).

As this discussion suggests, nurses' unions have been prompted by managed care to broaden the scope of bargaining beyond conventional subjects. Nurses have had some success to date in this area. This success undoubtedly is a function of the shortage of RNs found in virtually every region of the United States.

While most negotiations between unions representing RNs and hospital/health plan employers end in settlements, strikes by nurses do occur. Under the NLRA, such walkouts are permitted for nurses working for private-sector employers, but they are subject to the restrictions discussed earlier.

Among the most significant nurses' strikes in recent years were a fifty-nine-day walkout by 1,730 RNs at two Stanford University Hospitals ("Nurses' Strike" 2000), a forty-two-day work stoppage at Worchester Medical Center in Massachusetts, and a five-month strike at a community hospital in Nyack, New York (Stein 2000).[16] While nurses' strikes in the United States do occur, they remain relatively uncommon.[17]

In some cases, interest arbitration has been used to resolve disputes without disrupting patient care. An independent union of nurses signed an agreement with Rhode Island Hospital in 1997, allowing either party to invoke arbitration once the parties reached a bargaining impasse. In their next round of negotiations, the hospital chose to exercise that option, and an arbitrator resolved the issues in dispute (Kessler 2000). Arbitration does not appear to be gaining momentum as an impasse resolution procedure in nurse bargaining; however, it is an option that could limit the disruption of patient care, something about which both parties are concerned.

Union Threat and Wage Effect. As in most industries, collective bargaining settlements for unionized hospital employees impact their nonunion counterparts. The "union threat effect" comes into play most directly where some of the eight NLRB-designated unions in a hospital are represented by a union or association and some are not. In such a situation there are numerous incentives for a hospital's administration to provide equivalent compensation increases and benefits programs to prevent the unrepresented units from organizing. The same dynamics come into play for hospital systems, networks, and chains that have both organized and unorganized hospitals; for nonunion hospitals in proximity to unionized hospitals; and for nonunion hospitals in parts of the country where health care unions are actively organizing (Miller 1980).

A second economic phenomenon found in the hospital sector is the union wage effect. In 2000, the wage differential between unionized and nonunionized nurses was 13 percent. While substantial, the union wage effect is significantly less than the 28 percent differential for all occupations for that year. It is also less than the wage differential for all health care occupations (19 percent) and for LPNs (31 percent) (AFT 2001b). In the face of a significant nurse shortage, it is reasonable to expect the differential to become smaller still as nonunion hospitals are forced to raise wages to compete in the labor market.

Long-Term Care/Nursing Homes

The subjects of bargaining in the long-term care/nursing home sector are similar to those in the acute care hospital sector. These issues include wages and benefits, staffing levels, and mandatory overtime, as well as health and safety concerns and training opportunities. However, funding for the long-term care sector differs from the hospital sector, and this significantly affects the way the parties approach bargaining.

A substantial portion of the revenues that a long-term care/nursing facility receives for the care it provides comes from Medicaid. Because reimbursement rates are dependent on the amount of money individual states designate for this purpose, an employer's ability to meet union demands in this sector is dependent on the level at which that employer's state decides to fund Medicaid. For this reason, unions seeking wage and benefit increases often turn their attention to their state's governor and legislature in an effort to win such increases.

The unions representing long-term care/nursing home workers closely monitor the budget processes of state legislatures across the country. They regularly lobby legislators and governors for the maximum increase to Medicaid, as this provides a larger pool of funds over which to bargain (SEIU/1199 2001b).

This multilateral bargaining process was starkly depicted in the dispute between Connecticut nursing homes and SEIU/1199 mentioned earlier. With a March 15, 2001, contract deadline approaching for the state's forty-three unionized private nursing homes and nearly 6,000 workers, negotiations were at an impasse. The union was asking for pay raises and a decrease in the ratio of aides to patients. The nursing homes claimed that the only way they could meet these demands was if the state increased its Medicaid reimbursement rates for the coming years. The union then turned to the governor, calling on him to increase the amount of Medicaid funding he was asking the legislature for in his proposed budget. The governor refused and the nursing home employees walked off the job (Zapata 2001; Zielbauer 2001).

This strike differed from a typical private-sector strike in that the actual target was the governor, not the employers. By striking, the union hoped to convince the governor to seek an increase in Medicaid funding from the legislature. The union would then try to force employers to use at least part of the increase in funds to address the salary and under-staffing issues. The strike was eventually settled through binding arbitration. Although it failed to win the governor's support, the union did accomplish many of its goals when it convinced state legislators to accept and fund the arbitrator's award (over the strong opposition of the governor) (New England Health Care Employees Union 2001).

Since Medicaid is a state-funded initiative, the multilateral bargaining in the Connecticut nursing home sector is a phenomenon that is repeated in other states. In fact, SEIU, the dominant union in the long-term care/nursing home sector, has made an effort to form a "New Partnership" with employers in this sector, particularly the large chains, to pursue the common interest they have in increased Medicaid funding (SEIU 2001a).

The union argues that the "tarnished reputation and negative public image" of the large nursing home chains have made it difficult for the industry to gain "the public or political support necessary to win in-creased Medicaid funding" (SEIU 2001a:3). On the other hand, SEIU contends that it has a proven ability to "build the political support necessary to increase Medicaid reimbursement rates" (SEIU 2001a:3–4) at the state level and points to recent successes in Michigan, California, and Connecticut. It also points out that it has accumulated considerable resources that could be directed toward the kind of joint campaign it envisions in its New Partnership proposal (SEIU 2001a).

The union also proposes that, in addition to helping the industry build support for funding increases, it is prepared "to develop and imple-ment a recruitment, training, placement, and retention program to address the staffing crisis" (SEIU 2001a:8) that the long-term care/nurs-ing home sector faces. The union has already begun such programs in California, where it has reduced the turnover rate for certified nurse assistants from 100 percent to 60 percent. It argues that, based on the California program and another in Texas, it can develop similar programs in ten labor markets that would recruit and train 7,500 such assistants. The quid pro quo that the SEIU would expect from the industry would be organizing rights in the form of neutrality agreements and card check recognition (SEIU 2001a). Such a partnership would be a dramatic departure from business as usual in the long-term care sector, given the adversarial nature of union–management relationships.

Two factors may cause the industry to give more serious considera-tion to the union's proposal than it would have in past years. First, the long-term care/nursing home industry is in the midst of a financial crisis that has driven five of the seven largest chains into Chapter 11 bankruptcy in 2001, at least in part as a result of the change in Medicare reimbursement procedures and the shortfall of Medicaid funds. Second, if the industry declines to enter into this sort of venture with SEIU, it seems clear that the considerable resources the union has offered to put into the proposed partnership will be used to mount large-scale organizing drives against the industry. It is not clear at this point whether long-term care employers will join with SEIU in this new partnership.

As in virtually all industries, unions are able to increase wages for long-term care/nursing home employees above nonunion wage levels. However, compensation for nursing personnel in long-term care facilities historically has been lower than the wages in other health care settings. For example, in 1998, average hourly wages for RNs in long-term care varied between $16.64 and $17.69, according to different studies (Buck Consultants 1998; BLS 1998). These same studies reported the average wage of hospital RNs during that same year as ranging from $19.83 to $21.12. This discrepancy can be attributed, in part, to the fact that the majority of care in nursing homes is publicly financed by Medicare and Medicaid, government programs in which present payment is determined by historical cost. This leaves little room for increasing wages (AHCA 2001).

Public Policy Initiatives

Labor organizations have used the political process as a means of addressing the needs and interests of their members for decades. As a growing number of health care employees join unions in response to the enormous changes occurring in the health care industry, these organizations are increasingly turning to political action to bolster their collective bargaining efforts.

Virtually all unions organizing physicians and nurses have been active in trying to influence health policy following the introduction of managed care. Perhaps the most successful effort to date is a bill CNA pushed through the California state legislature in 1999 that would set nurse staffing levels for hospitals (Fisher 1999). Nurses' unions continue to push for legislation in other states and for federal legislation that would set staffing standards that they consider safe and reasonable. Such measures, at least as proposed by nurses' organizations, are generally opposed by health care employers because of the added costs and restrictions they would impose on management (California Healthcare Association 2002).

Nurses' unions have also mounted intensive lobbying campaigns to place restrictions on mandatory overtime. In early 2002 their efforts resulted in the enactment of the first such state law when the governor of New Jersey signed a bill barring compulsory overtime in the state's hospitals and long-term care facilities ("New Jersey Governor Signs Measure" 2002).

And at the national level, nurses' unions have also been successful in passing the Safer Needles Bill in 2000. This legislation created federal safety standards for needles that will help protect nurses and other health care workers from deadly needlestick injuries that can spread HIV and hepatitis C (SEIU 2001b).

The unions representing physicians have also been actively pushing a legislative agenda of their own. At the top of that agenda is H.R. 1304, the Campbell–Conyers Bill. This bill would ease the antitrust restrictions against doctors who are independent contractors and give them the right to band together to engage in collective bargaining with HMOs and insurance companies over the terms and conditions for providing health services to the companies' customers (Connair 2000). This bill passed the House of Representatives in July 2000 but has not been voted on by the Senate.

In addition, CIR/SEIU has employed a public policy strategy to win limits on the hours interns and residents can be forced to work. The union has lobbied for federal and state legislation and for Occupational Safety and Health Administration (OSHA) standards to regulate the work hours of these physicians (Public Citizen 2001).

Unions representing long-term care/nursing home workers are also active in the political and legislative arena. As discussed earlier, lobbying individual state legislatures to win increased funding for Medicaid has almost become an extension of the collective bargaining process. In addition, health care unions have had success in winning federal staffing standards for long-term care/nursing home facilities. These standards mandate a certain level of personnel, including at least one RN on every shift (SEIU/1199 2001b).

An additional example of how union efforts in the public policy arena impact the work lives of long-term care/nursing home workers is a recent settlement among SEIU, the Beverly nursing home chain, and OSHA. As a result of workplace injury charges brought by the union against Beverly, the company agreed in 2002 to a comprehensive change in the safety procedures employed in 270 long-term care facilities across the country. The settlement requires Beverly to implement new safety guidelines and purchase new equipment in these facilities in an effort to protect its employees from injury (SEIU 2002).

The Future

The U.S. health care industry has been going through a period of tumultuous change over the past several years. The continued growth of managed care ensures that the health care environment will be equally dynamic in the years to come. Collective bargaining in this industry is evolving in a manner that reflects these changes.

Change in the collective bargaining process in the hospital sector of the health care industry is expected to be particularly great, as both the process and many of the parties are relatively inexperienced. As the process and the parties mature in the years ahead, it is reasonable to expect that bargaining will operate more efficiently.

The multitude of problems RNs face as a result of the introduction of managed care, combined with the expected long-term shortage in that profession, suggests that this will probably be one of the fastest-growing areas for unionization and collective bargaining, at least in the early part of the century. Whether the right to bargain will be broadened for physicians and whether physicians will embrace that right, is more uncertain. Physicians' unions fly in the face of the culture of the profession to a greater degree than in any other segment of the health care industry. These unions have sprung up as an almost last-ditch response to the problems and challenges posed by managed care. Whether they prove to be the most effective mechanism through which the medical profession can confront managed care remains to be seen.

Collective bargaining in the long-term care/nursing home sector also appears to be going through a transition period largely brought about by changes in the way such care is funded. However, unions have a longer history in this segment of the health care industry and are better established and less fragmented than in the hospital sector. Bargaining in the long-term care/nursing home sector could be turbulent in the years ahead, but the evidence suggests that it will continue to be a significant part of this industry.

One clear trend apparent in both sectors of the health care industry is a move toward more centralized bargaining. In 1998, SEIU, the nation's largest health care union, initiated a strategic planning process called the President's Committee 2000. This process was motivated, in part, by the tremendous changes the union and its members faced in the health care sector. One of the key findings of this report was the recognition that the structure of the health care industry is changing. Whereas decisions involving the delivery of health care services were at one time made at the facility level, increasingly those decisions are being made at the top levels of giant health care systems or nursing home corporations. In its report, SEIU recognized the need to restructure itself to reflect the structural changes occurring among employers.

In the hospital sector this means greater cooperation and coordination among local unions in order to engage in regional bargaining. SEIU anticipates the possibility of both single-employer bargaining among members of a regional hospital network or a system and multi-employer bargaining among separate hospitals in a city or region.

In the long-term care/nursing home sector, centralized bargaining is likely to become more prevalent if corporate chains continue to increase the proportion of the sector they represent. This bargaining structure would also involve local unions across wide geographic regions joining together to bargain master agreements.

Given the importance of government programs like Medicare and Medicaid to both health care employers and employees, it is possible that the parties may join forces politically and legislatively to influence funding for these programs. The New Partnership proposed by SEIU in the long-term care/nursing home sector may prove to be a model for such programs across the industry.

In any event, health care is a vital and important industry on a number of levels. The evolution of collective bargaining in this industry in the years ahead promises to be both fascinating and instructive. For students of bargaining, it merits watching.

Notes

[1] There is a substantial public-sector health care industry in the United States. Of the 4,941 general hospitals operating in the United States in 1999, 1,448 were administered by an agency of the local, state, or federal government (American Hospital Association [AHA] 2001). Of the 16,995 nursing homes, approximately 1,190, or 7 percent, are government administered (American Health Care Association [AHCA] 2001). This paper will be limited to an examination of collective bargaining in the private-sector health care industry.

[2] A third distinct sector of the health care industry is home health care. This includes people, often elderly or disabled, who receive nursing care in their homes. It is a growing sector, with approximately 7 million Americans receiving such care, but is smaller than the hospital and long-term care/nursing home sectors and will not be addressed in this chapter.

[3] Acute care hospitals provide treatment for severe illness, disease, or trauma. They are distinct from long-term care hospitals that provide ongoing treatment for

elderly and other types of disabled patients. Psychiatric hospitals are included in the latter category.

[4] Generally, not-for-profit hospitals are defined as hospitals that reinvest any leftover moneys rather than distributing them to any persons or groups. Not-for-profit hospitals are usually built and financed by citizens or religious groups, with money for constructing facilities coming from individuals, charitable groups, the sale of tax-exempt bonds, and local and state government grants.

[5] Most of the physicians belonging to unions are in salaried positions. Estimates suggest that roughly half of the 700,000 physicians in the United States are employed by hospitals, clinics, health systems, or other employers. Since these physicians are much more likely to be eligible to be represented by a union than are physicians who are self-employed, the percentage of eligible employees who are union members is actually somewhat higher than 5 to 6 percent (Greenhouse 1999; Tschida 1999).

[6] Only private-sector employees are involved in NLRB elections. Also, the figures reported are for all health care workers. The NLRB does not break down this category into occupational categories. Thus, it is not possible to determine what percentage of these elections involved RNs or physicians, nor can the separate win rates for these two groups of workers be determined. However, there is no evidence that nurses or physicians have been any less successful in organizing bargaining units than the rest of their counterparts in the health care industry.

[7] Clearly, while these categorizations do not describe union types as well as they once did (i.e., many craft unions of the past have tended to move toward becoming more like industrial unions, and many industrial unions now might more accurately be classified as general unions), they still are somewhat helpful in describing labor organizations.

[8] Although these workers are public employees, this election was significant because it established a beachhead in a third sector of the health care industry in which unions have not been particularly successful—home health care.

[9] The ANA also includes nurse specialists (nurse practitioners, nurse midwives, etc.) and nurse managers among its membership. Historically, there has been tension between the nurse managers and that part of the ANA that has pursued collective bargaining.

[10] The ANA has fifty-four affiliates. These include the fifty states, as well as Guam, the Virgin Islands, the District of Columbia, and an affiliate for nurses working for the federal government.

[11] The eight states were Connecticut, Massachusetts, Michigan, Minnesota, Montana, New York, Oregon, and Pennsylvania.

[12] Traditionally, most physicians employed by hospitals fell into one of three specialties—anesthesiology, pathology, and emergency room medicine. The types of physicians, as well as the numbers of physicians, employed by hospitals have increased in recent years.

[13] Medical fellows usually serve in the same circumstances as interns and residents.

[14] Although federal law usually supersedes state law, a 1943 Supreme Court ruling stated that "states can supersede federal anti-trust law if there is a 'clearly articulated state policy and active state supervision'" (Haglund 1999:2).

[15] The difference in benefits is sometimes linked to the high percentage of women in the health care industry and the "conventional wisdom that women workers should rely on their husbands to provide them with health coverage and pension income" (AFT 2001b:71).

[16] The five-month strike in Nyack is identified in the press as the "longest nurses' strike on record" (Stein 2000). This statement could not be independently verified.

[17] Strikes by nurses occur with more frequency and on a greater scale in many other countries. Ireland, for example, suffered a national nurses' strike of 27,500 nurses in 1999. The Canadian provinces of Quebec, Saskatchewan, and British Columbia experienced nurses' strikes in 1999, and countries as diverse as New Zealand and Malawi saw nurses walk out in 2000. U.S. nurses have traditionally been reluctant to strike, seeing such action as unprofessional and jeopardizing patient care.

References

"Acceptable Nursing Home Care." 2000. *New York Times*, August 7, p. A-18.

Alberts, Tanya. 2001. "Supreme Court Decision Expands Definition of Supervisor." *American Medical News*, June 25, p. 1.

Amber, Michelle. 1999a. "ANA Delegates Strongly Approve Creation of Separate Labor Entity Within Association." *Daily Labor Report*, No. 119, June 22, p. A-8.

_____. 1999b. "NLRB Lets Stand Decision That HMO Doctors at AmeriHealth Are Independent Contractors." *Daily Labor Report*, No. 205, October 25, p. 1.

_____. 1999c. "SEIU Sees Record Growth." *Daily Labor Report*, No. 243, December 20, p. C-1.

_____. 2000. "Kaiser Permanente, 25 Locals Agree on Pact That Provides Joint Decision-Making Powers." *Daily Labor Report*, No. 243, September 20, p. AA-1.

_____. 2001. "Steelworkers, California Nurses Association Join Forces to Organize Healthcare Workers." *Daily Labor Report*, No. 50, March 14, p. C-1.

American Federation of Teachers (AFT). 2001a. "Nursing Shortage Will Be Worse Than Current Estimates." Press Release, April 19.

_____. 2001b. *The State of the Healthcare Workforce, 2001*. Washington, DC: AFT.

_____. 2002. AFT Healthcare Website. <http://www.aft.org/health care/>. [February 19, 2002].

American Health Care Association (AHCA). 1999. "Facts and Trends." *The Nursing Facility Sourcebook*. Washington, DC: AHCA.

_____. 2001. AHCA Website. <http://www.ahca.org/who/profile4.htm>. [February 19, 2002].

American Hospital Association (AHA). 1976. *Taft-Hartley Amendments: Implications for the Healthcare Field*. Chicago: AHA.

_____. 1988. *Hospital Statistics, 1986–87*. Chicago: AHA.

_____. 1992. *Hospital Statistics, 1991–92*. Chicago: AHA.

_____. 1998. *Hospital Statistics, 1996–97*. Chicago: AHA.

_____. 2001. *Hospital Statistics, 2000*. Chicago: AHA.

American Nurses Association (ANA). 1998. Analysis of 1984–1997 Elections Overseen by the NLRB for Bargaining Units with RNs and RNs with Other Health Care Advocacy.

———. 2001a. "Nurses Concerned Over Working Conditions, Decline in Quality of Care, ANA Survey Reveals." Press Release, February 6.

———. 2001b. "UAN Moves Forward with Historic AFL-CIO Affiliation." Press Release, May 3.

———. 2001c. "Restructuring." <http://nursingworld.org/uan/uarestr.htm>. [February 19, 2002].

Armstrong-Stassen, Margaret, I. Takac, Sheila Cameron, and M. Horsbaugh. 1997. "The Reactions of Nurses to Hospital Merger." Unpublished paper presented at Administrative Sciences Association of Canada Conference, St. John's, Newfoundland, June.

Bellandi, Deanna. 2001. "High Court Takes on Highly-Charged Issues of Nursing Duties vs. Union Eligibility." Modern Healthcare, February 26, pp. 8–9.

"Beverly Bid Futile to Get Labor Order Rescinded," Arkansas Democrat-Gazette, June 30, 2001. <http://www.ardemgaz.com>. [February 19, 2002].

Bronder, Edmund. 2001. "Collective Bargaining Agreements." American Journal of Nursing, August, Vol. 101, no. 8, pp. 59–61.

Bronfenbrenner, Kate. 1997. Testimony of Dr. Kate Bronfenbrenner Before the Town Hall Meeting Sponsored by U.S. Congress Members William Coyne, Mike Doyle, Lane Evans, and Frank Mascara, Pittsburgh, PA, May 19, 1997. Obtained from K. Bronfenbrenner.

Buck Consultants. 1998. 1998 Survey of Managerial, Supervisory, and Staff Positions in Nursing Homes. Secaucus, NJ: Buck Consultants.

Budrys, Grace. 1997. When Doctors Join Unions. Ithaca, NY: Cornell University Press.

Bureau of Labor Statistics (BLS). 1998. "Occupational Employment Statistics." <http://www.bls.gov/oes>. [February 19, 2002].

———. 2001a. "Occupational Employment Statistics." <http://www.bls.gov/oes>. [February 19, 2002].

———. 2001b. "Current Population Survey." <http://www.bls.gov/home.htm>. [February 19, 2002].

Bureau of National Affairs (BNA). 1998. "1199, Six New York City Hospitals Reach Tentative Contract Agreement." Daily Labor Report, No. 232, December 3, p. 1.

California Healthcare Association. 2002. "2001 Public Policy Positions." <http://www.calhealth.org/adv_positions.htm>. [April 19, 2002].

California Nurses Association (CNA). 1998. "Mercy Agreement Largest First Contract for RNs in Over a Decade." The Cal Nurse. <http://www.calnurse.org/cna/cal/april98/>. [February 19, 2002].

———. 2001. <http://www.calnurse.org>. [April 19, 2002].

Calkins, Andrew. 2002. Phone interview with Andrew Calkins, Policy Analyst, Minnesota Nurses Association. January 17.

Carlson, Robert. 1999. "Is There a Physician Union in Your Future?" Family Practice Management, January, pp. 21–25.

Carter, Janelle. 2002. "Health Spending Reached $1.3T." Washington Post, January 7, p. 1.

Clark, Paul F., Darlene A. Clark, David Day, and Dennis Shea. 2001. "The Impact of Healthcare Reform On Nurses' Attitudes Toward Unions: The Role of Climate for Patient Care." *Industrial and Labor Relations Review*, Vol. 55, no. 1, October, pp. 133–48.

Cleeland, Nancy. 1999. "Home-Care Workers Vote for a Landmark for Labor," *Los Angeles Times*, February 26, p. 1.

Cleeland, Nancy, and Sharon Bernstein. 2000. "Kaiser, Union Coalition Enter 5-Year Collaborative Contract," *Los Angeles Times*, September 26, p. 1.

Cochrane, John. 1999. "Are Unions the Future of Medicine?" *Integrated Healthcare Report*, February, pp. 1–12.

Collins, Gail. 2001. "Public Interests; Nursing a Shortage," *New York Times*, April 13, p. A-17.

Committee of Interns and Residents/Service Employees International Union (CIR/SEIU). 2001a. "Brookdale Hospital Doctors Win Collective Bargaining Agreement." Press Release.

_____. 2001b. "Los Angeles Housestaff Make Headway on Reforms." <http://www.cirdocs.org/news/default.htm>. [February 19, 2002].

_____. 2001c. "Oakland Residents Win Raise and Patient Care Fund." Press Release.

_____. 2001d. "Patient Care Funds." <http://www.cirseiu.org/>. [February 19, 2002].

Connair, Michael Pierce. 2000. "Congressional Staff HR 1304 Briefing," Federation of Physicians and Dentists. <http://www.fpdunion.org/Advocacy/CollectiveBargaining-National/CC-Update-6-15-00-Connair.htm>. [February 19, 2002].

Corey-Lisle, Patricia, Anita Tarzian, Marlene Cohen, and Alison Trinkoff. 1999. "Healthcare Reform: Its Effect on Nurses." *Journal of Nursing Administration*, Vol. 29, no. 3, pp. 30–37.

"Data on Bargaining to Date in 2002 Show 4.0 Percent Average Raise in New Contracts." 2002. *Daily Labor Report*, No. 16, January 24, p. D-1.

Decker, Frederic H., and Jeannine Dollard. 2001. *Staffing of Nurse Services in Long-Term Care: Present Issues and Prospects for the Future.* Washington, DC: American Healthcare Association.

Deshpande, Satish P. 2000. "Hospitals and Union Elections." *Healthcare Manager*, Vol. 19, no. 2, pp. 8–12.

Economic Policy Institute (EPI). 1997. "Results of 1995 and 1996 Census Survey." Washington, DC: EPI.

Federation of American Hospitals. 2002. *Building Healthy Communities: One Patient at a Time.* <http://www.fahs.com/publications/annual_report/FAHar.pdf>. [February 20, 2002].

Feldacker, Bruce. 2000. *Labor Guide to Labor Law.* 4th Edition. Upper Saddle River, NJ: Prentice Hall.

Fisher, Jean. 1999. "Hospitals Question Nursing Staff Law: Just Not Enough RNs, They Claim." *Sacramento Bee*, October 18. <http://www.sacramentobee.com/>. [February 20, 2002].

Gabrel, Celia. 2000. "An Overview of Nursing Home Facilities: Data from the 1997 National Nursing Home Survey," Advance Data—Center for Disease Control Website. <http://www.cdc.gov/nchs/data/ad/ad311.pdf>. [February 20, 2002].

Greenhouse, Steven. 1999. "Angered by H.M.O.'s Treatment, More Doctors Are Joining Unions." *New York Times*, February 4, p. M-1.

Groves, Bob. 2000. "Health-Care Workers Seek Fiscal Therapy," *Bergen Record*, January 2, p. 1.

Haglund, Mark. 1999. "Salaried Doctors Turn to Unions to Stem Losses of Income, Autonomy," *Medicine and Health Perspective*, June 21, pp. 1–4.

Healthcare Financing Administration (HCFA). 2001. "HCFA Data and Statistics."<http://www.hcfa.gov/stats/>. [February 20, 2002].

Herzfield, John. 1998. "1199, New York Hospital League Reach Early Agreement Covering 40,000 Employees." *Daily Labor Report*, No. 120, June 23, pp. 1–2.

_____. 1999. "1199 Nurses Reach Tentative Agreement with Group of New York City Hospitals." *Daily Labor Report*, No. 23, February 4, pp. 1–2.

Jaklevic, Mary, and Ed Lovern. 2000. "A Nursing Code Blue: Few Easy Solutions Seen for a National RN Shortage That's Different From Prior Undersupplies." *Modern Healthcare*, December 11, pp. 42–46.

Kangas, Sandra, Carolyn Kee, and Rebecca McKee-Waddle. 1999. "Organizational Factors, Nurses' Job Satisfaction, and Patient Satisfaction with Nursing Care." *Journal of Nursing Administration*, Vol. 29, no. 1, pp. 32–42.

Keating, Gregory. 1991. "Physician Unionization Efforts Gain Momentum, Support." *Healthcare Financial Management*, November, pp. 52–55.

Kessler, Martha. 2000. "Rhode Island Hospital Invokes Arbitration on Eve of Strike by Healthcare Workers," *Daily Labor Report*, July 5, No. 129, p. A-1.

Knight, Wendy. 1998. *Managed Care: What It Is and How It Works.* Gaithersburg, MD: Aspen Publishers.

Lerner, Maura. 2001a. "Nurses Notify Hospitals of Intent to Strike June 1." *Minneapolis-St. Paul Star Tribune*, May 22, p. 1.

_____. 2001b. "Nurses Gain Ground in Control Over Workloads." *Minneapolis-St. Paul Star Tribune*, June 3, p. 1.

Levin Associates. 1999. *The Health Care Acquisition Report.* New Canaan, CT: Levin Associates.

Lutz, Sandy. 1994. "Let's Make a Deal: Healthcare Mergers, Acquisitions Take Place at a Dizzying Pace." *Modern Healthcare*, Vol. 24, no. 51, pp. 47–50.

Managed Care Online. 2001. <http://www.mcol.com/>. [February 20, 2002].

Mangan, Katherine. 1999. "Academic Medicine Becomes a Target for Labor Organizing," *The Chronicle of Higher Education*, August 6, pp. A-14–A-16.

Metzger, Norman, and Dennis Pointer. 1972. *Labor Management Practices in the Health Services Industry: Theory and Practice.* Washington, DC: Science and Health Publications, Inc.

Miller, Richard. 1980. "Hospitals." In *Collective Bargaining: Contemporary American Experience*," Gerald Somers (ed.), Madison, WI: Industrial Relations Research Association.

National Doctors Alliance/Service Employees International Union (NDA/SEIU). 2001. Web page. <http://www.ndaseiu.com/>. [February 20, 2002].

National Labor Relations Board (NLRB). 1967. *Butte Medical Properties*, 168 NLRB 52.

_____. 1999a. *Boston Medical Center v. House Officers' Association/Committee of Interns and Residents*, 330 NLRB 30.

_____. 1999b. *AmeriHealth HMO v. UFCW, Local 56*, 326 NLRB 55.

New England Health Care Employees Union. 2001. "Legislature Approves Contract for 8700 State Healthcare Workers." <http://www.nehceu.org/contract.htm>. [February 20, 2002].

"New Jersey Governor Signs Measure Banning Mandatory Overtime in Hospitals."
2002. *BNA Health Care Daily Report*, January 3, p. 1.
Newman, Nathan. 2001. "Burying Healthcare in 'Supervisors': The Supremes Screw
Unions Once Again." *Progressive Populist*, July 15, p. 1.
"Nurses' Strike Causes $43M in Losses." 2000. *San Francisco Business Times*.
September 15.
<http://sanfrancisco.bcentral.com/sanfrancisco/stories/2000/09/18/weekinbiz.html>.
[February 20, 2002].
"Nursing Home Strike Now All but Inevitable." 2001. *Hartford Courant*. March 18.
<http://www.ctnow.com>. [February 20, 2002].
Owley, Candace. 2001. "The Deadly Effects of Overtime." *AFT/FNHP Healthwire*.
March/April. <http://www.aft.org/publications/healthwire/mar_apr01/critical.html>.
[February 20, 2002].
Pear, Robert. 2002. "9 of 10 Nursing Homes Lack Adequate Staff, Study Finds."
New York Times, February 18, p. A-1.
Physicians for Responsible Negotiation/American Medical Association (PRN/AMA).
2001. <http://www.ama-assn.org/ama/pub/category/2554.html>. [February 20,
2002].
Poznick, Jill. 2001. E-mail correspondence.
Preuss, Gil. 1999. *Sharing Care: The Changing Nature of Nursing in Hospitals*.
Washington, DC: EPI.
Public Citizen. 2001."Public Citizen, Medical Resident and Student Organizations
Petition OSHA to Limit Work Hours for Medical Residents." Press Release,
April 30. <http://www.publiccitizen.org/Press/pr-sid46.htm>. [February 20,
2002].
Raffel, Marshall, and Norma Raffel. 1997. "United States." In *Healthcare Reform in
Industrialized Countries*, Marshall Raffel (ed.), University Park, PA: Penn State
University Press, pp. 263–90.
Saphir, Ann. 2000. "Bigger Isn't Better." *Modern Healthcare*, July 24, pp. 20–32.
"SEIU Locals Bargain Neutrality, Card Check Agreement with New York Health
Consortium." 2001. *Labor Relations Week*, February 15, Vol. 15, no. 7, p. 18.
Service Employees International Union (SEIU). 1997a. *Behind the Headlines: How
Short Staffing and Underfunding Puts California Nursing Home Residents at
Risk*. Washington, DC: SEIU.
_____. 1997b. *Caring Till It Hurts: How Nursing Home Work Became the Most
Dangerous Job in America*. Washington, DC: SEIU.
_____. 1998. *The Staffing Crisis in Nursing Homes*. Washington, DC: SEIU.
_____. 2001a. *A New Business Strategy for America's Nursing Homes*. Washington,
DC: SEIU.
_____. 2001b. "SEIU Nurses Alliance."
<http://www.nursealliance.org/together/together/better_choice.cfm>. [February
20, 2002].
_____. 2002. "Historic Settlement with Nation's Largest Nursing Home Co. Sets
Most Comprehensive Guidelines Ever to Protect Health Care Workers' Safety."
<http://www.seiu.org/index.html>. [February 20, 2002].
Service Employees International Union/1199P (SEIU/1199). 2001a. "Beverly Workers Win Breakthrough Agreement."
<http://www.1199p.org/pages/nhtnews081001_1.html>. [February 20, 2002].

Service Employees International Union/1199 (SEIU/1199). 2001b. "Nationwide Nursing Home Staffing Campaign Launched." Press Release.

Sochalski, Julie, and Linda Aiken. 1999. "Accounting for Variation in Hospital Outcomes: A Cross-National Study." *Health Affairs*, May–June. <http://130.94.25.113/Library/v18/n3/s30.pdf>. [February 20, 2002].

Stein, Todd. 2000. "Crossing the Line: When Nurses Walk, More Hospitals Hire Strikebreakers." *Nurseweek*. June 24. <http://sanfrancisco.bcentral.com/sanfrancisco/stories/2000/09/18/weekinbiz.html>. [February 20, 2002].

Strahan, Genevieve. 1987. "Nursing Homes Characteristics: Preliminary Data from the 1985 Nursing Home Survey." *Advance Data*, March 27, No. 131.

_____. 1997. "An Overview of Nursing Homes and Their Current Residents: Data from the 1995 Nursing Home Survey." *Advance Data*, January 23, No. 280.

Thompson, Elizabeth. 2000. "Organized Doctors." *Modern Healthcare*, February 28, pp. 35–40.

Tschida, Molly. 1999. "Getting Organized: Nation's Largest Physician Union Forms under SEIU Umbrella." *Modern Physician*, April, p. 2.

UFCW. 2002. "Health Care." <http://www.ufcw.org/who/internal.cfm?subsection_id=62&internal_id=66>. [February 20, 2002].

U.S. Congress. 1947. *Congressional Record*, Vol. 93, Part 4, p. 4997.

U.S. Supreme Court. 1991. *American Hospital Association v. NLRB*. 499 U.S. 606.

_____. 2001. *NLRB v. Kentucky River Community Care*. 532 U.S. 706.

Vandermere, James. 1999. "Medalia: Why We Unionized." *Family Practice Management*, January, pp. 60–61.

Wascoe, Dan. 2001. "Hospitals Ponder Fallout of Higher Nurse Contract Costs." *Minneapolis-St. Paul Star-Tribune*, June 19, p. 1.

Wunderlich, Gooloo, Frank Sloan, and Carolyn Davis. 1996. *Nursing Staff in Hospitals and Nursing Homes: Is It Adequate?* Washington, DC: National Academy Press.

Zapata, Ron. 2001. "Nursing Home Strike May Last, Brass Says." *New Haven (Conn.) Register,* May 2, p. 1.

Zielbauer, Paul. 2001. "Nursing Home Strike Is Predicted by Both Sides." *New York Times,* March 16, p. B-8.

CHAPTER 4

Hotels and Casinos: Collective Bargaining During a Decade of Expansion

C. JEFFREY WADDOUPS AND VINCENT H. EADE
University of Nevada, Las Vegas

The hotel and casino industries in the United States are closely linked in only a handful of locations such as Las Vegas, Atlantic City, Reno, and Lake Tahoe, which have been traditionally known for legalized casino gambling and as destination resorts. More recently, the two industries are emerging in Biloxi and Tunica, Mississippi, and Shreveport, Louisiana, to create additional hotel–casino resort destination markets. Lodging, of course, plays a vital role in such locations because many of the customers are tourists. For example, the National Gambling Impact Study Commission (NGISC) cites research indicating that approximately 85 percent of gambling revenue generated in Las Vegas originates from tourists (NGISC 1998:7–17). Of course, for most hotels and motels in the United States, casinos play no role in their operations.

Over the last decade, casinos have opened on riverboats in the Midwest, in small towns in the West, and on tribal reservations scattered throughout the nation. These casinos generally maintain only limited, small-scale lodging operations, if any at all. Lodging is not in high demand because a majority of these casinos' customers reside in close proximity to the properties. Gazel and Thompson (1996) found that 85 percent of customers on riverboat casinos live within 50 miles of the establishments they patronize.

Collective bargaining is prevalent in two locations where the hotel and casino industries are closely linked. On the strip and downtown in Las Vegas and in Atlantic City, most nonmanagerial employees in hotel–casinos are unionized. Meanwhile, in Reno a movement to organize some of the larger hotel–casino properties appears to be nearing its final stages, and no collective bargaining exists in Lake Tahoe. Furthermore, in some casinos that generally are not as closely connected to lodging operations, collective bargaining has also begun to emerge. Workers in the new casinos in Detroit collectively bargain (only one of the three is connected to a hotel), as do employees on six of the eighty-two riverboats in the Midwest. One tribal casino in Southern California recently unionized, making it the only casino on tribal lands in which workers are represented by a union. With the exception of Detroit casinos, collective bargaining in the emerging gambling jurisdictions remains rare.

Workers in Las Vegas and Atlantic City comprise nearly 20 percent of the membership of the Hotel Employees and Restaurant Employees International Union (HERE), the main union representing workers in the hotel and casino industries. Moreover, about 75,000 workers represented by various affiliates of the HERE are casino workers, most of whom are employed in Las Vegas and Atlantic City but others of whom work on riverboats in the Midwest or in Detroit (NGISC 1998:7–8). Although a significant minority of the HERE's membership works in hotels with casinos, the bulk of hotel unionism still exists in major urban centers, generally outside the South in cities such as Boston, Chicago, Detroit, Honolulu, Los Angeles, New York, San Francisco, and Washington, DC (Cobble and Merrill 1994).

This chapter will assess the structures, trends, and economic outcomes connected with collective bargaining in these two interrelated industries. First, the economic performance of the hotel and casino industries during the 1990s will be assessed. Second, the structures of the industries and collective bargaining will be examined. Third, patterns of union representation will be outlined. Fourth, unique and emerging issues, such as tribal gaming, health and safety, civil rights, and labor–management cooperation, will be analyzed. Fifth, union and nonunion compensation patterns will be compared; and sixth, conclusions about the prospects for collective bargaining will be drawn.

Economic Performance During the 1990s

The lodging industry is a relatively small, yet growing, part of the economy. Data on gross domestic product (GDP) disaggregated by industry from over the past two decades indicate that the share of GDP attributable to "Hotels and Lodging Places" held steady at .8 percent until 1997 but increased to .9 percent in 1998 (U.S. Department of Commerce 2001). Inflation-adjusted GDP attributable to the industry rose from about $78 billion in 1990 to nearly $100 billion in 1999, a 28 percent rate of growth over the decade. Employment also increased during the 1990s, from just under 1.55 million to about 1.85 million workers (American Hotel & Motel Association [AH&MA] 2001).

Moreover, during the 1990s, lodging operations were restructured in response to the industry's dismal economic performance in the early part of the decade. Not only was the restructuring characterized by consolidation and concentration of ownership but also by a greater emphasis on niche marketing strategies. The industry reduced new investment in generic hotels or motels and increased investment in specialized establishments such as extended-stay properties. Another distinctive trend was the relative increase in shares of low-priced rooms in limited-service properties and a relative increase in the share of higher-priced rooms at resort destinations (Lomanno 2000). Restructuring at the industrial organization level, along with a prosperous economy, combined to transform the lodging industry into one of the most profitable sectors in the retail trade sector. The industry posted pretax profits in 1999 of nearly $22 billion, a substantial improvement from the losses of about $5.7 billion in 1990 (AH&MA 2001).

In contrast to the steady growth and return to profitability of the lodging sector, the rise of casino gambling in the United States during the 1990s was nothing short of meteoric. Before 1988, no legal casino-style gambling existed in the United States outside Nevada and Atlantic City. Currently, every state in the United States, except Utah and Hawaii, has approved some form of legalized gambling. Twenty-eight states have authorized casino gambling in the form of either commercial casinos or class III tribal casinos (NGISC 1998:2).[1] The NGISC documented the increase in gambling's popularity with estimates that U.S. residents doubled their spending on gambling activities, as a percentage of real personal income, between 1976 and 1997 (NGISC 1998:2). In the decade of the 1990s alone, spending on casino gambling soared from $8.3 billion in 1990 to $22.2 billion in 1999, an 11.6 percent annual growth rate (American Gaming Association [AGA] 2001). Employment in casinos expanded to meet the increased demand and stood at about 508,000 workers nationwide by the year 2000 (AGA 2001).

Although commercial casinos generated a large majority of gaming revenues in the United States, tribal casinos experienced a nearly twenty-fold growth in revenue, from about $500 million in 1988, when the Indian Gaming Regulatory Act was passed, to $9.6 billion in 1999. The eight largest of the 287 tribal gambling operations generated more than 40 percent of the revenue in 1997, according to research reported by the NGISC (1998:7–9). Not surprisingly, increases in revenue have led to substantial employment growth. Tribal casinos reported employment of about 152,000 workers nationwide in 1999 (National Indian Gaming Commission [NIGC] 2000).

Patterns of Collective Bargaining Among Employers

Hotels and Motels

Although analysts have segmented the lodging industry along a number of dimensions, one useful characterization of the sector is a division of establishments into segments by price and quality of service. Using a price–quality schema, some industry analysts have developed a four-segment structure: (1) high-priced "upscale" hotels, (2) mid-priced "full-service" properties, (3) lower-priced "economy" hotels and motels, and (4) low-priced "budget" establishments (e.g., *Hotels Magazine* 2000a). Typically upscale and full-service properties are relatively large and often located in urban centers or destination resorts. They cater to business and convention travelers and upper- to middle-income tourists, who are probably less price conscious than their counterparts patronizing economy or budget establishments but who also expect higher levels of service. The establishments in the economy and budget categories, usually much smaller, tend to be located in suburban or roadside locations—although they may also operate in urban areas—and attract customers less interested in high levels of service and who are more sensitive to price.

The existence of collective bargaining often depends on a property's location within the four-tiered segment structure. Most hotel unionism is found in larger urban hotels in the full-service and upscale segments (e.g., Starwood Hotels and Resorts Worldwide, Inc. 2000).[2] Unionization is more likely to be found in the top two segments for a number of reasons. First, the size of the establishments provides economies of scale to union activities, from organizing to contract administration, which makes representing workers at larger establishments more cost effective.

Second, upper-tier hotels tend to agglomerate in urban centers, which provides additional economies of scale to union activities and also provides the union with an incentive to organize all or most of the competing properties in the relevant submarket. Union leaders have long recognized that additional bargaining power can be obtained if most or all of the competitors in a given market are unionized, essentially taking wages and working conditions out of competition. With wages and working conditions removed from competition, firms compete by providing higher-quality products and services rather than by cutting wages and benefits.

Third, compared to lower-segment establishments, upper-segment establishments must deliver relatively high-quality service to their customers, which places a premium on a stable and more highly trained workforce. Empirical evidence leaves no doubt that a unionized workforce has lower turnover rates (Freeman and Medoff 1984). To the extent that employment relations in unionized firms leads to lower turnover rates, accumulation of firm- and industry-specific human capital is encouraged. Workers with greater amounts of human capital are more productive and can thus more effectively deliver high-quality service. If such reasoning applies to the hotel industry, then collective bargaining may be more consistent with building and maintaining the kind of workforces required in upscale and full-service properties compared to the economy and budget segments. Consequently, employers might be less likely to resist union activities, and higher union wages and benefits become more economically viable based on higher productivity (associated with more human capital) and lower recruitment and training costs (associated with lower turnover).[3]

On the other hand, location and market considerations appear to present obstacles to unionization in the economy and budget segments. First, smaller, more geographically dispersed establishments, often located outside urban centers, likely demand more resources of hotel unions per potential member. This makes representation of workers in such establishments less cost effective. Unions are less likely to expend their scarce resources in areas where organizing and representation activities may not be viable. Second, because customers of economy and budget properties tend to expect low prices rather than high levels of service, keeping costs and prices down becomes management's major imperative. Productivity related to lower turnover and the accompanying human capital accumulation thus become relatively less important in lower-segment properties. Consequently, employment relationships in a unionized environment are less consistent with maintaining a workforce compatible with the operations of lower-tier segments, suggesting a greater incentive to remain union free.

Although the segment in which the property competes partially determines patterns of collective bargaining, such patterns are also a function of geography. Hotels in urban centers in the South and in some locations in the West, despite being in the more heavily unionized upper segment of the industry, remain largely nonunion. At the same time, unionization is prevalent—although certainly not universal—in the upper-segment hotels located in urban centers of the Northeast and

Midwest. Region-specific customs of managerial and perhaps worker resistance—or indifference—to unionization, therefore, must also be recognized as potential determinants of the observed patterns of unionization.

Casinos

Researchers have also employed a segmentation structure to describe the casino industry. The NGISC (1998:7–8) reported on research conducted by the National Opinion Research Council (NORC), which surveyed casinos for the Commission's report. The NORC divided casinos into three segments: (1) the top 25 casinos based on revenue (almost all of which are destination resorts); (2) other commercial casinos, including, but not limited to, riverboats; and (3) tribal casinos. It must be noted that the NORC's segmentation scheme is not entirely consistent with the organization of the casino sector. For example, there is little doubt that most of the top 25 revenue-generating casinos are indeed correctly classified as resort destination properties; however, other casinos not listed in the top segment may also be appropriately classified as destination resorts. Classification problems notwithstanding, casinos in the resort segment offer a much greater variety of gambling products, ranging from sports books (in Nevada) to highly specialized state-of-the-art slot machines to a wide variety of table games. In addition, they provide other nongambling amenities, such as high-quality shows, fine dining, health spas, and other forms of recreation.

Although the NORC's report does not mention the physical location of the 25 responding properties in the top segment, it stated that 21 of the 25 were unionized and tended to offer better and higher-quality jobs relative to casinos in the other two segments (NGISC 1998:7–8). Because most of the NORC's top-segment properties are unionized, it can be inferred that a large majority are either located in Las Vegas or Atlantic City. Any other top-segment casinos outside Las Vegas and Atlantic City would have been nonunion (e.g., Foxwoods, a tribal casino in Connecticut, may have been on the list).

The prospect for unionization of a casino is generally tied to the union status of the hotel to which it is connected. Generally, the same unions that represent hotel workers also represent casino workers, where casino workers spend a majority of their time on the casino floor. For example, guest room attendants in a typical unionized Las Vegas hotel and cocktail servers in the hotel's casino are part of the same bargaining unit, which is represented by the HERE's Culinary Union Local

226. However, in nonunion resort destination hotel–casinos on the Las Vegas Strip (for example, the Venetian or the Aladdin), neither hotel nor casino workers are unionized.[4] Other commercial casinos operating outside the top segment of the market in Atlantic City, Las Vegas, and Reno may or may not be unionized. However, where there are unions, they almost always represent both casino and hotel workers.

On the other end of the size spectrum, small commercial casinos in Colorado and South Dakota, riverboat casinos in the Midwest and South, and nearly all tribal casinos have gambling operations that are more limited than those of the top segment. Not only are there fewer gambling products available, but there are usually lower betting limits and fewer nongambling amenities. Moreover, in the case of commercial casinos, higher tax rates are levied (at least compared to Nevada). In addition, as previously mentioned, casinos located outside tourist corridors are more likely to attract local residents as customers so that in some cases lodging establishments are not connected with casinos. Where lodging does exist, the establishments are generally smaller and less likely to be in the full-service or luxury segments of the industry.

Like their lodging counterparts, location and size of casinos affect unionization. Remotely located and smaller casinos that are not tourist destinations tend to attract customers interested in lower-stakes betting. Casino customers' demand for lower-stakes games limits the potential revenue and ultimately the potential productivity of casino workers, where productivity is usefully defined as revenue per employee hour. Establishments that generate low levels of revenue per employee may be less able to pay union scale wages and benefits, and thus may more strongly resist union organizing efforts. Furthermore, because of the isolation and smaller scale of operations, unions are likely to find organizing casino workers less cost effective. In the case of tribal casinos, the difficulty for unions is exacerbated because federal labor laws fail to protect workers' rights to organize and bargain collectively (NGISC 1998; Taylor 2001).

Differences in employment quality and outcomes are expected to vary based on the different economic conditions faced by casinos in the three segments. As an indicator of the differences, the NGISC reported average salaries for workers in the top segment to be about $26,000 annually, $20,500 in other commercial casinos, and $18,000 for workers in tribal casinos (NGISC 1998:7–8). The extent to which the reported wage differentials depend on a property's status as a top 25 casino is not entirely clear, nor is it clear how much of the wage differential results from collective bargaining. Waddoups (1999a) concludes that it is unlikely that large hotel–casinos and resorts operating nonunion in a largely nonunion location, such as Reno or Lake Tahoe, pay union scale wages. The large *nonunion* casinos in highly unionized locations, such as on the Las Vegas Strip (e.g., the Venetian and the Aladdin), however, generally do offer union scale wages and benefits.

Local Labor Markets and Decentralized Bargaining

Even though large (often) transnational corporate conglomerates own, franchise, or provide management services to lodging establishments, only the upper-level managers within the upscale and full-service segments generally compete in national or international labor markets. The vast majority of nonmanagerial jobs in hotels are filled by a range of skilled to unskilled workers competing in local labor markets. Consistent with the local nature of lodging and casino products and labor markets, collective bargaining is also localized, generally yielding establishment-specific collective bargaining agreements.

In some local hotel or hotel–casino markets, however, large corporations may own a number of properties, which may essentially bargain as a group with one or more unions. Thus, some qualities of local multilateral bargaining exist in the industry. For example, a majority of the workers in the Culinary Union Local 226's members are employed by five large corporations, the Mandalay Resort Group, Harrah's Entertainment, the MGM/Mirage Corporation, Park Place Entertainment, and the Boyd Group. Each of these firms owns several high-profile establishments on the strip or downtown. Bargaining is conducted among numerous unions and the individual properties owned by these corporations. The resulting labor agreements between the properties and unions are similar, although not identical, among properties within a given corporation and somewhat less similar across establishments owned by different corporations. Another example of multilateral bargaining is found in the San Francisco Hotels Partnership Project. Twelve hotels formed a multi-employer group and used an interest-based bargaining approach to arrive at a new contract with HERE Local 2 in 1999. Such multilateral bargaining structures, however, tend to be the exception (Chipkin 2001).

Patterns of Collective Bargaining: The Unions

There is not one common pattern of union representation of hotel and casino workers. A number of unions represent various types of workers in the lodging and casino sectors. The HERE, however, is the primary union representing hotel and casino workers, with a membership of about 265,000 (Chipkin 2001). A substantial majority of HERE members are employed in lodging establishments and casinos. Las Vegas has the largest concentration of HERE membership, where nearly 52,000 workers are covered under contracts negotiated by two HERE affiliated locals, the Culinary Union Local 226 and the Bartenders Union Local 165 (Taylor 2001). The HERE also has substantial locals in other large urban and tourist hotel markets, such as Boston, Chicago, Detroit, Honolulu, Los Angeles, New York, San Francisco, and Washington, DC.

Although the HERE is the primary union in the hotel and casino industries, other unions are also commonly present, often with bargaining units alongside an HERE local. Hotel and casino workers are represented by the International Brotherhood of Teamsters (IBT), the International Union of Operating Engineers (IUOE), and the International Alliance of Theatrical Stage Employees (IATSE). Skilled maintenance and construction workers often belong to the various building trades unions. Although the HERE represents workers at a number of major resort hotels in Hawaii, it shares the market with the International Longshore and Warehouse Union (ILWU), which organized most workers in Hawaii during the intense labor struggles in the mid-1900s.

As mentioned, the HERE also represents casino workers. The NGISC (1998:7–8) reported that the union represented about 75,000 casino workers in 1997. The organizing drive at the Rio All-Suite Hotel and Casino in Las Vegas recently added nearly 2,400 hotel and casino workers. In Detroit, cooperation among the HERE, United Automobile Workers (UAW), IUOE, and IBT resulted in the formation of the Detroit Casino Council (DCC), which, along with the Carpenters Union, now represents nonsupervisory workers in the three newly established casinos, one with a connecting hotel (*Daily Labor Report* 2001).

The HERE also has organized six riverboat casinos in the Midwest (Holtmann 2001). In a recent organizing drive that ended in representation for the workers, the HERE joined with the Service Employees International Union (SEIU) to unionize the President Casino on the *Admiral* riverboat in Saint Louis. In addition, the Viejas tribal casino in Palm Springs, California, became the first tribal casino to unionize when the Communications Workers of America (CWA) achieved recognition with a card check in March 2000 (Holtmann 2001).

Bargaining Units in Hotels and Casinos

Because the pattern of union representation varies in unionized lodging and casino establishments, one would also expect the occupational composition of bargaining units to vary. Indeed, in some cases, the HERE locals have "wall-to-wall" representation in hotels, such as the New Yorker Hotel that was recently organized in New York (HERE 1999:5). In other cases, especially among larger properties, several unions represent workers according to their occupations. Table 1 lists a number of major occupational categories in hotels and casinos and corresponding unions that often represent them. Keep in mind that the pattern of union representation outlined in the table does not describe all hotel and casino properties, nor does it suggest an optimal pattern of bargaining unit formation, but summarizes how typical hotel and casino bargaining units tend to be organized in large resort hotel–casinos.

TABLE 1

Occupational Composition of Bargaining Units in
Typical Resort Hotel–Casino, by Union[a]

Hotel Employees and Restaurant Employees International Union (HERE)	International Brotherhood of Teamsters (IBT)	International Union of Operating Engineers (IUOE)	International Alliance of Theatrical Stage Employees (IATSE)
Food preparation Kitchen sanitation Dining room staff Bell desk Housekeeping Slot change Cocktail servers Bartenders Bar backs	Front desk Telephone operators Valet parkers Warehouse Equipment operators Window washers	Maintenance staff Heating, air conditioning, ventilation	Staging staff Audiovisual
Carpenters Union	International Brotherhood of Electrical Workers (IBEW)	Painters Union	UAW
Construction Repair staff	Electricians	Painters Paper hangers	Casino dealers[b]

[a] Hotel workers are also represented by the International Longshore and Warehouse Union (in Hawaii), the Service Employees International Union, and Communications Workers of America (Viejas tribal casino).

[b] Only dealers in Detroit's casinos collectively bargain in the United States.

Table 1 indicates that food and beverage preparation, serving, baggage handling, housekeeping, and casino change personnel are generally in HERE locals. The IBT often represents front desk personnel, PBX operators, valet parkers, warehouse workers, window washers, and small-equipment operators. Workers maintaining the physical plant, such as heating, air-conditioning, and ventilation equipment, tend to be in IUOE bargaining units. The IATSE often represents stage hands and technical workers serving conventions and shows. Workers skilled in the building and construction trades employed in-house, such as carpenters, electricians, and painters, tend to be represented by their respective craft unions.

Dealers and Unions. Dealers operate table games such as roulette, poker, craps, black jack, and baccarat. In U.S. casinos they do not generally collectively bargain, except in Detroit, where the UAW represents them. Additional unionization of dealers may be on the horizon, however. In Las Vegas during 2000, the NLRB held elections in twelve major casinos to determine certification for the Transport Workers Union (TWU) as the dealers' bargaining agent. Dealers in three of the casinos voted for representation. Thus far no contracts have resulted from ongoing negotiations.

Another notable association of casino dealers, the International Union of Gambling Employees (IUGE), maintains a presence in Nevada but does not engage in collective bargaining. It primarily uses political and legal means to improve dealers' working conditions. For example, the IUGE has filed lawsuits against tobacco companies and casinos over health issues related to secondhand tobacco smoke. It has also publicized risks of repetitive-motion injuries faced by dealers, calling for OSHA to study the issue and set appropriate safety standards (IUGE 2001).

The virtual absence of collective bargaining among dealers in the United States remains a curious phenomenon. In contrast to the United States, casino dealers are unionized in Canada, France, Belgium, Australia, and Spain, among other nations. Several attempts to organize dealers in Nevada over the past forty years have not resulted in collective bargaining (Campbell 1989).

A number of factors explain why dealers in the United States generally are not unionized. First, employer opposition likely plays a role. Casino employers argue that "at-will" employment for dealers helps them to keep games "honest." If dealers are suspected of running dishonest games, they must be removed quickly to avoid serious financial damage. Due process procedures in labor agreements may allow cheating to continue, rendering companies vulnerable to unacceptable financial risk (Frey and Carns 1987).[5] Second, dealers' own perceptions of their jobs may be a factor. They generally see themselves as being in the occupation for less than five years, thus job protections provided by a union contract are less valuable in the long term. Third, the organization of dealing work complicates union organizing. In some cases dealers work part-time dealing games and part-time supervising them. The ambiguous position between management and frontline workers not only complicates the formation of traditional bargaining units but increases dealers' affinity with management (Frey and Carns 1987).[6]

Fourth, affinity with management may also originate from the path dealers have traditionally followed to obtain increasingly lucrative jobs over time. Upward economic and occupational mobility has typically required "juice" (network human capital) with managers in the industry (Binkley 2001). To the extent that dealers perceive support of a union as a threat to the "juice" that got them their jobs and that will be necessary to obtain better jobs, they may not support unionization (Frey and Carns 1987). More recently, as the industry has expanded, corporate-style human resource policies are gradually replacing the traditional system of patronage and "juice." Unions may become more attractive to dealers if such trends continue.

New Union Leadership and Aggressive Organizing

Progressive new leaders in unions representing hotel and casino workers have altered the industrial relations terrain in the hotel and casino industries over the past decade. The diversity of unions representing hotel and casino workers makes it difficult to conduct a complete assessment of union leadership, thus the focus will be on leadership in the HERE. As the balance of power in the union has shifted from the "old guard" to the "reformers," the union's reputation and its organizing strategies have changed as well. Reformers may be loosely defined as persons less likely to have worked in the industry as rank-and-file employees, and as more likely to be college educated "outsiders," to be optimistic idealists, and to be more interested in organizing than their old guard counterparts (Strauss 2000). An example of old guard leadership in the HERE is the former president Ed Hanley. John Wilhelm, who was just elected in 1998 but who has been influential in the union for over two decades, is an example of reformer leadership.

Wilhelm's earlier experiences as a union leader are consistent with Strauss's (2000) description of reformer. Shortly after graduating magna cum laude from Yale University, he was hired as an organizer and business agent for HERE Local 217 in Rhode Island and Connecticut. Within two years, he was elected secretary–treasurer of the local. After several years as secretary–treasurer, he became business manager of Local 34 at Yale, where he was instrumental in organizing and negotiating a contract for white collar support workers. Later he served as chief negotiator of major contracts in Boston, San Francisco, Los Angeles, and Las Vegas. A position that perhaps best exemplifies the respect he has garnered in the political sphere, the labor movement, and the hotel and casino industries was his appointment as commissioner to the high-profile NGISC in 1997 (HERE 2001b).

Organizing and Corruption. As a reformer leader, Wilhelm's ambitious plans to organize have included the use of innovative methods that often require coalitions with community groups and support of political leaders. Such coalitions and support are naturally more difficult to form and obtain when charges of corruption hang over the union. He appears, however, to have recognized the importance of openly and frankly addressing these allegations. The HERE has been plagued by allegations of corruption (Cobble and Merrill 1994; Strauss 2000). In fact, the HERE and the Department of Labor entered into a consent decree in 1995 that provided for a federal monitor to investigate and deal with charges of corrupt and undemocratic practices in the union. After almost five years (two years into Wilhelm's presidency), the federal monitor declared the need for extra-normal scrutiny no longer existed. It was ended by order of the Federal District Court in New Jersey on December 1, 2000 (HERE 2001c). Wilhelm's adroit leadership helped the union successfully navigate the critical period of federal monitoring. This not only helped to dissipate clouds of suspicion about the union's integrity but provided valuable political capital necessary for the union to more effectively employ its aggressive and innovative organizing strategies.

Wilhelm's work reforming the union and his emphasis on organizing were also consistent with the objectives of John Sweeney, who was elected to the presidency of the AFL-CIO on a reform platform that centered around organizing. Wilhelm and the leadership of the HERE continue to take organizing seriously. In HERE's 2001 convention, the union committed to organize 18,000 new workers per year until the next convention in four years (HERE 2001a).

Organizing with Neutrality Agreements and Card Checks. Under Wilhelm's leadership, the HERE has earned a reputation for aggressively organizing new properties without traditional NLRB election procedures. NLRB certification elections are costly and often ineffective. For example, in Las Vegas the Culinary Union Local 226 tried to organize the Santa Fe Hotel and Casino with an NLRB election. In spite of winning the election, a contract was not signed due to stiff management opposition and legal delays. Eventually, the property was sold to the Station Casino Group, a nonunion "neighborhood" hotel–casino chain, dealing a severe blow to the organizing effort.

NLRB election procedures are particularly problematic because of high turnover rates in the hotel and casino industries. Under current labor law, union certification elections can be delayed for years. Long delays, coupled with an annual turnover rate of 152 percent in the lodging industry, suggest that there may be very few workers who initiated the unionization effort remaining with the employer by the time an election occurs (AH&MA 2001). The need to organize and then constantly reorganize in response to high turnover because of protracted delays in elections and certifications has made traditional NLRB election procedures practically unworkable in many instances.

In place of elections, the HERE has adopted strategies that include intensive organizing among workers within establishments while attempting to secure neutrality agreements from employers. Although neutrality agreements take different forms, they typically contain language that provides union organizers access to the employers' facilities, agreements by the employer not to campaign against the union, card check recognition, arbitration of first contracts, accretion agreements that extend the employer's neutrality for purposes of organizing to other entities that may be acquired by the employer, and agreement by the union to not picket or disrupt business as the organization drive proceeds (Cohen 2001). Not only are neutrality agreements enforceable in federal court, but the HERE's recent experiences have also demonstrated that they dramatically increase the probability that a union will obtain NLRB certification.

The HERE and other unions use various strategies to secure neutrality agreements from employers. For example, in some cases the unions use their political power at the local level to affect zoning and tax decisions. In San Francisco the union persuaded the city commission to adopt a policy requiring any new hotel property that took advantage of tax concessions from the city to remain neutral in union organizing drives.[7] A similar agreement was obtained in Milwaukee, where the city provided the Sodexho Marriott Corporation with $2 million in development funds. In exchange, the company agreed to remain neutral when the HERE would attempt to organize the completed property (HERE 1998). Other strategies to obtain neutrality agreements have also been employed. In Jacksonville, Florida, the AFL-CIO invested funds from its Building Investment Trust (BIT) in the new Jacksonville Hilton and Towers. In exchange for the financing, the hotel signed a neutrality agreement. The Hyatt Regency Philadelphia at Penns Landing in Philadelphia also signed a neutrality agreement after receiving financing from the AFL-CIO's BIT funds (HERE 1999:14).

In another case, an accretion clause in an existing labor agreement provided for employer neutrality and card check recognition. The Rio All-Suite Hotel and Casino in Las Vegas was recently acquired by Harrah's Entertainment Corporation, which has such an agreement with the Culinary Union Local 226. Before its acquisition by Harrah's, Rio's management had resisted unionization and operated union free for nearly ten years. After its acquisition, the workers were unionized with a card check within several months (*Las Vegas Sun* 2001).

In Las Vegas, the largest hotel–casino market in the United States, virtually all new organizing has relied on employer neutrality and card check recognition. In all, nearly 30,000 hotel and casino workers have been added to HERE's membership rolls since 1990 without a traditional NLRB election (Greenhouse 2001).

Alliances with Other Unions. To increase its organizing ability, the HERE has forged alliances with other unions. In its 2001 convention, the HERE extended its organizing agreement with the SEIU for another four years (HERE 2001a). The two unions worked together recently to achieve union representation for workers of the President Casino on the *Admiral* riverboat in Saint Louis (HERE 1999:11). In addition, an alliance of the HERE, SEIU, and the IUOE continues to pursue a "labor peace" initiative (another name for a neutrality agreement) in its campaign to represent hotel, restaurant, and casino workers in New Orleans (Hotel and Restaurant Organizing Coalition 2001). As mentioned, the HERE local in Detroit combined with the UAW, IBT, and IUOE to form the DCC. The unions achieved recognition by means of a card check, with the nonsupervisory workers being represented by the unions roughly according to the occupational structure outlined in Table 1 (*Daily Labor Report* 2001).

Organizing and Immigrants' Rights. For Wilhelm and the HERE, new organizing and immigration law reform are complementary. The union supports reformed immigration laws that would allow undocumented immigrants to change their status more easily. Support of immigration reform corresponds with the interests of a substantial segment of HERE's members and potential members. About one-fourth of the workers in the lodging sector are not U.S. citizens, according to the authors' analysis of data from the Current Population Survey (CPS). Immigration law reform is also a platform for labor–management cooperation, as industry and union leaders are working together for such reforms.

The HERE's position on immigration reform has found its way into some labor agreements. In Los Angeles, San Francisco, and Las Vegas, contract provisions allow workers days off work specifically to handle immigration matters with the Immigration and Naturalization Service. One contract provides workers up to a one-year leave of absence without loss of job title or seniority if they need to travel to deal with immigration (Taylor 2001).

Under the leadership of Wilhelm, not only has the HERE improved its internal practices but it has adopted aggressive strategies to organize new workers, forged alliances with other unions, and worked to empower immigrant workers. Despite the successful reform movement within the union, a number of issues in organizing and bargaining remain to be addressed.

Issues in Organizing and Bargaining

Tribal Gaming

The number of casinos and casino-related operations on Native American tribal lands has grown rapidly in recent years. According to the Indian Gaming Regulatory Act of 1988, much of the regulation of tribal casinos has been left to tribal gaming compacts to be negotiated between tribes and the individual states. Tribal sovereignty has been interpreted to mean that federal employment laws, including labor laws, civil rights legislation, and laws regulating health and safety standards, are not enforceable in workplaces on Native American reservations (NGISC 1998; Taylor 2001; Green 2001). Without the protection of labor laws, organizing in tribal casinos has been exceedingly difficult.

Health, Safety, and Civil Rights

Job safety and civil rights in commercial casinos are receiving increased scrutiny by OSHA and the Equal Employment Opportunity

Commission. A particularly thorny safety issue is secondhand tobacco smoke. In 1993 the Environmental Protection Agency (EPA) declared that the bulk of scientific evidence implicates secondhand smoke as a carcinogen that increases the risk of lung cancer and other respiratory disorders (U.S. EPA 1993). As cited previously, the IUGE has sued tobacco and casino companies, with the eventual aim of eliminating the hazard (Ryan 2000; IUGE 2001). The potential danger of secondhand tobacco smoke is likely to remain at the forefront of debate on workers' health and safety in casinos.

Dealers may also be at risk for repetitive-motion injuries (IUGE 2001). There is still no consensus among medical and ergonomic experts, however, that the mechanics of dealing leads to such injuries (Benjamin 2000). Regulations promulgated by OSHA on potential hazardous working conditions in casinos are silent on potential ergonomic problems associated with the work of dealers (OSHA 2001).

Potentially unsafe working conditions may also affect other workers on the casino floor. For example, cocktail servers at some properties have been required to wear shoes with two- to three-inch heals. Activist groups in Reno, where collective bargaining in hotel–casinos is not prevalent, recently coordinated a "Kiss My Foot" campaign. The protest highlighted debilitating uniform requirements for cocktail servers and called for protective legislation (Griffith 2000). As with repetitive-motion injuries, the medical community does not agree on the danger of high heels to servers; however, the American Podiatric Medical Association has judged high-heeled footwear to be biomechanically unsound, stating that it can lead to foot, knee, and back injuries. In Las Vegas, the union has dealt with disputes over such uniform requirements on a case-by-case basis, usually in response to complaints by members. No contract language has arisen from the high-heel controversy because most properties have agreed to accommodate medical problems by allowing workers to wear lower-heeled shoes or have offered workers the choice to wear lower-heeled shoes (Strow 2000).

Uniform requirements may also raise a civil rights issue. Some casinos have required their cocktail servers to wear sexually provocative costumes. Workers' and women's groups argue that such uniforms encourage sexual harassment by customers. In a well-publicized case, a cocktail server working at the Rio All-Suite Hotel and Casino, where revealing uniforms were required, was sexually assaulted by a patron (Baird 2001). A lawsuit by the worker is pending against the company. The suit addresses whether hotel–casino firms are responsible for sexual harassment that may be encouraged by the uniforms servers are required to wear. A similar controversy erupted at the MGM Grand property in Las Vegas after executives decided to adopt more revealing uniforms for cocktail servers. After complaints by a number of servers, the union organized a meeting between the affected workers and their managers, which resulted in the property agreeing to offer the servers a choice between the new uniforms and the original, more modest uniforms (Berns 1999).

Labor–Management Cooperation and Conflict

Cooperation. Labor–management cooperation often depends on the maturity of the relationship between the two parties. Because some markets have experienced collective bargaining for decades, a level of trust has evolved that serves as a foundation for cooperation. Two particularly notable examples of labor–management cooperation are jointly operated training programs in Las Vegas and San Francisco. HERE locals in the two cities have established multi-employer agreements to create training trusts for potential and incumbent workers who want skills necessary for employment or upward occupational mobility. The curricula are wide ranging and flexible, encompassing courses such as English as a second language, techniques in housekeeping, cooking skills, and table-serving skills, among others. Hotels can also request programs that are tailored to meet their specific needs. The partnerships embodied in such programs have been singled out by the Working for America Institute, an AFL-CIO supported research organization that researches and highlights innovative, high-road partnerships among labor organizations, employers, and community groups (Working for America Institute 2001).

It is also useful to compare how controversial uniform standards for cocktail servers were dealt with in Reno and Las Vegas. In Reno, where unions are not prevalent, workers and community groups held a protest campaign calling for state legislation to ban shoes with heels over two inches. On the other hand, in Las Vegas, where the servers had union representation, the controversy appeared to have been settled expeditiously by members airing their grievances to management through their union representatives. The result was a change of uniform policy more acceptable to the workers.

Conflict. Not all controversies are resolved as easily, however. As managers of hotels and casinos search for strategies to become more competitive, changes in work organization have led to overt conflict. For example, in 1997 the newly opened New York–New York Hotel and Casino decided to subcontract some of its restaurant operations to ARK, a firm that provides catering services. ARK employees worked on the company premises but remained nonunion. Not only did ARK refuse to allow card check union recognition for its workers, but it paid wages and benefits well below the union scale (Bach 1997). The result was 10,000 protestors demonstrating in front of the property against subcontracting work to low-wage employers. The union contends that subcontracting is simply a pretense for union avoidance, while the hotel maintains that it had a right and a competitive interest to subcontract for food services on its property. Although no resolution to the controversy between the union and the New York–New York and ARK has been forthcoming, contract negotiations in 1997 at a number of other major resorts yielded contract language in which hotel–casino properties agreed not to subcontract food operations to employers that paid wages lower than the union scale (Caruso 1997).

Although some labor strife is to be expected in unionized, or unionizing, hotels and hotel markets, major local industry-wide strikes, such as those in Las Vegas in 1984 and New York in 1985, have not surfaced. The proximate cause for the sixty-seven-day strike in Las Vegas was a demand by properties that newly hired or transferred workers would be paid 80 percent of the contractually bargained rate for workers with less than a year of experience in an occupation. The union eventually relented to the demand. Both the local hotel industry and its unions were battered by the strike, but replacement workers were used to keep some of the strip and downtown properties operating. In addition, picket-line violence, decertifications, and substantial membership losses weakened the union. Similarly, hotels in New York were able to continue operating during the city-wide strike. One hundred sixty-five properties were struck by 25,000 union members in the twenty-six-day walkout in New York City. As in Las Vegas, a central issue was a lower starting wage (75 percent of union scale) for workers in their first year. To the surprise of union leaders, the strike failed to shut down the industry; nevertheless, workers obtained wage and benefit increases in exchange for more flexible job classification systems and the lower wage for first-year workers (Cobble and Merrill 1994). To the surprise of hotel owners and managers, the unions demonstrated a great deal of resilience during the conflict. The 1980s was generally an era of substantial union decline. The outcome of these strikes was not surprising. In fact, a similar strike in Reno several years earlier left the hotel and casino industries in that city virtually union free (Taylor 2001).

Isolated incidents of strikes, boycotts, and other labor unrest, however, have affected some hotel and casino properties. Perhaps most notable was the protracted strike at the Frontier Hotel and Gambling

Hall in Las Vegas in 1991. After the employer cut wages and payments to unions' health, welfare, and pension funds, 550 workers from five unions walked out in an unfair labor practice strike. By the time it ended in 1998, the strike had become the longest in U.S. history. Although no union workers crossed the picket line, the company continued to operate with replacement workers. The strike was finally resolved after the property was sold and the new employer recognized the union. An estimated 300 of the original strikers returned to work at The New Frontier Hotel and Casino (Berns 1998).

Overt conflict has also arisen when properties on Las Vegas's highly unionized strip have attempted to open and operate nonunion. The MGM Grand opened in 1994 without agreeing to remain neutral or to recognize a card check procedure. The union protested with informational pickets and by leafleting customers. A free-speech issue arose when the hotel–casino, which also owned the sidewalk surrounding the property, asserted its property rights to remove the protesters from the sidewalk as trespassers. Similar controversies are brewing at the new 3,000-room Venetian Hotel and Casino on the strip. In a recent federal court ruling, however, sidewalks owned by hotel properties were judged to be areas in which free speech—including union activities—are protected (U.S. Court of Appeals, Ninth District 2001).

Overt conflict over organizing has also been encountered in San Francisco and Los Angeles. San Francisco's HERE Local 2 achieved NLRB certification at the San Francisco Marriott Hotel in 1996, but contract negotiations have since stalled. The hotel has been placed on HERE's boycott list and has experienced several years of picketing ("SF Marriott Boycott" 2001). In Los Angeles, conflict has been ongoing for more than four years as HERE Local 11 has attempted to organize the New Otani Hotel and Garden. The union continues to conduct a corporate campaign, a boycott, and picketing to elicit a neutrality agreement with card check recognition from the hotel. Using a novel strategy, the *employer* sought an NLRB election, even though workers themselves had not filed for one. The NLRB, however, refused to hold an election without a petition from the workers (*Stokes and Murphy Trends* 2001).

Security

Although security in casinos is certainly not a new issue, the exposure of large sums of money to workers and the public makes it an important one. The State Gaming Control Board in Nevada has issued guidelines concerning collective bargaining agreements, mandating that no provision can contradict requirements of the Board. In light of Nevada's pioneering role in gaming control, it is likely that other states have adopted similar guidelines. Security measures in typical hotel– casino labor agreements include contract language that allows for locker checks conducted by management. Consistent with Weingarten rights, however, inspections can only be conducted after the union has been contacted (*National Labor Relations Board v. J. Weingarten, Inc.* 1975). In addition, contract language requires that shortages of cash must be documented before any disciplinary action can be taken against an employee covered under the agreement.

Workers and Labor Markets: Hotels and Motels

Employment in the hotel–motel industry includes a large proportion of relatively unskilled service workers. Without union coverage, such employees are often paid low, poverty-level wages, with few benefits (Waddoups 2001a). In fact many frontline hotel–motel jobs fit the profile of "nonstandard" work—part-time, contingent, and/or lacking in affordable fringe benefits—according to the definition of Carré et al. (2000). Evidence that many properties organize work according to "nonstandard" principles can be found in the 152 percent annual turnover rate for frontline lodging workers mentioned earlier (*Hotels Magazine* 2000b).

Wages, Union Density, and Other Worker Characteristics

While essentially flat between 1990 and 1997, real wages began to increase somewhat toward the end of the decade. Figure 1 shows the movement of real wages of hotel–motel workers during the 1990s using year 2000 dollars as the base. The upward trend is similar in the retail trade and services industries in general. Increasing real wages likely resulted from favorable labor market conditions, as indicated by unemployment rates that fell to around 4 percent in 2000. Mishel, Bernstein, and Schmitt (1999) also documented the trend in rising real wages of less skilled workers during the late 1990s.

Collective bargaining is closely connected with higher real wages for workers in both union and nonunion establishments in a given location. For example, in research on the Nevada hotel and casino industries, Waddoups (1999a, 2001b) compared median occupational wages of a number of occupations that were highly unionized in Las Vegas with identical occupations in Reno, which were largely nonunion. The comparison highlighted a marked difference in the wage structure of hotel–casino

FIGURE 1

Average Real Hourly Wages of Production Workers in the
Hotel–Motel, Retail Trade, and Service Industries,
1991–2000

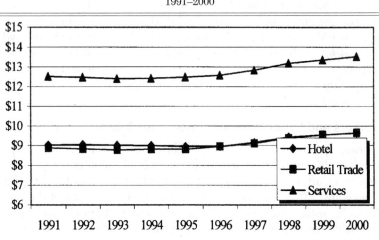

Source: U.S. Bureau of Labor Statistics (2001a).

firms in the two regions. Median wages for less skilled service jobs in Las Vegas were found to be more than 40 percent higher than their counterparts in Reno. When the union–nonunion differentials were estimated using multiple regression analysis to account for the possibility of product market differences between Las Vegas and Reno, the union–nonunion differential fell to 24 percent (Waddoups 2000). This percentage is closer to figures obtained using standard multiple regression approaches to estimate differentials (e.g., Curme and Macpherson 1991).

To see how unions affect wages in the U.S. hotel–motel industry, we gathered data on hotel–motel workers from the 1994–2000 Current Population Survey–Outgoing Rotation Group (CPS–ORG) data files. The data indicated union densities hovered between 11 and 12 percent for most of the decade (see Figure 2). In Table 2, summary statistics of selected worker characteristics in the union and nonunion sectors are displayed. The results indicate that, compared to the nonunion sector, unionized workers are less likely to be female and more likely to be married, Hispanic, and noncitizens. They are also less likely to reside in rural areas and small cities and much more likely to live in a large city or one of the metropolitan statistical areas (MSAs) we designated as a

FIGURE 2
Percentage of Hotel–Motel Workforce Covered by
Union Contract, by Year

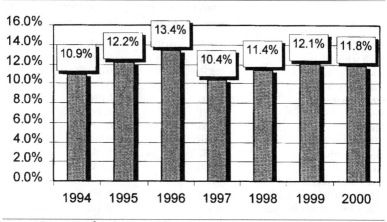

Source: CPS–ORG data (1994–2000).

"union city." In fact, about 70 percent of hotel–motel workers covered under a union contract reside in one of these MSAs.

Union–Nonunion Wage Differentials. Using a standard technique, we calculated union–nonunion wage differentials for hotel–motel workers. First, the natural log of weekly earnings for a group of unionized workers was estimated. Then, a corresponding equation for a group of nonunion workers was estimated using ordinary least squares regression. The two equations contained the standard controls for human capital and other characteristics that may affect wages. Regression results indicate a flatter age-earnings profile for union-covered workers and less of a return to education in the union sector. In addition, nonunion workers in highly unionized hotel markets enjoy higher wages than do nonunion workers in nonunionized markets. Belman and Voos (1993) argued that such patterns are expected for "local labor market industries" and demonstrated it empirically for employees in grocery stores across the United States. The results also suggest that female, African American, Hispanic, and noncitizens in both union and nonunion sectors earn lower wages, all else equal.

Using coefficient estimates and sample means, union–nonunion differentials evaluated at specified values of observed characteristics were

TABLE 2

Statistics (Selected Characteristics): Hotel–Motel Workers in the United States[a]

Variables	Covered by union contract		Not covered by union contract	
	Mean	Std. dev.[b]	Mean	Std. dev.
Age of respondent	39.239	10.982	36.388	11.814
High school	0.392	—	0.351	—
Some college	0.258	—	0.302	—
Bachelor's degree	0.087	—	0.133	—
Graduate degree	0.006	—	0.016	—
Female	0.491	—	0.592	—
Married	0.565	—	0.472	—
African American	0.146	—	0.128	—
Hispanic ethnicity	0.257	—	0.164	—
Noncitizen	0.260	—	0.155	—
Does not reside in MSA	0.082	—	0.223	—
MSA[c]: 150,000 to 499,999	0.034	—	0.104	—
MSA: 500,000 to 4,999,999	0.473	—	0.332	—
"Union city"[d]	0.713	—	0.240	—
Number in sample	1,157		6,967	

Source: Current Population Survey–Outgoing Rotation Group (1994–2000).
Respondents reporting employment in the hotel industry (SIC 762) during the survey week, weekly earnings of $20.00 or more, and being between the ages of 18 and 64 were included in the final sample.
[a] Summary statistics of all variables available on request.
[b] Std. dev. = Standard deviation.
[c] MSA = Metropolitan statistical area.
[d] Union cities have a substantial union presence according to Cobble and Merrill (1994) and our own analysis. Cities included are Atlantic City, Boston, Chicago, Detroit, Honolulu, Las Vegas, Los Angeles, New York, San Francisco, and Washington, DC.

calculated while holding other variables constant at their sample means. Table 3 contains selected results.[8] Workers with no high school education are helped more by union coverage than are their counterparts at higher educational levels. Union members not residing in an MSA enjoy a particularly large union wage premium. The union wage premium also appears to have diminished over the 1994–2000 period. Such a decline is likely a result of extremely tight labor markets toward the end of the decade, which drove market-mediated wages of nonunion workers up relative to their union counterparts' wages, which were more likely to be fixed by contract.

TABLE 3

Predicted Union–Nonunion Wage Differentials for Hotel–
Motel Workers by Selected Characteristics (%)[a]

Characteristic	Differential
Average	19.5
No high school	29.7
High school	18.6
Some college	19.1
Bachelor's degree	7.0
Graduate degree	24.2
Male	22.9
Female	17.0
Not married	25.9
Married	13.0
African American	18.7
Hispanic ethnicity	17.5
Noncitizen	15.4
Does not reside in MSA	39.1
MSA[b] between 150,000 and 499,999	26.3
MSA between 500,000 and 4,999,999	8.0
MSA larger than 5 million	19.3
Does not reside in union city	22.8
Resides in union city	12.4
Interviewed in 2000	13.5
Interviewed in 1994	22.4

Source: Differentials calculated using parameter estimates and summary statistics derived from the CPS–ORG data (1994–2000).
[a] Full results available on request.
[b] MSA = Metropolitan statistical area.

Gender, Race, Ethnicity, and Citizenship Status. Regardless of union coverage, the occupational structure in hotels still is characterized by high levels of occupational segregation by gender, race, ethnicity, and citizenship status (see Cobble and Merrill [1994] for corroborating evidence). Table 4 shows that, although 59.5 percent of production workers are female, females comprise 78 percent of sales counter clerks and 85 percent of maids and housemen, yet only 33 percent of the bartenders and 16 percent of security guards. African American workers are overrepresented as maids and housemen and underrepresented as front desk clerks, bartenders, and food servers. Hispanic workers tend to work disproportionately as maids and housemen and janitors and are underrepresented as front desk clerks, bookkeepers, and guards. In addition, noncitizens are overrepresented as maids and housemen and janitors and cleaners and underrepresented as front desk clerks, bartenders, and food servers.

TABLE 4

Employment by Selected Occupations and
Demographic Characteristics (%)

Selected occupations	Female	Characteristics Hispanic	Black	Noncitizens
Sales counter clerks	77.8	15.0	15.0	19.1
Hotel front desk clerks	74.5	8.2	9.7	3.5
Bookkeepers	67.3	7.2	6.5	7.2
Guards, protective services	15.7	6.7	13.3	5.8
Bartenders	33.1	8.0	5.2	10.3
Food servers	65.1	16.8	5.5	15.2
Cooks	23.6	23.9	14.2	22.9
Food preparation workers	31.5	43.8	15.9	39.9
Maids and housemen	85.1	29.8	23.1	31.6
Janitors and cleaners	16.0	34.3	14.2	32.0
Attendants	42.8	5.0	5.0	11.7
Porters and bellhops	13.1	11.2	16.3	16.2
Maintenance workers	2.7	12.3	4.1	9.5
Managers	51.5	17.7	6.7	6.9
All production workers	59.5	20.2	14.3	19.2
All hotel workers	57.8	17.7	13.0	17.0

Source: Authors' calculations using CPS–ORG (1994–2000) data on hotel–motel
workers.

Collective Bargaining and Nonwage Benefits

Collective bargaining, in general, results in more generous fringe benefit packages (Mishel, Bernstein, and Schmitt 1999). Furthermore, even
among enterprises that are nonunion but compete in a highly unionized
environment, competition for high-quality workers and the desire to fore-
stall unionization tends to compel firms to offer fringe benefit packages
that approach the levels of their unionized competitors.

Like other employers, lodging firms in markets where there is little
pressure to unionize have more flexibility to control costs. They do this
by keeping wages low, especially for their less skilled workers, and by
either not offering fringe benefits or by increasing out-of-pocket costs to
workers. In addition, firms in such markets can rely more on part-time
and contingent workers who are less likely to qualify for or be able to
afford fringe benefits offered by their employers.

Data from the 1992–2000 March CPS were examined to determine
the extent to which hotel–motel workers are offered fringe benefits, such
as health insurance and pension coverage. As with the CPS–ORG data,

the relatively few workers employed in the industry made it necessary to combine multiple years of data. The March CPS contains detailed questions about occupation and industry of employment, wages, employer-sponsored health insurance, and the existence of and participation in a pension plan sponsored by either an employer or a union.

To control for union status, MSAs characterized by highly unionized environments in the top segments of their local lodging industries were isolated. Cobble and Merrill (1994), using information from the HERE, suggested that Atlantic City, Boston, Chicago, Las Vegas, Los Angeles (County), New York City, San Francisco, and Washington, DC, are highly unionized. Our analysis of CPS–ORG data and interviews with union officials confirm Cobble and Merrill's (1994) findings. In addition, analysis of the CPS–ORG data also suggests that Honolulu is a highly unionized location in the industry, and Detroit was added because of its high union density. Using this information, a dummy variable (union city) was created. Such a procedure is likely to be an adequate control for union effects on benefits. Empirical evidence indicates that the union threat effect in more highly unionized environments causes hotel workers in unionized cities to receive wages, and presumably benefits, that are similar to those received by their union counterparts (Waddoups 1999b). According to the March CPS data, approximately 68 percent of the sample of hotel workers reside in one of the previously mentioned MSAs.

Health Insurance. Summary statistics of the proportion of employees with access to employer-sponsored health insurance are presented in Table 5. The data, available since 1995, show that approximately 46.6 percent of hotel workers had access to employer or union-sponsored health insurance. By comparison, a study by Cooper and Schone (1997) found that 75.4 percent of all employees in the United States were offered health insurance in 1996. Of those with access to insurance, 65.4 percent had either part or all of the premiums paid by their employer. The evidence suggests that the hotel–motel industry is substantially less likely to offer health insurance to its employees or to pay premiums for their employees than are employers in general.

Information is not available on the rate at which hotel–motel employees actually participate in their employment-based health insurance plans, but, in general, participation rates are substantially lower than offer rates. According to Cooper and Schone (1997), the rate at which workers typically participate in employer-sponsored health plans

TABLE 5

Proportions of Hotel–Motel Workers with Employer-Sponsored Health
Insurance and Pension Plan Coverage (1995-2000)

	Proportion/Mean	Number
Employer-Sponsored Health Insurance		
Employer sponsored health ins. available	0.466	2,972
All or part of health ins. premium paid	0.440	2,972
Average employer contribution	$877.80	2,972
Pension plan		
Pension offered by employer or union	0.464	2,972
Total pension participation	0.283	1,431
Pension participation (given plan offered)	0.609	—

Source: Authors' calculations using CPS (March 1995–2000) data on hotel–motel
workers.

was 80.1 percent. This would suggest that 40 percent is a reasonable
estimate of the rate at which hotel–motel workers participate in such
plans.

To determine the factors that correlate with the probability of health
insurance being offered and paid for by employers, probit regressions
were used. The first omits "weekly wage" as a covariate, and the second
includes "weekly wage" to determine if an empirically detectable trade-
off exists between wages and benefits. Partial results of the probit estimations are listed in Table 6.

Human capital variables "age" and "education" are positively corre-
lated with the availability of health insurance, other things equal.
Female and African American workers are approximately ten and seven
percentage points less likely to have health insurance available, respectively. Residing in a union city increases the likelihood that insurance is
available by nearly 18 percent. Firm size is also a significant determinant of the availability of insurance. Employees in firms with 100 employees or more are 40 to 50 percent more likely to be offered health insurance or to have a union that offers it.

Estimations of the probability that the firm pays all or part of the premiums for health insurance closely mirror the previous results. Co-
efficients on human capital variables, and demographic, union, and demand-
side variables have similar signs and magnitudes. Again, notice that hotel
workers residing in a union city are about 23 percent more likely to have
all or part of their insurance paid by their employer.

TABLE 6

Probability That Health Insurance Is Offered or Paid for by Employer or Union:
Selected Partial Derivative Estimates

Variable[a]	Health ins. offered		Health ins. paid	
	Coefficient[b]	z statistic	Coefficient	z statistic
Age	*0.011*	11.606	*0.010*	10.852
High school	*0.117*	4.220	*0.113*	4.064
Some college	*0.141*	4.581	*0.138*	4.476
Bachelor's degree	*0.223*	5.390	*0.210*	5.046
Graduate degree	0.096	1.142	0.023	0.273
Respondent is female	*-0.104*	-4.784	*-0.079*	-3.578
Respondent is married	0.018	0.870	0.019	0.908
Respondent is African American	*-0.075*	-2.325	-0.059	-1.806
Respondent is Hispanic	-0.013	-0.504	-0.004	-0.167
Resides in "union city"[c]	*0.187*	7.785	*0.226*	8.721
Between 10 and 24 employees	0.078	1.182	0.031	0.412
Between 25 and 99 employees	*0.333*	5.980	*0.306*	4.968
Between 100 and 499 employees	*0.406*	7.606	*0.356*	6.018
Between 500 and 999 employees	*0.445*	7.425	*0.390*	5.868
Over 1,000 employees	*0.501*	10.193	*0.471*	8.594
Number in sample		2,978		2,978
Log-likelihood		-1,687		-1,682
Chi-square		753.586		754.201

Source: CPS (March 1995–2000).

[a] Other variables controlled for in the regression equation are region, occupational categories, and year of interview. Full results available on request.

[b] Bold and italicized print indicates statistical significance at .05 level or less.

[c] Union cities have a substantial union presence according to Cobble and Merrill (1994) and our own analysis. Cities included are Atlantic City, Boston, Chicago, Detroit, Honolulu, Las Vegas, Los Angeles, New York, San Francisco, and Washington, DC.

Pension Coverage. The impact on labor market outcomes of employer-sponsored pensions has been treated extensively in the literature (Allen, Clark, and McDermed 1992; Gustman, Mitchell, and Steinmeier 1994). Such programs offer advantages to employers by eliciting additional work effort from employees who would suffer a substantial capital loss if they were fired before vesting in the pension plan. They also give the firm more control over turnover rates. Lower turnover reduces the loss of firm-specific human capital that it may have invested in its workers. On the other hand, pensions are desirable for workers because they offer a convenient, tax-deferred means for retirement savings and insurance against disability and old-age poverty.

While traditional defined benefit pensions became common for "standard" jobs between World War II and 1980, researchers began to detect a change in type and incidence of pension coverage during the move toward increased flexibility in the employment relationship, a transformation that began to occur roughly in the 1980s. For example, Even and Macpherson (1994) documented a decline in firms' pension coverage and participation in such programs during the 1980s. An important factor in the decline was the emergence of 401(k) pension plans in which participation is voluntary. Younger workers were found to be especially prone to decline participation in voluntary plans.

Data from the 1995–2000 March CPS indicate that 46.4 percent of workers in the hotel–motel industry were offered some kind of pension plan, and of those offered a plan, 60.9 percent participated (see Table 5). In all, approximately 28.3 percent of the hotel–motel workforce participated in a pension program during the period.

Probit models were also used to estimate the probability that an individual is offered a pension as a function of a group of explanatory variables. As with the health insurance models, the results indicate that age and human capital characteristics are positively related to the probability that a pension plan is offered. They also suggest that female and Hispanic workers are less likely to have access to a pension plan (see Table 7). Residing in a union city adds seven percentage points to the probability that a pension is offered. Employer size is the most important determinant of such a probability. Workers in larger firms are substantially more likely to be offered pension coverage.

Even and Macpherson (1994) suggested that part of the decline in coverage among male workers is due to a reduction in participation in employer-sponsored plans. To assess such employee behavior in the hotel–motel industry, a separate probit model was estimated in which the dependent variable was the probability of participation in a pension plan conditioned on one being offered. The results suggest that age is a positive predictor of participation, as is marital status, where married workers are approximately ten percentage points more likely to be participants. The union city estimate is large, adding nearly twenty percentage points to the probability of participation. Also notable is the importance of company size as a determinant of employee participation. Workers employed in larger companies generally exhibit a statistically discernable increase in the probability of participation in a pension plan than their counterparts in smaller organizations.

TABLE 7

Probability of Hotel–Motel Workers being Covered by a Pension:
Selected Partial Derivative Estimates

Variable[a]	Pension available Coefficient[b]	z statistic	Particip. if avail. Coefficient	z statistic
Age	0.003	3.591	0.012	9.282
High school	0.081	3.019	0.091	2.288
Some college	0.153	5.120	0.125	2.952
Bachelor's degree	0.149	3.739	0.147	2.678
Graduate degree	0.106	1.233	0.041	0.366
Respondent is female	-0.076	-3.583	-0.063	-2.121
Respondent is married	0.045	2.176	0.100	3.547
Respondent is African American	0.004	0.127	-0.044	-0.972
Respondent is Hispanic	-0.097	-3.832	-0.056	-1.562
Respondent resides in "union city"[c]	0.072	3.082	0.225	7.178
Between 10 and 24 employees	0.121	1.740	0.211	1.314
Between 25 and 99 employees	0.279	4.724	0.311	2.263
Between 100 and 499 employees	0.449	7.987	0.214	1.629
Between 500 and 999 employees	0.462	7.428	0.319	2.325
Over 1,000 employees	0.622	11.838	0.317	2.482
Number in sample		2,978		1,433
Log-likelihood		-1,768		-813
Chi-square		587.73		276.00

Source: March Current Population Survey, 1995-2000.
[a] Other variables controlled for in the regression equation are region, occupational categories, and year of interview. Full results available upon request.
[b] Bold and italicized print indicates statistic significance at .05 level or less.
[c] Union cities have a substantial union presence according to Cobble and Merrill (1994) and our own analysis. Cities included are Atlantic City, Boston, Chicago, Detroit, Honolulu, Las Vegas, Los Angeles, New York, San Francisco, and Washington, D.C.

Workers and Labor Markets: Casinos

Although CPS data allow us to estimate the effects of unions on wages and benefits for workers in hotels and motels, similar data, unfortunately, are not available on casino workers. Not only do the CPS data not contain a three-digit industry code for casino workers, but the small number of workers in the early 1990s also would have made it difficult to find sufficient observations even if the coding existed. Instead of CPS data, occupational wage surveys conducted yearly in various casino jurisdictions are used to examine wages and benefits of casino workers (International Gaming Institute 2000a, 2000b, 2000c). Table 8 contains average occupational wages of common casino (and some hotel–motel) occupations in Las Vegas (representative of a highly unionized location), riverboat, and tribal casinos.

TABLE 8

Average Occupational Wages in Casinos:
Selected Occupations and Jurisdictions

| Occupation | Average hourly wages ($) | | | % Difference | |
	Las Vegas[a]	Tribal	Riverboat	LV/Tribal	LV/River.
Dealer	5.49	6.09	5.69	-9.9	-3.5
Slot technician	18.89	11.07	12.20	70.6	54.8
Slot floorman	11.89	9.53	9.40	24.8	26.5
Change attendant	9.21	7.54	7.51	22.1	22.6
Front desk clerk (hotel)	11.68	8.33	7.97	40.2	46.5
Valet parking attendant	7.52	6.45	5.75	16.6	30.8
Guest room attendant	9.79	7.44	7.31	31.6	33.9
Cook	12.23	8.96	8.44	36.5	44.9
Food server	7.71	6.48	5.52	19.0	39.7
Busperson	7.74	6.75	6.35	14.7	21.9
Bartender	11.83	7.18	5.67	64.8	108.6
Cocktail server	7.65	5.76	4.70	32.8	62.8
Kitchen worker	9.69	7.30	6.85	32.7	41.5

Sources: Las Vegas Casino/Hotel Survey (2000); Tribal Casino/Hotel Wage Survey (2000); and Riverboat Casino/Hotel Wage Survey (2000); International Gaming Institute, William F. Harrah College of Hotel Administration, University of Nevada, Las Vegas (International Gaming Institute 2000a, 2000b, 2000c).
[a] Forty-one casinos in Las Vegas, forty-six tribal casinos, and nineteen riverboat casinos participated in the surveys.

Wages. Unfortunately the results in Table 8 do not make a direct comparison of wages in union and nonunion properties possible. The union–nonunion distinction is not much of a problem in the tribal casino segment because virtually no such establishments are unionized. The riverboat casino data are more problematic because six of the eighty-two riverboat casinos are unionized (Green 2001). It is impossible, however, to determine how many of these six properties actually participated in the survey. It is safe to infer that a distinct minority of riverboat casinos in the sample are unionized and that arithmetic average wages would lean toward the market-mediated nonunion wage. As for the data on Las Vegas, previous work has demonstrated that union and nonunion wages of hotel and casino workers are nearly the same, probably because of the union threat effect (Waddoups 1999b).

It is apparent that a significant wage differential exists between Las Vegas and the other two locations in virtually every occupation. Whether the differentials are driven by a stronger union presence in Las Vegas or qualitatively different product and labor market conditions is difficult to determine with the data available. It is interesting to note, however, that wages on tribal casinos and riverboats diverge by about 11 percent (an unweighted average), where tribal casinos' wages are somewhat higher, a result that runs counter to the findings of the NGISC's (1998) report, as previously noted. In addition, differences in occupational wages, which are calculated as the percentage by which average occupational wages in Las Vegas exceed wages in other locations, appear similar to the percentage differences in the relevant occupations reported in Waddoups (2001b), where he compares detailed occupational wages in Las Vegas and Reno, Nevada. Thus, it would appear that the occupational wage structure in riverboat casinos, tribal casinos, and casinos in the mostly nonunion Reno area (where hotel–casinos are generally larger) is similar. Such a finding suggests that the nonunion wage structure among casino workers is relatively constant regardless of the establishment's size or geographic location. Union density in a region, rather than other market characteristics, appears to be a better predictor of relatively high wages.

Employer-Sponsored Health Insurance. Data on casino workers' access to, and participation in, fringe benefits programs are described qualitatively in the wage surveys. All riverboat casinos responding to the survey indicate that they offer employer-sponsored health insurance of some kind to their full-time workers (forty hours or more per week). Of the twenty-one respondents, eleven reported offering health insurance to part-timers (twenty-four to thirty-two hours per week). The types of plans differ substantially among respondents, as do the percentages of workers who participate. No information, however, is given on the proportion or number of workers who are qualified for health insurance benefits.

The incidence of health insurance offered to workers on tribal casinos is almost the same as on riverboats. Of the forty-four casinos responding, all but one offered some sort of health insurance package to its full-time workers (again defined as forty hours per week). Only twenty-four employers offered insurance to part-timers (defined in this case as from twenty to thirty-three hours per week). As with the riverboat casinos, a range of coverage plans are offered both within and across firms, and the rates of worker participation also varied substantially by property and plan type. And similar to riverboat properties, no information about the percentage of workers who qualified for insurance was reported.

Pensions. All responding riverboat casinos offered 401(k) pension plans, and all included some kind of employer match. It was not specified, however, whether part-time workers were qualified to participate, nor was the rate at which employees participated given. Tribal casinos are less likely to offer pension plans than are casinos on riverboats. Thirty-seven of the forty-four tribal casinos reported offering a 401(k) pension plan, most with some kind of employer matching scheme. The other seven did not report offering a pension. No information is given on whether part-timers are qualified to participate in the program or to receive the matching contribution. In addition, no numbers are available on the proportion of workers who actually participate in the pension plans.

Conclusion: The Future of Collective Bargaining

Hotels and Motels

Prospects for collective bargaining among hotel–motel and casino workers look moderately bright; however, these prospects depend on the ability of the HERE and other unions to continue finding creative strategies to organize workers through means that may deviate from the traditional NLRB election machinery. The HERE affiliate in Las Vegas has virtually abandoned NLRB-sponsored elections in favor of neutrality agreements and card checks to achieve recognition. Other locations have followed their lead. A majority of recent organizing successes by HERE locals have relied on neutrality agreements and card checks.

Supporting training centers is another strategy that has helped the HERE ensure that its members' higher wages and benefits do not adversely affect the economic viability of firms in the industry. Joint training programs also serve as a platform for labor–management cooperation. The economics of on-the-job training suggests that employers may be reluctant to offer socially optimal amounts of general training to their workers because skills are portable to other, perhaps competing, firms. The problem is especially acute for hotel–motel properties where competitors are located within close geographic proximity and where turnover is especially high. For example, once an individual firm trains workers to clean rooms, the workers can take their skills and increased productivity to any competing hotel or motel, leaving the original hotel without a return on its training investment.

Much as unions operate apprenticeship training programs in the construction industry, hotel unions are in a unique position to coordinate training programs for entire locations (or perhaps segments within locations) of the industry so that any one firm does not have to bear the risk of losing its investment in general on-the-job training because of turnover. The training may also be thought of as a screening device by which potential workers who may not be suitable for work in the industry discover that fact before firms expend resources hiring and training them. Given the high turnover rates and the substantial recruitment costs, training that may reduce turnover by better screening and by offering avenues for upward mobility has the potential to be valuable to hotel firms.

Casinos

As with hotels, casinos located in resort destinations enjoy relatively good prospects for unionization. The notable exceptions, however, may be the few occupations that have traditionally remained nonunion, such as dealers. The prospects are not as bright for collective bargaining in smaller commercial and tribal casinos. It appears almost inevitable that additional smaller commercial and tribal casinos will begin operation, especially given that only 35 percent of tribes currently operate casinos (NIGC 2000). As the number of gambling establishments increases and casinos become more common, the potential for extra-normal profitability will likely diminish. Lower profitability would not bode well for unions in smaller commercial and tribal casinos. This is especially true in outlying areas where unions must expend substantial resources to organize and administer collective bargaining agreements for relatively small bargaining units. The outlook for collective bargaining in tribal casinos is even dimmer because of the lack of federal protection for bargaining rights.

Alternatively, the proliferation of gambling throughout the country appears to have changed the tastes and preferences of the public for gambling, making it more socially acceptable. An increased demand for gambling in tourist destinations is likely to be a boon to both the hotel and casino sectors and the collective bargaining that already exists in those areas. Furthermore, increases in demand for lodging and gambling at destination resorts in largely nonunion locations, such as those in Mississippi and Louisiana, make such locations more attractive organizing targets for unions. The customary resistance to unionization in the South, however, will likely remain an obstacle.

Epilogue

The bulk of this chapter was written before the terrorist attacks on September 11, 2001. The attacks prompted a sharp reduction in demand for travel and travel-related services, as well as the demand for labor in lodging establishments, restaurants, and casinos. By October 2001, the HERE reported that about one-third of its membership had been laid off and that many more had been placed on reduced schedules (Greenhouse 2001). Substantial numbers of hotel and casino workers in other unions and in the nonunion sector were laid off as well. For perspective on the potential impact of the attacks on collective bargaining in the lodging and casino industries, consider that nearly one-third of HERE's membership would amount to roughly 88,000 workers. Job losses reported by the U.S. Bureau of Labor Statistics (2001b) since the attacks until the end of November were estimated at around 800,000. The numbers suggest that job losses among HERE members could account for nearly 11 percent of all jobs lost in the economy since the September 11 attacks. When one considers that hotel and casino jobs account for less than 2 percent of total employment in the United States, the disproportionately large negative impact on workers, their unions, and the industry in general is evident.

At this stage, it is impossible to forecast when, or whether, the demand for labor in hotels and casinos will reach pre-attack levels. For now, however, excess capacity, lagging demand for travel and tourism-related services, and the recession that officially began in March 2001 will likely lead to hard bargaining as contracts expire and unions struggle to protect their gains in representation, wages, and benefits, and as hotel and casino companies attempt to maintain economic viability. These circumstances suggest that the trend of rising real wages of the four years since 1997 will probably be reversed.

In the conclusion section written before September 11, we indicated that the prospects for collective bargaining looked "moderately bright." The new reality suggests a more cautious and less sanguine assessment. It is in the tourist and convention sector of the industry where union density is highest, collective bargaining relationships have been most secure, and a disproportionate downturn in demand has occurred. Thus, not only are there fewer workers in the industry, but it is likely that proportionately fewer now are covered by collective bargaining contracts. Collective bargaining in the industry will not disappear, but the bargaining power of hotel and casino workers and their unions will no doubt be reduced.

Notes

[1] Class III gambling is described by the National Indian Gaming Commission (NIGC) as "full scale casino-style gaming," including traditional table games such as black jack, roulette, and craps, as well as slot machines.

[2] Starwood Hotels and Resorts Worldwide, Inc., a hotel management company that specializes in ownership and management of properties in the upper two segments, has about 60,000 employees under its management at various properties across the United States. The company's stockholder report indicates that about one-third of its employees are covered by union contracts, which is more than double the union density for hotel–motel workers in general.

[3] One must also recognize that union contracts may also impose additional costs in the form of restrictive work rules that potentially reduce productivity in a unionized environment. If workers in unionized settings are less productive than their counterparts in the nonunion sector, the pattern of unionization observed may be better explained in terms of monopoly power in product and/or labor markets and perhaps in terms of region-specific customs regarding union activity.

[4] There are some exceptions. For example, a small bargaining unit of warehouse workers at the Aladdin in Las Vegas just voted to be represented by the Teamsters.

[5] Over the years, dealers have been involved in pilferage by palming chips, slipping chips up their sleeves or behind the faces of watches, hiding chips in pockets or behind collars or neckties, placing chips in their mouths, and perpetrating scams with players. If stolen chips are in $100 or $500 denominations or scams are not detected quickly, a casino's losses could quickly become large.

[6] A conversation between one of the authors and a dealer about the TWU organizing drive suggested that occupational duality may have been deliberately manipulated to complicate the union organizing effort. The dealer's suggestion, of course, was perception only and was not corroborated by further investigation.

[7] One of the issues in the HERE Local 2's boycott of the Marriott in San Francisco is an alleged violation of a neutrality agreement the company signed to obtain zoning permission to build the hotel.

[8] The coefficient estimates and many of the summary statistics of variables used in the regression equations are omitted. In addition, only selected coefficient estimates are displayed for equations estimated in Table 2. The full results and a technical appendix are available upon request.

References

Allen, Steven G., Robert L. Clark, and Ann A. McDermed. 1992. "Pensions, Bonding, and Lifetime Jobs." *Journal of Human Resources*, Vol. 28, no. 1 (Winter), pp. 463–81.

American Gaming Association. 2001. "State of the States 2000: The AGA Survey of Casino Entertainment 2001."
<http://www.americangaming.org/survey2001/overview/over_view.html>. [December 31, 2001].

American Hotel & Motel Association (AH&MA). 2001. "Information Center."
<http://webprod.ahma.com/ahma/infocenter/lip.asp>. [February 1, 2001].

Bach, Lisa Kim. 1997. "Food Workers Cut Off at the Pass." *Las Vegas Review-Journal*, April 18, p. D1.

Baird, Kirk. 2001. "Skin City: Getting an Eyeful of Those Revealing Uniforms Worn by Casino Cocktail Waitresses." *Las Vegas Sun*, February 3, p. E1.

Belman, Dale L., and Paula B. Voos. 1993. "Wage Effects of Increased Union Coverage: Methodological Considerations and New Evidence." *Industrial and Labor Relations Review*, Vol. 46, no. 2 (January), pp. 368–80.

Benjamin, Caren. 2000. "Dealers Illnesses Called Frequent." Las Vegas Review-Journal, January 29, p. B1.

Berns, Dave. 1998. "It's a New Frontier." *Las Vegas Review-Journal*, February 1, p. A1.

_____. 1999. "MGM Waitresses Air Concerns about Uniforms." *Las Vegas Review-Journal*, February 9, p. D1.

Binkley, Christina. 2001. "In Drive to Unionize, Casino Dealers Defy a Las Vegas Tradition." *The Wall Street Journal*, March 6, p. A1.

Campbell, Douglas N. 1989. "Lost in the Storm: Culinary Union Local 226 and the Las Vegas 'Strip' Resorts." Unpublished paper, Gaming Studies Research Collection, University of Nevada, Las Vegas.

Carré, Francois, Marianne A. Ferber, Lonnie Golden, and Stephen A. Herzenberg. 2000. "Nonstandard Work: The Nature and Challenges of Changing Employment Arrangements." In Francois Carré, Marianne A. Ferber, Lonnie Golden, and Stephen A. Herzenberg, eds., *Nonstandard Work: The Nature and Challenges of Changing Employment Arrangements.* Champaign–Urbana: Industrial Relations Research Association.

Caruso, Monica. 1997. "Slow Negotiations Frustrate Culinary." *Las Vegas Review-Journal*, September 22, p. D1.

Chipkin, Harvey. 2001. "Reorganized Labor: Will Changing Union Strategies Lead to Changing Industry Strategies?" *Lodging*, Vol. 26, no. 6 (February), pp. 63–66.

Cobble, Dorothy Sue, and Michael Merrill. 1994. "Collective Bargaining in the Hospitality Industry in the 1980s." In Paula B. Voos, ed. *Contemporary Collective Bargaining in the Private Sector.* Madison, WI: Industrial Relations Research Association, pp. 447–89.

Cohen, Charles I. 2001. "Neutrality Agreements: Will the NLRB Sanction Its Own Obsolescence?" presented to the American Bar Association Committee on Development of Law under the National Labor Relations Act. <http://www.morganlewis.com/art012800.htm>. [December 12, 2001].

Cooper, Philip F., and Barbara Steinberg Schone. 1997. "More Offers, Fewer Takers for Employment Based Health Insurance: 1987 and 1996." *Health Affairs,* Vol. 16, no. 6 (November/December), pp. 142–49.

Curme, Michael A., and David A. Macpherson. 1991. "Union Wage Differentials and the Effects of Industry and Local Density: Evidence from the 1980s." *Journal of Labor Research*, Vol. 12, no. 3 (Fall), pp. 419–27.

Daily Labor Report. 2001. "Greektown Casino in Detroit Grants Recognition to Detroit Casino Council." April 16, p. A2.

Even, William E., and David A. Macpherson. 1994. "The Decline of Male Pension Coverage in the 1980s." *Industrial and Labor Relations Review*, Vol. 47, no. 3 (April), pp. 439–53.

Freeman, Richard B., and James L. Medoff. 1984. *What Do Unions Do?* New York: Basic Books.

Frey, James H., and Donald E. Carns. 1987. "The Work Environment of Gambling Casinos." *Anthropology of Work Review*, Vol, 8, no. 4 (December), pp. 38–42.

Gazel, Ricardo C., and William N. Thompson. 1996. *Casino Gamblers in Illinois: Who Are They?* Chicago: Better Government Association.

Green, Marian. 2001. "Labor Pains." *International Gaming & Wagering Business*, Vol. 22, no. 2 (February), p. 1.

Greenhouse, Steven. 2001. "A Labor Leader on the Rise as His Workers Are Down." *New York Times*, October 13, p. A8.

Griffith, Martin. 2000. "Women in Reno to Rally Against Casinos' High Heel Policy." *Las Vegas Sun*, May 13. <http://www.lasvegassun.com/sunbin/stories/text/2000/may/13/510252336.html>. [December 12, 2001].

Gustman, Alan L., Olivia S. Mitchell, and Thomas L. Steinmeier. 1994. "The Role of Pensions in the Labor Market: A Survey of the Literature." *Industrial and Labor Relations Review*, Vol. 47, no. 3 (April), pp. 417–38.

Holtmann, Andy. 2001. "Are Unions in the Cards? A Look at the Past, Present, and Future of Labor Unions in the Casino Industry." *Casino Journal*, Vol. 14, no. 2 (February), pp. 30–34.

Hotel and Restaurant Organizing Coalition. 2001. "What Is Labor Peace?" <http://www.hotroc.org/articles/laborpeace.html>. [December 13, 2001].

Hotel Employees and Restaurant Employees International Union (HERE). 1998. "Organizing Agreement with New Marriot." *Catering Industry Employee.* (November/December), p. 24. [November 17, 2001].

———. 1999. *Catering Industry Employee.* <http://www.hereunion.org/newsinfo/cie/CIE_Summer99_.pdf>. [November 17, 2001].

———. 2001a. "Convention Resolutions." <http://www.hereunion.org/newsinfo/convention/resolutions.asp>. [December 8, 2001].

———. 2001b. "John W. Wilhelm General President." <http://www.hereunion.org/about/bios/>. [December 8, 2001].

———. 2001c. "Order of Dismissal." <http://www.hereunion.org/newsinfo/news/orderofdismissal.pdf>. [December 8, 2001].

Hotels Magazine. 2000a. "Global Update." Vol. 34, no. 3 (July), p. 6.

———. 2000b. "People Matters: Employee Recruitment and Retention Tactics." Vol. 34, no. 3 (March), p. 28.

International Gaming Institute. 2000a. *Las Vegas Casino/Hotel Wage Survey.* Las Vegas, NV: International Gaming Institute, University of Nevada, Las Vegas.

———. 2000b. *Riverboat Casino/Hotel Wage Survey.* Las Vegas, NV: International Gaming Institute, University of Nevada, Las Vegas.

———. 2000c. *Tribal Casino/Hotel Wage Survey.* Las Vegas, NV: International Gaming Institute, University of Nevada, Las Vegas.

International Union of Gaming Employees (IUGE). 2001. "Dealers Seeking Class Action Lawsuit Against Big Tobacco." <http://www.nfge.com/news/2001/dealers_seeking_class_action.htm>. [December 13, 2001].

Las Vegas Sun. 2001. "Rio Workers Choose Union Representation." January 11, p. C3.

Lomanno, Mark. 2000. "A Decade of Change: A Look at the Industries Growth from 1990-1999." <http://www.lodgingnews.com/lodgingmag/2000_9/2000_9_34.asp>. [April 17, 2001].

Mishel, Lawrence, Jared Bernstein, and Michael Schmitt. 1999. *The State of Working America, 1998-99.* Washington, DC: Economic Policy Institute.

National Gambling Impact Study Commission (NGISC). 1998. *National Gaming Impact Study Commission Report.* Washington, DC: National Gaming Impact Study Commission.

National Indian Gaming Commission (NIGC). 2000. *Biennial Report.* Washington, DC: National Indian Gaming Commission.

National Labor Relations Board v. J. Weingarten, Inc. 1975. 420 U.S. 251, S. Ct. 959.

Occupational Safety and Health Administration (OSHA). 2001. "Ergonomics Guidelines: A Casino." <http://www.osha-slc.gov/SLTC/ergonomics/ergonomicsreports_pub/lt981029.html>.

Ryan, Cy. 2000. "Dealers Take Case Against Tobacco to Supreme Court." *Las Vegas Sun*, September 15, p. B6.

"SF Marriott Boycott: Labor Dispute in San Francisco." 2001. <http://www.sfmarriottboycott.org/>. [December 13, 2001].

Starwood Hotels and Resorts Worldwide, Inc. 2000. *Starwood Hotels & Resorts Worldwide, Inc. Is One of the World's Largest Hotel Operating Companies* (Company's 10-K). <http://www.starwoodlodging.com/html/comp_over.html>. [March 27, 2001].

Stokes and Murphy Trends. 2001. "The Twists and Turns of New NLRB Decisions." Atlanta: Stokes and Murphy Law Firm.

Strauss, George. 2000. "What's Happening Inside U.S. Unions: Democracy and Union Politics." *The Journal of Labor Research*, Vol. 21, no. 2 (Spring), pp. 211–25.

Strow, David. 2000. "Casino High-Heel Policies Targeted." *Las Vegas Sun*, February 11, A1.

Taylor, D. (Staff Director, Culinary Union Local 226). 2001. Interview by C. Jeffrey Waddoups and Vincent H. Eade. April 6, Las Vegas, Nevada.

U.S. Bureau of Labor Statistics. 2001a. "Bureau of Labor Statistics Data." <http://146.14.4.24/cgi_bin/surveymost.>. [March 13, 2001].

_____ "United States Economy at a Glance." <ftp://ftp.bls.gov/pub/economy.us.txt>. [December 19, 2001].

U.S. Court of Appeals, Ninth District. 2001. *Venetian Casino Resort, LLC v. Local Joint Executive Board of Las Vegas, Culinary Workers, Local 226 et al.*, no. 00-15136, D.C. no. CV-99-00276-pmp, July 12.

U.S. Department of Commerce: Bureau of Economic Analysis. 2001. "Gross Domestic Product By Industry." <www.bea.doc.gov/bea/dn2/gpox.htm>. [January 29, 2001].

U.S. Environmental Protection Agency. 1993. *Secondhand Smoke: What You Can Do about Secondhand Smoke: Parents, Decision-Makers, and Building Occupants,* form EPA-402-F-93-004. Washington, DC: Environmental Protection Agency.

Waddoups, C. Jeffrey. 1999a. "Union Wage Effects in Nevada's Hotel and Casino Industry." *Industrial Relations*, Vol. 38, no. 4 (October), pp. 577–83.

_____. 1999b. "Union-Nonunion Wage Differentials in the Hotel Industry: The Cases of Las Vegas and Other Large Hotel Markets." *Proceedings of the Fifty-First*

Annual Meetings (New York, January 3–5, 2000). Champaign–Urbana: Industrial Relations Research Association, Vol. 1, pp. 161–68.

———. 2000. "Unions and Wages in Nevada's Hotel-Casino Industry." *Journal of Labor Research*, Vol. 21, no. 2 (Spring), pp. 345–61.

———. 2001a. "Unionism and Poverty-Level Wages in the Service Sector: the Case of Nevada's Hotel-Casino Industry." *Applied Economics Letters*, Vol. 8, no. 3 (March), pp. 163–67.

———. 2001b. "Wages in Las Vegas and Reno: How Much Difference Do Unions Make in the Hotel, Gaming and Recreation Industry?" *Gaming Research & Review Journal*, Vol. 6, no. 1, pp. 7–21.

Working for America Institute. 2001. "Community Partnerships: Building Good Jobs in Strong Communities." <http://www.workingforamerica.org/documents/journal/page4.htm>. [November 9, 2000].

CHAPTER 5

Newspapers: Collective Bargaining Decline Amidst Technological Change

HOWARD R. STANGER

Canisius College

In the early hours of the morning, October 2, 1975, pressmen and stereotypers at *The Washington Post* stormed out of the building in response to their contract's expiry and management's demands to alter work and overtime rules. On the way out, they damaged a number of presses and assaulted a foreman. In response, management locked out most unions, airlifted printing mats to a remote printing facility, and continued to publish and distribute newspapers using supervisors, nonunion personnel, and replacement workers. After a few months, unionized printers, mailers, and a number of Newspaper Guild journalists crossed picket lines. By the end of February 1976, management was in control of production and distribution, lucrative wage and benefit packages had been scaled back, the pressmen's union had been decertified, and other unions were in disarray and weakened. In the end, the *Post* required only 184 press operators, down from 205 before the strike; overtime premiums were cut to almost zero; and only thirty striking press operators came back to work.

A similar and equally nasty conflict emerged twenty years later in Detroit when, in July 1995, six unions, representing 2,500 workers, struck the *Detroit Free Press*; *The Detroit News*; and its joint management company, the Detroit Newspaper Agency. The main issues included changes in the distribution system, which would eliminate 59 of 189 Teamster district manager jobs, and the substitution of a merit pay system for across-the-board wage increases for Guild-represented newsroom workers. Other unions struck in support of the Teamsters and Newspaper Guild. Production and distribution of the newspapers continued shortly after the strike began. Despite huge drops in circulation, however, the parent companies—Gannett (*News*) and Knight Ridder (*Free Press*)—held firm, forcing the unions to end their strike on February 14, 1997. The unions continued their battle with boycotts and legal actions. Initially, the unions appeared vindicated when, in a mixed decision in 1998, the NLRB ruled that management's unfair labor practices caused the strike and ordered the strikers reinstated. But in July 2000, a three-judge panel of the U.S. Circuit Court of Appeals in Washington reversed the Board, stating strongly that the *News* had not unilaterally imposed a merit pay system on the Guild. Instead, it contended that the Guild was not prepared to bargain seriously over the proposal (Fitzgerald 2000b).

The strike hurt all parties, perhaps irrevocably. The newspaper agency lost more than one-third of its daily circulation, $100 million, and much good will with readers. The number of employees shrunk by 766, all unions agreed to open-shop clauses and less restrictive work rules, merit pay replaced annual wage increases for Guild members at the *News*, and wage growth stalled or declined. To a large extent, management won what they had sought from the unions in 1995 (S. Greenhouse 2000).

The Detroit strike contains many of the same elements as *The Washington Post* strike. In both cases management sought to regain control over the labor process by limiting restrictive work practices that inflated labor costs; establishing plans to continue both production and distribution with the aid of technology, replacement workers, nonunion personnel, and outside firms that specialized in continuing production; dividing labor's ranks; and changing the tenor of labor relations practices to increase shareholder value. Do the similarities between the two strikes imply that little has changed in the industry's labor relations since 1976? If not, what has happened in the intervening years?

The years between these strikes—1975 to 2000—witnessed the continuing erosion of union power in the face of increased industry concentration, the rise to prominence of the intent of publicly owned newspaper/media companies on realizing and sustaining high profit margins, labor-saving technological changes, and public policies that favor public newspaper companies. Unions have, at times, made matters worse with intra- and interunion rivalries that prevented them from becoming larger, stronger, and more vibrant. Evidence of union decline can be seen in a number of different ways, including union merger activity, deunionization, labor disputes, pay-related issues, and the rise of long-term job security contracts.

Yet, despite union weakness and decline, there are some recent trends that offer the potential for a resurgence of union power. But some of these same developments—shared union jurisdiction, online union jurisdiction, and the conversion of independent contractors to union employees—also could spell further union atrophy if organized labor cannot capitalize on them.

The Unions

Three major international unions currently represent newspaper workers. The more than 600,000-member Communications Workers of America (CWA) includes more than 27,000 reporters; copyeditors; photographers; and advertising, marketing, and customer service employees of the Newspaper Guild, who work at eighty-nine U.S. dailies. In addition, the CWA includes about 30,000 printers; mailers; and related trades, formerly of the International Typographical Union (ITU), which it absorbed in 1987. Both the ITU and Guild operate as semiautonomous sectors within the CWA. The Graphic Communications International Union (GCIU) represents mainly press operators, platemakers, engravers, paperhandlers, and other noncomposing room personnel. Of the GCIU's 87,000 members, roughly 8,600 work at about seventy-three daily newspapers in the United States. The third major union, the 1.2 million-member International Brotherhood of Teamsters (IBT), represents roughly 20,000 drivers, mailroom workers, and district managers of distribution. Teamster members are found mainly at big-city newspapers, except in New York and Los Angeles (Gifford 1998; Rudder 1999).

Traditionally, the skilled crafts wielded tremendous power in newspaper plants. Without their labor, newspapers could not be produced. Moreover, without unionized drivers and their intimate knowledge of routes, newspapers could not be delivered. However, changes in production technologies have eliminated entire crafts and/or severely deskilled them. This has enabled companies to produce newspapers during strikes. Moreover, changes in readership patterns have resulted in a shift from evening editions to morning ones. This change in the production cycle has led to alterations in the distribution system away from localized "bread truck" routes, with youth carriers delivering evening papers, toward centralized distribution depots, where adult carriers—mostly nonunion independent contractors—pick up morning newspapers for delivery from large tractor trailers. The use of independent carriers, who are ineligible for union membership, has enabled companies to weaken the drivers' unions. All of these changes have enabled publishers to produce and distribute newspapers during most strikes.

The Newspaper Guild's newsroom workers have historically been more ambivalent about unionism, given their levels of education and their job-related social connections. While many Guild locals have been strong and militant, picket line crossing has been a problem at times. In addition, given the changes in computerization, companies make greater use of freelance journalists, shared resources, and wire reports, and are thus able to produce a newspaper, at least in the short term, in the event of a strike.

Industry Characteristics

The newspaper industry produces more than $59 billion worth of economic activity; employs more than 440,000 people; and is roughly the same size as petroleum and coal products, lumber and wood products, and textiles industries. It is the oldest and one of the most profitable media segments in the United States. Industry experts consider newspapers to be excellent investments, given their financial stability, strong cash flows, stable and predictable revenues and costs,[1] and general lack of competition (Picard 1998).

During the 1980s, operating profit margins averaged 17 percent and peaked at 22 percent during the middle of the decade. The average profit margin before taxes for public-company newspaper operations in 2000 was more than 22 percent. The typical profit margin for industry in general, including manufacturing, is between 8 and 9 percent (Liebeskind 1999; Morton 1999a).

Newspaper companies are somewhat unique in that they simultaneously manufacture a product (news) and provide a service (advertising) that have short life spans—twenty-four hours for daily newspapers and seven days for Sunday editions. These two markets, however, are interdependent (Picard and Brody 1997).

There were about 1,480 daily newspapers in existence in 2000, an all-time low. But between 1950 and 1980, the number of dailies held steady at about 1,750. Since then the number has dropped as a result of the closing of afternoon editions of morning papers in response to changing work and commuting habits, recessions, and a spike in newsprint prices. The percentage of evening papers has fallen from 80 percent in 1980 to 54 percent by 1997. In 2000, for the first time, the number of morning newspapers surpassed evening newspapers. At present, forty-nine of the largest fifty daily newspapers publish in the morning or all day (Asher and Roberts 2000).

Total daily circulation peaked in 1985 at 62.7 million but has declined throughout the 1990s and into 2000, when it stood at 55.7 million. Most dailies are small, averaging roughly 38,000. About 85 percent of the nation's papers have daily circulations below 50,000, while only 1 percent top 500,000. The largest papers, such as *The New York Times*, the *Los*

Angeles Times, The Wall Street Journal, and *USA Today* exceed 1 million (Picard 1998). Monopoly and its concomitant market power characterize the industry. At present there are only 29 cities that have two or more daily newspapers with separate staffs. Of these, two have the same ownership and thirteen operate as part of joint operating agreements. In the early 1920s, however, 502 cities had competing dailies. In the few places where a second daily exists, duopoly, not competition, best describes industry structure. Dailies face very limited competition in circulation, advertising, and content from suburban dailies and weeklies and shoppers (Picard and Brody 1997; Picard 1998).[2]

The domination of group or chain ownership, originating with the birth of the Scripps McRae League of Newspapers in 1890, became more significant after World War II. For example, in 1968, 159 groups owned 828 dailies, or 47 percent of the total. Consolidation began to occur in the 1980s, and by 1997, 120 groups controlled 77 percent of the dailies and 81 percent of daily circulation (see Table 1) (Lacy and Simon 1993; Picard 1998). As chains have mushroomed, the number of independent properties has fallen from 1,650 in 1920 to 300 in 1998 (Risser 1998). Many newspaper companies also own portfolios containing other media properties.

TABLE 1

Top Twenty U.S. Newspaper Companies by Circulation

	Daily circulation	Number of dailies
Gannett Co.	7,287,914	99
Knight Ridder	3,867,512	34
Tribune Co.	3,650,429	11
Advance Publications Inc.	2,903,225	27
The New York Times Co.	2,402,797	17
Dow Jones & Co.	2,356,615	20
MediaNews Group Inc.	1,772,554	46
The Hearst Corp.	1,670,970	12
The E.W. Scripps Co.	1,521,356	22
The McClatchy Co.	1,347,779	11
Cox Newspapers Inc.	1,210,255	18
Freedom Newspaper	1,127,233	29
Community Newspaper Holdings Inc.	1,055,913	115
Belo	880,162	5
Media General Inc.	879,970	25
The Washington Post Inc.	865,329	2
Morris Communications Corp.	730,873	30
Hollinger International Inc.	704,557	7
The Copley Press Inc.	683,956	7
Lee Enterprises Inc.	654,275	27

Source: Newspaper Association of America (NAA) (2001).

Overall, three trends in ownership have occurred: decline of intracity competition, increased consolidation and concentration of ownership, and geographic clustering of smaller newspapers to streamline administrative costs and provide advertisers with greater circulation than a single property can provide. These industry trends have been aided by a number of public policies.

Public Policies

Taxes

When publishers began converting to photocomposition and offset printing techniques in the early 1960s, production costs dropped and profits increased. The Internal Revenue Service subsequently raised newspaper valuations, making it nearly impossible for heirs of deceased publishers to meet their estate tax obligations. This led to the sale of 587 family-owned papers between 1960 and 1980. A subsequent change in income tax law further accelerated chain growth by encouraging owners to retain earnings to fuel additional acquisitions (which could be depreciated over time) instead of paying dividends to shareholders. Family owners could not afford to do this because of future estate tax liabilities, nor could they afford to invest in the new technology the way chains could. The combined forces of estate and gift taxes, the excess accumulation surtax, and the cost of new technology set off a selling frenzy of family-owned papers to emerging chains such as Gannett. Moreover, between 1969 and 1973, more than a dozen newspaper companies became publicly traded companies (Neiva 1996).

Tax Law Changes and Newspaper Transactions

The 1990s was the busiest decade ever for newspaper transactions. Compared with the 1980s, when 413 properties changed hands, the 1990s witnessed 856 deals. Of these, only 114, or 13.3 percent, involved independent newspapers. Instead, big groups participated in strategic acquisitions. For example, groups sold to other groups 85 percent of the time. In the two previous decades, independent newspapers sold to groups 80 percent of the time (*Presstime* 2000).

Newspaper ownership in 2000 became even more consolidated. For example, ten companies own newspapers that distribute more than 51 percent of the nation's weekday circulation. The Gannett Company, Knight Ridder, and the Tribune Company claim 25 percent of newspaper circulation in the country. Other forces driving ownership consolidation include the relaxation of rules for cross-ownership of different media, the U.S. Justice Department's recent approvals of sales of suburban newspapers to major metros, and the sale of family-owned groups to public companies (Asher 2001; Kunkel and Roberts 2001).

Tax Law Changes and Geographic Clustering

Underlying newspaper transactions during the 1990s was the strategy of geographic clustering. Clustering involves the geographic concentration of newspaper functions to share resources among newspapers under the same ownership in order to reduce operating costs, including head count, consolidate administrative functions such as accounting for employee benefits, and improve advertising revenues by offering large retailers a regional buy and higher circulation (Morton 1997a). Clusters also are used as a defensive strategy against competition from other media, including weekly newspapers. Clusters of smaller suburban properties also may compete with metro newspapers (Lallande 2001). The use of satellite and other technologies to transmit production matter has made this business strategy possible.

In 1990, only 17 percent of all dailies were part of clusters; by late 2000, 35 percent were. In 2001, there were roughly 125 clusters containing more than 400 properties. The impact of clusters is greater in terms of circulation; in 1990 clustered properties distributed 5.6 million daily papers, but by 2000 that number jumped to 9.7 million (Bass 1999; Lallande 2001). Newspaper financial analyst John Morton describes the recent phenomenon of chains swallowing chains as "an industry approaching the final stages of ownership concentration, a process that came late to the newspaper industry . . ." (Morton 1997b:52).

Workers and unions may not be better off within clusters. For example, Singleton's purchase of the *Long Beach Press-Telegram* and Knight Ridder's acquisition of Scripps Howard's *Monterey County Herald* illustrate some of the labor implications from clustering. In 1997, Singleton purchased the struggling *Press-Telegram* in an asset sale. Asset sales reduce taxes and allow the new owner to void existing labor agreements under certain conditions. For example, the company has to recognize the union if the old contract contains a "successor clause" but *only* if 51 percent of the union's members are rehired. And then, a new contract has to be negotiated from scratch, which is what happened in Long Beach. Singleton cut the salaries of most editorial employees by 20 percent, almost to parity with his larger (Los Angeles) *Daily News*. There, however, Singleton promised no firings, while more than 200 noneditorial jobs were slashed at the *Press-Telegram*. One year later, more than half of the paper's editorial staff had left. Three years after the sale, the Guild and the *Press-Telegram* finally agreed to a three-year contract (Neuwirth 1997).

A similar outcome occurred in 1997 when Knight Ridder added the small *Monterey County Herald* to its cluster of six other dailies in the Bay Area, including the *San Jose Mercury News*. A few days after announcing the deal, Knight Ridder set aside all union contracts as a condition of the asset sale. The company fired its entire staff, including 160 Guild members. All were invited to reapply for their jobs at the same base pay but without the old benefits, night differentials, and job security protections. Roughly 90 percent of those who reapplied were rehired, while twenty-four voluntarily left the newspaper.

In response, the unions took successful strike votes, began a community support campaign, and filed unfair labor practice charges against Knight Ridder. One complaint asserted that when Knight Ridder acquired the nonunion *San Luis Obispo Telegram-Tribune*, it did not make workers reapply for their jobs. In April 1998, the NLRB ruled in favor of Knight Ridder, supporting its right to set new terms of employment because its motivations were economic not discriminatory when it reduced compensation for *Herald* employees and left untouched wages and benefits at the *Telegram-Tribune*, which had much lower labor costs (Goetz 1997; *Labor & Employment Law Letter* [*L&ELL*] 1998). No contract has yet been reached in Monterey.

Even without asset sales, clustering can cause invidious wage comparisons between richer union contracts and nonunion pay packages and work rules. This can be seen in Wisconsin, where the Thomson chain has amassed a cluster near Sheboygan. Unionized editorial workers in Sheboygan with five years' experience earned $717 per week, or $37,284 per annum, while nonunion workers in Oshkosh, a paper with similar circulation, made $28,000 per year. The pay gap has made labor relations more difficult since Thomson took over (Bass 1999).

Joint Operating Agreements

Public policy also has contributed to the decline of competition with the passage of the Newspaper Preservation Act in 1970. The Act provides for antitrust exemptions to newspapers that participate in joint agreements. The law's intent, according to its sponsors, was to maintain "a newspaper press editorially and reportorially independent and competitive in all parts of the United States." (quoted in Farhi 1999:50). Thus, covered newspapers must maintain separate editorial staffs as part of the joint operating agreements (JOAs).

Under a JOA, most operations, such as printing, advertising, and distribution, are combined. The firms do not merge; instead, they either contract for services from each other or form a separate, jointly owned company. JOAs have been found to engage in price fixing, profit pooling, and market allocation (Busterna and Picard 1993). A number of JOAs provide for the split of profits between 50 and 100 years, even if the weaker paper closes. Some publishers have chosen to shut down a JOA paper in the interest of profits (for example, see the case of Advance Publications, Inc. in Miller 2000).

At the peak, there were twenty-eight cities with JOAs. Seven JOAs formed between the mid-1970s and 1990. In 2000, *The Rocky Mountain News* and *The Denver Post* formed the first new JOA in a decade. However, joint agreements in San Francisco and Honolulu ended after recent changes in ownership. At present only twelve JOAs remain, with a few more likely to be terminated in a few years (Moses 1999; Fitzgerald 2000a). Most JOAs dissolve because of a downward "circulation spiral" as one paper gets a circulation lead and attracts more advertisers to it (Lacy and Simon 1993). The trailing paper gets caught in a cycle of declining ads and circulation until it closes. In general, JOAs appear to delay the inevitable demise of the weaker newspaper. However, the death of a JOA does not eliminate competition. Instead, metro dailies now compete with community weeklies (Moses 1999).

Laws and tax codes favorable to public newspaper companies have created an industry structure virtually free of direct competition. At times the companies that manage JOAs have tried to use their market power to exact concessions from unions, forcing strikes in Pittsburgh (1992), San Francisco (1994), and Detroit (1995). Despite previous protests, six unions, representing 3,000 members and operating as the Denver Council of Newspaper Unions, assisted the Denver newspapers in ensuring JOA status. The Guild, the largest of the unions with 1,400 members at both papers, supported the JOA because the newspapers satisfied the union's desire for separate editorial voices. The union also won the guarantee that, should the JOA end, both papers would continue publishing. In the seven-year deals, the unions also received no layoff pledges for two years and additional job security measures for seven years (Bureau of National Affairs [BNA] 2000).

Technological Changes

Economists Dertouzos and Quinn note: "Since the early 1960s, [the newspaper] industry has been swept by a technological revolution that has dramatically reduced production costs by reducing the amount of labor required to compose a newspaper" (1985:v). This "cold type" revolution displaced "hot type," as computerization replaced mechanical typesetting machines. Combined with offset printing techniques, which replaced letterpresses during the 1970s and 1980s, cold type has yielded much greater output, with far fewer employees and less maintenance than hot type (Dertouzos and Quinn 1985). It has also wrought skill degradation and homogenization among the crafts. In general, skill requirements have converged around the less skilled mailers (Kalleberg et al. 1987).

Cold type diffused rapidly throughout the industry between the mid-1970s and early 1980s. In 1970, for example, more than 10,000 hot metal line casters (mostly Linotypes) were used in American Newspaper Publishers Association plants. In 1982, only 194 were in use, while 46,000 video display terminals (VDTs) were employed. By contrast, only 23 VDTs were in operation in 1970. By 1983, 99 percent of the sampled firms in one study used photocomposition, while 92 percent of the editorial departments used VDTs. (Dertouzos and Quinn 1985). At present, workstations linked to networks are quickly replacing VDTs (Picard and Brody 1997).

The microelectronic revolution, including the use of satellite, telephone, and microwave links to transmit print matter, also has altered spatial relations between departments. The new technology has allowed companies to separate production departments from editorial ones. *The Wall Street Journal* was the first newspaper to do this in 1968. Other newspapers have followed this pattern since then (Picard and Brody 1997; Sleigh 1998). Advanced telecommunications networks also have made online newspapers and geographic clustering possible.

Industry concentration and consolidation, made possible by public policies favorable to publishers, combined with technological changes, has shifted collective bargaining power from the unions to the publishers. This dramatic shift may be seen by a number of outcomes discussed below.

Major Developments and Bargaining Outcomes

De-Unionization

Total newspaper employment grew between 1975 and 2000, from 376,800 to 445,000. In between, however, employment fluctuated. After peaking in 1991 at 485,900, industry employment fell through 1997, when it began to rise again (Newspaper Association of America [NAA] 2001). Newsroom employment, however, has risen by 28 percent between 1978 and 1998, from 43,000 to 54,700, according to the American Society of Newspaper Editors (Terry 1998). In both cases, net employment growth underlies turmoil in production areas, newsrooms, and distribution. For example, technological changes have reduced production labor requirements since the 1970s. A sample of 493 composing rooms revealed a drop in employment, from about 14,500 to roughly 6,900, between 1970 and 1983. As the major union representing these workers, the ITU has also suffered. Between 1970 and 1982, total ITU membership fell from 105,300 to 77,100, a decline of 27 percent. Total active membership fell by 40 percent and the number of apprentices by 27 percent (Dertouzos and Quinn 1985).

In newsrooms, recessions, mergers and closures, and a spike in newsprint prices led to downsizing twice during the 1990s and again during 2000. In response to shrinking profit margins, more than forty newspapers announced layoffs and permanent dismissals affecting more than 1,000 employees during the early 1990s (Chang 1993). Layoffs, early retirements, buyouts, and hiring freezes were again used in 1994 and 1995 when newsprint prices spiked. In 2000, widespread layoffs, buyouts, and other newsroom cuts occurred in response to weakening advertising revenues, rising newsprint prices, and the quest for higher profit margins (Wenner 2000).

The U.S. Census Bureau's Current Population Survey (CPS)—Outgoing Rotation Group data reveal that, after peaking at 20 percent in 1978, union density rates in newspapers dropped to 13.6 percent in 1985 and to 13.0 percent in 1990. By 2000, density rates fell to 9.9 percent (see Table 2). In comparison, density rates for private-sector manufacturing fell by 59 percent between 1975 and 2000. This drop is much greater than for the newspaper industry, but sampling problems limit definitive conclusions. The widespread use of lifetime job security agreements in the newspaper industry may have mitigated the effects of de-unionization.

Currently, the NAA reports that unions operate at roughly 21 percent of the 1,669 member papers in North America (including Canada) and at 72 of the 106 (68 percent) North American papers with circulation exceeding 100,000 (Burroughs 1998). In general, unions are found in larger, big-city papers. For example, the Newspaper Guild still represents workers at 41 of the nation's largest 100 newspapers (Dotinga 1998b), while the Teamsters can be found in just about all of the major dailies.

TABLE 2

Union Density, 1975–2000

Newspapers Versus Private-Sector Manufacturing

	Newspapers		Private-sector manufacturing	
Years	Membership (%)	Coverage (%)	Membership (%)	Coverage (%)
1975	17.80	NA	36.00	NA
1976	17.40	NA	35.60	NA
1977	17.60	NA	35.50	37.60
1978	20.00	NA	34.20	36.70
1979	19.70	NA	35.40	38.20
1980	19.20	NA	32.30	34.80
1981[a]	NA	NA	31.30	33.80
1982[b]	NA	NA	NA	NA
1983	17.70	21.40	27.80	30.50
1984	14.40	16.10	26.00	28.40
1985	13.60	14.90	24.80	26.90
1986	14.10	15.80	24.00	25.80
1987	16.30	18.20	23.20	24.70
1988	12.80	14.80	22.10	23.80
1989	13.20	14.30	21.60	23.10
1990	13.00	14.50	20.60	22.20
1991	14.20	15.20	20.30	21.80
1992	13.40	15.60	19.70	21.10
1993	12.70	13.90	19.20	20.30
1994	15.10	17.30	18.20	19.60
1995	8.90	10.20	17.60	18.70
1996	10.40	11.10	17.20	18.30
1997	10.80	11.70	16.30	17.20
1998	13.10	15.10	15.80	16.80
1999	12.40	14.00	15.60	16.60
2000	9.90	10.20	14.80	15.60

Sources: Kokkelenberg and Sockell (1985) provide three-year averages for data for the years 1975 to 1980. Data for the years 1983 to 2000 are from Hirsch and Macpherson (1993–2000).
[a] Three-year moving averages from 1975 to 1980 make no data available.
[b] No union information available.

Unit decertification and limited organizing efforts also have contributed to declining density rates. Newspaper decertifications became more commonplace after 1970, as in other industries, but had their own distinctive catalysts. For example, technological change, "sensitive" employee relations policies, and internal union dissent have been noted (Newsom 1988). Industry data suggest other causes of decertifications: the loss of majority support for representation, unions disclaiming interest in representation, department shutdowns, and changes in union affiliation (L&ELL 1981–2000).

Over the past two decades, newspaper union win rates are similar to those from a national data set (49 percent), but decertification loss rates are slightly higher (80 percent versus roughly 70 to 75 percent nationally). For all industries, and in newspapers, the peak year for decertification elections occurred in 1983. Moreover, election activity has declined since the early 1980s in the national data set but since 1990 in newspapers. When all newspaper representation proceedings are considered since 1990, the percentage of union victories averaged about only 23 percent and ranged from zero percent in 1992 to 36 percent in 1994 (Jelf and Dworkin 1997; L&ELL 1981–2000). The organization of 326 workers by the Milwaukee Newspaper Guild in 1984 was the largest successful organizing drive since 1952, when the Guild organized 400 commercial department employees at Baltimore's *Sun* newspapers (BNA 1984).

All of the major unions have had multiple units decertified at small and large papers alike. After fending off decertification attempts in 1995 at the *Cincinnati Enquirer* and at the *Detroit Free Press* in 1998, the Guild lost a large unit in 1998 at the *San Diego Union-Tribune*, then the nation's twenty-first largest paper and the Guild's tenth largest unit. It was its biggest loss since 1970 and one of five newsroom decertifications in the 1990s (Dotinga 1998a). There are only two units left at the *San Diego Union-Tribune* since three other units have been decertified since 1994. The pressmen have been without a contract since 1992 and the Teamsters since 1993. Before the Guild was voted out, it had been without a contract since 1994, owing to conflict over management's desire to replace annual wage changes with merit pay. Having represented workers at the paper for more than sixty years, the Guild faced a month-long campaign by the company to sway employees to vote out the union. According to the union, the company took workers to dinner at expensive restaurants, held hotel and country club affairs, promised improvements in the retirement plan, and allowed workers to gather decertification petition signatures on company time (BNA 1998).

Since the mid-1980s, the former ITU lost major units in Cleveland, Columbus, Houston, San Antonio, San Diego, and Dallas, among others, many to the Teamsters. The GCIU lost units in Rochester, New York; Los Angeles; Houston; and Syracuse, to name a few. At the *Fort Lauderdale News and Sun Sentinel*, workers have voted out five units since 1981 (L&ELL 1981–2000).

Union Mergers

The combination of increased corporate power, an unfavorable legal and political climate, and technological changes led newspaper unions to undertake seven mergers between 1964 and 1997 (see Table 3). Moreover, all the major unions were also involved in a number of merger attempts that in the end failed. For example, between 1977 and 1987, the ITU attempted five mergers with all the major newspaper unions before agreeing to be absorbed by the CWA. Enough bitter feelings grew out of merger proceedings to keep workers divided by craft loyalty and prevent additional mergers. Even among unions, merger negotiations led to intense political battles. The ITU's attempt at finding a viable merger partner is an example.

Between 1977 and 1981, the ITU and the Newspaper Guild engaged in merger talks. However, the unions disagreed over dues and local autonomy, and Guild members feared their interests would be neglected once absorbed into the larger ITU. After talks collapsed in 1981, they resumed in 1982 until both unions held referenda votes in 1983. ITU members voted to reject the Guild and explore the GCIU as a partner. In the meantime, the Teamsters had designs on the ITU to gain a foothold in organizing the printing industry. However, the AFL-CIO sought to create a single printing union, and at the time, the Teamsters were not part of the AFL-CIO.

The 1983 ITU presidential elections resulted in a contested election. A rerun election was held in 1984. In the meantime, talks between the ITU and the GCIU broke down, leading the ITU's merger committee to continue negotiations with the Teamsters. The AFL-CIO ran a strong campaign opposing the merger. In a repeat election, anti-Teamster Robert McMichen defeated pro-Teamster Joseph Bingel. McMichen supporters also won control of the executive board. McMichen quickly renewed merger talks with the GCIU.

In March 1985, however, faced with poor financial projections related to the ITU's shrinking membership base, the GCIU's officers rejected the merger proposal. The Teamsters then renewed its campaign for the ITU, but in April 1985, the ITU's membership rejected the Teamsters. Finally, in 1986, the ITU agreed to be absorbed by the CWA. The ITU became the semiautonomous Printing, Publishing and Media Workers sector within the CWA (Chaison 1996).

Bitter feelings by the Teamsters led it to conduct nineteen successful raids of ITU mailer units between July 1986 and March 1987, adding about 3,000 members to Teamster ranks (*Presstime* 1987). In addition, when ITU members struck the *Chicago Tribune* in 1985, Teamsters crossed their picket lines in retaliation for not voting for the merger, thus contributing to a major union defeat (Chaison 1996).[3]

TABLE 3

Union Mergers: Printing and Publishing, 1964–1997

Year of merger	Unions involved	Membership at merger	New union
1964	International Photoengravers Union; Amalgamated Lithographers of America	IPU (17,000) + ALA (39,000) = 56,000	Lithographers and Photoengravers International Union (LPIU)
1972	International Brotherhood of Bookbinders; Lithographers and Photoengravers International Union	IBB (62,500) + LPIU (60,000) = 122,500	Graphic Arts International Union (GAIU)
1973	International Printing Pressmen and Assistants Union of North America; International Stereotypers', Electrotypers' and Platemakers' Union	IPPAU (127,900) + ISEPU (8,800) = 136,700	International Printing and Graphic Communications Union (IPGCU)
1979	International Typographical Union; International Mailers Union	ITU (81,300) + IMU (3,100) = 84,400	IMU absorbed by International Typographical Union (ITU)
1983	International Printing and Graphic Communications Union; Graphic Arts International Union	IPGCU (112,000) + GAIU (82,500) = 194,500	Graphic Communications International Union (GCIU)
1987	International Typographical Union; Communications Workers of America	ITU (40,000) + CWA (515,000) = 555,000	ITU absorbed by CWA
1997[a]	The Newspaper Guild; Communications Workers of America	TNG (22,000) + CWA (480,000) = 502,000	TNG absorbed by CWA

Sources: Dewey (1971); Janus (1978); Adams (1984); Williamson (1995); Gifford (1998)

[a] Guild members agreed to a merger at a 1995 referendum. The merger was finalized at TNG's June convention (*Daily Labor Report*, 6/19/97, 6/23/97).

Overall, incomplete union mergers and strained interunion relations have helped maintain outdated narrow, decentralized bargaining structures in an industry that has become more centralized and dominated by powerful media companies. The AFL-CIO's plan for one media union has yet to be realized. The following bargaining outcomes show how power relations have shifted since the mid-1970s.

Labor Disputes

Strike activity across industries has declined precipitously since 1980, according to the Bureau of Labor Statistics (www.bls.gov). Labor dispute trends in the newspaper industry have followed these larger strike patterns. After reaching a peak of thirty in 1978, newspaper strikes have become increasingly rare. NAA data indicate that between 1970 and 1978, on average twenty-five strikes occurred per year. The ten strikes of 1979 were the fewest recorded since 1961, while the two in 1983, both lasting one day, matched 1943's total. Moreover, the absence of strikes in 1986 had never before occurred since the trade association began collecting data in the 1930s. For the remainder of the 1980s, workers struck once a year. In 1995 two long-term strikes began in Detroit and Ellwood City, Pennsylvania (*Presstime* 1980–1990; *L&ELL* 1997). Not until 2000 did another newspaper strike occur.

On November 21, 2000, employees struck JOA papers in Seattle—the *Seattle Post-Intelligencer* and *The Seattle Times*—over wages, pensions, and health benefits. The Guild and its 900 news, advertising, and circulation employees at the *Times* and some 130 news and business department employees at the *Post-Intelligencer* had been without a contract since July 2000. Despite attempts at mediation, workers struck for the first time at the *Times* since 1953 and since 1936 at the *Post-Intelligencer*. Unable to prevent the papers from publishing and distributing newspapers and with some 25 percent of Guild members crossing picket lines, workers at the *Post-Intelligencer* ended their strike thirty-eight days after it had begun. Guild workers at the *Times* continued striking for another eleven days. In the end, the Guild signed a six-year contract that included wage changes initially offered by the companies before the strike began. It also failed to end the merit pay scheme in effect since 1987.

However, the union secured gains in pension contributions and health insurance, the elimination of a two-tier wage scale for suburban reporters after three years, and salary upgrades for lower-paid circulation employees. It also maintained an agreement that 90 percent of all new hires be required to join the union. The economics of the *Times*' contract was identical to the *Post-Intelligencer*'s. The parties also worked out a deal for the gradual removal of most replacement workers at the *Times* (the *Post-Intelligencer* did not use replacements) and a joint effort to regrow circulation that had suffered from union-sponsored boycotts. Circulation decline led the *Times* to announce 10 percent staff cuts in the strike's wake (*L&ELL* 2001).

Since *The Washington Post* strike in 1975–76, unions have been able to impede only production (Philadelphia in 1985) or distribution, such as in New York City (1990–91), Pittsburgh (1992), and San Francisco (1994). In most of these cases, unionized drivers prevailed by preventing the companies from establishing viable alternative delivery systems. In Chicago in 1985 union drivers crossed compositors' picket lines, effectively ending any chance of a union victory. Even strong union solidarity, as evidenced in major strikes at Wilkes-Barre, Pennsylvania, in 1978 and in 1995 in Detroit, has not been able to overcome the powerful combination of management resistance, union-busting law firms, permanent replacement workers, unfavorable labor laws, and new technologies. Industry expert John Morton explains union weakness in the following way:

> Union power at newspapers began to wane . . . as the computer-driven revolution in newspaper technology swept through the industry in the 1970s and 1980s. . . . The bitter truth for the strikers is that they have been replaced by fewer workers than even management had thought possible, replaced by technology and by a decisive shift in the balance of power. (1996:51, 56)

Writing on the 1978 Wilkes-Barre strike against Capital Cities (one of the earliest media conglomerates and one of the first companies to take an aggressive stand against unions at its newspapers), Thomas Keil (1988) contends that antiquated bargaining structures also have been detrimental to unions. He keenly observes that newspaper unions developed at a time when local families owned the vast majority of newspapers. The narrow, decentralized bargaining structure covering many separate trades has become grossly outmoded in the face of media conglomerates and newspaper chains. When companies can shift human and capital resources at will, suffer big circulation declines, and continue to realize sufficient corporate profits to appease shareholders, unions stand little chance of winning strikes or favorable contracts.

Media economist Robert Picard places recent strikes at the (New York) *Daily News* and in Pittsburgh, San Francisco, and Detroit in a larger historical context: "In all . . . cases, the unions struck to hang on to labor-friendly contract terms that management had agreed to a few decades before, at the time of the second phase of strikes" (cited in Peterson 1997:D9). (The first wave occurred during the big organizing drive of the 1930s.) The second wave occurred during the 1950s and 1960s, when new technology slowly began entering composing and mailrooms. In that era, when many families owned newspapers, labor peace was traded for job security provisions.

By the 1970s, management sought to eliminate costly "featherbedding" practices that had originated in the 1950s under a different set of economic conditions, at a time when unions had the power to shut down newspapers with strikes. For example, pressroom contracts specified "mandated" positions that exceeded those needed to run the presses; printers' contracts required printers to reset type that had already been processed by Linotypes. This "bogus" work often represented the difference between machine-set and hand-set type. Mailroom contracts set a fixed distance between bundles of newspapers coming off the press line on conveyor belts, even though the gaps could be closed; and some distribution workers received a full day's pay even if their job required just a few hours of work. Often, labor agreements also called for mandatory overtime, exacerbating labor costs (Morton 1996).

Pay-Related Issues

The decline of union bargaining power also can be observed through pay-related outcomes. Data from the Bureau of Labor Statistics' establishment wage surveys and the Guild provide the best gauges. Table 4 reveals that between 1976 and 2000, average nominal wages for newspaper production workers rose from $6.14 per hour to $13.81, a gain of 125 percent. Real wages (in 2000 dollars), however, fell over the same period from $18.58 to $13.81, a decline of 25.7 percent. In comparison, the average manufacturing wage rose from $5.22 to $14.71, or 182 percent, but real wages fell by only 6.8 percent. The average American worker's real wage fell 13.8 percent between 1976 and 1996 (U.S. Department of Labor 1998). Looked at another way, the ratio of the average newspaper production worker's wage to that of the average manufacturing worker fell from 1.17 in 1976, to 1.02 in 1991, to .94 by 2000, a relative decline of 20 percent since 1976. Aside from reduced bargaining power, two-tier wage plans have slowed the growth of newspaper production workers' wages.

Guild-represented workers' wage changes since 1977 (the first year for which data are available) can be evaluated similarly. Guild wages

TABLE 4

Production Worker Hourly Wages, 1976–2000

Newspaper and Manufacturing

Year	Newspaper hourly wage ($)	Newspaper real hourly wage ($)[a]	Avg. mfg. worker hourly wage ($)	Avg. mfg. worker real hourly wage ($)[a]	Ratio of newspaper to avg. mfg. real hourly wage
1976	6.14	18.58	5.22	15.79	1.17
1981	8.35	15.82	7.99	15.14	1.05
1986	10.05	15.79	9.73	15.29	1.03
1991	11.36	14.36	11.18	14.14	1.02
1996	12.52	13.81	12.78	14.03	0.98
2000	13.81	13.81	14.71	14.71	0.94

Source: U.S. Department of Labor, Employment, Hours, and Earnings (2000).
[a] In 2000 dollars; CPI-U 1982–84 = 100.

(average top minimum weekly wages) exclude merit and incentive pay. While nominal wages have grown 141 percent, from $329.72 in 1977 to $796.17 by 2000, real wages (in 2000 dollars) fell 15 percent (Newspaper Guild, various years) (see Table 5). In sum, Guild members have fared better than newspaper production workers, but both have fallen behind both the average production and American worker.

With unions on the defensive, some newspaper companies have attempted to reduce pay growth by implementing merit pay plans, especially in newsrooms.[4] This phenomenon began in the mid-1980s and was part of a larger trend across industries. Former journalist and industry critic Doug Underwood (1998) argues that the rise of the public newspaper company, with its emphasis on marketing and the bottom line, has led management to introduce new performance systems that seek to codify newsroom productivity quantitatively under a factory model of production. More employees are being covered by incentive plans across occupations and job levels in order to contain payroll costs that range between 26 and 47 percent of total costs. No data exist that measure the extent of these changes, however (Burroughs 1998). Merit pay also may be seen as a way for management to exert control over the workforce.

Since its birth in 1933, the Newspaper Guild has had a history of negotiating minimum "livable" salaries, with additional merit pay for members to be negotiated on top. It supports the concept of merit pay but only if wage scales keep up with productivity and price changes, and with the caveat that merit pay not be used to selectively reward a chosen

TABLE 5

Newspaper Guild Average Weekly Top Reporter Minimums, 1977–2000

Average top reporter minimum earnings	Nominal ($)	Real wages ($)[a]	CPI-U 1982–84 = 100
April 1, 1977	329.72	829.20	60.60
April 1, 1978	351.23	820.97	65.20
April 1, 1979	373.25	783.52	72.60
April 1, 1980	396.38	733.11	82.40
April 1, 1981	432.33	724.83	90.90
April 1, 1982	461.36	728.61	96.50
April 1, 1983	492.05	752.90	99.60
April 1, 1984	519.98	762.70	103.90
April 1, 1985	547.66	775.68	107.60
April 1, 1986	567.44	789.03	109.60
April 1, 1987	585.70	785.75	113.60
April 1, 1988	608.32	783.67	118.30
April 1, 1989	628.10	771.96	124.00
April 1, 1990	645.96	753.21	130.70
April 1, 1991	678.47	759.17	136.20
April 1, 1992	690.06	749.57	140.30
April 1, 1993	703.44	741.90	144.50
June 1, 1994	714.53	734.78	148.20
June 1, 1995	713.73	713.73	152.40
December 1, 1996	741.02	719.77	156.90
April 1, 1997	745.73	708.10	160.50
April 1, 1998	783.98	733.00	163.00
April 1, 1999	791.03	723.61	166.60
April 1, 2000	796.17	704.62	172.20

Sources: Newspaper Guild; *The Guild Reporter* (various years); CPI data from Bureau of Labor Statistics.
[a] In 2000 dollars.

few while bargaining unit wages erode. Further, it adamantly opposes merit pay discrimination against women, minorities, and union activists (Newspaper Guild 1997, 1998).

Merit pay has become a highly contentious bargaining issue at many newspapers. Moreover, the courts have heard a number of cases, most involving disputes that originated in the 1980s. The most significant case involved two California papers owned by McClatchy—*The Sacramento Bee* and *The Modesto Bee*—and the Northern California Newspaper Guild Local 52. In 1986, the company sought to eliminate all across-the-board wage adjustments once workers reached top scale, in favor of a management-controlled merit pay plan not subject to grievance arbitration. After thirteen months of fruitless negotiations, McClatchy implemented its final offer at impasse, and the union voted down McClatchy's final offer, 163–0. The NLRB heard the case twice, before the D. C. Appeals court decided the case in December 1997. After consolidating the cases into one, it decided against the company, ruling that there were limits to a company's ability to implement its final offer at impasse. Siding with the Board the second time around, the court found McClatchy in violation of the law since the union lacked information necessary to meaningfully challenge the plan in later bargaining sessions. In short, the plan was too discretionary.

The McClatchy "exception" to posting conditions at impasse was at issue in Detroit. On July 7, 2000, the U.S. Court of Appeals for the D.C. Circuit reversed the Board's decision that the twenty-month Detroit strike between 1995 and 1997 was an unfair labor practice strike. Had the court upheld the Board, the unions would have won a major victory. Instead, the court agreed with *The Detroit News* that it had outlined specific parameters during negotiations with the Guild, including a 1 percent annual increase for everyone and average maximum payouts. Merit was tied to a detailed evaluation system. The Guild, the court opined, made no counteroffers and opposed the concept of merit pay outright (Terry 2000:63).

Given the industry's intent on increasing the significance of merit raises and guidelines set in *McClatchy*, we can expect difficult negotiations over merit raises in the future. Faced with the drop in union membership, the inability to strike, corporate downsizing, and downward wage pressures, job security has become more important since the 1970s.

The Rise of Long-Term Job Security Contracts

The implementation of new computerized production processes during the 1960s and 1970s led management to seek concessions from unions in work processes and work rules. In return, often following strikes, production unions, mainly the ITU, got lifetime job guarantees, opportunities for retraining, and early retirement incentives as part of long-term agreements.

The New York City ITU led the way in 1974, when it signed an eleven-year deal with *The New York Times* and the (New York) *Daily News*. The newspapers won the unlimited right to introduce automated typesetting procedures, the contract ended manning provisions on equipment and placed limits on transfers and assignments, and the ITU agreed to end the practice of "bogus" work—the resetting of advertising set by outside shops (*Monthly Labor Review* 1974). In return, 1,400 "regular" and 385 "substitute" printers were given lifetime job security. Similar long-term contracts followed in Minneapolis (1975), Dayton (1976), Buffalo (1977), and Baltimore (1980) (BNA 1980). By 1980, the ITU reported that 13 percent of its 980 contracts contained some form of absolute job guarantee (Newsom 1981).

Subsequent long-term deals have been concluded that involve other craft unions.[5] Still, not all contracts are alike, as cases from Minneapolis; Washington, DC; and Cleveland illustrate. The "Minneapolis Concept," as it became known, originated in 1975 and involved a number of unions in the implementation of new technology. To deal with overstaffing, Cowles Media, owner of the *Star* and *Tribune*,[6] two separate papers until 1987, reduced the workforce through attrition and retirement incentives. The ITU was the first union to sign a long-term deal. Other production unions entered into extended contracts in subsequent years.

The ten-year ITU contract signed in 1975 provided lifetime jobs for 389 regular printers and future job opportunities for 42 substitutes. Management gained complete control over the implementation of all new technologies but agreed to a "plant pattern" for determining wages over the ten years, such that, when one unit negotiated a wage increase, all units received that amount. In addition to offering termination incentives, Cowles started a publishing company, Tri-Star Graphic, to employ redundant printers. The company lasted until 1984, when it closed after losing $1 million. When Cowles opened a state-of-the art production facility during the late 1980s, it continued its cooperative labor relations approach with its unions, involving its unions in decision making. The *Star Tribune's* humane approach to the use of new technology and the role of unions can be contrasted with the Tribune Company, which attacked its unions in Chicago in 1985 prior to opening its modern production facility, Freedom Center (Sleigh 1998).

In contrast to the friendly but stern approach to labor relations in Minneapolis, the Washington Post Company took advantage of its bargaining power to radically alter labor relations traditions between it and a former ITU local at its flagship *Washington Post* newspaper in 1991. As was typical of these deals, the ten-year contract gave union printers job security in exchange for absolute management control over the implementation of new technology. It also offered $75,000 buyouts to twenty-four printers, reducing employment to 210, from about 800 in

1974. However, union concessions ran deeper in Washington. For example, management won total control over hiring; established a tiered pay scale and merit pay; deleted all remaining ITU general laws, including the rule that all foremen be union members; and, for the first time, subjected compositors to progressive discipline. Most of these union controls hark back to the nineteenth century and were vestiges of the closed-shop era (Gersh 1991).

In 1996, an "historic" and "unprecedented" ten-year contract went into effect between *The* (Cleveland) *Plain Dealer* and ten separate units. The 900 affected workers overwhelmingly ratified the agreements by a 94 percent vote. These contracts are noteworthy because they involved long-term contracts for ten *separate* unions, all of which agreed not to strike nor seek arbitration over wages when the scheduled raises end after six years. A Cleveland Teamsters official called his contract "a first class contract for the best newspaper workers in America," (Fitzgerald 1996a:15) while the newspaper's publisher hailed the ten agreements as "eloquent testimony to the mutually respectful and mature relationships" (Fitzgerald 1996a:53) between labor and management. These contracts represent a middle ground between the friendly approach taken by Cowles and the more aggressive stance taken by the Washington Post Company. In the context of the ongoing conflict in Detroit and in the aftermath of the closing of the *Cleveland Press* in 1982, the deals made sense to union members and management alike (Fitzgerald 1996b:4).[7]

Lifetime job security contract language has enabled the former ITU to preserve a shrinking pool of jobs for those with high seniority. The union recognizes it is a dying institution but continues to protect its more senior members. However, since the early 1980s, there have been seven court cases that have questioned the legality of lifetime contracts. Most of them involved fundamental business changes and management's desire to end contracts often signed by previous ownership. A few of these cases advanced to the U.S. Supreme Court.

The first major case occurred at *The Cincinnati Post*, when 100 ITU printers filed suit in December 1977, after management informed them that they would no longer have jobs when the paper entered into a JOA with *The Cincinnati Enquirer*, which would produce the newspaper. However, in 1974, E. W. Scripps, the *Post*'s owner, had signed an automation pact with the Cincinnati Typographical Union No. 3, granting composing room workers lifetime jobs. Yet, one month after the JOA went into effect in 1979, Scripps closed down its composing room and fired its printers. The U.S. Court of Appeals for the Sixth Circuit ruled that Scripps had violated the 1974 contract. Had the *Post* closed permanently, the company might have won. The U.S. Supreme Court refused to hear the case on appeal (BNA 1982).

Other cases followed the *Post* case in Toledo; Cleveland; Roanoke; Sacramento; and Escanaba, Michigan.[8] The most recent major court case involved the (New York) *Daily News* and the former ITU Local 6 in 1992. The dispute dealt with a change in ownership and the bankruptcy status of the paper. The Appeals Court for the Second Circuit, overruling the district court, decided in December 1992 that the federal bankruptcy judge did not err when she canceled the union's lifetime contract with the *Daily News*. This was a necessary precondition to allow Mortimer Zuckerman to purchase the ailing paper from the deceased previous owner, Robert Maxwell (BNA 1992). The irony of this case was that the printers' union crossed picket lines a year earlier to honor its lifetime contract when drivers and other units struck the newspaper.

Overall, these court cases illustrate that, in a dynamic industry such as newspapers, lifetime contracts may be illusory under certain conditions. It appears that so long as the newspaper continues to publish and is not in bankruptcy proceedings, jobs will be protected. Short of strikes and legal proceedings, management will continue to make use of termination incentives and attrition to further reduce their workforces.

Despite the preservation of union jobs in outmoded crafts, these arrangements have not spurred new union growth areas. Instead, they have slowed the inevitable decimation of certain trades and certain production departments, notably compositors, owing to technological and work rule changes.

Summary, Emerging Issues, and the Future of Newspaper Unions

Since the 1970s, the combined forces of technological change, federal tax policies, the profit-seeking behavior of public newspaper companies, and internal union problems have dramatically shifted the balance of power in the newspaper industry toward employers and away from unions. In 2001, these same factors remain important. Yet, new issues have emerged during the mid-1990s that may possibly spark a union revival. Among the most relevant issues are shared union jurisdiction, online union jurisdiction, and the conversion of "stringers" (part-time journalists) to employees and union members . These issues have all arisen from the continuing advance of technology or, in the case of stringers, from changes in public policy.

Shared Jurisdiction

Beginning with the automation pacts during the 1970s, innovative arrangements have continued to be worked out by labor and management. In all cases, new technology had blurred traditional union jurisdictions and made traditional craft rules anachronistic. To maximize work process efficiency and preserve labor peace, shared jurisdiction agreements have developed since 1994 at a handful of newspapers.

In most cases, workers become crosstrained in one or more additional skill sets, are required to work across skill areas as needed, and are paid equal wages. For example, at the *Minneapolis Star Tribune*, a new digital imaging center, designed to streamline the flow of photo preparation, is jointly staffed by members of Guild Local 2 and the GCIU Local 229. At *The Denver Rocky Mountain News*, the *Toledo Blade*, and *The Buffalo News*, CWA printer and GCIU photoengraver units have negotiated shared work agreements in the prepress area. At *The Seattle Times*, CWA printer and Guild units agreed to share jurisdiction covering electronic composition of display advertising in the creative services department. The unions also agreed not to file grievances over new work assignments but in return will not suffer any job loss. A joint committee, composed of representatives of both unions and the *Times*, will resolve disputes over staffing ratios, although the publisher reserves the right to settle all outstanding issues. The committee also will oversee related training programs. Finally, the parties agreed to modify the arbitration process, in effect weakening the unions' ability to grieve certain issues (NAA 1997a).

These cases reveal that the efficient use of new technology has required changes to traditional labor relations practices and structures. Faced with the reality of further job and wage erosion, the unions involved have agreed to concessions related to jurisdiction, staffing, dispute resolution language, and other areas, but the affected workers maintain union membership. Companies receive contractual flexibility to deploy labor and maximize staff effectiveness and productivity. With more than 300 collective agreements set to expire by 2001 (Rudder 1999), it is expected that such agreements will become more common. New jurisdiction issues also are likely to emerge. One such case involves workers producing online papers.

Online Newspapers

The advent of the digital newspaper has created a host of new labor relations issues, including union recognition and jurisdiction, employee status, and the ownership of and compensation for reuse of work.[9]

It was estimated that by 2000 more than 67 million households would have Internet access. Moreover, the Pew Research Center found that the percentage of Americans getting news online at least once a week tripled between 1996 and 1998 to more than 36 million. In response, newspaper companies have increased their online offerings to meet the new demand. In 1994 there were 20 online editions; in 1997, there were 1,500 worldwide. By mid-2001, more than 1,300 North American dailies had an online presence. Knight Ridder has the most involved operation with forty-five websites and 400 employees. With many different types of media concerns establishing classified websites and with low barriers to entry, newspaper companies' forays into this business are part defensive and part evolutionary. Many digital newspapers have been losing money, but companies are willing to take losses to preserve their classified ad base, a $15 to $18 billion a year business, making up between 25 to 50 percent of total revenue.

By focusing on how the product (information) is produced, not delivered, the Newspaper Guild has developed a number of strategies to bring online newspaper workers into the union fold. Preliminary evidence shows they are making headway. In 1999 the Guild had approximately twenty agreements covering online workers, all where the Guild had prior representation rights (Rudder 1999).

Guild strategies include the following. Some locals have written *strong jurisdiction clauses* that make it easy for them to argue that the development of editorial copy and advertising for electronic publications is similar to the unit's traditional work and that jurisdiction should be extended to the new products. Examples include contracts at the *Toledo Blade*, the *Chicago Sun-Times*, and *The Rocky Mountain News*. In these cases, the number of online employees is small and employers did not resist. At *The* (Eugene, Oregon) *Register-Guard* and *The Knoxville News-Sentinel*, the Guild has used *recognition clauses* that identify only job classifications and departments covered by an agreement to cover workers doing online work.

Guild units also have negotiated *modified jurisdiction language* to incorporate work related to technological advances, including online publications, and *supplemental language* to enable its members to do online work similar to the work performed by the existing unit. Examples of the former include the (Minneapolis) *Star Tribune* and the *San Francisco Chronicle*, while examples of the latter appear at the (Akron) *Beacon Journal*, the *Milwaukee Journal Sentinel*, and the *Pittsburgh Post-Gazette*.

Given the uncertainties and risks related to online publishing, some publishers have taken both cautious and hostile approaches to union jurisdiction. In some cases, as at the *Portland* (Maine) *Press Herald* and the *San Jose Mercury News*, publishers have agreed to *experimental* and *temporary* clauses that extend jurisdiction to the Guild for a fixed time (Needham 1998). At *The Pueblo Chieftain*, a dispute arose in 1996 following the company's creation of the *Pueblo Chieftain Online*. The workers in question were HTML coders who, the company argued, were part of a separate venture and not part of the bargaining unit. An arbitrator ruled in August 1998 that these workers did "soft coding,"[10] work similar to the tasks they performed as paginators who code text when laying out newspaper pages. As such, the arbitrator directed the company to include online workers in the extant Guild unit (*The Guild Reporter* 1998). At *The Providence Journal* and *The* (Baltimore) *Sun*, where negotiations and grievance and arbitration hearings have failed to produce settlements, the parties have used the NLRB and the courts to resolve jurisdictional disputes.

The dispute at *The Providence Journal* began in the summer of 1994, after the company established a dial-in online service initially called *Rhode Island Horizons*. Soon after, the company moved the operations to the World Wide Web and changed the name to *projo.com*. The union claimed representation rights, but the company argued that the online jobs were different from those of the print version and, thus, fell outside of the union's control. In response to failed negotiations, the union filed a grievance in May 1995, eventually taking the case to the full NLRB in Washington.

In a case watched closely by the union and newspaper companies, the Providence newspaper reversed course and settled with the union short of a Board ruling, allowing seven editorial and two advertising workers to fall under the Guild's contract. The company attributed its reversal to the rapid growth of the Internet and the need to have both papers and their respective employees housed in the same building to maximize efficiencies in news and advertising (Noack 1998a).[11]

The most contentious case to date arose in the summer of 1996 at *The* (Baltimore) *Sun*, following the conclusion of a contract with the Washington–Baltimore Guild that failed to include language dealing with online and events promotion employees at the *Sunspot*, an online venture that had not yet been launched. The union filed a unit clarification petition in August and, after the *Sunspot* commenced operations in September, a separate one seeking jurisdiction over the ad/marketing department in October. At the end of 1996 the NLRB's regional director consolidated both cases. The Guild argued that the work performed by online workers was similar to that done at the *Sun*, while the company argued that the union failed to file the petition in a timely manner. In December 1997, almost one year after the union's petition, the regional director ruled for the union, arguing that both sets of workers shared a "community of interest" strong enough to accrete *Sunspot* employees to the larger unit. The Guild also won the right to represent workers in the promotions and events department. At the time, the union represented reporters, advertising staff, and maintenance workers at the *Sun*. The Times-Mirror Company, then owner of the properties, filed an appeal to the full Board on January 15, 1998 (Noack 1998b).

On April 7, 2000, a three-member panel of the Board ruled that *The Sun* violated the Act by refusing to bargain with the Washington–Baltimore Newspaper Guild for employees working at *Sunspot* following their accretion to the unit in the 1997 unit clarification decision (*L&ELL* 2000). But, in July 2001, the U.S. Court of Appeals for the Fourth Circuit ruled that the Board erred in ordering the company to add employees in its website department to an established bargaining unit. The justices applied the two-prong test set out in *Safeway Stores* (1981). Following *Safeway*, the Board may issue an order to accrete employees into an existing bargaining unit when employees have "little or no separate identity and thus cannot be considered to be a separate appropriate unit, and the community of interest between the employees and the existing unit is 'overwhelming.'" (Safeway Stores 1981) In this case, the court contended that the Web employees were different from newsroom employees because they did not work on preparing the newspaper, they were paid differently than other employees, and they needed a different set of skills and expertise from traditional newspaper workers. Moreover, the court found that the Web-based workers shared little community of interest with *Sun* employees (BNA 2001a).

Despite the legal defeat at *Sunspot*, the Guild has done a good job of extending its jurisdiction into the online segment of the industry over the last six years, although the first electronic papers to come under its jurisdiction were the *Minneapolis Star* and *Minneapolis Tribune* in 1980, following a twenty-seven day strike by the mailers and the Guild (*New York Times* 1980; Fitzgerald 1998; Rothman 1999). There are, however, some high hurdles for the Guild to clear in order to organize a critical mass of the online newspaper sector: cutbacks at many properties; organizational flux; employer resistance; and too many ventures that employ only a handful of eligible employees, making cost–benefit calculations unfavorable. Nonetheless, if online newspapers become either substitutes or strong complements to the printed version, the Guild needs to have a significant presence at them.

From Independent Contractor to Union Employee

The use of independent contractors in the newspaper industry is concentrated in distribution where, since 1996, the number of adult carriers has surpassed that of teenage carriers. For example, the teen force fell from a high of about 800,000 in 1980 to 373,269 in 1990, and to 206,136 by 1996, the last year for which data exist. Whereas adults made up 32.3 percent of the carrier workforce in 1990, they comprised 51.1 percent in 1996. Moreover, the shift to adult carriers, who handle bulkier morning papers, has resulted in fewer carriers overall. Besides the general shift to morning delivery and earlier deadlines, issues of safety, child labor laws, and streamlined delivery systems have reduced the demand for child carriers (Neuwirth 1998; Strupp 1999a).

The vast majority of home deliverers are independent contractors, mainly adults, who buy and resell newspapers. In 1994, they comprised 94 percent of all carriers. There are also agents who receive a fee for delivering papers but who never take ownership of them and fewer employees who are entitled to employment and labor law protections. The industry estimates that it saves hundreds of millions of dollars in payroll costs, taxes, benefits, insurance liability, and administrative expenses by using independent contractors. Some publishers claim these added costs could put them out of business (Gyles 1999). Newspapers also can avoid unionization.[12]

There have been hundreds of legal cases over the years involving the status of independent contractors. Most involve carriers and are won by the companies. One major exception that could increase organizing activity in the near future involved carriers and haulers at the *St. Joseph* (Missouri) *News-Press*. On September 6, 2001, an NLRB administrative law judge, applying standards applied by previous Board cases, ruled that these workers were employees covered by federal labor laws, not independent contractors. During the Teamsters' organizing drive that began in October 1999, the company had fired four union activists and committed other unfair labor practices, according to the Board. Should the union win likely appeals, it could potentially make hundreds of thousands of similar workers at other newspapers organizing targets (BNA 2001b).

To a far lesser extent, cases have involved editorial freelancers or "stringers," who argue for overtime pay and the right to unionize and bargain with management. The most significant and successful of these involved suburban correspondents and photographers at *The Philadelphia Inquirer* over a ten-year period between 1988 and 1998. Their path to unionization and their first labor agreement unfolded in three main phases. First, in the summer of 1988, the NLRB's Philadelphia office ruled that stringers were in fact employees and entitled to organize a union. Stringers complained of low pay and benefits for full-time work that was equivalent to regular *Inquirer* workers' responsibilities. They often worked thirty-two hours a week covering the *Inquirer's* expanded suburban beats but received only half the pay and benefits of staff reporters. Initially there were two unions attempting to represent full-time stringers: The Newspaper Guild of Greater Philadelphia and the newly formed Newspaper Reporters of the *Philadelphia Inquirer* District 1.

On January 13, 1994, after six years of legal wrangling, stringers voted 107–37 to be represented by the Newspaper Guild of Greater Philadelphia Local 10. The bargaining unit was separate from the Guild's main 1,200-member unit at Knight Ridder's Philadelphia Newspapers, Inc. (PNI) and included 175 part- and full-time nonstaff correspondents. Union organizers noted that this was the first time since 1986 in Scranton, Pennsylvania, that the Guild organized a group of former independent contractors (Garneau 1994).

The third phase ended four years later when the union secured its first contract, a twenty-six-month deal, with the *Inquirer's* publisher, PNI. The contract was an historic one, the first to cover a group of stringers, since the Scranton unit never won a contract. Except for 15 full-timers, the 130-person unit was largely composed of part-timers working four days per week. The unit voted 78–12 on June 17, 1998, to accept the contract, which provided lucrative wage and benefit improvements, a grievance and arbitration procedure, and language to create more full-time jobs. PNI won less than full parity pay and benefits between workers on staff and those on suburban assignments (Caparella 1998).

The Future of Newspaper Unionism

The main factors that have contributed to union weakness since the mid-1970s—rapidly advancing technology, industry consolidation and concentration, the prominence of publicly traded media companies, and certain public policies—are not expected to be reversed any time soon.

For unions to regain power in this tough environment, they must continue to merge and work toward the formation of a single media union. This is no easy task, however, given earlier conflicts among some of the unions. Clustering also brings new challenges to unions. Clustered properties may be easier and less costly to organize than geographically dispersed properties, but it is likely that many newspaper companies will continue to resist union organization. Where organized, unions could work to centralize bargaining units into regional and/or chainwide structures. Here too, unions face long odds. Legal scholar Jim Atleson (1985) argues that certain union tactics—secondary boycotts and coordinated bargaining efforts, among others—designed to change bargaining structures and broaden the scope of bargaining to deal with power imbalances in the workplace and society have been stymied by unrealistic and illogical NLRB rulings. His work—and case law—shows that, if employers do not want to alter existing bargaining structures, it is almost impossible for unions to effect such change. Perhaps unions stand a better chance with clusters where no unions currently exist.

Above all, the future of the newspaper itself could determine the fate of newspaper unions. Since the 1970s, newspaper companies have sought to limit union control of the labor process by weakening production unions through implementing new technologies and then by rationalizing the distribution process, hurting unionized drivers and related personnel. Recent strikes at the (New York) *Daily News* (1990–91)[13] and at the JOAs in Pittsburgh (1992), San Francisco (1994), and Detroit (1995–97) involved management's desire to streamline and control the distribution function. With the exception of Detroit, union drivers in other cities were successful in stopping distribution, although they paid a price in terms of lost jobs. For example, Pittsburgh Teamsters agreed to cut 40 percent of their 627 delivery jobs over five years after staying out for eight months in 1992 (Fitzgerald 1992). A twelve-day strike at both papers in San Francisco in 1994 cut the number of youth carriers, as well as 150 driver jobs, most by attrition (BNA 1994).

Until, and if, the digital newspaper comes to dominate over the print version, the power base of the newspaper unions will lie within the unionized drivers since they have the best chance of preventing the distribution of newspapers during strikes. Should the digital newspaper supersede the print newspaper, the production of the newspaper once again becomes contested terrain for control of the labor process. While this may be years away, the Guild's ability to organize online workers is essential to its survival and perhaps the survival of all newspaper unions.

Notes

[1] Advertising accounts for between 70 and 85 percent of operating revenue, while circulation brings in between 15 and 30 percent. Newspapers receive roughly 27 percent of all dollars spent on advertising, the largest of any media sector. Overall, newspaper advertising expenditures have grown from $1.16 billion in 1946 to $38 billion by 1996. The largest single expenses are mechanical (13 to 15 percent) and newsprint (20 to 35 percent) (Picard and Brody 1997; Picard 1998).

[2] Research also shows that there is limited competition for advertising dollars between daily papers and other media such as radio, television, and cable. In general, newspapers face the most intense advertising competition from media forms that can provide the greatest market penetration, such as total market coverage papers and direct mail (Picard and Brody 1997).

[3] The Teamsters crossed picket lines to honor its contract with the *Tribune*. But, in the same year, when the Guild struck Knight Ridder's two newspapers in Philadelphia for forty-six days, all unions stood firm, *despite* having contracts in effect at the time (BNA 1985).

[4] The NAA reports that merit pay is much less common in composing, press, and mailrooms. Variable pay, largely through tiered-pay structures, is more prevalent in these work areas (NAA 1997b).

[5] Examples where more than two units have signed long-term deals, around ten years, include *The New York Times*, *Newsday*, *The* (Newark) *Star-Ledger*, *The Buffalo News*, and the *St. Louis Post-Dispatch*.

[6] In 1997, McClatchy paid $1.4 billion dollars for the Minneapolis paper. It remains to be seen whether the Minneapolis Concept will be maintained when these contracts expire (Fitzgerald 1997).

[7] Toward the end of 1997, the Boston Typographical Union signed its second ten-year agreement with *The Boston Globe*. The union ceded more control over work and personnel in exchange for pay and benefit improvements and job security. Minimum staffing levels will be reduced from 125 in 1987 to 50 at the end of the current contract. The owner, the New York Times Company, will use both retirement incentives and low entry wages to reduce both wage costs and employment (*The Boston Globe* 1997).

[8] For information on these other cases, see *Labor & Personnel Relations Letter* (*L&PRL*) 1984 for Sacramento; *L&PRL* 1986b for Cleveland; *L&PRL* 1990 and BNA 1991 for Toledo; *L&PRL* 1986a for Roanoke; and *L&PRL* 1986c for Escanaba, Michigan.

[9] On June 25, 2001, the U.S. Supreme Court ruled 7–2 in favor of freelancers that a group of newspaper and magazine publishers infringed the copyrights of the freelancers' work by making their articles available on electronic databases without permission. The Court did not rule on the remedy (L. Greenhouse 2001).

[10] Soft coders use a computer program to convert stored data, including text and graphics, into HTML code. Hard coders write HTML code directly from a keyboard into a computer.

[11] An emerging trend in Internet operations is for companies to consolidate their operations across the country into a single operation that may eventually be spun off into a separate public company. Some newspapers are partnering with others in close geographic proximity to share a website and also are entering joint ventures with traditional Internet concerns (Morton 1999b).

[12] Some independent contractor–status carriers have been seeking union representations, such as those affiliating with the Independent News Carriers Association of Northeast Ohio, itself part of CWA Local 4390. These Ohio carriers have sought union protection in response to the decision of The (Cleveland) Plain Dealer to lower subscription rates to people who pay the company directly, instead of their carriers (Strupp 1999b).

[13] See Jennings (1993) and Sleigh (1998) for details on this strike.

References

Adams, Larry. 1984. "Labor Organization Mergers 1979–1984: Adapting to Change." *Monthly Labor Review* (September), pp. 21–27.

Asher, David M. 2001. "Who Owns What?" *Presstime* (January), pp. 46–47.

Asher, David M., and Melanie M. Roberts. 2000. "Good Morning!" *Presstime* (June), pp. 40–44.

Atleson, James B. 1985. "Reflections on Labor, Power, and Society." *The Maryland Law Review*, 44, 3, pp. 841–72.

Bass, Jack. 1999. "Newspaper Monopoly." *American Journalism Review* (July/August), pp. 64–77.

Bureau of National Affairs (BNA). 1980. "Typographical Union Ratifies 10-Year Pact Guaranteeing Jobs at Baltimore Newspapers." *Daily Labor Report*, DLR No. 220 (November 12), p. A-5.

_____. 1982. "Justices Decline Review of Ruling on Lifetime Job Security Guarantee." *Daily Labor Report*, DLR No. 100 (May 24), p. A-7.

_____. 1984. "Newspaper Guild Wins Bargaining Rights for Employees at Two Milwaukee Papers." *Daily Labor Report*, DLR No. 101 (July 9), p. A-3.

_____. 1985. "Philadelphia's Longest Newspaper Strike Ends as Teamsters, Typographers Reverse Vote." *Daily Labor Report*, DLR No. 205 (October 23), p. A-6.

_____. 1991. "Justices Dent Review in Case Preserving Union Role in Early Retirement Decision." *Daily Labor Report*, DLR No. 10 (January 15), p. A-6.

_____. 1992. "*Post-Gazette* Reaches Agreement with Teamsters." *Daily Labor Report*, DLR No. 248 (December 24), p. A-9.

_____. 1994. "San Francisco Newspaper Employees Ratify Five-Year, Strike-Ending Pacts." *Daily Labor Report*, DLR No. 218 (November 15), p. D-16.

_____. 1997. "Newspaper Guild Locals Chartered by CWA as Merger Nears Completion." *Daily Labor Report*, DLR No. 118 (June 19), p. D-10.

_____. 1998. "Employees at San Diego Union-Tribune Vote to Decertify Newspaper Guild Local." *Daily Labor Report*, DLR No. 114 (June 15), p. D-20.

_____. 2000. "Unions Endorse JOA for Denver Papers, Negotiate Seven-Year Labor Agreements." *Daily Labor Report*, DLR No. 137 (July 17), p. A-9.

_____. 2001a. "NLRB Erred in Accreting Web Site Workers into Newspapers Bargaining Unit, Court Says." *Daily Labor Report*, DLR No. 139 (July 20), p. A-12.

_____. 2001b. "NLRB Judge Finds Newspaper Carriers Are Employees, Not Independent Contractor." *Daily Labor Report*, DLR No. 182 (September 21), p. A-6.

Burroughs, Elise. 1998. "Pay's New Package Deal." *Presstime* (May), pp. 55–60.

Busterna, John C., and Robert G. Picard. 1993. *Joint Operating Agreements: The Newspaper Preservation Act and Its Application*. Norwood, NJ: Ablex Publishing.

Caparella, Kitty. 1998. "Philly Correspondents Get Contract." *The Guild Reporter* (June 19), pp. 1–2.

Chaison, Gary N. 1996. *Union Mergers in Hard Times: The View from Five Countries*. Ithaca, NY: ILR Press/Cornell University Press.

Chang, Elizabeth. 1993. "The Buyout Boom." *American Journalism Review* (July/August), pp. 17–21.

Dertouzos, James N., and Timothy H. Quinn. 1985. *Bargaining Responses to the Technology Revolution: The Case of the Newspaper Industry*. R-3144-DOL. Santa Monica, CA: Rand.

Dewey, Lucretia. 1971. "Union Merger Pace Quickens." *Monthly Labor Review* (June), pp. 63–70.

Dotinga, Randy. 1998a. "Will 850 Union-Trib Workers Vote Out Their Guild?" *Editor & Publisher* (June 6), pp. 8–9, 12.

_____. 1998b. "Guild Divisions Contributed to Ejections." *Editor & Publisher* (July 25), pp. 20–21, 40.

Farhi, Paul. 1999. "The Death of the JOA." *American Journalism Review* (September), pp. 49–53.

Fitzgerald, Mark. 1992. "Union Concessions." *Editor & Publisher* (December 5), p. 12.

_____. 1996a. "Decade of Stability." *Editor & Publisher* (October 19), pp. 15, 53.

_____. 1996b. "Labor Statesmanship." *Editor & Publisher* (November 2), p. 4.

_____. 1997. "Twin City Slickers." *Editor & Publisher* (November 22), pp. 8–9, 37.

_____. 1998. "Unions Gain Ground at Paper Web Sites." *Editor & Publisher* (September 12), p. 46.

_____. 2000a. "Sleight of Hand." *Editor & Publisher* (June), pp. 20–26.

_____. 2000b. "Strikers in Detroit Dealt a Blow." *Editor & Publisher* (July), p. 8.

Garneau, George. 1994. "Stringers Unionize in Philadelphia Suburbs." *Editor & Publisher* (January 29), pp. 17, 38.

Gersh, Debra. 1991. "The Changing Role of the Typographer." *Editor & Publisher* (June 8), pp. 80–82, 102.

Gifford, Courtney. 1998. *Directory of U.S. Labor Organizations: 1996–97 Edition*. Washington, DC: Bureau of National Affairs.

Goetz, Thomas. 1997. "Knight-Ridder's Rampage." *In These Times* (December 14), p. 9.

Greenhouse, Linda. 2001. "Freelancers Win in Copyright Case." *The New York Times* (June 26), p. A14.

Greenhouse, Steven. 2000. "After 5 1/2 Years, a Labor War Ends at 2 Detroit Papers." *The New York Times* (December 19), p. A20.

Gyles, Barbara Z. 1999. "Carrier 2000." *Presstime* (March), pp. 43–48.

Hirsch, Barry T., and David A. Macpherson. 1993–2000. *Union Membership and Earnings Data Book*. Washington, DC: Bureau of National Affairs.

Janus, Charles. 1978. "Union Mergers in the 1970's: A Look at the Reasons and Results." *Monthly Labor Review* (October), pp. 13–23.

Jelf, Gregory S., and James B. Dworkin. 1997. "Union Decertification Research: Review and Theoretical Integration." *The International Journal of Conflict Management*, 8, 4 (October), pp. 306–37.

Jennings, Kenneth M. 1993. *Labor Relations at the New York Daily News*. Westport, CT: Praeger.

Kalleberg, Arne L., and Michael Wallace et al. 1987. "The Eclipse of Craft: The Changing Face of Labor in the Newspaper Industry." In Daniel B. Cornfield, ed., *Workers, Managers and Technological Change: Emerging Patterns of Labor Relations*. New York: Plenum Press, pp. 47–71.

Keil, Thomas J. 1988. *On Strike!* Tuscaloosa, AL: University of Alabama Press.

Kokkelenberg, Edward C., and Donna R. Sockell. 1985. "Union Membership in the United States, 1973–1981." *Industrial and Labor Relations Review*, 38, 4 (July), pp. 497–533.

Kunkel, Thomas, and Gene Roberts. 2001. "Leaving Readers Behind." *American Journalism Review*. (May), pp. 32–41.

Labor & Employment Law Letter (L&ELL). 1981–2000. "Representation Elections." (December).

———. 1997. "Strikes." (December), pp. 238–239.

———. 1998. "NLRB Actions—Newspaper." (August), pp. 138, 140.

———. 2000. "Board Holds Company's Refusal to Bargain for Accreted Web Site Employees Violated Act." (April), pp. 102–03.

———. 2001. "Guild Members Ratify Company's Contract Offer and End Seven-Week Strike" (January/February), p. 16.

Labor & Personnel Relations Letter (L&PRL). 1984. "Supreme Court Declines to Review Lifetime Job Guarantee Dispute." p. 67.

———. 1986a. "Supreme Court Denies Review of Job Security Suit Remanded for Arbitration." (April), p. 84.

———. 1986b. "Sixth Circuit Upholds Denial of Job Guarantees for Former *Cleveland Press* Printers." (August), p. 180.

———. 1986c. "Lifetime Job Guarantees Survived Expiration of Contract, District Court Rules." (October), pp. 226–27.

———. 1990. "Insisting to Impasse on Right to Bypass Union Over Employee Buyouts Violated the Act." (October), pp. 223–24.

Lacy, Stephen, and Todd F. Simon. 1993. *The Economics and Regulation of United States Newspapers*. Norwood, NJ: Ablex Publishing.

Lallande, Ann. 2001. "The Art of the Deal." *Presstime* (January), pp. 38–45.

Liebeskind, Ken. 1999. "Veronis, Suhler Report Highlights Newspapers' Healthy Revenue Gains." *Editor & Publisher* (January 9), pp. 8, 45.

Miller, James P. 2000. "Pulitzer Alters Ownership Deal at Newspaper." *The Wall Street Journal* (May 2), p. B12.

Monthly Labor Review. 1974. "Printers Okay Automation in 11-Year Pact." (August), p. 89.

Morton, John. 1996. "Newspaper Strikes: Bad News for Employees." *American Journalism Review* (September), pp. 51, 56.

———. 1997a. "A Flurry of Deals to Create Clusters." *American Journalism Review* (March), p. 52.

———. 1997b. "Chains Swallowing Other Chains." *American Journalism Review* (July/August), p. 52.

_____. 1999a. "Everything Is Coming Up Profits for Papers." *American Journalism Review* (June), p. 80.

_____. 1999b. "Web Spawns Talk, But Newsprint Turns Profit." *American Journalism Review* (October), p. 100.

Moses, Lucia. 1999. "Do JOA's Still Work? (Have they ever?)." *Editor & Publisher* (September 11), pp. 18–19.

Needham, Marian. 1998. "Jurisdictional Agreements in New Media." The Newspaper Guild–CWA Sector Conference (Hyatt Regency, Chicago) The Newspaper Guild, pp. 9–34.

Neiva, Elizabeth MacIver. 1996. "Chain Building: The Consolidation of the American Newspaper Industry: 1953–1980." *Business History Review*, 70 (Spring), pp. 1–42.

Neuwirth, Robert. 1997. "Singleton on California Roll." *Editor & Publisher* (December 13), pp. 12–13.

_____. 1998. "Adults Eclipse Kids in Carrier Force." *Editor & Publisher* (September 12), p. 7.

Newsom, Clark. 1981. "Buyouts of Printers May Have Peaked." *Presstime* (November), pp. 42–43.

_____. 1988. "Union Decertifications Increase." *Presstime* (January), p. 30.

Newspaper Association of America (NAA). 1997a. Labor Relations and Technology Seminar—Pertinent Cases. Vienna, VA.

_____. 1997b. "Merit and Variable Pay Summary Reports."

_____. 2001. "Facts About Newspapers: A Statistical Summary of the Newspaper Industry." Vienna, VA.

Newspaper Guild. 1997, 1998. *Collective Bargaining Manual*.

New York Times. 1980. "Unions Vote to End Strike at Minneapolis Newspapers." (October 11), p. 6.

Noack, David. 1998a. "*Projo.com* Goes Union, Settlement Avoids Ruling." *Editor & Publisher* (August 8), p. 9.

_____. 1998b. "NLRB Says Web Workers are Editorial." *Editor & Publisher* Interactive. Accessed website. <http://www.mediainfo.com/ephome>.

Peterson, Iver. 1997. "Recalling Three Waves of Newspaper Strikes After the Devastation in Detroit." *The New York Times*, February 24, p. D9.

Picard, Robert G. 1998. "The Economics of the Daily Newspaper Industry." In Alison Alexander, James Owens, and Rod Carveth, eds., *Media Economics: Theory and Practice.* Mahwah, NJ: Erlbaum, pp. 111–30.

Picard, Robert G., and Jeffery H. Brody. 1997. *The Newspaper Publishing Industry.* Boston: Allyn and Bacon.

Presstime. 1980–1990. "Strike Summary." (February).

_____. 1987. "Growing Number of Mailer Units Renounce CWA." (April), p. 60.

_____. 2000. "A Decade of Deals." (February), pp. 33–34.

Risser, James V. 1998. "Endangered Species." *American Journalism Review* (June), pp. 19–34.

Rothman, Carol. 1999. "At 65, the Guild Is Far From Retirement." *The Guild Reporter* (May), p. 7.

Rudder, Gregory S. 1999. "After Detroit." *Presstime* (November), pp. 60–64.

Safeway Stores (256 NLRB 918, 107 LRRM 1338 (1981).

Sleigh, Stephen R. 1998. *On Deadline: Labor Relations in Newspaper Publishing.* Bayside, NY: Social Change Press.

Strupp, Joe. 1999a. "Delivered at Dawn." *Editor & Publisher* (April 24), p. 14.

Strupp, Joe. 1999b. "Direct-Pay Options Drive Carriers to Organize." *Editor & Publisher* (October 30), pp. 10–11.

Terry, Carolyn. 1998. "Minority Journalists Gain Slightly." *Presstime* (May), p. 72.

_____. 2000. "Merit-Pay Proposal Ruled Fair." *Presstime* (September), p. 63.

The Boston Globe. 1997. "Globe Printers Recommend New Contract to their Board." (December 22), p. F2.

The Guild Reporter. 1998. "Arbitrator's Ruling Penetrates Internet." Vol. 65, no. 8 (August 21, 1998), p. 8.

U.S. Department of Labor. 1994. *Employment, Hours, and Earnings, United States, 1909–94,* Volume 1. Bulletin 2445. Washington, DC: Bureau of Labor Statistics.

_____. 1995. *Employment, Hours, and Earnings, United States, 1990–95.* Bulletin 2465. Washington, DC: Bureau of Labor Statistics.

_____. 1998. *Handbook of U.S. Labor Statistics,* 1st ed. Washington, DC: Bureau of Labor Statistics.

_____. 2000. Employment, Hours, and Earnings, United States. Washington, DC: Bureau of Labor Statistics. <ftp://ftp.bls.gov/pub/suppl/empsit.ceseeb2.txt> [January 9, 2001].

Underwood, Doug. 1998. "Assembly-Line Journalism." *Columbia Journalism Review* (July/August), pp. 42–44.

Wenner, Kathryn S. 2000. "Slimming Down." *American Journalism Review* (December), pp. 38–41.

Williamson, Lisa. 1995. "Union Mergers: 1985–1994 Update." *Monthly Labor Review* (February), pp. 18–25.

CHAPTER 6

Professional Sports: Collective Bargaining in the Spotlight

JAMES B. DWORKIN
Purdue University

RICHARD A. POSTHUMA
University of Texas at El Paso

Introduction

Even the casual reader of almost any daily newspaper is well aware that professional athletes have been heavily involved in collective bargaining for many years. Strikes, lockouts, arbitration, free agency, salary caps, revenue sharing, competitive balance, antitrust laws, franchise relocations, new economically viable stadiums, and a myriad of other related topics are familiar turf for sports fans and labor relations specialists alike. The purpose of this chapter is to focus on current developments in collective bargaining and the future challenges these developments pose to professional sports, especially baseball, basketball, football, and hockey.

To accomplish this goal, the chapter is divided into six sections. Section I describes the professional sports industry and provides our assessment of the industry's opportunities and threats. Section II describes the major parties involved in the collective bargaining process in the sports industry. Section III covers players and the labor markets they face. Section IV examines the bargaining history between owners and players, with an emphasis on major developments since the 1980s. Section V predicts the issues that will shape the next rounds of bargaining in this industry. Finally, section VI elaborates on the possible future scenarios for union–management relationships in the industry.

Section I—The Industry

Many industries have unique institutional factors that influence how they operate, and the professional sports industry is no exception. Perhaps more public attention is given to professional sports than any other industry. In addition, professional sports wields enormous market control in the sectors in which it operates. Professional sports also exercises more control over the allocation and use of its employees (the players) than any other industry does. Finally, the professional sports industry is characterized by a need for the competing teams to cooperate so that everyone may survive and prosper. Each of these features of this industry is discussed in the following sections.

Public Attention to Professional Sports

Why are Americans and people around the world so fascinated with professional sports? U.S. professional sports have sales of about $2 billion per year. Yet, this pales in comparison with the revenues produced by major U.S. companies. Thus, it's not the size of the industry that generates so much attention (Quirk and Fort 1999; Fort 2000). This high interest level may be related to four other factors.

First, many people grow up actively participating in a variety of sports for recreational purposes. People can relate to professional athletes more easily than they can relate to people assembling a car or inventing new software for a high-technology company. The media fuels vicarious participation in the sports industry by keeping us constantly informed of the daily events in each major sport. It's true that many also watch the activity on the New York Stock Exchange and the NASDAQ as a daily routine. Yet, during the important formative years of one's youth, few children traded stocks and bonds. Most were actively participating in the product of the sports industry (baseball games, football games, etc.).

Second, professional sports teams are a source of pride for communities. People are proud of their teams and come to identify with their players and their successes or failures. The Dodgers left Brooklyn for Los Angeles in the 1950s, yet even today people in Brooklyn still talk about Walter O'Malley's move west.

Third, competition on the playing field is captivating. One of the alluring aspects of professional sports is the fascination surrounding games with uncertain outcomes. Think how tedious games would be if one team always was the winner. With the possible exception of Los Angeles Dodger fans, who are notorious for arriving late and leaving early, a close contest typically is more interesting and has fans glued to their seats until the final out or until the clock ticks off the last second of play.

Fourth, sports teams provide a model for teams in the workplace. Often, managers seek to emulate the team model to manage their workplaces. They try to assemble a winning team, to facilitate cooperation among team members, and to celebrate successes when their teams win out over the competition (Katz 2001).

The Industry Wields Strong Market Control

There is no other industry like the professional sports industry in terms of market control mechanisms. In professional sports, there is exclusive geographic franchise control. Through bylaws and rules, sports leagues control which teams operate in which markets, when teams can relocate, where they can relocate, and when new franchises can enter the market. By contrast, in the retail industry, Wal-Mart may open a new store, and one of its competitors is free to locate nearby. There are no restrictions against this kind of competitive activity. This control over both team movement and team location provides the professional sports industry with power not possessed by any other industry. This power allows team owners to make demands on cities for new, economically viable stadiums to be paid for by local taxpayers. To balk at such a request is to risk losing a team, a risk many cities are unwilling to take. Often other host cities wait in the wings, offering enticing packages to existing teams that are considering a franchise relocation.

Each professional sports league operates teams *only* in those markets (cities) in which it chooses to enter. No competition is permitted. Challenges to this market control have arisen when rival leagues were formed. But generally they had little or no success. One exception was the American Basketball Association, which prospered for several years and was able to assimilate several of its better teams into the NBA (Naismith 1996; Gould 1998). In all other sports, the success of one team or league in terms of attendance did not have much impact on the other league.

Control Over Allocation and Use of Players

Professional sports has a unique control over new player talent entering the league. This control is exercised via a number of rules and regulations governing the drafting of rookie players. Actually, until the player unionization movement took hold, teams were able to control their players over their entire careers through what economists refer to as monopsony power (one buyer and many sellers). This control was enforced through the reserve clause in each player contract. Players were reserved to one team into perpetuity. This control has been challenged and weakened over the years. The players in all professional sports have finally achieved a modicum of control over their careers through a series of collective bargaining events that will be described in this chapter. Yet, it is still true today, as it was 100 years ago, that the leagues have vast power over entering talent through the rookie draft procedures.

Competition and Cooperation

The economics of professional sports leagues is peculiar (Neale 1964). Leagues operate by a set of rules whereby the teams within a league cooperate in order to prosper and survive. Teams use a set of common playing rules (instant replay, strike zone, three-point shot, penalties for slashing) and enforcement mechanisms. Yet, cooperation also entails agreeing to league rules about franchise relocation and the allocation of television revenues. The agreed on control of gate and television revenue-sharing arrangements varies across leagues, from complete revenue sharing in football to a more complicated and problematic system of partial revenue sharing employed in baseball.

This cooperation is in juxtaposition to the ongoing competition among the teams. Teams compete to win but also to make profits, often at the expense of other teams in the league. Competition among teams within a league is essential, but too much economic competition could kill the golden goose. This results in an industry that needs a moderate degree of competitive balance to enable all teams to share in the success of the industry (Sherony, Haupert, and Knowles 2001).

Many of the woes facing baseball continue to stem from the small-market versus big-market team competitive issues. Can a small-market team like Milwaukee, with limited local TV and radio dollars, really compete with a large-market franchise like the New York Yankees? The Yankees might have as much as $100 million per season in local TV and broadcast rights. The large-market teams generate large revenues that can be used to buy the best players. Therefore, the leagues struggle with supporting smaller markets to ensure that a reasonable level of competition continues.

Section II—The Parties

Within this industry, several key parties exert significant influence. These parties are the leagues, the teams, the players and their unions, and the government. Therefore, the next section focuses on each of these parties (Dunlop 1993; Aaron and Wheeler 1991).

Employer Groups—The Leagues

Professional sports leagues in hockey, football, basketball, and baseball engage in many functions, such as scheduling games, arranging for games to be officiated, and hiring the officials. Besides these crucial functions, however, all leagues also impose strict rules and codes on all member teams that limit economic competition. By limiting competition among league teams and restricting entry into the league by newer teams, these cartel organizations are better able to maximize profits. The league grants each member team what is referred to as an exclusive territorial franchise. While the concept varies from league to league, it generally means that a team located in a specific location has a monopoly over that area. No other teams are permitted to invade that territory.

In addition, once a team is situated in a particular location, movement to another location is not permitted without a significant majority of support from all league teams (e.g., 75 percent of all teams in football). Table 1 presents a summary of the number of franchise moves in each league since the 1950s. The data suggest that there is only about one franchise relocation per year (Quirk and Fort 1999). Many move to communities that allure teams with economically viable stadiums financed by cities and citizens. Yet, many more teams threaten to move than actually do. Often, just the threat of moving results in local support for a new arena or stadium.

Table 1
Franchise Relocations by Sport, 1950s to Present

Decade	Baseball	Football	Basketball	Hockey	Total
1950s	5	0	4	0	9
1960s	4	2	5	0	11
1970s	2	0	7	3	12
1980s	0	3	2	2	7
1990s–present	0	4	1	4	9
Totals	11	9	19	9	48

Sources: League guides and Quirk and Fort (1999).

The league's restriction on entry of new teams has led to threats of new or rival leagues. These include such ill-fated attempts as the World Hockey Association, the World Football League, the Mexican League in baseball, and others. Yet, it's hard to find examples of successful rival leagues. The rival leagues have a big disadvantage because of lack of resources, poor player talent, and inadequate playing facilities. None-the-less, there have been a few successes, such as the American League in baseball; the American Football League (AFL); and, of course, the American Basketball Association (ABA) (who can forget the red, white, and blue ball?). The most curious thing about these successful rival leagues is the way the competition was resolved. In each case, the competing leagues were merged into or assimilated with the existing league. These combinations reestablished the former monopoly powers of the premerged single league. In essence, after competition the leagues were right back where they started, as anticompetitive, profit-maximizing cartels.

The story of the ABA is just one example. In terms of player salaries, the ABA could do two things. The ABA's first approach was to hire college stars for big money. Yet, the NBA teams could pay higher salaries. The ABA's second approach was to encourage established NBA players to switch leagues. Some players did jump leagues. Yet, most players were able to reap the benefits of interleague competition by merely threatening to jump leagues. As Koppett (1999) and others have pointed out, interleague rivalry was not in their best interests. The result was a minimerger in which the NBA did accept several of the ABA's strongest franchises.

Individual Employers—The Teams

While the leagues play a crucial role in establishing market power and in rule-making/enforcement procedures, the major employers in the professional sports industry are the teams within the leagues.

Team ownership has changed significantly over the years. Early owners tended to be former players who accumulated enough capital to get into the management side of the game. For example, in football the Chicago Bears were owned and coached by former player George Halas, and the Green Bay Packers were owned and coached by former player Curly Lambeau. A more recent example is Michael Jordan and the Washington Wizards basketball team. However, the days of former players as owners have mostly passed into history.

Today, owners tend to be billionaire business tycoons like Paul Allen, owner of the Portland Trailblazers and the Seattle Seahawks; Philip Schutz, owner of the Los Angeles Kings and the Los Angeles Lakers; and John McGraw, owner of the Vancouver Canucks, the Vancouver (now Memphis) Grizzlies, and partial owner of the Seattle Mariners. This list could go on and on, but the essential point is that team owners in professional sports leagues today are fabulously wealthy! While some argue about the profitability of these team franchises, the value of a franchise is illustrated by its selling price. In today's market, you can't buy a franchise for much less than $100 million. This is much more than the prices paid for even the most elite teams in the recent past. Table 2 gives a few examples of the increased selling prices for teams.

TABLE 2

Examples of Team Sales Prices[a]

Team	Sport	Price (year last sold	Previous sales price (year)
Texas Rangers	Baseball	$250.0 (1998)	$97.8 (1989)
Minnesota Vikings	Football	$250.0 (1998)	$100.0 (1991)
Philadelphia 76ers	Basketball	$125.0 (1996)	$12.0 (1981)
Edmonton Oilers	Hockey	$85.0 (1998)	$7.5 (1979)[b]

Sources: Quirk and Fort (1999); Quirk and Fort (1992).
[a] Sales prices in millions of dollars.
[b] Fee paid for entry into league.

In the past, profitability was a primary goal of most franchises. However, for today's millionaire and billionaire owners, it's not clear that profitability is the primary objective. Owning a team may be more of a rich person's hobby. Just as the big-game hunter spends big bucks to bag an exotic animal, today's team owners want winning teams, even if it means sometimes operating at a net loss. It is quite possible to spend huge sums of money to acquire players just to win a championship. Consider the recent case of Wayne Huizenga of Blockbuster Video. His Florida Marlins won the 1997 World Series after Mr. Huizenga spent millions of dollars to hire the best talent. Having accomplished that goal, the championship club was dismantled and it finished *last* the very next season.

Also consider the case of basketball as another example. Table 3 illustrates how team salaries are related to team winning percentages. In the 1997–1998 season, total team salaries averaged $33.4 million. There is a significant and positive correlation between total team salary and team winning percentage for the 1997–1998 season ($r = .51$). The higher the salaries the better the team's winning percentage.

The big question is whether team owners today are just in it for fun—or to make money. Table 4 presents data for operating income in each of the four sports covered in this chapter. As shown in Table 4, owning a major league team is not a remarkably profitable endeavor. Several individual players earn a single season salary in excess of the total operating revenue of many teams. Also, the variance in operating revenue from team to team is quite large. Some teams do well, while others, typically in smaller markets, are hard pressed to break even. This large income disparity was a major factor affecting recent collective bargaining

TABLE 3

NBA Team Income, Team Salaries, and Team Winning Percentages, 1997–1998

Team	Team income, 1996 ($ in millions)[a]	Projected team income, 1997 ($ in millions)[a]	Team salary 1997–1998 ($ in millions)[b]	Team winning percentage, 1997–1998[c]
New York Knicks	99.9	118.6	56.5	52.4
Chicago Bulls	86.8	103.0	61.7	75.6
Portland Trail Blazers	86.1	102.2	28.5	56.1
Los Angeles Lakers	81.3	96.5	36.6	74.4
Phoenix Suns	78.8	93.5	42.1	68.3
Detroit Pistons	77.3	91.8	27.1	45.1
Boston Celtics	64.6	76.7	27.4	43.9
Cleveland Cavaliers	64.5	76.6	27.8	57.3
Houston Rockets	62.8	74.5	28.0	50.0
Orlando Magic	62.8	74.5	45.8	50.0
Utah Jazz	61.4	72.9	28.5	75.6
San Antonio Spurs	59.7	70.9	42.9	68.3
Seattle SuperSonics	55.7	66.1	36.7	74.4
Charlotte Hornets	53.7	63.7	27.8	62.2
New Jersey Nets	52.9	62.8	34.1	52.4
Sacramento Kings	50.4	59.8	27.1	32.9
Toronto Raptors	49.4	58.6	25.3	19.5
Golden State Warriors	48.2	57.2	34.2	23.2
Indiana Pacers	47.8	56.7	38.9	70.7
Washington Wizards	45.9	54.5	40.9	51.2
Philadelphia 76ers	44.6	52.9	28.5	37.8
Miami Heat	44.3	52.6	34.6	67.1
Minnesota Timberwolves	44.0	52.2	27.3	54.9
Denver Nuggets	43.6	51.8	25.9	13.4
Vancouver Grizzlies	42.3	50.2	25.5	23.2
Dallas Mavericks	42.2	50.1	27.0	24.4
Atlanta Hawks	41.3	49.0	32.1	61.0
Milwaukee Bucks	36.4	43.2	24.9	43.9
Los Angeles Clippers	35.5	42.1	24.1	20.7
Totals	**1,664.2**	**1,975.4**	**967.8**	

[a] *Source:* Hoover's Online Database. Projected = 1996 income plus 18.7%.
[b] *Source: USA Today,* Statistical Archives <http://www.usatoday.com>.
[c] CNN *Sports Illustrated* (http://www.cnnsi.com/basketball/nba/stats/1998/stats.nbaatt.html).

negotiations in baseball, basketball, and hockey. Small-market owners have had major confrontations with their richer counterparts over changes in labor market rules and mechanisms. It seems clear that the big winners lately have been the players and their unions. We now turn our attention to these key actors.

TABLE 4

Estimates of Operating Income, 1996[a]

	Baseball	Football	Basketball	Hockey
Best	Yankees $38.3	Cowboys $30.2	Trail Blazers $33.5	Blackhawks $26.9
Worst	Reds -$14.0	Jets -$8.0	Bucks -$3.5	Coyotes -$11.7
Average	$7.3	$5.5	$11.2	$3.5

Source: Financial World (1997). Operating income equals revenues less costs for the year for each team. From operating income, teams subtract interest costs and player contract depreciation. Whatever is left over after these deductions is the pretax profit for the club in a particular year.
[a] Millions of dollars.

The Unions and the Players

Much has been written about the history of player unionization in professional team sports (Dworkin 1981). Players have overcome rather oppressive conditions and a monopsonistic labor market, where each player was owned—in perpetuity—by the club for which he played. The result of a monopsonistic labor market was control of player salaries. In the early years, collective bargaining did not exist, and individual salary negotiations were typically not very successful. A player seeking a higher salary had few options. He could *not* threaten to play for another team in his own league. In the absence of a rival league, he could *not* threaten to jump to the other league. He could threaten to hold out for more money, but, in so doing, he faced a situation of severe resource imbalance. His team had a much greater ability to withstand his holdout due to far greater resources. Finally, a player could always quit the game and go into another (probably less lucrative) occupation. Players were in a difficult position. Collective bargaining has changed the players' labor market fortunes.

Probably one of the most interesting differences between labor relations in professional sports and that of other industries covered in this book is that wage bargaining in the sports industry occurs at two levels. Through collective bargaining, the players' union and league management set minimum salaries for players with fewer years of service. These minimum salaries set the floor for the important individual negotiations that go on between each player and his club.

Today most players employ agents to negotiate their individual contracts. The high salaries that have resulted are legendary. Michael Jordan earned $33 million playing for the Chicago Bulls in 1997–1998. Kevin Garnett signed a six-year $126 million dollar contract with the

NBA's Minnesota Timberwolves. Table 5 illustrates just how high salaries have become. Nevertheless, while average player salaries are high, there is a lot of variation between the highest and lowest paid players. Most teams have a few players earning the professional minimum ($100,000 to $200,000), while the team superstar earns more than $10 million for a single season. There is also a lot of variance between the highest average team salary and the lowest average team salary.

TABLE 5
Average Salaries in Professional Sports[a]

	Baseball (1998)	Basketball (1997–1998)	Football (1997)	Hockey (1997–1998)
High team[b]	$2,555	$4,115	$1,091	$1,766
Low team[c]	352	1,603	593	831
Average	1,443	2,175	789	1,125

Sources: Various websites, Sports Illustrated, USA Today.
[a] In thousands of dollars.
[b] Baltimore Orioles, Chicago Bulls, Oakland Raiders, New York Rangers.
[c] Montreal Expos, Los Angeles Clippers, Carolina Panthers, New York Islanders.

Two questions immediately come to mind. Are these players worth the money? How did salaries get this high? Economic theory suggests that a club would be willing to pay a player in salary the extra amount of revenue he would bring in for the club. This extra revenue might come in the form of greater ticket sales, better TV contracts, and the like. Extremely popular superstars like Wayne Gretzky, Michael Jordan, Roger Clemens, and Brett Favre add real magic to their teams' economic fortunes. The trick for each team is to balance these highly paid super-stars with the remaining roster of "bargain basement" athletes and still have a club that can compete for a championship.

Under the labor market systems that existed in the past, players had severely restricted opportunities. Player reserve clauses gave the player's current team the right to require that the player sign with them again when his contract expired. In negotiation terminology, a player did not have a very good "BATNA," or best alternative to a negotiated agree-ment (Lewicki, Saunders, and Minton 1997). If a player could not play for another team, no other team could bid for his services. Perhaps his BATNA was to work at JCPenney's for $15,000. This would not be a very attractive alternative for the ballplayer, who would probably sign again with the same team for a relatively low salary.

But now, in the year 2002, all players in all sports enjoy free agency and in some cases salary arbitration, as well. These factors have significantly improved players' BATNAs and have enabled them to negotiate for much higher salaries. These improved alternatives are a direct result of the collective bargaining process. Through negotiations the players have significantly curtailed the labor market restrictions they faced for so long.

The case of baseball illustrates the importance of the two most important changes players gained: free agency and salary arbitration. For example, if the current club offers the player $1.3 million, his best alternative may be to go the route of free agency and be paid $1.8 million by another team. Free agency or even the threat of negotiating with another team has made the labor market for players much more competitive. In baseball, salary arbitration has been a second major alternative available to players. If the player is not able to obtain a satisfactory salary through negotiation, he may invoke binding arbitration and have his salary determined by an independent third-party arbitrator.

To summarize, all professional athletes today in baseball, basketball, football, and hockey are represented by a union—their players' association. The union negotiates over a traditional set of labor–management issues, such as minimum wages, hours of work, and other terms and conditions of employment. Players typically employ agents to negotiate their individual salaries. The unions have largely been responsible for the major gains players have seen in compensation over the years because free agency and salary arbitration provisions resulted from collective bargaining. These basic structural changes to the players' labor market have altered the game tremendously. However, while player unions have had a significant influence, we cannot ignore the role that government has had. It is to this final party in the system that we now turn our attention.

The Government

State, local, and federal government policies have profoundly affected all professional sports leagues. This issue has been covered in depth by other authors (Abrams 1998; Quirk and Fort 1999; Dworkin 1981), so here we summarize the key points.

A critical factor for small-market franchises is the generation of sufficient revenues to meet skyrocketing player payroll costs. One way to generate more revenue is through new stadium facilities, with lucrative skybox arrangements. In fact, it is possible to decrease the total number of stadium seats while increasing revenues through the construction of

more economically viable arenas. In addition, teams with expiring stadium or arena leases put pressure on local and state officials, threatening to relocate unless "better" facilities are built. Quirk and Fort (1999)
relate the story of the $210 million baseball stadium built for the Balti-
more Orioles, Camden Yards. As Hamilton (1997) and Kahn (1992)
have demonstrated, Camden Yards has been a great success for the Orioles, making them one of the most profitable baseball franchises since it
opened in 1992. Interestingly though, the stadium authority running the
facility loses almost $10 million per year. It's the taxpayers in the state of
Maryland who pay the tab.

Like Camden Yards, most recently built stadiums and arenas are single sport in nature and are publicly financed. These financing arrangements are negotiated with local and sometimes state officials. Often the
citizens get involved through the public referendum process. The bottom line from the labor relations perspective is that the revenue-generating aspects of new playing facilities provide player unions and player
agents the opportunity to demand a larger share of an increasing revenue
pie. As a result, the players' unions need to be sensitive to the public relations aspects of their sport so that public support is maintained. In the
decade of the 1990s alone, at least 40 different cities built or were in the
process of building new facilities (Jozsa and Guthrie 1999). Table 6 summarizes some of this activity to suggest the magnitude of what has
occurred.

TABLE 6
Recent Arena and Stadium Construction

City/year	Financing[a]	Seating capacity
Baltimore 1992 (baseball)	$210 publicly financed	48,000
Baltimore 1998 (football)	$200 publicly financed	65,000
Boston 1995 (hockey/basketball)	$160 privately financed	17,565
Boston 1997 (football)	$200 privately financed	76,000
Chicago 1994 (basketball)	$175 privately financed	21,711
Denver 1995 (baseball)	$215.5 publicly financed	50,100
Jacksonville 1996 (football)	$137 publicly financed	73,000
Milwaukee 1995 (baseball)	$250 publicly financed	42,500
Philadelphia 1991 (hockey/ basketball)	$210 privately financed	41,000
Tampa Bay 1996 (hockey)	$139 publicly financed	19,500
Tampa Bay 1998 (football)	$265 publicly financed	65,000

Sources: Various newspaper reports. Also see Noll and Zimbalist (1997).
[a] In millions of dollars.

The federal government has also been an important actor in professional sports labor relations. Most of this involvement has centered on the applicability of federal antitrust statutes to the various professional sports (Abrams 1998; Waller, Cohen, and Finkelmen 1995). Going back to the *Federal Baseball Club* Supreme Court decision in 1922, baseball has been exempted from antitrust law coverage (*Federal Baseball Club v. National League* 1922). Congress held many hearings over the years to address baseball's exemption, but it was not until 1998 that a major change occurred. That year, Congress passed and President Bill Clinton signed the Curt Flood Act (1998). The statute was named in honor of the famous baseball player, the late Curt Flood, who sat out one year in 1970 in order to avoid the restrictions of the player reserve clause (Flood and Carter 1970). The statute amended the nation's antitrust law to remove the exemption that baseball had enjoyed. However, the statute only removed the exemption as it applied to issues "directly relating to or affecting employment of major league baseball players" (Curt Flood Act 1998). In other respects, baseball continues to be exempted from the antitrust laws.

Other professional sports have not enjoyed baseball's antitrust exemption (Dworkin 1987). However, Congress also acted on antitrust issues involving other professional sports. While the inaction of Congress strengthened market power in baseball, its action strengthened the leagues' market power in football and basketball. Congress exempted football from antitrust laws when the NFL and AFL merged. The same approach was employed during the NBA–ABA merger negotiations. However, Congress has not done much to improve the market power of players in any sport.

Thus, the legal system, local and state politics, and the U.S. Congress have been important actors affecting labor relations in professional team sports. Much of the activity herein has taken place at the local level. No major federal statutes regulate the sports industry overall. Of course, this industry is covered by other federal statutes much the same as is all commerce in the United States.

Section III—Workers and Labor Markets

Each of the professional sports teams and leagues covered in the chapter employs several types of personnel. At the league level, we find managerial employees associated with conducting the business of the sport, ancillary personnel, and game officials. At the team level the basic types of employees are managerial (club officials); other employees involved in such things as ticket sales, promotions, concessions, and so on; and, of course, the players themselves. The two groups of employees most involved in labor relations issues have been the officials and players.

Officials

First, let us briefly consider the case of game officials. There have been several collective bargaining events involving sports officials, including the recent NFL officials' walkout, which ended when the officials voted, by e-mail, to approve the terms of a new contract. However, perhaps the most noteworthy event involving officials was the boggled attempt at a strike—of sorts—by the baseball umpires in 1999. A little background sets the stage for this event. Officials belong to unions for the purpose of collective bargaining with the respective leagues. The baseball umpires formed the Major League Umpires Association (MLUA) in 1978. Over the years, the umpires engaged in several job actions (1979, 1984, 1991), and the leagues imposed a lockout in 1995.

The precipitating factor for the 1999 umpires' job action was the incident involving Roberto Alomar, of the Baltimore Orioles, and umpire John Hirschbeck, on September 27, 1996. Alomar spit in Hirschbeck's face after he was ejected from the game for arguing a third-strike call. Umpires were enraged by the light five-day suspension meted out to Alomar by then–American League president Gene Budig (Dworkin and Staudohar forthcoming). Further incensing the umpires was the decision by Major League Baseball to hire Sandy Alderson as executive vice president of baseball operations. Alderson's responsibilities would include labor relations dealings with the umpires group. Power and authority would thus be consolidated in one person versus the older approach where each league president (National League—Len Coleman, American League—Gene Budig) dealt with labor matters separately. Umpires were also riled about baseball wanting the rulebook "high" strike to be called. Management was also pressing to change the postseason work rules, whereby 75 percent of all umpires had been guaranteed postseason work. This system was better for the umpires than were the arrangements used in hockey, football, and basketball, where only the highest graded officials in the regular season were entitled to work in the postseason.

What happened next was absolutely amazing. The collective bargaining agreement (CBA) was set to expire on December 31, 1999. Because the season would be over, the union realized that an effective strike could not occur when the contract expired. In a serious tactical mistake, MLUA executive director Richie Phillips persuaded fifty-five umpires to resign on September 2, 1999. This would mean they would not work the last work weeks of the regular season, nor the play-offs.

This tactic was designed to pressure Major League Baseball to accede to the terms of a new collective bargaining contract that would be favorable for the umpires. The strategy failed badly on two counts. First, baseball was ready with a supply of talented replacement umpires. Second, the umpires' union did not have the solidarity of purpose necessary to pull off an action of this sort successfully.

Many of the umpires who resigned later rescinded their resignations. While 55 percent of the National League umpires rescinded their resignation and were rehired, only 36 percent of the American League umpires followed suit. Yet, fan support was running strongly against the umpires and in favor of Major League Baseball.

The leagues hired a total of twenty-five replacement umpires. Twenty-two umpires had their resignations accepted by the two leagues. The umpires' union tried several things to get jobs back for its members who had resigned. A suit in U.S. District Court in Philadelphia to acquire a court order allowing umpires to rescind their resignations was unsuccessful. Another unsuccessful ploy was an unfair labor practice claim filed against Major League Baseball, contending significant changes in terms and conditions of employment by shifting authority over umpires from league presidents to the commissioner's office. Both the unfair labor practice charge and the lawsuit were later dropped.

For twenty-two lost jobs, all the union obtained in the final settlement was a split of the $1.36 million postseason bonus among all umpires, whether still working or not. The union also received the right to arbitrate the issue of whether the twenty-two terminated umpires were treated in a discriminatory or recriminatory fashion.

In November of 1999, the umpires voted in an NLRB supervised election to decertify their union and replace it with a new one, the World Umpires Association. Their first president is John Hirschbeck and their executive director is player–agent Ron Shapiro. Thus ended one of the most abortive job action attempts ever witnessed in professional sports. In addition, the positions of American League and National League president were eliminated in favor of the consolidation of power in the office of the commissioner. The strike zone has been enlarged. The final chapter to this bizarre event was written when arbitrator Alan Symonette ordered Major League Baseball to rehire nine of the twenty-two umpires who had been terminated in 1999. The terminations of the other thirteen umpires who had resigned and later rescinded their resignations were upheld.

Players

Players have been studied in terms of their education and skills, their compensation, and racial and demographic issues. Each of these topics is discussed in the following sections.

Education and Skills. Most players in baseball and hockey are developed through extensive minor league systems. Some players in these two sports come into the minors (or majors) after completing a college career. But for the most part, baseball and hockey players tend to be high school educated with some college. By contrast, in basketball and football the vast majority of players finish four years of college eligibility before entering the professional ranks. Colleges serve as the minor league training grounds for both basketball and football players. These two sports do not have an extensive system of minor league franchises. Thus, on average, education levels are higher for basketball and football players than for hockey and baseball players.

In terms of skill level, major league players have incredible and unusual talents. It is highly unlikely that any of the millions of children playing sports will eventually become a college athlete. Only the very best of that talented lot of players are lucky enough to have the skills to propel them to a college athletic scholarship or a minor league contract. Every once in a while, a superstar high school athlete may jump directly to a professional league, but this is a rare event. In terms of skill level, what we find in the professional sports leagues are the best of the best (Sullivan 1992; Marburger 1997).

This small number of persons with incredible skills generate large earnings. By contrast, officials only earn a fraction of the million dollar salaries of the players. Yet, there are a lot more people who have the necessary skills to become umpires than there are people who can become players. Fewer people possess the necessary traits to enable them to become professional athletes. Those who do possess such skills are therefore appropriately compensated for their scarce skills and talents. Perhaps some of the on-field tension between umpires and players described earlier in this chapter can be attributed to jealousy or animosity over these pay differentials.

Compensation. The earnings of professional athletes are illustrated by the empirical data in Table 5. Salaries have soared since restrictive labor market practices of the past have been abolished. For just one brief example, consider the situation in baseball on opening day of the

2001 season. The average salary of a professional player now exceeds $2 million for the first time. The precise average pay for a baseball player on an opening day roster in 2001 was $2,264,403, which represents a large 14 percent increase over opening day 2000. Table 7 contains some interesting data on average baseball player salaries over the years. This table illustrates that in the year 2001 baseball players' salaries were twenty-two times greater than they were in 1979. By contrast, average household incomes in the United States in 2001 were not quite three times greater than they were in 1979. The highest paid baseball player in 2001 was Texas shortstop Alex Rodriguez, at $22 million. A distant second was Los Angeles Dodgers pitcher Kevin Brown, who earned $15.7 million in 2001. The three highest team payrolls in 2001 belonged to the Yankees ($109.8 million), the Red Sox ($109.5 million) and the Dodgers ($109 million). The average player on one of these three clubs earned in excess of $4 million. At the other end of the spectrum were the Minnesota Twins, with a total payroll of $24.4 million. An average Minnesota player in 2001 earned less than $1 million.

TABLE 7
Baseball Player Salaries

Year	Average salary (baseball)	Average household income
1979	$100,000	$19,554
1992	1,000,000	38,804
2001	2,264,403	54,842

Sources: USA Today Baseball Weekly (April 11–17, 2001); U.S. Bureau of the Census.

In 2001 there were thirty-five players at the top of the earnings ladder, making in excess of $9 million. Only nine players had earnings at that level in 1999, while twenty players exceeded that mark in the 2000 season. At the bottom of the salary ladder there were just thirty-nine players on opening day rosters in April of 2001 who earned the major league minimum salary of $200,000. This number declined from forty-six in the 2000 season and sixty-eight players in 1999.

This illustrates how player salaries in all professional sports continue to spiral upward. How high can these salaries soar? Is there an end in sight? Will collective bargaining continue to help players achieve greater and greater financial success, or will the entire labor relations system come crashing to a sudden halt? The answers to these questions will be explored later, when we describe the bargaining context in the four major professional sports.

Race and Demographics. Now let's turn our attention to demographics and racial discrimination in the labor market for professional athletes. Much of the useful writing on this topic has been done by Lawrence Kahn (2000). The data reveal that in the 1990s baseball players were about 30 percent black, with another large Hispanic group. In the NFL, blacks made up 65 percent of the player rosters, while in the NBA this figure was as high as 80 percent (Staudohar 1996). Indeed, much progress has been made compared to the pre–Jackie Robinson era in baseball and other professional sports. Many black and Hispanic athletes are among the highest paid in their cohort group. In other jobs, like managerial and front office positions, minorities have not fared as well (Fizel, Gustafson, and Hadley 1996; Zimbalist 1992).

Many authors have addressed the question of racial discrimination, and a review of the literature suggests some conclusions. There have been studies in baseball, basketball, football, and hockey (Christiano 1986, 1988; Dey 1997; Kahn 1992; Jones and Walsh 1988; Lavoie 2000; Longley 2000). Gary Becker (1957) suggested partitioning discrimination into three types: employer, coworker, and customer. For example, some baseball teams exhibited employer discrimination by being very slow to bring black ballplayers to the major leagues. Teams quick to employ blacks typically had greater success on the field of play. Coworker discrimination was exhibited when certain white players threatened to strike or not play against or with black players. Customer discrimination was exemplified by threatening letters to great players like Jackie Robinson and later to Hank Aaron (Tygiel 1983; Aaron and Wheeler 1991).

The empirical evidence on salary discrimination has been striking. In basketball, Kahn and Sherer (1988) showed whites received 25 percent higher salaries, controlling for productivity. Hamilton (1997) also found some evidence of racial discrimination in the 1994–1995 NBA season but only for star players. By way of contrast, recent empirical work has not found much evidence of salary discrimination against minorities in baseball, hockey, or football (Kahn 2000).

Discrimination can also be looked at from other angles. Do black players get drafted based on their talent levels? Do they receive the same kinds of marketing endorsements and commercial opportunities as similarly situated white players? What about assignment discrimination? There is some evidence that most quarterbacks are white. Of course, quarterbacks on average are the highest paid NFL players. Hoose (1989) documented how positional or assignment discrimination is prevalent in professional sports.

Finally, a word about tenure, or what might be called retention discrimination. Are minority ballplayers likely to have shorter careers than their white counterparts, ceteris paribus? All professional athletes tend to have short playing careers. This shortness of career heightens the importance of (a) earning as much as possible during one's playing career and (b) having a college degree or marketable skills for that inevitable moment when one's career ends. Empirical evidence suggests exit discrimination against black athletes. One study by Jiobu (1988) found that black players in baseball had significantly higher exit rates than their white counterparts. Hoang and Rascher (1999) report similar empirical findings for black NBA players. In an occupation where career length is short to begin with, a loss of two years due to the color of one's skin can have major economic consequences.

In summary, there is evidence that minorities have progressed a long way in the field of professional sports. Many blacks and other minorities earn huge salaries as professional athletes. The evidence on salary discrimination suggests that the problem of lower salaries for blacks, ceteris paribus, has subsided considerably. Other more subtle aspects of discrimination still need to be addressed. There seems to be fairly strong evidence of discrimination against blacks in areas such as position assignment, tenure, and even fan racial preferences. Until black and white athletes are treated equitably on all of these dimensions, the professional sports industry will still have to wrestle with the problem of racial bias.

Section IV—The Bargaining Context

In this section we will take each of the four sports and bring the reader up to date on the major developments in bargaining since the 1980s. Recent critical issues will be examined, with an eye toward the future of labor relations and bargaining in each sport. Since much of the earlier material on this subject has been covered elsewhere, historical events will be briefly summarized with references provided for the interested reader.

Baseball

The history of baseball unionization goes back to the days of John Montgomery Ward in the late nineteenth century (Dworkin 1981). Since all of this historical material is found elsewhere (Miller 1991; Miller 1990; Kuhn 1987; Lowenfish 1991; Scully 1989, 1995), suffice it to say that the unionization of baseball players came about because of player concerns over poor salaries (Feinstein 1993). These poor salaries were basically due to the reservation system that the owners had implemented (Koppett 1998). Both Koppett (1998) and Costas (2000) provide interesting summaries of the labor relations situation in baseball since the 1980s. Earlier events, such as the initial unionization efforts, establishment and eventual elimination of the player reservation system, and collective bargaining negotiations up to the 1981 strike, are thoroughly discussed in Dworkin (1981).

The Major League Baseball Players Association (MLBPA) survived the 1981 strike in good shape. Free agency was preserved. Future rounds of negotiation would feature some minor tweaking of the system, but for several years free agency was a major impediment to player movement. Long-time MLBPA leader Marvin Miller retired in 1982 (Miller 1991). It would not be at all surprising to someday soon find a bust of Marvin Miller in Cooperstown. A new union leader was chosen. Donald Fehr had been with the MLBPA since 1976 and was well prepared to take on this important leadership role. His first challenge was to be the 1984 negotiations.

In these negotiations, the idea of a salary cap was proposed by the clubs. For their part, players wanted increased contributions to their pension funds based on greater TV revenues. Rhetoric heated up and a midseason strike date of August 6, 1984, was set. In early August Commissioner Peter Ueberroth got involved and resisted the owners' proposed salary cap. Of course, this action by *their* commissioner did not make the owners very happy. The players did strike briefly on August 6 and 7, but a quick settlement ensued. A bit of rescheduling allowed for the entire 162-game season to be completed.

The settlement terms were unremarkable. As expected, the salary cap idea went nowhere. Players did receive a doubling of their pension contributions and a higher minimum salary. More importantly, the issue that caused the 1981 strike, compensation for teams losing a free agent player, was gone. However, the owners did gain something in the area of salary arbitration. The new pact specified that it would henceforth require three years of major league service, instead of two, for players to qualify for salary arbitration. This concession has proved to be significant for the owners, as they retained an additional season of labor market monopsony power before the player could invoke salary arbitration.

After the 1985 season something strange happened. It seemed like the market for free agents had totally dried up, as players were not receiving any offers, except from their own teams. The players suspected something was amiss and filed a grievance claiming collusion among the teams. The union eventually prevailed at arbitration in three separate cases. The impact of these collusion cases is being felt many years later (Greenberger 2001). The Indians paid eight players a total of $610,000 in 1994, as additional compensation for collusion that had occurred in the 1986 season. The Indians also paid fourteen players $1.5 million in collusion damages for the 1987 season. The team argued in court that it should owe social security and unemployment insurance withholding taxes based on the lower rates in effect in 1986 and 1987. In a decision written for the Supreme Court, Justice Ruth Bader Ginsburg wrote that the IRS has consistently interpreted the rules "to require taxation of back wages according to the year the wages are actually paid, regardless of when those wages were earned or should have been paid" (*United States v. Cleveland Indians* 2001).

It turns out that these collusion rulings also had a big impact on the next round of negotiations in baseball in 1990. Baseball management had yet another new plan to attempt to restrict skyrocketing player salaries. This plan would designate a certain percentage of baseball revenues to be spent on player salaries (39 percent). Another part of the plan would set up a classification system with salaries based on seniority and performance criteria (Hendricks 1994).

The players and their union wanted no part of this frontal attack on their free agency system (Jennings 1997). Once again the baseball commissioner, now Fay Vincent, stepped in on the side of the players. His goal was to simply see the games continue without a major altercation. Negotiations stalled and 1990 spring training began almost one month late. The parties were able to truncate the spring training season and managed to play a full 162-game schedule in 1990. Minor changes to the CBA included higher minimum salaries, more pension money, and some players with less than three years of major league service would now be eligible for salary arbitration. But no changes were made to the free agency system. The contract was to run for four years with a re-opener on major issues after three years. The parties also set up a panel of experts to study the economics of the industry. Finally, the parties agreed that the penalty for future collusion violations by the owners would be triple damages.

The next big confrontation would occur in 1994, but the stage was set many months earlier. Table 8 lays out the interesting chronology of events leading up to the biggest battle of all. The stage was set, but neither side thought their opponent would actually allow a strike to interrupt the season. The players didn't believe that the owners would risk losing the lucrative postseason games. The owners didn't believe that the players would strike in the middle of a championship season. Both sides were wrong!

TABLE 8

Chronology of a Strike in Baseball

Date	Event
12/7/92	Baseball owners vote 15–13 to reopen contract.
12/8/92	Owners notify players of possible lockout.
2/17/93	Owners link revenue sharing to salary cap.
8/12/93	Owners unable to agree on revenue sharing plan.
	Owners promise no lockout through end of 1994 season.
8/16/93	Players agree not to strike during 1993 season.
12/31/93	1990 collective bargaining agreement expires.
1/18/94	Owners agree on revenue sharing—still tied to salary cap.
1/19/94	Commissioner's office put in charge of collective bargaining.
3/7/94	Players told that a salary cap is a must.
6/8/94	Owners decide they must have a 3/4 vote (21–7) to approve any CBA reached during a strike.
6/14/94	Owners present their proposals.
7/18/94	Players reject these proposals and make counterproposals.
7/27/94	Owners reject counterproposals from players.
7/28/94	Players set August 12, 1994, strike date.

Source: Koppett (1998).

The entire remainder of the season was cancelled due to the ongoing dispute. There was no World Series in 1994 for the first time in ninety years. The World Series had even gone on during the tumultuous years of World War II. Yet, this was a labor war and all play was halted. Many proposals and counterproposals were exchanged. President Clinton got involved by appointing a well-known federal mediator, Bill Usery, to facilitate negotiations. Of course, once the season was lost in 1994, all eyes turned toward 1995. What would happen? Would baseball be permanently damaged from this labor–management strife (Burk 2001)?

The rhetoric continued to heat up. The owners threatened to hire replacement players. This strategy had been employed unsuccessfully in professional football and also once before in baseball at the time of the so-called Ty Cobb strike (Dworkin 1981; Burk 1994). The replacement player strategy was set to go, except in Toronto, where Canadian law forbade the use of replacements. Also, Baltimore Orioles owner Peter Angelos maintained that his team would not use replacement players. Thus, the owners' strategy had a couple of flaws in it from the very beginning.

On December 23, 1994, the owners declared an impasse in bargaining and asserted that their final offer, including a salary cap, the elimination of salary arbitration, and a restricted free agency plan, would be put into effect. The players filed unfair labor practice charges, claiming management had not bargained in good faith over mandatory subjects of bargaining, including wages. The fact that the NLRB was likely to uphold the players unfair labor practice complaint caused the owners to take pause and reevaluate some of their strategies.

The owners opened spring training camps on March 2 with replacement players. The NLRB ruled in favor of the players on the unfair labor practice charge. The NLRB general counsel then went before a federal court judge (Sonia Sotomayor) to seek an injunction against baseball's use of new rules and to reinstate all of the terms of the expired labor agreement until a new one was reached. The players agreed to end their strike if this injunction was granted. Judge Sotomayor granted the injunction on March 31, 1994, and the strike ended. But what happened?

The 1995 season started with the old CBA in effect. Of course, the season started late and the total number of games played would be 144. The new labor agreement wasn't signed until December 1996. This new pact covered 1996 through 2000, with a provision to continue it through the 2001 season if the players agreed. The agreement was in fact extended through the 2001 championship season.

Who won in this most recent round of negotiations in baseball? The players held on to free agency and salary arbitration (Abrams 2000). Minimum salaries were once again increased. The MLBPA demonstrated once again the solidarity of strength it had in terms of player acceptance of the union's objectives.

Two new concepts emerged from the 1996 negotiations. First, the two parties agreed on an experiment to try interleague games during the regular season. These games have proved to be popular in the ensuing years. Second, the parties created a payroll tax to be charged to any team whose player salary costs exceeded a certain specified amount. These revenues would go into a special fund where the monies could be distributed from the richer large-market teams to the poorer small-market clubs. Not a lot of money was involved here, but at least the concept of revenue sharing among the clubs was finally addressed.

It is noteworthy that club revenue sharing is a management issue that could be resolved unilaterally. The clubs had tried to tie revenue sharing to the idea of a salary cap. No salary cap exists in baseball, but the owners did decide on their own to experiment with a revenue sharing plan. Whether this will be sufficient to address the huge problems baseball faces in the battle of haves and have-nots will be addressed in the next section of this chapter. The next round of negotiations in professional baseball is set to begin after the 2001 season concludes. The key future issues facing baseball and all sports will be considered later in this chapter. The game has gone through a fascinating journey, but the future harbors many uncertainties (Phalen 2000; Anderson 2000; Waller, Cohen, and Finkelman 1995).

Basketball

The history of NBA labor relations has been extensively covered by Staudohar (1996) and Dworkin (1981). While not having the 100 years plus of player unionization history found in baseball, basketball players have been unionized for many years. As Staudohar (1996) reports, Bob Cousy helped form the National Basketball Players Association (NBPA) in 1954. Not much happened in the way of collective bargaining until the players hired attorney Lawrence Fleisher as their general counsel in 1962. The first CBA between the league and the players was signed in 1973.

As in baseball, a big issue in NBA labor relations was the concept of the perpetual nature of the reserve clause in each player's contract. However, this player control mechanism was eliminated as part of the court-approved settlement in class action litigation dealing with antitrust issues and the merger of the ABA and the NBA (*Robertson v. National Basketball Association* 1976). After that case was resolved, the two sides agreed on a new collective bargaining contract in 1976. Key terms were damages paid to 500 players to the tune of $4.5 million, the elimination of the option (reserve) clause, the establishment of a first refusal system for players receiving offers from other teams, and the gradual elimination of the compensation system for teams losing free agents.

Before this settlement, a team losing a free agent was entitled to some compensation for its loss in the form of draft choices, cash, or roster players. That system was gradually phased out. The alternative was the first refusal approach, which allowed a team to retain one of its free agent players by matching the offer made by another team.

The next agreement was reached in 1983. There was no player strike in the NBA that year, but the referees did walk out for two months over salary issues. There were high expectations that a player strike was going to occur in 1983. However, both sides negotiated in good faith and an agreement was reached on March 31, 1983. A major stumbling block was the high salaries paid to NBA players. To address this concern, the parties agreed to spend a maximum of 53 percent of gross revenues on player salaries. They also agreed on the concept of a salary cap. Table 9 provides data on salary cap levels for the twelve-season period, from 1984–1985 through 1995–1996. The idea behind the salary cap was to create balance among rich and poor teams. No rich-market team would be able to buy up all of the best talent and win the league championship year after year. Teams would have a budget to manage. Of course, a team did not have to spend up to the level of the cap. The cap was supposed to set a maximum spending level per team for player personnel.

TABLE 9

NBA Salary Cap

Season	Salary cap
1984–85	$3,600,000
1985–86	4,233,000
1986–87	4,945,000
1987–88	6,164,000
1988–89	7,232,000
1989–90	9,802,000
1990–91	11,871,000
1991–92	12,500,000
1992–93	14,000,000
1993–94	15,175,000
1994–95	15,974,000
1995–96	23,000,000

Source: Staudohar (1996); National Basketball Association.

The problem with this approach has been what are referred to as loopholes, or ways to get around the salary cap and spend more money on player salaries. As just one example, teams are allowed to retain at *any* price one of their players who becomes a free agent. Many teams spent a lot of time and effort figuring out innovative ways to live within and beyond their salary cap.

The 1983 pact expired on June 15, 1987, with three major issues looming. The big three were the aforementioned salary cap, the right of first refusal, and the college draft. While threats of strikes and union decertification were heard, in the end cooler heads prevailed, and a new six-year contract was reached in April 1988, without a major confrontation. The parties resolved the college draft issue by reducing the number of rounds from seven to three and eventually to just two. Veteran players would no longer be subject to the right of first refusal. That is, they could sign with a new club without having their old club match their new offer. Finally, while the salary cap was retained, there were still opportunities for clubs to exceed their agreed on limits. The abuse of the salary cap has led to major problems in negotiations.

The 1988 collective bargaining contract expired on June 23, 1994. By this time the NBPA had seen enough and sought to eliminate the draft, the salary cap, and first refusal. Peace was restored temporarily as the players agreed to finish out the 1994–1995 season without a new labor agreement in place. Yet, lingering antagonisms remained and both sides were ready to do battle. The owners filed a lawsuit in which they claimed a continuation of the 1988 CBA would not violate antitrust laws. The owners also sought a ruling that the salary cap, draft, and right of first refusal were valid even if antitrust law was applied. Players argued that once their CBA expired, the antitrust law labor exemption no longer was in effect.

Several players, led by Michael Jordan, filed a union decertification petition with the NLRB. The idea was to remove the labor exemption to the antitrust laws by no longer having a union. The players eventually voted 226–134 against decertification, so this tactic did not succeed. The league feared a lengthy antitrust battle should decertification occur and, thus, decided to take the offensive by calling for a lockout on June 30, 1995. Would Commissioner Stern really use the lockout tactic and threaten the start of the NBA season? Baseball had just lost part of a season plus a World Series to a labor battle. Was the same going to occur in basketball? Not this time! For the time being basketball was able to maintain its record of never having to cancel a game due to a strike or lockout.

An agreement was reached whereby the players' share of gross defined revenues increased from 53 to 55 percent. Players also received additional licensing revenues, and the salary cap increased incrementally to $32 million in the last year of the contract. The salary cap remained flexible with many of the loopholes the players so desired. The owners won smaller annual pension contribution increases plus an important cap on rookie salaries.

The biggest battle of all was looming in the upcoming 1998 negotiations. In earlier negotiations both sides had agreed that the 53 percent of the revenue cap should not be a hard cap. Exceptions would be allowed. One of these important exceptions was referred to as the "Larry Bird exception" (Zimbalist 2000). This exception allowed a team to re-sign one of its own players at *any* salary, regardless of the impact on the team's salary cap. The clubs readily used the Larry Bird exception. It allowed them some measure of roster stability. This was especially important in light of the reverse-order-of-finish draft procedure utilized by the NBA. Teams were able to keep superstar players and were also building stronger fan loyalty. Other teams usually would not have enough room within their own salary caps to make a huge offer to a free agent. The home team had a big advantage in retaining star players, so the salary cap idea seemed to work for the clubs.

As the 1998 negotiations approached, the key issue again was soaring player salaries. Commissioner David Stern claimed that the NBA, as a whole, had lost $30 million in the previous season and could no longer afford these huge losses (Fatsis and Weinbach 1999). By now the owners also thought that the Larry Bird exception was part of the problem and wanted to eliminate it. Perhaps the clubs also felt they might take advantage of the internal strife the union had gone through in the previous round of talks in 1995–1998. When negotiations with the union stalled, the owners instituted a lockout on July 1, 1998. Table 10 gives a brief chronology of the 1998 NBA lockout.

TABLE 10
1998 NBA Lockout

Date	Action
3/23/98	Owners vote 27–2 to reopen the CBA after the 1997–1998 season.
6/22/98	Negotiation session ends after thirty minutes, with players saying no to the idea of a "hard cap."
6/30/98	NBA announces lockout to begin next day.
7/1/98	Third lockout in NBA history begins.
8/6/98	Talks resume but owners walk out.
9/24/98	NBA cancels twenty-four exhibition games and postpones training camps.
10/5/98	NBA cancels remainder of exhibition season.
10/8/98	Bargaining session ends with little progress. First two weeks of regular season cancelled.
10/20/98	Arbitrator Feerick rules owners do not have to pay on guaranteed contracts during a lockout.
11/20/98	Thirteen-hour negotiation session ends with real progress.
12/27/98	NBA makes final proposal.
1/4/99	Union makes final proposal.
1/6/99	Stern and Hunter reach new agreement to end lockout the day prior to NBA's drop dead date for cancelling the entire season.

Source: Associated Press.

The NBA, for the first time in its history, cancelled regular-season games due to a labor dispute. In all, 437 games were called off due to the lockout. The season resumed in early February 1999 and was 52 games in length rather than the regular 82-game schedule. Nevertheless, the new pact was received as a victory of sorts for Mr. Stern and the NBA in that the main goal of curbing runaway salary increases was achieved. How was this achieved? The NBA clubs for the first time won limits on the maximum amounts of money a team could pay to an individual player! This concept was unprecedented. Never before had a collective bargaining agreement in professional sports set a maximum on individual player salaries. Unions in all sports have negotiated minimum salaries. After that, agents have taken over and negotiated individual player salaries with the respective teams. No other major professional sport has yet embraced the notion of a maximum player salary.

In the end, the NBA players, led by former federal prosecutor Billy Hunter, agreed to a season-saving deal to avert further losses. The lockout had already cost the players $500 million in salaries and the NBA $1 billion in league revenues. What sweetened the deal for the players was the concession the owners made to give them 55 percent of the NBA's total revenues in the last three years of the pact. The league also allowed for exceptions to the salary cap that would benefit midrange players. Minimum salaries were now to be tied to years of service in the NBA.

The owners won significant gains too. Players with less than ten years of NBA service could earn no more than $11 million per year. Recall that in a single season alone Michael Jordan's salary had been $33 million! Also, free agents who remained with their home team would be limited to annual pay increases of no more than 12 percent.

The final terms were contained in a six-year contract. It included an escrow system to go into effect after the first three years of the new pact. This system was set up so that beginning with the 2001–2002 season, player salaries would be reduced if total salaries and benefits exceed 55 percent of a carefully defined concept of revenue called basketball related income (BRI). As noted earlier, several salary cap exceptions, such as the Larry Bird exception, the $1 million exception, and a new creature referred to as the middle class exception, were either retained or established through the process of collective bargaining.

The middle class exception is particularly interesting and has been the focus of recent research (Hill and Groothuis 2001). Those authors argue that the new salary cap exceptions tend to reduce the skewness of the distribution of NBA salaries by redistributing income from the highly paid superstars to the average players. This indicates a shift in the union's strategy away from the highest salaries possible for superstars toward greater concern for an equitable internal distribution of player salaries. It will be very interesting to see if other unions follow their pattern and negotiate provisions to correct salary skewness (Gramlich 1994).

The parties also agreed that maximum salary increases for Larry Bird exception contracts would be limited to 12.5 percent, while for all other contracts the maximum increase per year was set at 10 percent. Players with zero to six years of experience could receive a maximum salary of $9 million. Those with seven to nine years could receive a maximum of $11 million. Finally, a player with ten or more years could receive a maximum salary of $14 million per season.

The agreement also contains a sliding scale minimum for rookies and other players. The rookie minimum salary was set at $275,000. This minimum salary scale increases to $1 million for players with ten or more years of NBA service.

The midlevel exception to the salary cap was set at $1.75 million for the initial year of the new contract and thereafter increases to 108 percent of the average NBA salary for the prior season. This exception can be used once per year and is again specifically designed to increase the salaries of middle range players. This is consistent with the median voter model described by White (1986).

The jury is still out on the outcome of the NBA 1998–1999 negotiations. The two biggest union concessions were the agreements to limit individual player salaries and to accept a hard salary cap at 55 percent of BRI. The big player gain was in salary distribution. All middle range basketball players will benefit from this new collective bargaining pact in the years to come. More players in the NBA are now earning salaries in the $1 to $2 million range, while fewer players in the NBA today earn less than $1 million per season.

Perhaps hockey, baseball, or football might emulate aspects of the new NBA collective bargaining agreement. The next round of bargaining in baseball is set for 2002, while in the National Hockey League a new deal will be negotiated in 2003. It will probably take some time to fully assess the most recent NBA negotiations (Hyman 2001a). Is the NBA hurting? If so, how much? While the labor scene may be calm, the NBA has had a thuggish image and fan interest (TV ratings) is waning. TV ratings are 35 percent lower than in the Michael Jordan era. The NBA's current $2.6 billion TV deal expires after the 2001–2002 season. A big question is whether NBC will renegotiate that contract and at what level. Chances are that NBC and the NBA will reach a new deal. Television revenues are a crucial part of the NBA's financial health picture. A big issue for the future health of the NBA is whether the league will be able to increase revenues from the network television agreement. Can the NBA have the same success in these negotiations as it did in its most recent labor negotiations?

Football

In football, the first players' union was conceived by Cleveland Brown players Abe Gibron and Dante Lavelli (Staudohar 1996). The actual founding of the National Football League Players Association (NFLPA) occurred in 1956. Their first aggressive union leader, Edward Garvey, was hired in 1971. In the early years, Garvey led the union to shut down training camps for forty-two days in 1974. The NFLPA was also the first sports union to become affiliated with the AFL-CIO (1979). Perhaps Mr. Garvey is best remembered for his success in getting the courts to nullify the so-called Rozelle Rule.

Prior to 1976 football players were subjected to the same monopsonistic labor market rules that existed in other professional sports. Staudohar (1996) and Dworkin (1981) have covered the various legal challenges the players made against this player control system. An early decision established the principle that pro football was covered under antitrust laws (*Radovich v. NFL* 1957). In 1962 player R. C. Owens, of the San Francisco 49ers, played out his option and signed with the Baltimore Colts. To prevent further player movement of this type, the owners promulgated the Rozelle Rule. This rule allowed the commissioner at that time, Pete Rozelle, to award whatever he deemed to be fair compensation (e.g., draft choices, cash, players) to any team losing a player to a new team after that player had played out his option year. The huge amount of uncertainty caused by the guessing over what fair compensation might be brought the signing of "free agent" players to a standstill. In fact, over the thirteen-year period, from 1963 to 1976, only four such players were able to play out their options and sign with a new club.

Legal challenges brought by Joe Kapp (*Kapp v. NFL* 1979) and John Mackey (*Mackey v. NFL* 1977) finally brought an end to the Rozelle Rule. Players were at last able to become free agents without the onerous compensation barrier previously described. The 1977 collective bargaining process included a new method of determining compensation payments. The 1982 CBA liberalized free agency a bit more, but in truth, things were really not that much better than in the earlier days of the Rozelle Rule. In the ten-year period, between 1977 and 1987, only one free agent was able to sign with a new team.

In earlier years NFL teams had no real incentives to spend huge amounts of money on player salaries. Players had little leverage. As described earlier with reference to baseball players, NFL players did not have many alternatives. They could play in Canada or threaten to not play at all. One NFL player typically will not have the superstar value or impact on team success found in other sports like basketball. A big break for NFL players came with the formation of the USFL. As in other sports, NFL teams had to raise salaries significantly to prevent league jumping and to sign the top college stars.

Football players have been no strangers to job actions. They struck in 1968 over pensions and again over pensions and grievance procedures in 1970. The much longer training camp strike in 1974 primarily dealt with the Rozelle Rule issue previously discussed. A bitter outcome from this 1974 episode was some loss of union solidarity as veteran players crossed picket lines to return to work. Power and victory seemed to be on the side of the owners entering the 1982 negotiations.

In 1982 the players demanded a fixed percentage of NFL gross revenues (55 percent) for their salaries. This demand was later modified into a wage scale based on seniority. With little progress made in their talks, the players walked out after the second week of the 1982 season. The strike lasted fifty-seven days and ended because both sides feared that the entire season would be cancelled if a deal was not reached quickly. In this strike, player solidarity again waned as the stalemate dragged on. The strong solidarity found among unionized baseball players did not seem to transfer to their NFL brethren. Times are always difficult when some players support their union while others do not. The recent movie *Replacements* (2000) depicts what happens when a football players' union is so divided.

The outcome of this confrontation was a $1.28 billion guaranteed wage package over five years. No substantial changes were made to the free agency system. Most observers claim correctly that this settlement was a victory for the owners (Staudohar 1996), allowing them to be quite profitable. For example, in the 1982–1986 period, the average annual TV income per team was $13.6 million (Wulf 1993). The average player salary during that same time was $100,000, and total payroll costs averaged around $5 million per team. This was far less than the annual TV revenues, to say nothing of the income from packed stadiums each Sunday. The NFL was a profitable enterprise!

The 1982 CBA was set to expire on August 31, 1987 (Staudohar 1987). The big question was whether another job action would take place. The owners came to the 1987 negotiations well prepared for any contingency. The owners' strategy was formulated by a veteran labor negotiator, Jack Donlan. Mr. Donlan had arranged for a $150 million line of credit to cushion the blow of a potential strike. The owners had several other advantages. There was no longer a USFL, so players who wanted to jump leagues had no other option but the Canadian Football League. The NFL was also well prepared with replacement players. Each team roster contained many extra players just in case of a walkout. The NFLPA was not well prepared. Instead of building up strike funds and loan commitments, the union concentrated on the issue of maintaining player solidarity. This was not a bad idea, but it took NFLPA Executive Director Gene Upshaw away from the bargaining table as he visited player camps across the country.

A strike did occur. To the union's credit, the vast majority (84 percent) of the league's 1,585 players stayed out on strike for the entire duration of the conflict. The strike ended on October 15, 1987, after some high-profile players threatened to return to work. The NFL did not allow these returning players to play that first weekend, citing their lack of conditioning and risks of injury. Perhaps the only victory the NFLPA could claim from the 1987 strike was the NLRB's ruling, which awarded $30 million in back pay to strikers who were not allowed to play on October 18. Yet, this unfair labor practice victory was a small one compared to what the union lost. The NFLPA really gained no ground on free agency in 1987, nor on much else for that matter.

In fact, a new CBA was not signed until January 1993! When players returned to work after their 1987 job action, it was under the terms of the 1982 collective bargaining contract. While the players returned to work in 1987 without much bargaining success, their eye was still on the much bigger prize of free agency. The very day that the 1987 strike ended, the NFLPA filed an antitrust lawsuit challenging the restrictions on free agency and the college draft as being anticompetitive practices in the player labor market.

The union wanted real free agency for players whose contracts with their clubs had expired. To achieve this end several tactics were utilized. First, the NFLPA tried again in court to have the labor exemption nullified. The thinking was that with an expired CBA the labor exemption should no longer hold. The players also decertified their union on the pretense that without a union the NFL could no longer claim the labor exemption from antitrust laws.

Possibly the NFL began to feel a bit of heat as it unilaterally established the new "Plan B" free agency system for players. This new system was similar to the original baseball reservation system, as teams could protect a majority of their roster players. These protected roster players could become free agents, but the old compensation rules applied. The remaining roster players were unprotected and could become free agents and change clubs without compensation.

The free agency situation was a bit better for the players, but the superstar players did not benefit from the newer system. A restricted free agent player, Freeman McNeil, joined with seven other players to challenge Plan B under antitrust law. While the NFL also was under legal attack because of its player draft and policies on franchise movement from city to city, and from the USFL, it is undoubtedly true that the McNeil case (Staudohar 1992) was the prime factor responsible for the new collective bargaining pact in 1993. This decision found the NFL's Plan B free agency system in violation of the antitrust laws. Two basic features of this agreement were (a) liberalized free agency and (b) a salary cap. These two factors serve to offset one another.

Players with five years of NFL service were now able to change teams without compensation or other restrictions after their contracts expired. One franchise player is exempted per team, but that player must be offered the average of the top five players at his position by his home team. Free agency has helped players to switch teams.

The salary cap, on the other hand, has helped owners maintain control over player personnel costs. The parties agreed to an NBA-type salary cap, where the players received a maximum of 58 percent of the designated gross revenues in the form of salaries. The NFL cap is referred to as a "hard" cap, as there are few loopholes like those that exist in the NBA. While players have been able to switch teams, the new team always has to be conscious of salary cap concerns.

Today a spirit of cooperation seems to exist between owners and players in the NFL. The newest CBA was extended through the 2003 season, with an option to be extended by both parties for the 2004 season. The parties are working together on several issues, ranging from promoting the game to young people, helping the United Way, and trying to provide pensions for older retired players who had no such NFL retirement plan when they retired from the game.

Free agency is a reality in the NFL. Restricted free agents have three accrued seasons. A season is defined as six or more games on a club's active/inactive, reserve-signed, or "physically unable to perform" lists. A restricted free agent can receive what is referred to as a qualifying offer from his current club. The amount of this offer is determined in the CBA. The player is then free to accept an offer sheet from any rival team. However, his current club has the right of first refusal, the ability to match any competing offer and keep the player. Of course, the nice thing from a player's perspective is the ability to be paid the higher amount in salary, whether it be from his current team or a new team. If the player's current team decides not to match the offer made by the new team, draft choice compensation may be available based on the amount of the current club's qualifying offer.

Players with four years of NFL service are referred to as unrestricted free agents. This type of free agent can sign with any club without compensation due his old club. The only condition is that this signing must occur prior to July 15 of each year. If the player does not sign with a new club by this date, his current club can make him a tender offer, which amounts to 110 percent of his salary in the previous season. The player must then be signed by November 7, or he has to sit out the entire season. The new collective bargaining contract contains other rules on transition players and franchise players, but the key point has already been made. Players in the NFL have more freedom of movement than ever before through free agency. Yet teams also have a cost control mechanism in the form of the salary cap. For the 2000 season, the salary cap was set at 63 percent of leaguewide defined gross revenues, or $62.1 million per club. Relations between owners and players in football are as peaceful as they have been in years. While several problems do exist in the game, owners and players have a good working relationship and seem to be able to work out their differences through collective bargaining.

Hockey

The most recent CBA in the NHL was signed on January 13, 1995. The agreement followed a four-month lockout during the 1994–1995 season. The 1995 pact was initially scheduled to expire at the completion of the 1999–2000 championship season. As part of a deal to expand the NHL from twenty-six to thirty teams, both parties agreed to extend the CBA until September 15, 2004. Still it is clear that if salaries continue to escalate, another labor war may ensue some time in the future. For now, hockey fans can rest easy knowing that the contract extension has guaranteed labor peace until 2004. Just how did professional hockey players and the NHL get to this point in the history of their labor relations?

It all started back in 1957 when the players, led by Detroit Red Wing Ted Lindsay, formed the National Hockey League Players Association (NHLPA). Players in those early days were relatively well paid and had an established pension system. The union was mainly interested in promoting the popularity of the game, as a better television package would potentially mean more money for them. Players were miffed when early TV contracts did not provide them with an appropriate share of these league revenues. Player unrest convinced the owners to change this situation, but the early days of the NHLPA were marked by meager economic gains for players.

The earliest NHLPA legal counsel was the same J. Norman Lewis who had represented baseball players. In 1967 the players hired Alan Eagleson to head their union. While he led the NHLPA to many gains, Eagleson was also controversial because he also served as a player agent. He stepped down in 1992 and two years later was charged with racketeering, embezzlement, and fraud for activities during the time he was the union's director. Eagleson's deputy at the NHLPA since 1990 had been Bob Goodenow. When Eagleson resigned Goodenow took over as the executive director of the NHLPA. Goodenow was to prove to be a formidable adversary in labor negotiations with team owners.

The NHL and the NHLPA had reached earlier CBAs in 1975, 1982, and again in 1986. The 1986 agreement was set to expire on September 15, 1991. Not surprisingly, the big player issues in this round of negotiations were in the areas of free agency and player draft procedures. Professional hockey players were dissatisfied with their limited free agency rights and the rather stiff compensation awarded to teams losing free agent players. The players also wished to cut the annual player draft from twelve rounds to six. It was hoped that in doing so more players could sign as free agents and command higher salaries.

The 1991–1992 season began, but the play-offs approached with little progress in the negotiations. Players were polled and authorized a strike. The strike began on April 1, 1992, with the players voting 560–4 in favor of a walkout. The strike lasted only ten days. This was the first strike in NHL history (Romain and Diamond 1987). No games were actually missed, as all postponed contests were eventually rescheduled and made up. The changes on the two big issues previously described were not overwhelming. The draft was reduced from twelve to eleven rounds. Players could now become unrestricted free agents at age thirty, where previously this occurred at age thirty-one. Free agency compensation was changed slightly to favor the players. Other settled issues included a two-year agreement, more money in the players' play-off fund, and union input into the choice of arbitrators. Perhaps both sides could claim victory, but both also realized they would live to do battle another day.

That day was set to come on September 15, 1993. However, the players agreed to play the entire 1993–1994 season without interruption. The eventual confrontation was put off for an additional year. When the conflict erupted it came in a big way. The owners instituted a lockout that lasted 103 days, causing the cancellation of 468 games! A major issue in the negotiations was a familiar salary cap proposal. The cap proposal in hockey was a bit different from other sports. In hockey, salaries were not capped by team or league. The intent was the same as in the other sports, to control spiraling player payroll costs. But NHL owners proposed a so-called payroll tax on the higher-spending teams. Those teams with high-spending appetites for star players would contribute some of their revenues to the smaller-market teams, which could not afford high spending on player salaries. The NHLPA proposed a much more restrictive tax that only applied to the top sixteen teams.

The lockout ended in January 1995 and a partial season was saved. Instead of eighty-four games, the teams would play a highly truncated forty-eight-game schedule. The agreement was set to last for six years but has recently been extended until 2004. The player draft was further reduced from eleven to nine rounds. Several changes were made to the salary arbitration system, most notably the restriction of player access until the age of twenty-six or twenty-seven is reached, depending on the player's age when he first entered the league.

While hockey players have some freedom of movement from team to team, they still face the most restrictive free agency system of the major professional sports. The CBA signed in 1995 gives the clubs control over their players for their first twelve league seasons. The key stumbling block for these so-called restricted free agents is the compensation that must be paid to their former clubs if a player changes teams. The compensation is included in a specifically negotiated schedule. Free agent compensation is based on the player's salary in the previous season. It can range from as little as a third-round draft pick for a player whose salary was between $401,000 and $550,000 all the way up to three first-round draft picks for a player whose salary was above $1.7 million in the previous year. This hefty free agent compensation sharply restricts player movement from team to team. Unrestricted free agents are those players who have reached age thirty-one. The signing of an unrestricted free agent does not require compensation to the team losing the player.

Labor peace in the NHL may be short-lived. Even though the extended CBA does not expire until September 2004, players and the NHL already seem to be gearing up for their next battle. For example, San Jose Shark player Owen Nolan has a clause in his player contract that gives him an extra year if a labor dispute in 2004–2005 limits him to less than forty games. This type of lockout protection clause is certain to be challenged either through arbitration or in court. Many people believe that when the current contract expires in September 2004 the entire NHL season may be lost to yet another labor dispute.

Section V—The Future of Bargaining

The major issues likely to shape the future of collective bargaining in professional sports have a familiar ring to them. For many years the single most contentious issue between owners and players has been the division of the revenues generated by the game. Simply put, both sides have struggled to garner a greater portion of the revenue pie. Through legal challenges and collective bargaining, players in all four sports have made enormous strides. Yet, there are major differences among salaries, arbitration, and free agency rights for players in baseball, basketball, football, and hockey. A major question is whether major labor market restrictions such as those that still exist in hockey will precipitate further conflicts. Labor strife of the type discussed in this chapter is likely to occur when current contracts expire.

Another major issue is competitive balance. Do the fans only want winning teams, or will we see more of the Chicago Cubs phenomenon or the NFL scenario, where ballparks are packed in spite of mediocre win–loss records? In some sports, where revenues are split relatively evenly, perhaps competitive balance is not a major factor. Yet, recent research in baseball suggests some interesting conclusions (Schmidt and Berri 2001). With all the talk lately about the gap between large-market and small-market teams in baseball, these authors found that the decade of the 1990s was one of the *most* competitive in baseball history on the field of play. The authors found a statistical relationship between aggregate league competitive balance and attendance. Close games and pennant races lead to higher attendance, which in turn means more revenues going into the game. It seems that competitive balance does matter (Bassa 2001), and thus it is likely that we will see both sides working on this problem in the future in an integrative manner (Rosenthal

2001). Achieving better league competitive balance can be a winning proposition for both sides, to say nothing of how much the fans will appreciate closely contested games and championships.

Tangential to the competitive balance issue is the notion of who pays for new stadiums and how this capital structure impacts team performance. Recent research by O'Roark (2001) has addressed this question. His research suggests that public ownership of a stadium negatively affects the winning percentage of the home team that plays in that facility. O'Roark (2001) found that teams perform better in privately owned than in publicly owned arenas. It may be that the incentive to field a winning team is far greater with private residual claimancy of a stadium. Publicly financed stadiums do not present team owners with the same types of incentives to field a competitive team. As the major sports grapple with ways to create playing field parity among teams, this finding needs to be kept in mind. Coupling this notion with what we saw earlier about attendance being linked to parity and on-the-field success, privately owned facilities may be a good option to consider for small-market teams.

The Yankees and Tigers, while in larger market areas, are interesting examples of teams whose stadiums changed hands from private to public ownership without franchise relocation. The results before and after the change of ownership support the contention about private ownership and winning. The Yankees won a World Series once every 2.4 years prior to 1971, when the famous Yankee Stadium was turned over to New York City. Since 1971 the Yankees have still won but at the rate of one World Series every 5.4 years. The Detroit Tigers won three of five World Series prior to the sale of Tiger Stadium to the City of Detroit in 1977. Since that time the Tigers have only been to the World Series once.

Forces for change in professional sports abound. But for all the changes in our world in technology and mobility of assets, professional sports contests are played within a fairly stable environment. The rules of the games change somewhat over time, but the objective remains to put more points, runs, or goals on the scoreboard than the opposing team. Ownership has changed greatly over the years, from the privately held or family team operation to the billionaire owners of today. Given this change, some suggest that the value of winning is not just to generate profits. Owning a team has become a nice hobby for the fabulously wealthy.

But there is a darker side that all parties need to address through collective bargaining. Fans become disgruntled over lost games due to strikes and lockouts. Labor relations confrontations have given each sport a bad reputation. To date, the parties have been able to withstand some hard times and come back both financially and competitively after the resolution of labor disputes. Fans seem to be forgiving, as they want the games to go on.

However, each sport has lingering problems both on and off the field. In baseball the issue of minority players flared up several years ago after the Al Campanis interview with Ted Koppel on *Nightline*. Baseball has done better, but blacks are still underrepresented in managerial positions. The other problem area for baseball is player substance abuse. In particular, baseball players have had a lot of bad press due to alcohol and drug abuse. Professional sports as an industry is no different from other commercial enterprises when it comes to employee substance abuse. The trick is to walk the fine line between discipline for abusing players, while recognizing the illness aspects of substance abuse addiction as a disease.

Football players also have tarnished the image and reputation of their game through documented cases of substance abuse. The use of amphetamines and cocaine by football players led to an NFL program emphasizing education and rehabilitation for drug users. Alcohol has also been a problem in the NFL, which in 1991 established a disciplinary policy for alcohol-related misconduct.

NBA players have also been associated with illegal drugs. Some feel that the NBA's drug policy is too harsh on the players, but it has made some innovative strides by emphasizing voluntary admission of a drug problem, followed by education and treatment. The NBA has also been plagued by other concerns such as gambling and violence. In years past, gambling may have involved point shaving and even direct betting on games. Since 1982 the NBA has been aggressively involved in educating players about the dangers of gambling and drug abuse.

Finally, violence has also given the NBA a black eye. To curb on-court violence, the NBA instituted three referees per game in the 1988–1989 season. Recent incidents with Vernon Maxwell punching a heckler in the stands and Dennis Rodman kicking a cameraman at courtside have only exacerbated the notion that basketball is a violent sport.

Hockey has always been known as a very violent sport. Other problems like drug abuse, alcohol abuse, and gambling have not been as widely reported in the NHL as in other sports. When one thinks of problems in the NHL, the primary focus is on player violence with sharp skates, sticks, and fists. The NHL's approach to this problem has been to impose stricter rules against fighting on the ice, including ejections from games. To the NHL's credit, these tougher sanctions have reduced fighting to a fraction of what it used to be.

Another problem brought to public light by basketball player Magic Johnson's case is the issue of acquired immunodeficiency syndrome (AIDS) in professional sports. Most professional leagues now provide education in the form of seminars and literature to their players and to potential players as well. As in other occupations, there will be players in professional sports leagues who are infected with the human immunodeficiency virus (HIV). The leagues and player unions will have to work together in the future to continue their policy on education about and prevention of the spread of the AIDS virus.

Whether we focus on AIDS, drug abuse, alcohol abuse, gambling, or violence, it all translates to one very important concept to both owners and players—image! The future health of all professional sports leagues will, in no small part, be determined by the image fans have of the game and its players. All leagues and players must realize that their public image can do much to help or harm their industry. The problems are indeed societal ones; but, in a high-profile industry like professional sports, which is in the news on a daily basis, such problems become magnified. The owners and players truly have a great opportunity to take action that can serve as a model for employer–employee relationships in many industries.

Section VI—Conclusion

What does the future hold for the sports industry and its union–management relationships? Relationships between management and labor typically vary on a scale that ranges from extreme adversarialism on one end to extreme cooperation on the other. Unfortunately, most of the history of labor–management relations in professional sports has been adversarial. In other industries, labor–management cooperation has been successfully used in many settings. One example is a greenfield site like Saturn in Springhill, Tennessee, where both the United Auto Workers and General Motors agreed to try a newer, more cooperative relationship at a new facility.

Sometimes parties cooperate when they join forces to fight a common enemy. In poor economic times, concession bargaining or other attempts by both labor and management have saved entire plants, jobs, and even industries. The question is whether things have progressed to the point in professional sports where the parties see common enemies or threats that will motivate them to collaborate to prevent their mutual demise.

Players' unions have had extraordinary success in enhancing salaries and benefits of professional athletes. How far can these salary and benefit increases go? As previously mentioned, many of the leagues appear prepared to go to war again, in the old-fashioned adversarial way. For example, baseball's executive vice president Sandy Alderson is widely credited for helping MLB beat the umpires' aborted resignation attempt in 1999 (Hyman 2001b). He is also in charge of the new strike zone enforcement by major league umpires. As baseball moves toward its next confrontation after the 2001 season, having Alderson involved in labor relations matters with the players seems to signal more adversarial relations ahead.

The next labor war will be in baseball after the 2001 season. Some argue that the game has never been better (Costas 2000). Others fear that Commissioner Bud Selig's cheers for the game do indeed have a hollow ring (Mariotti 2001).

Another troubling aspect of today's game is individual player celebrity status and lack of identification with one team. Elgin Baylor was a Laker. Johnny Bench was a Cincinnati Red. Today's superstars seem to care more about the money than the team. There are numerous examples of players who have played for several teams. Fans hardly learn one lineup before their favorite players are free agents signing with another club.

So it is in all professional sports leagues. Negotiations will continue to be heated and there will be strikes and lockouts. Growth may continue with expansion onto other continents. The older problems of how to split revenues between owners and players will continue to highlight the talks between the parties. Issues will come and go, but the process of collective bargaining will remain intact. Union–management relationships will vary from extreme hostility to periods of cooperation. Yet, the collective bargaining process can handle all of these mood swings. The bottom line is that the future of the industry looks challenging, but there are many opportunities for mutually beneficial gains. Union–management relationships in baseball, basketball, football, and hockey are maturing. With age, hopefully will come wisdom and the ability to focus on the big picture to achieve equitable solutions for all parties. Let us hope that in the case of the professional sports industry, out of conflict shall come eventual accord.

References

Aaron, Hank, and Lonnie Wheeler. 1991. *I Had a Hammer: The Hank Aaron Story*. New York: Harper Collins Publishers.

Abrams, Roger I. 1998. *The Money Pitch: Baseball Free Agency and Salary Arbitration*. Philadelphia: Temple University Press.

_____. 2000. *The Money Pitch: Baseball Free Agency and Salary Arbitration*. Philadelphia: Temple University Press.

Anderson, David W. 2000. *More Than Merkle: A History of the Best and Most Exciting Baseball Season in Human History*. Lincoln: University of Nebraska Press.

Bassa, Allen. 2001. "Fair Ball?" *The Wall Street Journal*. April 13, p. W12.

Becker, Gary S. 1957. *The Economics of Discrimination*. Chicago: University of Chicago Press.

Burk, Robert F. 1994. *Never Just a Game: Players, Owners and American Baseball to 1920*. Chapel Hill, NC: University of North Carolina Press.

_____. 2001. *Much More Than a Game: Players, Owners and American Baseball Since 1921*. Chapel Hill, NC: University of North Carolina Press.

Christiano, Kevin J. 1986. "Salary Discrimination in Major League Baseball: The Effect of Race." *Sociology of Sport Journal*, 3 (June), pp. 144–53.

_____. 1988. "Salaries and Race in Professional Baseball: Discrimination 10 Years Later." *Sociology of Sport Journal*, 5 (June), pp. 136–49.

Costas, Bob. 2000. *Fair Ball; A Fan's Case for Baseball*. New York: Broadway Books.

Curt Flood Act, P.L. 105-297; 112 Stat. 2824 (1998).

Dey, Mathew S. 1997. "Racial Differences in National Basketball Association Players' Salaries: Another Lock." *The American Economist*, Vol. 41, no. 2, pp. 84–90.

Dunlop, John T. 1993. *Industrial Relations Systems* (2nd ed.). Boston: Harvard Business School Press.

Dworkin, James B. 1981. *Owners Versus Players: Baseball and Collective Bargaining*. Boston: Auburn House Publishing.

_____. 1987. "Professional Sports." In David B. Lipsky and Clifford B. Donn, eds., *Collective Bargaining in American Industry: Contemporary Perspectives and Future Directions*. Lexington, MA: Lexington Books.

Dworkin, James B., and Paul Staudohar. (forthcoming). "Even Umpires Sometimes Strike Out." *NINE: A Journal of Baseball History and Social Policy Perspectives*.

Fatsis, Stefan, and Jonathan B. Weinbach. 1999. "NBA, Players Reach Accord, Saving Season." *The Wall Street Journal*, January 7, p. A3.

Federal Baseball Club v. National League, 259 U.S. 200 (1922).

Feinstein, John. 1993. *Play Ball: The Life and Troubled Times of Major League Baseball*. New York: Villard Books.

Fizel, John, Elizabeth Gustafson, and Lawrence Hadley (Eds.). 1996. *Baseball Economics: Current Research*. Westport, CT: Praeger.

Flood, Curt, and Richard Carter. 1970. *The Way It Is*. New York: Trident Press.

Fort, Rodney. 2000. "Market Power in Pro Sports; Problems and Solutions." In William S. Kern, ed., *The Economics of Sports*. Kalamazoo, MI: W. E. Upjohn Institute for Employment Research.

Gould, Todd. 1998. *Pioneers of the Hardwood*. Bloomington and Indianapolis: Indiana University Press.

Gramlich, E. M. 1994. "A Natural Experiment in Styles of Capitalism: Professional Sports." *Quarterly Review of Economics and Finance*, Vol. 34, no. 2, pp. 121–30.

Greenberger, Robert S. 2001. "Cleveland Indians Draw Goose Egg in Tax Case." *The Wall Street Journal*, April 18, p. B2.

Hamilton, Barton Hughes. 1997. "Racial Discrimination and Professional Basketball Salaries in the 1990's." *Applied Economics*, Vol. 29, no. 3, pp. 287–96.

Hendricks, Randal A. 1994. *Inside the Strike Zone*. Austin, TX: Eakin Press.

Hill, J. Richard, and Peter A. Groothuis. 2001. "The New NBA Collective Bargaining Agreement, the Median Voter Model, and a Robin Hood Rent Redistribution." *Journal of Sports Economics*, Vol. 2, no. 2, pp. 131–44.

Hoang, Ha, and Don Rascher. 1999. "The NBA, Exit Discrimination, and Career Earnings." *Industrial Relations*, Vol. 38, no. 1, pp. 69–91.

Hoose, Phillip M. 1989. *Necessities: Racial Barriers in American Sports*. New York: Random House.

Hyman, Mark. 2001a. "How Bad Is the NBA Hurting?" *Business Week*, May 7, p. 123.

_____. "Speak Bluntly and Carry a Big Bat." *Business Week*, April 16, pp. 58–59.

Jennings, Kenneth M. 1997. *Swings and Misses: Morbund Labor Relations in Professional Baseball*. Westpoint, CT: Praeger.

Jiobu, Robert M. 1988. "Racial Inequality in a Public Arena: The Case of Professional Baseball." *Social Forces*, Vol. 67, no. 2, pp. 524–34.

Jones, J. C. H., and William D. Walsh. 1988. "Salary Determination in the National Hockey League: The Effects of Skill, Franchise Characteristics and Discrimination." *Industrial and Labor Relations Review*, Vol. 41, no. 4, pp. 592–604.

Jozsa, Frank P., and John J. Guthrie. 1999. *Relocating Teams and Expanding Leagues in Professional Sports*. Westport, CT: Quorum Books.

Kahn, Lawrence. 1992. "The Effects of Race on Professional Football Players Compensation." *Industrial and Labor Relations Review*, Vol. 45, no. 2, pp. 295–310.

_____. 2000. "A Level Playing Field: Sports and Discrimination." In William S. Kern, ed., *The Economics of Sports*. Kalamazoo, MI: W. E. Upjohn Institute for Employment Research.

Kahn, Lawrence M., and Peter D. Sherer. 1988. "Racial Differences in Professional Basketball Players' Compensation." *Journal of Labor Economics*, Vol. 6, no. 1, pp. 40–61.

Kapp v. NFL, 390 F. Supp. 73 (1974); 441 U.S. 907 (1979).

Katz, Nancy. 2001. "Sports Teams as a Model for Workplace Teams: Lessons and Liabilities. *Academy of Management Executive*, Vol. 15, no. 3, pp. 56–67.

Koppett, Leonard. 1998. *Koppett's Concise History of Major League Baseball*. Philadelphia: Temple University Press.

_____. 1999. *24 Seconds to Shoot: The Birth and Improbable Rise of the NBA*. Kingston, NY: Total Sports Illustrated Classics.

Kuhn, Bowie. 1987. *Hardball: The Education of a Baseball Commissioner*. New York: Times Books.

Lavoie, Marc. 2000. "The Location of Pay Discrimination in the National Hockey League." *Journal of Sports Economics*, Vol. 1, no. 4, pp. 401–11.

Lewicki, Roy J., David M. Saunders, and John W. Minton. 1997. *Essentials of Negotiation*. Chicago: Irwin.

Longley, Neil. 2000. "The Underrepresentation of French Canadians on English Canadian NHL Teams: Evidence From 1943-1998. *Journal of Sports Economics*, Vol. 1, no. 3, pp. 236–56.

Lowenfish, Lee. 1991. *The Imperfect Diamond: A History of Baseball's Labor Wars.* New York: Da Capo Press.

Mackey v. NFL, 543 F.2d 644; 434 U.S. 801 (1977).

Marburger, Daniel M. (Ed.). 1997. *Stee-Rike Four! What's Wrong with the Business of Baseball?* Westport, CT: Praeger.

Mariotti, Jay. 2001. "Selig's Cheer Has a Hollow Ring." *Sporting News*, Vol. 225, no. 15, p. 8.

Miller, James E. 1990. *The Baseball Business: Pursuing Pennants and Profits in Baltimore.* Chapel Hill, NC: University of North Carolina Press.

Miller, Marvin. 1991. *A Whole Different Ball Game: The Sport and Business of Baseball.* New York: Birch Home Press.

Naismith, Jones. 1996. *Basketball: Its Origin and Development.* Lincoln and London, NE: University of Nebraska Press.

Neale, Walter. 1964. "The Peculiar Economics of Professional Sports." *Quarterly Journal of Economics*, Vol. 78 (February), pp. 1–14.

Noll, Roger, and Andrew Zimbalist (Eds.). 1997. *Sports, Jobs and Taxes: The Economic Impact of Sports Teams and Stadiums.* Washington, DC: Brookings.

O'Roark, J. Brian. 2001. "Capital Structure and Team Performance in Professional Baseball." *Journal of Sports Economics*, Vol. 2, no. 2, pp. 168–80.

Phalen, Rick. 2000. *A Bittersweet Journey: America's Fascination with Baseball.* Tampa: McGregor.

Quirk, James, and Rodney Fort. 1992. *Pay Dirt: The Business of Professional Team Sports.* Princeton, NJ: Princeton University Press.

————. 1999. *Hardball: The Abuse of Power in Pro Team Sports.* Princeton, NJ: Princeton University Press.

Radovich v. NFL, 352 U.S. 445 (1957).

Robertson v. National Basketball Association, 72 F.R.D. 64, Trade Cas. (CCH) P 61029 (S.D.N.Y. 1976); aff'd, *Robertson v. National Basketball Association*, 556 F.2d 682, 1977-1 Trade Cas. (CCH) P 61474, 23 Fed. R. Serv. 2d (Callaghan) 798 (2d Cir. N.Y. 1977).

Romain, Joseph, and Don Diamond. 1987. *A Pictorial History of Hockey.* New York: Gallery Books.

Rosenthal, Ken. 2001. "MLB Owes It to the Teams to Build Level Playing Field." *The Sporting News*, April 16, p. 17.

Schmidt, Morton B., and David J. Berri. 2001. "Competitive Balance and Attendance: The Case of Major League Baseball. *Journal of Sports Economics*, Vol. 2, no. 2, pp. 145–67.

Scully, Gerald W. 1989. *The Business of Major League Baseball.* Chicago: University of Chicago Press.

————. 1995. *The Market Structure of Sports.* Chicago: University of Chicago Press.

Sherony, Keith, Michael Haupert, and Glenn Knowles. 2001. "Competitive Balance in Major League Baseball." *Nine: A Journal of Baseball History and Culture*, Vol. 9, no. 102, pp. 225–36.

Staudohar, Paul D. 1987. "The Football Strike of 1987: The Question of Free Agency." *Monthly Labor Review*, Vol. 111, no. 8, pp. 27–31.

————. 1992. "McNeil and Football's Antitrust Quagmire." *Journal of Sport and Social Issues*, Vol. 16, no. 2, pp. 105–106.

_____. 1996. *Playing for Dollars: Labor Relations and the Sports Business*. Ithaca, NY: Cornell University Press.

Sullivan, Neil J. 1992. *The Diamond Revolution: The Prospects for Baseball After the Collapse of Its Ruling Class*. New York: St. Martin's Press.

Tygiel, Jules. 1983. *Baseball's Great Experiment*. New York: Oxford University Press.

United States v. Cleveland Indians, 532 U.S. 200 (2001).

Waller, Spencer Weber, Neil B. Cohen, and Paul Finkelman (Eds.). 1995. *Baseball and the American Legal Mind*. New York: Gaylord Publishing.

White, M.D. 1986. "Self-Interest Redistribution and the National Football League Players Association." *Economic Inquiry*, Vol. 29, pp. 669–81.

Wulf, Steve. 1993. "Out Foxed." *Sports Illustrated*, December 27, p. 19.

Zimbalist, Andrew. 1992. *Baseball and Billions*. New York: Basic Books.

_____. 2000. "Economic Issues in the 1998-99 NBA Lockout and the Problem of Competitive Balance in Professional Sports." In William S. Kern, ed., *The Economics of Sports*. Kalamazoo, MI: W. E. Upjohn Institute for Employment Research.

CHAPTER 7

Telecommunications: Collective Bargaining in an Era of Industry Reconsolidation[1]

JEFFREY KEEFE
Rutgers University

ROSEMARY BATT
Cornell University

Introduction

In the two decades following the breakup of the Bell System in 1984,[2] the telecommunications services industry has witnessed a profound transformation—an explosion of new services in wireless, data, video, and Internet communications; dramatic employment declines in some segments and rapid growth in others where digital skills are in high demand; and de-unionization, growing wage inequality, and the unraveling of the traditional social contract that exchanged employment security for loyalty. Between 1984 and 1992, old Bell System companies eliminated between 30 and 60 percent of their core workforce, while hundreds of small upstarts promised to provide better and cheaper services in deregulated markets.

Yet oddly, despite deregulation, the legacy of the Bell System continues to dominate the industry, with the former Bell affiliates employing the majority of the core industry's workforce and comprising the majority of the industry's market capitalization. Moreover, from the mid-1990s on, corporate mergers and acquisitions have led to the reconsolidation of the industry into a handful of dominant integrated carriers providing long distance, local, wireless, data, and Internet services. The top five integrated carriers in the country are all former Bell System affiliates. And despite a drop in unionization from 56 percent of the total workforce in 1983 to 28 percent in 1998, the industry remains one of the most unionized in the country. The Bell System legacy of union–management cooperation, torn apart in the early years of deregulation and restructuring, reasserted itself in the mid-1990s among some of the major corporate players and unions in the industry—the Communications Workers of America (CWA),[3] with about 300,000 industry members, and the International Brotherhood of Electrical Workers (IBEW),[4] with about 40,000 industry members.

In this paper, we examine the reconsolidation of the industry, between 1995 and 2001, focusing on the merger, acquisition, and business strategies of the major corporate players; union responses to those strategies; and the resulting evolution of union–management relations and collective bargaining outcomes.[5] We argue that the nature of the industry and technology, coupled with its institutional legacy, provides incentives for consolidation and recentralization of the ownership structure. In this process over the last decade, former Bell affiliates have sought union support before regulatory commissions, and the unions have leveraged their political power to make important gains in collective bargaining and in organizing new members. As a result, the outcomes for union members and prospects for union institutional viability are more positive than they otherwise would have been.

The paper is organized as follows. First, we review the extent of reconsolidation of the industry through mergers and acquisitions, analyzing why some companies won and some lost in the context of unexpected growth and opportunity based on the explosion of wireless and Internet communications. Then, we examine the reemergence of labor–management partnerships, based primarily on corporate need for union support for merger activity before regulatory commissions. We discuss the successes and failures of those efforts by comparing the rise of SBC Communications (the former Southwestern Bell, Pacific Bell, Ameritech, and Southern New England Telephone companies) and Verizon (combining the former NYNEX, Bell Atlantic, and GTE), as trendsetters in union–management relations, and the decline of AT&T, traditionally the pattern setter for the former Bell affiliates. In the last section, we review the outcomes of collective bargaining in the current period. Throughout the paper, we draw on our qualitative field research over several years, collective bargaining agreements, industry data, and our own 1998 nationally representative survey of establishments in the industry.

Industry Restructuring and Reconsolidation

The telecommunications services industry provides bidirectional or multidirectional communications over a network, making it distinct from the unidirectional broadcast industries, such as television and radio broadcasts. Telecommunications services (SIC 481 and 484)[6] is composed of five submarkets: (1) interexchange toll markets (long distance), (2) wireline local exchange access, (3) wireless local exchange access, (4) cable television distribution, and (5) customer premise equipment (CPE). Cable TV is included in the industry because, unlike broadcast television, it is transmitted over wire networks, which may be used for two-way communications.

Three Phases of Technology-Driven Restructuring

This industry's revolution has been driven by advances in technology but constrained within a highly regulated structure. Regulatory changes have lagged behind technological breakthroughs, but the structure has evolved to promote some competition rather than to set prices and control entry. Historically, the regulated monopoly AT&T (with its twenty-two local affiliates) dominated the long distance, local, and CPE markets. Cable television and wireless markets were undeveloped. Industry restructuring began in the 1970s and proceeded through three stages. The first stage in the 1970s initiated competition in equipment markets; the second, in the 1980s and early 1990s, brought competition to long distance markets; and the third phase, from the early 1990s on, has involved the deregulation of local access markets and the rise of wireless and Internet services. Below, we briefly review the first and second phases before focusing on the third phase in more detail.

The first stage involved innovations in local data networks, accompanied by a Federal Communications Commission (FCC) policy to allow competition in the markets for business telecommunications equipment and leased line services. Some customers began to purchase their own PBX equipment from competitors of AT&T's Western Electric rather than lease it from a Bell company. Over time, other innovations in computer networking would fundamentally change the nature of all telecommunications networks. The most important innovation was the development of local area networks (LANs), which were the first data networks to rely on routers rather than circuit switches. Because they were located on a single business's premise, they did not fall under common carrier regulations, but they could interconnect over leased telephone lines with mainframes or other LANs. The opening of the network and data equipment markets to competition seriously challenged the role of AT&T's Western Electric, as the sole source for telecommunications equipment, and Bell Labs, as the source of all technical innovation in the industry.

Today, data networks based on the LAN design concept are the standard for communications networks and carry approximately 75 percent of all telecommunications traffic. The CPE market has become very heterogeneous. It includes networked computers in LANs, voice-data integrated networks, automated and menu-driven call distributed networks on the corporate side, and simple inside wiring of other generic customer equipment in the residential market.

The second stage of industrial restructuring began with the deregulation of long distance markets, which proceeded on an erroneous set of technological forecasts. The Justice Department insisted on breaking up AT&T in 1984 in order to launch an era of competition—one premised on the use of inexpensive and decentralizing technologies based on satellite and microwave transmission networks (Rosenberg 1994). Microwave network technology, however, was largely obsolete by the time AT&T divestiture occurred; and satellite communications were soon relegated to a secondary technology used for paging or communicating with remote areas of the world. In the meantime, a digital revolution was under way. Advances in customer premise business equipment induced a digital revolution in network switching and architecture, and the deployment of fiber optic trunks dramatically increased digital transmission capacity.

To complete the long distance revolution, regulators needed to confront the cross-subsidy problem in the AT&T natural monopoly rate structure. The old system was designed to provide universal service through cross subsidies: long distance prices were set above their cost in order to subsidize local rates, which were set below their cost. With the AT&T breakup, the regulators created a new system called access pricing. Access pricing requires long distance companies to compensate local access providers for the use of their facilities in the completion of long distance calls. Access pricing enables more open access to the long distance market without either bankrupting the local companies or resulting in unacceptably high local service rate increases. The innovation allowed competitors such as MCI and Sprint to enter the long distance market in the 1980s, using AT&T's network while they were building their own network trunks.

Once opened to competitive entry, the long distance market immediately segmented into its wholesale and retail sectors. AT&T, MCI, and Sprint served both the wholesale and retail markets, while some 500 resellers entered the retail market. Many resellers owned no network facilities but instead repackaged and resold the wholesaler's long distance service. In addition, wholesalers such as WorldCom, Level3, and Qwest also began selling network capacity to the retailers, large corporate service providers, and even the major network providers. During the late 1990s, wholesalers rapidly expanded network capacity, as a variety of energy firms plowed in fiber cable along their networks. As a result, wholesale prices dropped, and many companies experienced financial distress or bankruptcy. By 2000, there was a considerable overbuild of fiber optic network capacity. This allowed wireless firms to offer long distance as part of fixed-price minutes packages, as wholesale long distance prices plummeted. Verizon, SBC, and BellSouth purchased long distance network assets from bankrupt and distressed firms at substantially discounted prices, which greatly facilitated their entry into long distance markets.

The third stage of restructuring, the focus of this paper, has involved dramatic growth and transformation of local access markets, accompanied by changes in state and federal legislation. It began with the explosive growth in wireless service, which rose from 4.4 million access lines in 1990 to over 110 million access lines by 2001, a 42 percent average annual rate of growth (Freedman 1999). In addition, in the once saturated market for wireline access (basic telephony), the Internet stimulated demand for second lines, leading to an unanticipated annual growth rate of 6 percent (from 134 million lines in 1990 to 192 lines in 2000) (FCC 2001). Digitalization of cable TV distribution also accelerated local access competition by making possible bidirectional communications through cable TV lines.

On the regulatory side, state Public Service Commissions (PSCs), with responsibility for regulating local telephone service, redesigned rate structures to provide incentives to reduce costs and make innovations. Finally, the federal Telecommunications Act of 1996 was designed to encourage competition in the local loop: the incumbent local exchange carriers are allowed to enter long distance service in exchange for opening their local access monopolies to competitors such as AT&T, MCI, and Sprint. (Under the original divestiture order, all former Bell affiliates were allowed to enter the then-infant cellular industry, but AT&T could not enter local access markets and the regional Bells could not enter long distance markets). The 1996 Act mandated the unbundling of local access networks into elements (such as facilities, switches, routers, transmission equipment, signaling systems, lines, poles, information sufficient for billing, and local loop to the customer premises). The purpose of unbundling was to promote network facilities–based competition: each competitor would build or own some network elements rather than entirely relying on leasing or reselling of the existing network (primarily owned by the former Bell monopolies).

Nevertheless, the 1996 Telecommunications Act was accompanied by a wave of mergers and acquisitions that reorganized the industry into a handful of megacarriers that provide a full range of voice and data services, wireless and wireline access, and integrated high-capacity backbone networks. For example, Verizon (the dominant carrier in twelve northeastern and mid-Atlantic states and Washington, DC) is a composite of several former regional Bells: New York Telephone merged with New England Telephone to form NYNEX, which was acquired by the former Bell Atlantic; the merged entity joined with GTE (itself composed of numerous independent telephone companies from across the United States) to form Verizon in 2000. In addition, after an unsuccessful bid to acquire AirTouch (the former wireless properties of Pacific Telesis and US West), Verizon Communications entered into partnership with Vodaphone, the successful bidder for AirTouch, to form Verizon Wireless. SBC (formerly Southwestern Bell) is now the dominant carrier in thirteen states. It acquired Pacific Telesis (serving California and Nevada), Southern New England Telephone (SNET, serving Connecticut), and Ameritech (serving five north-central states). It would become the dominant partner with BellSouth (the local provider in nine southeastern states) to form Cingular Wireless. US West (covering fourteen Rocky Mountain and northwestern states) was acquired by the long distance upstart Qwest, which is headed by a former AT&T executive.

Moreover, mergers, acquisitions, divestitures, carve-outs, and joint ventures accelerated in the wake of the Telecommunications Act not only among the former Bell companies but among new entrants as well. For example, WorldCom merged with MCI despite a heated debate before the FCC that the merger posed a substantial threat to competition in global Internet markets (Keefe 1998). Qwest bought out US West in 2000, and in 2001 Alltel was attempting to acquire Century.

Thus, despite almost three decades of deregulation—a public policy committed to the promotion of competition and the repudiation of the theory of natural monopoly—the former Bell affiliates continue to dominate the industry. They comprise more than 80 percent of the industry's market capitalization (Table 1). The former Bells still dominate local access by providing 88 percent of the retail local wireline service (Table 2). Under the 1996 Telecommunications Act, they also have become wholesalers of local service to new entrants in the industry, such as competitive

TABLE 1

Market Capitalization and Average Stock Price of Telecommunications Carriers

	Market capitalization, 7/01 (billions)	Average stock price			Percentage change 1997 to peak	Percentage change 1997 to 7/01
		1997	1999	2001		
Integrated carriers						
Verizon	149.0	38	60	55	110	75
SBC	137.0	30	60	42	140	60
AT&T	84.0	25	64	20	160	-10
BellSouth	77.0	20	50	44	130	90
Qwest ($40 billion US West)	51.0	10	48	30	800	375
WorldCom	43.0	20	55	15	250	-10
Alltel	19.0	30	70	60	200	100
Sprint	18.0	22	45	23	190	-15
Broadwing (Cincinnati Bell)	5.0	25	38	24	60	-5
Independent wireless						
Nextel	12.0	15	20	18	700	80
Independent interexchange carrier						
Global Crossing	8.0	NA	50	9	400	-15
Level 3 Communications	2.0	30	90	5	250	-90
Independent LECs						
Century	4.0	18	40	30	80	15
Citizens	3.0	10	8	12	80	15
CLECs and DLECs						
McLeodUSA	2.0	3	10	3	800	0
Allegiance	2.0	NA	10	15	1,100	60
Time Warner Local Communications	1.0	NA	30	33	230	10
Metromedia	1.0	1	50	2	3,000	0
RCN	0.5	15	25	5	450	-75
XO	0.5	5	10	2	1,000	-50
Covad	0.2	NA	25	0	225	-99
Adelphia	0.2	NA	20	5	250	-80
Equipment manufacturers						
Cisco	141.0	10	30	20	1,000	200
Qualcomm (royalties for standard)	48.0	1	5	64	3,000	1,000
Motorola	37.0	22	22	17	120	-30
Nortel	29.0	12	20	9	630	-10
Lucent	23.0	12	55	7	340	-70
JDS	17.0	1	20	20	4,000	100
Ciena	12.0	20	10	40	550	70
Juniper	10.0	NA	10	31	1,300	100
Total market capitalization	**619.4**					
Total market capitalization for former AT&T–Bell System companies	**503.0 (81%)**					

Note: Italics indicate former AT&T–Bell System companies.

TABLE 2

Telecommunications Industrial Structure and Union Representation Status

Telecommunications wireline access	Millions of wire loops	Percentage of market share	Union status
Verizon (former Bell Atlantic, NYNEX, and GTE)	62.3	34	CWA-IBEW
SBC (former Southwest Bell, PacTel, Ameritech, SNET)	58.9	32	CWA-IBEW
BellSouth Telecommunications, Inc.	24.8	13	CWA
Qwest (formerly US West)	16.9	9	CWA
Sprint Corporation	7.9	4	CWA-IBEW
Top 4 (former Bell companies)	**162.9**	**88**	
Top 5 wireline access providers	**170.8**	**92**	

Telecommunications wireless access	Millions of subscribers	Percentage of market share	Organizing status—CWA
Verizon Wireless (formerly GTE, BA Mobility, Airtouch)	23.8	31	Card check
Cingular (formerly CellularOne, BellSouth Mobility)	16.5	22	Card check
AT&T Wireless	9.5	12	Expedited election
Sprint PCS	5.7	7	Antiunion
Top 4 wireless companies	**55.5**	**73**	

Long distance carriers	Revenue (billions $)	Percentage of market share	Union status
AT&T Consumer and Business Services	40.2	41	CWA
WorldCom–MCI	23.4	24	Antiunion
Sprint	9.7	10	Antiunion
Verizon	3.1	3	CWA
Top 3 long distance carriers	**73.3**	**74**	

TABLE 2—(*Continued*)

Telecommunications Industrial Structure and Union Representation Status

Cable television broadband networks	Revenue (billions $)	Percentage of market share	Union status
AT&T Broadband (formerly TCI and MediaOne)	16	23	Expedited election
AOL Time Warner	12.7	19	Antiunion
Comcast	7.7	11	Antiunion
Charter	6.4	9	Antiunion
Cox	6.2	9	Antiunion
Adelphia	5.7	8	Antiunion
Top 6	**49**	**80**	

Sources:

Wireline: FCC, *Trends in Telephone Service*, December 21, 2000. Table 8.3 (as of December 31, 1999): Telephone Loops by Holding Company

Wireless: http://www.wow-com.com/industry/stats/bearstearn/ David Freedman, Bear, Stearns & Co. Telecommunication Untethered, Q4 1999

Long distance: FCC: *Statistics of the Long Distance Telecommunications Industry*, January 2001. Table 1: Total Toll Service Revenues by Carrier

Cable TV: Respective corporate division websites.

local exchange carriers (CLECs) and digital local exchange carriers (DLECs). The CLECs and DLECs often supply some network elements but largely rely on the incumbent carrier to provide most of its access facilities and resources. Also, led by Verizon Wireless, SBC–BellSouth's Cingular, and AT&T Wireless, the former Bell affiliates provide more than two thirds of wireless access in a market with six national service providers. The others are Sprint PCS, Deutsche Telecom's Voicestream, and Nextel. Finally, the former Bell System companies still provide the majority of long distance service, as AT&T remains the leader in the long distance market, and Verizon has quickly become the fourth largest long distance carrier as it gains long distance rights under Section 271 of the Telecommunications Act. The only industry segment where the former Bell affiliates do not dominate is cable television, but AT&T Broadband alone holds almost one quarter of the market share in that segment.

After five years of consolidation following the 1996 Telecommunications Act, the former regional Bell companies are the winners under the new regulatory regime. They are building national and international marketing capabilities and network facilities. In 2001, Verizon was the largest integrated carrier, followed by SBC, AT&T, BellSouth, and Qwest/US West. The regional Bell companies were well positioned to take advantage of the 1996 Act. Unlike the long distance carriers, they had a primary relationship with customers by providing local service, as well as access to long distance providers. While agreeing to open their local markets to competition, they are leveraging their embedded base to rapidly expand service offerings in long distance and provide bundled packages and billing plans.

Despite the fact that AT&T continues to be a major player, it has had a more difficult adjustment to the new environment, as have the other incumbent long distance carriers, such as WorldCom–MCI and Sprint. After enjoying an initial boom, which they used to make a variety of acquisitions, they have faced increasing competition in their core markets. AT&T's constant metamorphoses are indicative of its failed corporate strategy. In 1996, it divested itself of Lucent Technologies, its then highly profitable manufacturing subsidiary, and NCR, its second unsuccessful venture into the computer industry. In 1998, it acquired TCI and MediaOne to form the largest cable television company, AT&T Broadband, only to subsequently dispose of those assets at substantial discount to Comcast in 2002. AT&T also spun off AT&T Wireless in 2001, a business it acquired from Craig McCaw in 1992.

Why Reconsolidation?

The first round of local competition has largely failed as the CLECs and DLECs participated in the financial boom that by 2001 had turned into a big telecom bust. These small upstarts played an important role in the industry by accelerating the deployment of the digital subscriber loop (DSL) technology. They also disrupted established practices in market segments, forcing the Bells to deploy new technologies before they were fully ready or tested. Some of these technologies are unreliable and difficult to integrate into the existing network.

Initially, the success of the DLECs in determining new methods, technologies, and approaches to competition was measured by their market valuations at acquisition or merger. Nonetheless, the difficulties associated with successfully rolling out DSL technology were soon measured by bankruptcy and liquidation sales. For example, Metromedia's stock price exploded from one dollar per share to fifty dollars per share, only to crash at two dollars per share in 2001. Other firms, including RCN, XO, Covad, and Adelphia, lost between 50 and 100 percent of share price (see Table 1).

The bankruptcies of these firms cascaded into the network equipment market. Major equipment makers such as Cisco, Lucent, Alcatel, and Nortel had not only sold equipment to these upstarts but they had advanced substantial amounts of credit to finance their equipment sales. At the time of sale, the DLECs and CLECs boasted substantial market capitalization after their initial public offerings exceeded all expectations. Their rapid descent into bankruptcy or financial distress has impaired the FCC's policy of facilities-based competition and has created long-term problems for telecommunications equipment manufacturers, who must retrench even though the technology continues to advance. As a result, the initial phase of competition has actually strengthened the monopolistic tendencies within the core of the industry.

Relatively untouched by the turmoil in the industry were the regional Bell operating companies, particularly Verizon, SBC, and BellSouth. One explanation for this level of industry concentration is an institutional one: the legacy of the Bell System continues to dominate the industry. This would suggest that there is a time lag due to institutional inertia and that over time the power of institutional forces would erode, for example, as new entrants come into the market and de-unionization continues. However, this does not fully explain the abundance of mergers and consolidations among new entrants such as MCI and WorldCom.

Another explanation is that the nature of the product markets and technology provide incentives for merger and consolidation. That is, the network economics once thought to give rise to a natural monopoly still constrain the evolution of competition and technological innovation. Firms that operate network production processes are subject to economies of scale. They invest in costly communications networks, which represent a substantial sunk fixed cost. Furthermore, all participants in the industry face substantial uncertainty as they build, modernize, and maintain their networks. The evolution of data networks as they supplant the traditional circuit-based telephone network creates technological and economic uncertainty. The majority of the industry's revenue is generated by the circuit switched network; however, more than 75 percent of the traffic is carried by data networks that feature considerable excess capacity and declining prices as a result of the recent overbuild.

There is also uncertainty created as local access technologies are digitized and begin competing with each other. At the time of the AT&T divestiture in 1984, local access technologies were analog. Wireless access was delivered by the newly formed cellular service companies at high prices with large clunky mobile sets, and wireline access was supplied by the traditional telephone companies, which were still thought of as natural monopolies. Cable TV's coaxial distribution networks were only capable at that time of unidirectional broadcasts. Each of these technologies is now in the early stages of digitization, which has created the condition for competition among local access technologies. For consumers this offers many more options, while for providers it creates many more uncertainties. Betting on the wrong technology or media is likely to have dire consequences. The economic advantages and disadvantages among the competing media are ever changing, which makes forecasting a nightmare but unavoidable when investing in long-lived network elements.

In sum, several factors have driven industry reconsolidation. Bringing competition into the industry has been complicated by the presence of network externalities, scale economies, excess capacity, and technological uncertainty. These factors create incentives for companies to merge, form partnerships, and diversify across competing technologies.

Employment and Union Implications of Restructuring

The extensive change in telecommunications technologies has led to a blurring of industry boundaries, making precise determination of employment trends difficult to calculate on the basis of existing national data series. The overwhelming bulk of employment in the industry is captured under SIC code 481 (telephone communications, including wireline and wireless segments). Between 1983 and 1998, employment grew from 1.15 million to 1.3 million (Current Population Survey [CPS] 1999). In addition, cable TV employment has remained relatively stable, at about 150,000 employees. Employment in Internet services and customer premise equipment is more difficult to track because these segments cut across various industries; but they are much smaller than either the wireless or cable TV segments. Our best estimate, therefore, is that employment in the five market segments grew from about 1.3 million in 1983 to 1.6 million in 1998, a 23 percent overall increase, or about 1.5 percent annually.

We calculated a breakdown of employment by occupational group and industry and customer segments, based on our own 1998 survey of a nationally representative sample of establishments in the industry.[7] Among customer service and sales centers, the wireline segment employs 70 percent of the workforce, while the wireless industry employs 14.6 percent; cable TV, 11.1 percent; and the Internet, 4.8 percent. It is also noteworthy that the majority of the workforce (53 percent) serves the residential or mass market segment, where wages are lower, work is more routinized, and working conditions are more onerous than in centers serving business customers (see Batt 2000). Among the technical workforce, 76 percent work for wireline local exchange carriers, 6 percent for long distance wireline carriers, 7.6 percent for Internet providers, 5.5 percent for cable TV, and 3.2 percent for wireless. Thus, the overwhelming bulk of the workforce continues to be employed in wireline services (Table 3).

Despite this seeming stability, dramatic employment shifts have occurred in this industry, which have led to serious declines in unionization. For the telephone communications industry alone (SIC 481), unionization declined from 55.5 percent to 27.7 percent of the entire workforce between 1983 and 1998 (CPS 1999). However, de-unionization accelerated in the third phase of restructuring due in part to the dramatic growth in demand for Internet and wireless services. Unionization fell by a total of 23 percent, from 55.5 to 42.5 percent between 1983 and 1991, but 35 percent (42.5 to 27.7 percent) between 1991 and 1998. For the key nonmanagement occupational groups, unionization fell from 63 percent to 32 percent for customer service and sales workers and from 67 percent to 48 percent for technical workers between 1983 and 1998.

The accelerating decline in unionization is accounted for by three factors. First, the former Bell companies substantially downsized the unionized workforce in their regulated wireline operations, by 60 percent at AT&T and about 30 percent among the regional Bell companies (Keefe and Batt 1997). Second, employment grew dramatically in new nonunion wireless, data, and Internet enterprises, both among the former Bell affiliates and the new entrants. New entrants in the long distance, cable TV, and wireless industries have been fiercely antiunion. It is only recently that the CWA is gaining membership in the long distance segment, as Verizon and SBC become long distance providers under the provisions of the 1996 Telecommunications Act. Third, former Bell companies successfully classified new technical and professional positions as managerial and outside the collective bargaining unit despite the fact that the jobs did not contain supervisory responsibilities. The unions have challenged these classifications through grievance and arbitration procedures and in collective bargaining but have reclaimed only a small number of positions through these processes. Managerial employment has grown at almost a 5 percent annual rate since 1984, while nonmanagement employment has declined at a 2 percent annual rate during the same period (Keefe 1999).

These changes not only have led to de-unionization but have profoundly reshaped the union's base of power in the industry. Increasingly, the unions are isolated on a wireline island. For example, based on our 1998 national survey of establishments, we found that 98.5 percent of unionized customer service and sales workers work in the wireline segment, and 95.6 percent of unionized technicians work on the local wireline infrastructure (Table 3). In addition, unionized workers increasingly are concentrated in the less skilled occupational groups. Historically, the unions represented all nonmanagerial employees, ranging from the most skilled to the least skilled occupational groups. The shift has occurred over time as new technologies have led to the demand for new skills and former Bell companies have defined the new occupational positions as outside of bargaining unit employment.

For example, historically the most skilled groups were the network technicians who installed and maintained the analog transmission and switching equipment. Among the technical workforce, the shift from analog to digital systems has led to the employment of thousands of technical workers with computer skills who frequently have job classifications defined as managerial. In our 1998 survey, none of the establishments that hired college-educated technicians were unionized. Among

TABLE 3

National Survey of Telecommunications Services Establishment: Distribution of
Employment and Unionization by Industry Segment

Occupational group	No. of establish-ments	No. of workers	% of Establish-ments	% of Workers	% Distribution of union establish-ments	% Distribution of union workers
Customer service and sales reps						
Industry segment						
Wireline	187	26,349	52.8	69.5	92.6	98.5
Wireless	85	5,514	24.0	14.6	1.9	1.0
Cable TV	57	4,197	16.1	11.1	5.5	0.5
Internet service providers	25	1,834	7.1	4.8	0.0	0.0
Subtotal	354	37,894	100.0	100.0	100.0	100.0
Technicians						
Industry segment						
Wireline local	94	19,800	45.2	75.9	83.1	95.6
Wireline long distance	24	1,553	11.5	6.0	6.5	1.0
Wireless	17	835	8.2	3.2	1.3	0.3
Cable TV	23	1,435	11.1	5.5	2.6	0.7
Internet service providers	39	1,989	18.8	7.6	1.3	0.9
Customer premise equipment	11	475	5.3	1.8	5.2	1.6
Subtotal	208	26,087	100.0	100.0	100.0	100.0

customer service and sales workers there has been a growth of sales jobs
(filled by college-educated account managers and sales executives) serving business customers, which similarly have been defined as outside of
the collective bargaining unit. Based on our 1998 survey, we found that
only 8 percent of these workers are unionized. Finally, in operator services, an historic union stronghold, ongoing automation has led to
employment decline. While operators represented 60 percent of all
telephone employment in the 1920s and 45 percent in the 1950s, they
represent less than 5 percent in 2000.

Labor–Management Relations: Consolidation and the Viability of Partnership Strategies

The structure of collective bargaining and the tenor of relations
between the unions and management have been profoundly influenced

by the course of industry restructuring over the past thirty years. At the beginning of the first phase of restructuring, for example, the unions and AT&T had just agreed to a two-tiered national bargaining structure (as opposed to the prior system of local telephone company bargaining). Between 1973 and 1984, AT&T bargained with the CWA and the IBEW at two levels. At the national level, Bell System–wide agreements standardized wage increases, benefits, and employment security. At the local bargaining level, individual Bell Operating Companies bargained with local union leadership over work administration and work rules. Local bargaining issues included overtime policy, posting of schedules, steps in the grievance process, health and safety, and absence pay.

In the second phase of restructuring brought on by the breakup of the Bell System, however, the structure of collective bargaining became the most contentious issue in bargaining. When the companies rejected the CWA's proposal for centralized bargaining, CWA pressed for continuance of the two-tier structure, with the first tier at the enterprise level (AT&T and the regional Bells) and local bargaining remaining at the operating company level. Eventually, all the RBOCs would opt for this two-tier structure. However, AT&T succeeded in removing itself from the common expiration dates established in telephone bargaining. It renegotiated the termination date of its 1983 contract to May 31, 1986, while the RBOC contracts all expired on August 9, 1986. In the subsequent four rounds of bargaining (1986, 1989, 1992, and 1995), AT&T would remain the economic pattern setter under a loose pattern framework (Keefe and Boroff 1994; Batt and Keefe 1999). The core issues in the loose AT&T pattern bargaining structure were compensation, health care, employment security, and union institutional security, including the right to organize at new subsidiaries.

In the third phase of restructuring, however, as the market power and success of AT&T has declined, so too has its role as a labor relations leader and pattern setter. In its place, the leading integrated megacarriers, Verizon and SBC, have emerged as not only the largest service providers but the innovators in collective bargaining and labor relations. Part of this change is accounted for by the political maneuvers of the unions in legislative and regulatory arenas. Because the regional Bell companies are regulated by the state public service commissions (PSCs), the unions historically have been able to go to state regulators to push for PSC intervention in instances where consumer and labor interests coincide (for example, where staffing levels are too low to meet service quality standards). In the 1990s, however, the opportunities for union political leverage increased as Bell companies sought changes in state rate structures, as they sought PSC approval of plans to open their local markets to competition (as required by the 1996 Telecommunications Act), and as they sought state and federal approval of their mergers and acquisitions. The CWA decided it was willing to enter into strategic partnerships to support Verizon's and SBC's business plans, on condition that these companies provide decent contracts, employment security, and neutrality and card check at all subsidiaries. The union's organizing strategy relies on using its existing relationships with the incumbents in the traditional wireline businesses to gain access to the new markets and employees.

The process and outcomes for the parties at Verizon and SBC, however, have been radically different. At Verizon, the process of merger among NYNEX, Bell Atlantic, and GTE has undermined strategic partnerships that were emerging between the unions and NYNEX and GTE prior to their merger into the larger entity. Despite major union gains in collective bargaining, a series of strikes and labor–management distrust have led to ongoing fights over agreed-upon contract language, preventing implementation of a partnership strategy. At SBC, by contrast, the partnership strategy emerged incrementally over several years, through several rounds of conflicts that have nonetheless been settled through negotiation. While union wages and benefits do not quite match those in the Verizon contract, the hallmark of CWA–SBC partnership is union institutional security in exchange for union support of mergers and corporate growth. Since 1996, SBC has kept its commitments to neutrality and card check language for workers in its nonunion enterprises, resulting in union organizing victories for 11,000 workers at SBC's Cingular wireless operations. In the sections following, we examine in more detail the development of these partnership efforts and the explanation for their successes and failures.

Verizon–CWA: Failed Partnership

In the 1980s, a partnership strategy was not part of the union–management landscape in the Northeast. While all other CWA districts accepted health care concessions in the 1980s, CWA District 1 in New York and the IBEW in New England joined forces in 1989 to retain traditional health care coverage. Through a bitter seventeen-week strike, the unions forced NYNEX to continue providing full health care coverage, without a copay or HMO. The win was due in large part to new mobilization strategies developed in the postdivestiture environment and borrowed from the public sector where workers do not have the right to strike. Union member mobilization coupled with public mobilization resulted in the denial of NYNEX's request for a rate increase before the New York State PSC.

CWA's Mobilization Strategy. CWA's member mobilization at NYNEX began shortly after 1986 bargaining. The issue was straightforward: preserve your health benefits. Mobilization consisted of workplace campaigns to involve every union member in actively representing his or her interests through collective action. Mobilization tactics included rallies, petitions, one-on-one postcard messages, wearing red clothing or arm bands, workplace coordinated stand-ups, work-to-rule campaigns, organizing nonmembers, information picket lines, electronic picket lines, and community support activities.

CWA also needed to put public pressure on the company in order to win the strike. In New York, the union had been actively involved in local and state politics for decades. CWA President Morty Bahr was an early supporter of Mario Cuomo when he entered political life. In 1989, Cuomo was the governor of New York. When it came to state regulatory issues, historically the union had either passively or actively supported the company. When the 1989 strike began, however, the union launched a public mobilization campaign to defeat NYNEX's request for rate increase before the state PSC. The public mobilization involved citizen petitions, alliances with consumer groups, publicly exposing poor-quality service in the Bronx and Brooklyn, ads in newspapers, and filings before the New York State PSC.

Public mistakes committed by the company earlier in the year greatly aided the union's public campaign. NYNEX had been convicted of criminally inflating its rate base to overcharge customers through the rate-setting process. The adverse publicity was accentuated when several executives of a deregulated subsidiary were caught sponsoring sex parties in Florida for some of their major clients. This gained NYNEX considerable attention from the New York tabloids. The union's public campaign against the company was further fueled by the death of a picketer in Westchester. The daughter of a company director who was crossing a picket line to work during the strike panicked and accidentally drove her vehicle into a picketer, killing him. The very public funeral was widely covered by the press and was followed by a spontaneous rank-and-file network sabotage campaign in Westchester County, the home of major corporations such as IBM.

The unions' concerted attack on NYNEX was successful when the PSC denied the rate increase. Since New York accounted for 65 percent of company revenue, the denial put considerable pressure on NYNEX, which was already the worst financially performing RBOC. Competition became another source of financial pressure that was unfamiliar to the company. In Manhattan, the most lucrative telecommunications market in the world, Teleport made a substantial effort to take the "high-cap" market by offering quick installation of high-capacity fiber links to major Wall Street firms.

After seventeen weeks of strike and the direct intervention of the governor, NYNEX relented, and the union-represented workforce retained their traditional health benefits. A considerable amount of internal CWA analysis, discussion, and debate followed the union's success. What made this strike different from its failed seven-month strike in 1971? The union concluded that its success was a result of the changing political economy of the industry, its political involvement throughout the state of New York, and the public mobilization campaign. Defeating the rate increase was the decisive step in the union victory.

Since 1989, CWA's mobilization programs in telecommunications have steadily improved in their effectiveness. In 1992, rather than strike, CWA continued to bargain after contracts expired at AT&T, Bell Atlantic, Pacific Telesis, and US West. Member mobilization was coordinated through electronic town meetings, conference calls, and taped telephone messages, which kept members involved and informed about bargaining progress. At AT&T, the unions threatened an electronic picket line by getting all their supporters to pledge to switch their long distance phone service to another carrier until a contract was signed. Some CWA locals increasingly demonstrated their mastery of information technologies in getting the union's story out to their members and to management. CWA also further developed its in-workplace strategies. The union believed that these tactics grow in power as employers increasingly rely on a committed and involved workforce to provide superior customer service.

CWA Wins 1995 Contract Through Public Relations Campaign. In the 1995 negotiations, mobilization again proved an effective tool to support the union's bargaining objectives. This time, the key contract fight occurred at Bell Atlantic, which then covered New Jersey, Pennsylvania, Delaware, Maryland, Virginia, West Virginia, and Washington, DC. The company launched an aggressive concession strategy. The circumstances were particularly difficult because, in contrast to NYNEX, the CWA and IBEW did not form a coalition against Bell Atlantic. Instead,

Bell Atlantic first bargained with IBEW and reached an agreement that guaranteed job security in exchange for a two-tier wage structure.[8] The CWA was outraged that Bell Atlantic forced an agreement in this manner and destabilized bargaining structure. In addition, CWA did not view a strike as viable because the union at Bell Atlantic was only able to maintain picket lines for about three weeks in 1989 before accepting the company's proposal.

Given these circumstances, the union developed a strategy linking internal mobilization, the threat of a regionwide strike, a public relations campaign, a lobbying effort on service quality at the state PSCs, and a national-level initiative to postpone signing the Telecommunications Act into law. The 1995 CWA national convention also passed a resolution providing the leadership with access to the strike fund to conduct public relations campaigns in support of collective bargaining.

At Bell Atlantic, employees worked without a contract from August 7, 1995, until January 1996. The union built an internal mobilization that gained national visibility when more than 1,000 Bell Atlantic of Pennsylvania employees were suspended for wearing T-shirts proclaiming, "We Won't Be Road Kill on the Information Superhighway." Workers reported high levels of acrimony at work, and they particularly resented the unilaterally imposed forced overtime policies and widespread use of subcontractors to perform traditional telephone work. After several well-placed leaks to the news media, the state PSCs investigated service quality during this period, found repeated violations of service standards, and ordered the company to hire an additional 500 customer service representatives, among other things.

Most effective, however, was the CWA's coordinated public relations campaign that relied on newspaper, radio, and television ads. The union commercials attacked the company's public-image making and questioned whether Bell Atlantic was "the Heart of Communications or Just Heartless?" In December 1995, CWA began to air a television ad about Larry—a slob of a subcontractor instead of a well-trained technician, who could be sent to your house by Bell Atlantic. Rude and poorly trained, Larry could destroy your home. The humorous ad was an immediate success; customers who called for installations or repairs emphasized that they did not want Larry sent to their home. Radio and newspaper ads encouraged customers to check for identification to see if technicians were real Bell Atlantic employees.

Shortly after Larry appeared, negotiations resumed, with Bell Atlantic vice chairmen Jim Cullen and Larry Babio at the table. Larry, the name of the central character in the ad, was chosen because the union believed Larry Babio, along with Ray Smith the CEO, represented their major roadblock. Bell Atlantic's aggressive contract concession strategy backfired after six months of intense union–management hostility and negative publicity. The contract was settled within the AT&T lead pattern, although CWA was forced to accept BACCSI, except in Pennsylvania. Nevertheless, CWA was able to achieve an 11 percent wage increase over three years, no retiree copay for health insurance, a 12 to 14 percent pension increase, and no two-tier settlement. The national CWA union then settled the remaining contracts with regional Bell companies in accordance with the AT&T pattern.

NYNEX Pays to Reign in the Union's Public Mobilization Tactics. At NYNEX, the bitter 1989 strike led the company to rethink its labor relations strategy and attempt a more positive bargaining relationship. In 1991, NYNEX hired James Dowdall as the vice president of labor relations. During his many years with AT&T labor relations, he had developed a good working relationship with Morty Bahr, president of CWA. Dowdall immediately sought to break the dynamics of mobilization and strike at NYNEX by extending the existing contract until 1995 and by providing generous 4 percent annual wage increases.

Similarly, when NYNEX decided to downsize 22,800 employees in December 1993, it followed up with early bargaining in spring 1994, which resulted in the most far-reaching retraining, transfer, and employment security system in the industry. As detailed in the next section, Collective Bargaining Outcomes, the 1994 contract provided a special retirement incentive, no layoff clauses, and an extensive retraining and transfer program. In return, CWA District 1 in New York signed a cease and desist letter of understanding, surrendering its ability to fight the company legislatively or before the PSC and to cease its public relations campaign against NYNEX. They would also eventually support the company's merger with Bell Atlantic, its petition at the New York PSC to become the first Bell company to gain access to the long distance market, and the Bell Atlantic merger with GTE. In 1997, NYNEX merged with Bell Atlantic. The merged company retained two labor relations vice presidents, one for the North (the former NYNEX) and one for the South (the former Bell Atlantic). In 1998, Bell Atlantic pursued early bargaining but with separate negotiations for the North and South.

In the North, the key issue was a contract clause requiring the company to offer to every eligible employee, prior to the contract expiration in August 1998, the 1994-negotiated pension enhancement. While estimates of eligible employees ranged from 6,000 to 14,000, both parties knew that Bell Atlantic North could not operate its network if all eligible employees accepted the buyout. The company sought to postpone the offer date for two years, a proposal the union accepted in exchange for substantial pension enhancements and decent wage gains. By April 15, 1998, the two sides had hammered out an agreement, but the union would not sign it until the Bell Atlantic South agreement was worked out.

Bargaining in the South stalled on three key issues: forced overtime, subcontracting, and organizing rights. Forced overtime dominated the agenda. The issue was a holdover from 1995 bargaining when CWA in the Potomac region had used overtime strikes (workers refused to work overtime as a tactic in its 1995 internal mobilization) when it worked without a contract. In response, the company implemented forced overtime, assigning employees specific days they were required to be available to work. Hundreds of employees were suspended for refusing to work during this period; but because they were without a contract the union could not take these cases to arbitration. The company continued the practice of forced overtime after the contract was settled in 1996. CWA would allege in an arbitration case following the strike that the company was violating a long-standing past practice in continuing to force its members to work overtime once the contract was settled. In 1997, however, the union lost the arbitration case. In 1998 bargaining, therefore, the union demanded that forced overtime be eliminated. Local bargainers would eventually settle for a ten- to fifteen-hour cap on forced overtime comparable to language in other agreements.

Nonetheless, these three outstanding issues in the South resulted in a regionwide strike on August 7 and 8, involving both the North and South and requiring the CEO, Ivan Seidenberg, to intervene. Seidenberg quickly accepted the union demands on subcontracting, neutrality, and card check, with one exception. Bell Atlantic Mobile (the company's staunchly antiunion cellular subsidiary) would be exempt from the organizing rights language. Although the contract contained many generous provisions, the membership in the South remained dissatisfied with the overtime provisions and in 1999 voted out incumbent leaders in the five largest locals in the district. The Bell Atlantic–CWA relationship, however, would be increasingly standardized on the NYNEX model. In exchange for these advances, the CWA became an important ally in Bell Atlantic's effort to merge with GTE and form Verizon, while simultaneously making some progress toward bringing GTE into the newly emerging pattern.

Failed Partnership at Verizon. With the formation of Verizon in spring 2000, just before bargaining was to begin, the prospects for union–management partnership initially looked promising. The management table was to be led by Randy McDonald, the head of human resources at GTE and co-architect (with Morty Bahr) of a successful partnership between GTE and the CWA. McDonald and Bahr had developed a personal relationship of trust and did road shows together to illustrate the viability of their joint strategy—one built on the union's support for technological innovation and corporate mergers before regulators in exchange for good wages, benefits, and employment and union security. McDonald was handpicked by Chuck Lee, the former CEO of GTE, and appeared to have good support among managers at GTE and the former Bell Atlantic. Just before bargaining began, however, McDonald mysteriously left Verizon for the top HR position at IBM, leaving a vacuum in bargaining leadership that was not filled.

Both management and the unions had the complex challenge of uniting disparate units behind a common agenda. It turned out that the unions had a more difficult task of uniting its leadership in districts 1 (NYNEX), 2 (the Potomac region), and 13 (Pennsylvania). The union's main issue was neutrality and card check at Verizon Wireless in the former Bell Atlantic North and South regions (covering thirteen states and Washington, DC). On the day the contract was to expire, the company conditionally agreed to card check and limited neutrality at Verizon Wireless in return for no strike at the newly formed Verizon Communications. Nevertheless, a regionwide CWA and IBEW strike commenced that night: though wage and benefits issues were settled, a variety of work administration and employment security issues remained.

During the first five days of the strike, regionwide issues on employment security and a special agreement covering service representatives at call centers were completed. Local issues dominated the remainder of the strike, after the neutrality and card check issues were once again finally concluded. Frustration over forced overtime in the South would eventually block a settlement and lead to a schism between North and South. Many of the new local leaders in CWA District 2 (in the Potomac region) had run on a platform of no forced overtime—a position the company consistently and adamantly rejected. On Thursday of the second week of the strike, the company agreed to an eight-hour cap on forced overtime. The regional bargaining leaderships then instructed the local bargainers to wrap up their negotiations by Sunday night of the second week, when the strike would end. Thinking that the strike would soon conclude, the national leadership, including Bahr, departed for Anaheim, California, where the CWA national convention would open the following week.

On Sunday afternoon, however, the bargaining committee in the South rejected the proposed settlement, largely on the forced overtime issue. The South would remain on strike for an additional four days, as the North, both CWA and IBEW, returned to work. During the next several days, busloads of picketers from the South would be sent to New York in an effort to block their return to work. The CWA leaders in the North were surprised and outraged. Toward the end of the strike's second week, the CWA district vice presidents and other officers had met and agreed to accept the proposed contracts and return to work on Sunday evening. CWA in the North and the IBEW in turn informed management that they accepted their contracts pending ratification and, consequently, were legally obligated to order their members to return to work. Ultimately, the South was forced to settle their continuing strike without any additional improvements. The union leaders in the South, however, would blame the North for the continuance of forced overtime in their contracts.

In the wake of 2000 bargaining, all parties felt betrayed. Even though the union gained desired language, CWA failed to advance its goal of a strategic partnership with the industry leader, Verizon. Instead, the company stiffened its arms'-length dealings. Eighteen months into the neutrality and card check agreement at Verizon Wireless, no employee had yet gained the right to collective bargaining under card check, as a variety of disputed issues were in arbitration. In response, CWA opposed Verizon's entry into long distance in Pennsylvania. At the local level, a large number of dismissals were also meted out for alleged strike-related violence and sabotage. After Verizon agreed to arbitration, most of the discharged strikers were reinstated. Nonetheless, these skirmishes consumed the first year of postbargaining labor relations.

Clearly, strategic partnership has not arrived at Verizon. Instead, a low-trust relationship prevails at the higher levels of the union and management, based on pervasive hostility that is fueled both by a mutual sense of betrayal and by internal political conflict and animosity within both CWA and Verizon.

SBC Communications—CWA's Strategic Partner?

In contrast to the chaotic union–management relations at Verizon, the CWA (initially District 6 and now expanded to districts 4 and 9) and SBC have stabilized a strategic partnership that exchanges union organizing rights for union support of corporate regulatory and legislative efforts. In 1998, SBC and the CWA settled an early contract that broke with the AT&T pattern. The SBC neutrality and card check language and the SBC–CWA relationship set the standard for the industry. Following the CWA–SBC settlement terms were contract agreements at Pacific Telesis and Ameritech, which had merged with SBC. These contracts each provided for significant wage improvements and expansive union organizing rights. Each SBC company also agreed to thirty-two-month contracts with CWA that would expire off the August cycle, in April 2001. In addition, in 1998 the Connecticut Telephone Workers Union (representing workers at SNET) merged with the CWA and was represented for the first time as a CWA affiliate. After a one-month strike, the union signed a thirty-two-month contract, bringing them into the SBC bargaining orbit, as SNET merged with SBC.

The SBC–CWA partnership emerged as a result of a concerted union effort, beginning in 1992, to reconstruct their relationship based on mutual support. CWA had always supported SBC's (then Southwestern Bell) positions in the state legislature and PSCs. However, in 1992 when the union tried to organize workers in the company's wireless subsidiary, Southwestern Bell Mobile Systems (SBMS), it met with classic antiunion suppression campaigns. The union explained it could not continue to provide political support for the company's regulatory agenda nor cooperate in the traditional wireline business while the company set up antiunion subsidiaries, particularly in wireless, that tenaciously fought unionization.

During the next five years, the CWA in District 6 undertook a sustained public and internal mobilization campaign to organize SBC Wireless. Internally the union had to educate members about the strategic importance of organizing the growing wireless business and to gain their participation in organizing campaigns. Externally, the union conducted demonstrations, filed board charges, and bargained hard over its participation in SBC legislative and regulatory affairs. Early on, the CWA decided on a policy of balanced participation and assistance conditioned on progress at the wireless subsidiary. In 1993, for example, SBC was pressing for state legislation that would regulate providers who were trying to access the SBC infrastructure and require them to build a certain amount of the infrastructure in every state served by SBC. CWA helped SBC pass the legislation in Kansas in exchange for an agreement on union job growth in the state (CWA 1997).

However, the "partnership" only emerged through a series of corporate antiunion campaigns and union organizing defeats, internal mobilizing and angry public demonstrations by the union, and incremental gains in neutrality agreements negotiated over five years. For example, despite an initial neutrality agreement signed in 1992, the SBMS continued to hire consultants to run antiunion campaigns and successfully defeat union elections through 1994. The campaigns surprised and angered CWA members who traditionally viewed the company as paternalistic. The corporation's behavior fueled member activism, and, by 1994, the union had trained 350 member organizers and counted fifteen locals directly involved in campaigns. In 1995, to redress specific violations at one site, the company signed expanded neutrality agreements that included mediation and arbitration of disputes. The union, in turn, helped mobilize 5,000 members to lobby for SBC before the state legislature. In another instance, the SBC asked CWA for help when it learned the city council of San Antonio was accepting bids to lease its fiber optic ring to a Canadian consortium. The CWA's San Antonio local turned out 200 members at one meeting, and 600 at a second, leading to the proposal's defeat (CWA 1997).

In a fourth agreement, the company approached the union because it wanted to open pilot stores to sell both wireline and wireless services ("one-stop shopping") in Houston and Austin. The company offered to accept card check recognition at these sites if, after one year, the company decided to continue the operation. Yet, in 1996, a new antiunion regional manager in SBMS again ran a tough antiunion campaign, leading to a union defeat in the election. Then, with the passage of the 1996 Telecommunications Act, SBC again approached the union to gain support for its efforts to regulate competitors' access to local service in five states. By 1997, it also sought CWA support for its merger with Pacific Telephone. After talks with CWA leaders in districts 6 and 9 (representing Pacific Telephone), SBC announced the formation of two new subsidiaries and gave CWA recognition to both. It then negotiated card check agreements for the other SBC subsidiaries. The agreement covered all lines of business, including current and future subsidiaries for all in-region operations of SBC. It granted worksite access for organizers, card check recognition by a simple majority, bargaining units based on the earliest date that appears on the cards turned in to the American Arbitration Association (AAA), and arbitration of all disputes. Since then, this language has been extended to all U.S. subsidiaries of SBC, even those operating outside the SBC regional footprints. SBC has gained the complete support of CWA in regulatory, legislative, and political affairs (CWA 1997).

In 2001 bargaining, SBC's contracts with CWA were scheduled to expire in April. SBC was interested in getting bargaining accomplished prior to the expiration. The CWA informed the company that many of the 10,000 workers that the CWA organized at SBC's wireless subsidiary (now called Cingular) were without first contracts. Early bargaining would be contingent on settling these first contracts. Larry Cohen, CWA's executive vice president, led the negotiations at Cingular. These talks produced surprisingly decent first contracts in wireless units in several states in the Midwest, New England, and mid-Atlantic regions. With wireless bargaining completed, the CWA and SBC units at Southwest Bell, Pacific Bell, Nevada Bell, Ameritech, and SNET negotiated a new contract, incorporating the key economic features of the Verizon agreement—wages, pensions, and special provisions for call centers. Negotiations were completed a month before contract expiration. Later, in August 2001, the CWA in District 3 (BellSouth) succeeded in negotiating a card check and neutrality agreement for 10,000 additional workers at Cingular Wireless in the nine-state BellSouth region, while also incorporating key features of the Verizon agreement.

Downward Departure from the Pattern: AT&T and Qwest/US West

As Verizon and SBC have become the consolidated industry giants, the union has sought to use contract gains with these companies to set new national patterns. AT&T, by contrast, has lost its pattern-leading position. By the late 1990s, however, pattern bargaining in general has eroded. While a loose relationship exists among Verizon, SBC, and BellSouth, their contracts no longer have common expiration dates. AT&T, Qwest, and Lucent have diverged more substantially, both in terms of content and expiration dates.

AT&T has continued to grapple with its long-term inability to grow revenue in core telecommunications. Its erratic business strategy has been accompanied by a consistent labor strategy: shedding union employees and cutting labor costs. The company's union workforce dropped from 250,000 at divestiture to 103,000 in 1994, to 48,000 in 1998, and 31,000 in 2001. AT&T's only unionized operation is AT&T long distance, which has remained the largest long distance company but has struggled with excess capacity, declining prices for its services, and new competition from Verizon and SBC. While the CWA negotiated a neutrality provision and expedited election process at AT&T and has organized about 3,000 workers in broadband and local service divisions, management often resists the process and forces issues into arbitration.

To force AT&T to reverse its labor relations practices, CWA sued the company in 2001. The union filed a shareholder rights lawsuit, charging that AT&T was trying to adopt an illegal process to amend its charter so that only a simple majority of shareholder votes, not the required two-thirds, could authorize AT&T's major restructuring. Management's plan to split AT&T into three companies with four separate stock listings—broadband, wireless, business services, and consumer long distance—was drawing considerable criticism, as its plan to acquire TCI and MediaOne had done earlier. According to CWA, the restructuring plan would move AT&T even further from a bundled telecommunications services strategy, a successful strategy adopted by all of its major competitors (CWA 2001). To fight AT&T's decision, CWA mobilized a public campaign leading up to the AT&T stockholders meeting. The union also conducted a conference call to numerous Wall Street firms in which it criticized the details of the AT&T divestiture plan. Publicly, the union criticized AT&T management for running the company for the benefit of themselves and the investment bankers who benefit enormously from the mergers, acquisitions, divestitures, and carve-outs.

The union's public mobilization strategy was successful in that it compelled AT&T senior management to negotiate with the CWA. This resulted in a temporary reversal of AT&T's policies. In return, CWA withdrew its lawsuit and its opposition to the AT&T plan. Nonetheless, as the downsized and fractured AT&T struggles to define its business strategy, it is increasingly in conflict with the CWA. As the union prepared for 2002 bargaining, it openly challenged CEO Michael Armstrong's alleged mismanagement: CWA opposed the proposed merger between AT&T Broadband and Comcast, which values the AT&T Broadband assets below half of what AT&T recently paid for them. At the same time, the merger provides Armstrong with the job of chairman of the new merged entity. The union wanted BellSouth to acquire AT&T, which would make it the third megacarrier in the industry.

At Qwest, CWA also conducted a two-week strike in 1998 to oppose the implementation of individual-based performance pay and to place limits on forced overtime. The union conducted a public mobilization campaign, focusing on the growing number of US West service failures. The union had not adequately prepared for its public mobilization campaign and was unable to defeat the individual-based compensation plan. However, it did limit forced overtime to sixteen hours a week in 1999 and eight hours per week in 2001. The Qwest/US West agreement is the only Bell contract where management has gained individual-based performance pay for technicians and commission pay for service representatives.

In 2000, Qwest/US West bargained early and reached a settlement in November, which fell short of the other major contracts in the industry.

The agreement provides a contract extension until August 2003. It provides for 3.5 percent and 5 percent wage increases and improved pensions. The contract did not modify the individual-based compensation plan and lacks any provisions for neutrality, card check, expedited election, or access of organizers to nonunion worksites at Qwest. The company was able to get a federal judge to enjoin the workplace mobilization practice of wearing black armbands. As a condition of the settlement, Qwest requested that the injunction be lifted. Qwest has been accused of highly aggressive accounting procedures in the wake of the Enron bankruptcy and may be implicated in the bankruptcy of Global Crossing.

Collective Bargaining Outcomes

Our review of collective bargaining in the postdivestiture telecommunications industry examines wage levels and compensation strategies, employment security, union institutional security, and agreements specific to service and sales centers, where working conditions have become particularly onerous since divestiture. We draw on collective bargaining agreements and analyses of trends in the CPS data. We also compare human resource management strategies in union and nonunion workplaces by drawing on our 1998 national survey of telecommunications establishments.

Wage Outcomes and Compensation Strategies

Several trends in compensation stand out in the postdivestiture period. First, the Bell companies and unions have negotiated wage increases that basically track the consumer price index. In fact, in successive rounds of bargaining, across-the-board wage increases rose as a percentage of base pay between 1986 and 2000. Second, despite the fact that collective bargaining was decentralized to the enterprise level, Bell companies continued to offer wages and benefits that formed a pattern until the late 1990s, when the pattern began to break down. Third, the union/nonunion wage gap was fairly small until 1990 but grew significantly in the 1990s due to falling real wages in nonunion companies. Finally, the downward pressure of the union/nonunion compensation differential has led AT&T and the RBOCs to seek reductions in health care costs and to introduce various forms of contingent pay.

Table 4 compares negotiated wage raises at AT&T and the regional Bell companies. The postdivestiture trend shows a steady increase in each successive contract. Across-the-board wage increases averaged 2.8 percent between 1986 and 1994, but they rose on average from 2.2 percent

Table 4
Changes in Wage Compensation in CWA Collective Bargaining Agreements

	Percentage annual change										Average annual postdivestiture wage changes
	1986–88	1989–91	1992–94	1995–98	1996	1997	1998	1999	2000	2001	
AT&T	2.7	3.0	3.9	3.5	3.5	3.4	3.8	3.8	3.8	3.9	3.4
SBC Ameritech	2.0	2.5	3.5	3.5	3.5	3.5	3.5	3.6	3.6	4.3	3.1
Verizon Bell Atlantic	2.7	2.5	3.9	3.7	4.0	3.5	3.8	4.0	4.0	3.0	3.4
BellSouth	1.7	2.0	2.5	3.5	3.5	3.4	3.6	4.1	4.1	3.1	2.8
Verizon NYNEX	1.5	2.8	4.0	3.5	3.5	3.0	3.8	3.8	4.0	3.0	3.1
SBC Pacific Telesis	2.0	3.1	3.7	3.5	3.5	3.4	3.5	3.6	3.6	4.3	3.3
SBC Southwest Bell	2.0	3.0	3.0	3.5	3.5	3.4	3.5	3.5	3.6	4.3	3.1
Qwest/US West	1.8	3.3	3.7	3.5	3.5	3.5	3.9	3.5	3.5	3.5	3.2
Average change	2.1	2.7	3.6	3.5	3.6	3.4	3.7	3.7	3.8	3.8	3.2
Average CPI change	3.3	4.6	2.8	2.6	3.0	2.3	1.6	2.7	3.4	2.7	3.1
Real wage change	-1.2	-1.8	0.8	0.9	0.6	1.1	2.1	1.0	0.4	1.1	0.1

in 1986 to 3.3 percent in 1994. Slight variation in the pattern existed among the Bell companies, with BellSouth consistently negotiating the lowest annual increases (averaging 2 percent annually) and AT&T negotiating the highest (3.2 percent on average). Previously negotiated cost-of-living adjustments were restricted, suspended, or eliminated in all companies in 1986 bargaining. Loose pattern wage bargaining produced wage gains that were below the rate of inflation in the late 1980s, but by the mid-1990s, real wage gains had returned.

Each company also pursued some form of contingent pay, which the unions resisted and treated as company add-ons outside of the basic economic package. By 1992, all of the former Bell affiliates, with the exception of NYNEX and US West, had negotiated one of these plans, which consisted of either profit sharing or "team" incentive awards (based on operational performance at an establishment or business unit level). In the 1990s, some companies shifted from profit sharing and team awards to stock ownership plans, while others (Verizon and SBC) offered both. All companies have also pushed for individual sales plans, which we discuss in the following section on service and sales workers. In addition, there has been an increased reliance on signing bonuses to ensure ratification. The former Bell Atlantic, Southwestern Bell, and US West introduced these bonuses in the 1980s. By 1995, five of the seven major contracts offered signing bonuses of between $500 and $1,500.

The unions have negotiated various parameters for the contingent pay plans. For example, in 1992 and 1995, District 9, representing Pacific Telesis workers, negotiated trials of a group incentive plan with joint union–management team oversight. The union insisted that there be no take-aways, that the plan be self-funding (based on a productivity gains fund), and that it be easy to understand. In 1994, the NYNEX contract established a bonus based on meeting "team" (division-level) service and sales objectives. Data for 1995 to 1997 show that employees received stock and cash bonuses amounting to 3.23 percent. The 1995 (former) Bell Atlantic contract allowed the company to create "team" incentive plans linked to operational objectives at the second-manager's level or above and limited to 5 percent of annual base pay (extended to 10 percent in 2001), but since they were not funded by the agreement, no bonuses have been paid.

The Union–Nonunion Wage Gap and Wage Inequality. Given the significant decline in unionization, one might expect that union wages would converge toward nonunion rates. However, the opposite has occurred as indicated in Table 5.[9] As de-unionization accelerated between

TABLE 5

Growth of Wage Inequality Within Union and Nonunion Segments, by Occupation:
Telecommunications Industry, 1983–1998

	1983	1998	Change (%) 1983–90	1990–98	1983–98
Clerical and sales workers					
Union real weekly earnings[a]					
Median earnings	$261	$368	1.0	0.9	1.8
10th percentile	$223	$205	-3.9	-4.2	-8.1
90th percentile	$446	$507	3.0	10.7	13.7
Nonunion real weekly earnings[a]					
Median earnings	$382	$307	-5.7	-13.9	-19.6
10th percentile	$221	$153	-13.4	-8.8	-22.2
90th percentile	$729	$650	-16.0	13.0	-3.0
Ratio					
Union/nonunion median					
real earnings	0.95	1.20	7.1	19.5	26.7
Ratio of 90th to 10th percentile					
Union	2.00	2.47	7.1	16.5	23.7
Nonunion	3.30	4.12	-3.0	27.8	24.8
Technical workers					
Union real weekly earnings[a]					
Median earnings	$488	$515	0.4	5.1	5.6
10th percentile	$351	$283	-12.9	-6.6	-19.5
90th percentile	$602	$736	1.6	20.6	22.2
Nonunion real weekly earnings[a]					
Median earnings	$502	$405	-2.5	-16.9	-19.3
10th percentile	$241	$215	1.6	-12.5	-10.9
90th percentile	$753	$706	1.6	-7.9	-6.3
Ratio					
Union/nonunion median real					
earnings	0.97	1.27	2.9	28.1	30.9
Ratio of 90th to 10th percentile					
Union	1.71	2.60	16.7	35.2	51.8
Nonunion	3.13	3.29	0.0	5.1	5.1

Source: CPS merged annual earnings files (1999).
[a] CPI–U adjusted. For methodological notes, see endnote 5.

1990 and 1998, so too did the rise in the union/nonunion wage gap.
Among clerical and sales workers, the ratio was .95 in 1983, 1.00 in
1990, and 1.20 in 1998, a 19.5 percent rise from 1990 to 1998 and 26.7
percent in total. Among technical workers, the ratio of union to
nonunion median weekly wages was .97 in 1983, 1.00 in 1990, and 1.27
in 1998, a 28 percent rise from 1990 to 1998 (31 percent rise overall).

These trends are due almost entirely to the precipitous fall in real wages of nonunion workers of over 19 percent over the period, for both technical and clerical and sales occupations. By contrast, union workers experienced small rises in the real wages over the period (5.6 percent for technical workers and 1.8 percent for clerical and sales workers over the period). These figures underestimate the differences in total compensation, however, by failing to take into account the higher levels of nonwage benefits for union workers and the greater use of part-time and contingent staffing among nonunion employers.

In addition, wage dispersion within both the union and nonunion segments increased. For clerical and sales workers, the 90/10 ratio of median weekly earnings rose to 2.47 for union workers (a 24 percent rise over the period) and to 4.12 for nonunion workers (a 25 percent rise). Among technical workers, the 90/10 ratio of median weekly earnings rose to 2.60 for union workers (a 52 percent rise) and to 3.29 for nonunion workers (a 5 percent rise). Among nonunion technical workers, wages fell for both the 90th and the 10th percentiles, but they fell somewhat more for the 10th percentile. Among union technical workers, they rose 22 percent for the 90th percentile group, but fell dramatically by 19.5 percent for the 10th percentile group.

Employment Security

Prior to divestiture, Bell System employees, union-represented and management alike, had secure jobs. Employment security was achieved by careful human resources planning and managed deployment of labor-displacing technology. AT&T retained employees in whom it had substantial human capital investments. The employees were decidedly loyal to the Bell System and its mission of providing universal, reliable telephone service. The spirit of service was the guiding shared value. Furthermore, the union leadership readily accepted technological advances in the workplace. A job control unionism, seeking security through highly detailed job classifications, never emerged in the industry. Instead, most job classifications were extremely broad, making work assignments easier and the workforce more flexible.

As a result of the Bell System's social contract, employment security issues were not paramount in predivestiture negotiations at the national level. There were several income protection programs bargained, notably the Supplemental Income Protection Program (SIPP) and the Voluntary Income Protection Program (VIPP), primarily to aid adjustment in Western Electric manufacturing. The former provided incentives for early retirement; the latter provided separation income to junior employees who opted to resign. Furthermore, in 1980 AT&T signed an understanding with its unions that it would not subcontract "traditional telephone work," where such subcontracting could directly result in layoffs, downgrading, or part-timing of regular employees.

At the local level, contracts did contain language on force adjustments, layoff procedures, and layoff pay. These provisions, generally, were "idle" in the contract, with the major exception of the employees in Western Electric's factories. This group of employees experienced the ups and downs of business cycles. The main workers permanently dislocated by automation were operators, who could transfer to clerical or other office jobs, sometimes locally and sometimes if they were willing to move to a different region.

Following divestiture, employment security became a central issue as AT&T cut 40,000 positions by 1985. As a result, AT&T and the CWA created what became the model for training and career assistance: a jointly owned, nonprofit corporation, the Alliance for Employee Growth and Development, designed to provide training and career development for both displaced workers and active employees. The parties also bargained an automated employee transfer system, called AT&T Transfer System (ATS), providing active and laid-off employees with real-time information about job openings nationwide. Between 1986 and 1992, the Alliance spent about $80 million serving 59,451 union members (60 percent of whom were active employees) (Batt and Osterman 1993). The Alliance was widely recognized as performing an heroic task on a small budget (compared to AT&T's annual training budget of $300 million). Several of the regional Bell companies negotiated similar training and internal transfer programs, though not as well financed as the Alliance. Ongoing downsizing in the 1980s and early 1990s occurred almost entirely through attrition (with the exception of AT&T), and companies offered good severance and early-retirement packages. Pacific Telephone and Southwestern Bell agreed to no-layoff clauses. Table 6 summarizes employment security provisions at the RBOCs and AT&T.

A new industry standard for employment security was negotiated in 1994 by NYNEX and the CWA, and extended in 1998 in the contract covering former NYNEX employees. The 1994 contract provided a special retirement incentive that added six years to both service and age. It also included a 30 percent social security supplement until age 62 or a $500 annual bonus, whichever is greater. The incentive program was designed to reduce the nonmanagement workforce by 30 percent (16,800

TABLE 6

CWA's Postdivestiture Employment Security Bargaining Outcomes

	1986	1989	1992	1995	1998
AT&T	Job information center. Alliance created. Income protection enhanced.	Automated transfer system. Displaced worker priority. Income protection enhanced.	Access to nonunion subsidiaries for transfer. Income protection enhanced.	No change	No change
Ameritech-SBC	No change	Relocation allowance increased. Medical benefits of laid-off employees expanded. Incentives for early retirement.	Priority placements for displaced workers. Income protection enhanced.	Hometown jobs—employment guarantees within market area.	Hometown jobs—employment guarantees within market area. Seniority strengthened.
Bell Atlantic-Verizon	Job information center for displaced employees.	Employee career resource centers. Income protection enhanced.	Income protection enhanced.	Job security for some occupations.	No layoffs, downgrades, or forced transfers; 3,000 temps made permanent.
BellSouth	Career continuation program.	Employment security partnership.	Joint committee on subcontracting. Improved early retirement income.	Increase mobility rights. Extend bargaining unit.	Increase mobility rights. Extend bargaining unit. Commitment to 600 techs; limits on temps and term employees.
NYNEX-Bell Atlantic North-Verizon	Priority placement for displaced workers. Income protection program enhanced.	Incentives for early retirement.	Incentives for early retirement.	No layoff—broad transfer rights. Add 6 years to service and seniority for pension eligibility.	No layoffs, downgrades, or forced transfers; 3,000 temps made permanent. Extension of the buyout deadline to 2000.
Pacific Telesis-SBC	No layoff agreement.	No layoff agreement. Transfer and relocation assistance improved.	No layoff agreement. Automated transfer system. Early-retirement severance increased.	Improved workforce movement. Improved income protection and separation benefits.	Hire 500 outside techs.

TABLE 6—(*Continued*)
CWAs Postdivestiture Employment Security Bargaining Outcomes

	1986	1989	1992	1995	1998
Southwest Bell-SBC	Career resource center. Notice increased to 90 days. Incentives for voluntary separation.	No layoff agreement. Early-retirement income improved.	Voluntary severance expanded.	Hometown jobs—find jobs in market area.	Hometown jobs—find jobs in market area.
US West/Qwest		Upgrade and transfer plan. Enhancements for voluntary separation.	Joint committee on skill needs. Enhancements for voluntary separation.	Transfer to mobile hiring hall for techs.	No change

Source: CWA.

of 57,000) at a cost of over $2 billion, or $77,000 per participating employee. For the surviving workforce, NYNEX committed itself to no layoffs due to organizational or technological changes, internal transfer rights to all divisions, and first rights to jobs in new subsidiaries. It also funded an innovative two-year associate's degree program in telecommunications technology, open to all bargaining unit employees. Participating employees work four days a week and go to school the fifth day on company time, with all educational expenses paid by the company. Upon graduation, employees receive a fifty dollar a week increase. NYNEX's strategy recognizes that it is a high labor cost supplier, and it offsets this cost disadvantage with a highly educated, flexible, and productive workforce. In the first two years of the program, roughly 1,100 employees enrolled (Clifton 1999). In addition, employees with five years of service are eligible for a two-year educational leave, with educational expenses funded at $10,000 per year, while retaining full benefits, seniority, and a guaranteed job when they return.

At Ameritech and Southwestern Bell in 1995, the CWA developed another innovative approach to employment security, known as "hometown jobs." The companies agreed that all surplused employees would have a right to reassignment in their local labor market. This provision continued in the 1998 and 2001 contracts. This gain was critical for members because much of the restructuring in the decade involved consolidation of offices into new geographic locations. Many workers could not, or would not, "follow the work" because their spouses worked or because they did not want to uproot their children.

Employment security receded as a key issue in the mid-1990s on, as demand for telecommunications services exploded. The former Bell affiliates miscalculated market demand. Most downsized too much and lost their most experienced workers, who often took their early-retirement packages and went to work for Bell competitors. The Bell companies scrambled to hire replacements, poured money into new hire training, and experienced high levels of absenteeism and turnover unlike they had ever encountered. Short staffing led to forced overtime, which, as indicated previously, became a major strike issue in 1998.

To handle their staffing problems and cut costs, the former Bell affiliates also have resorted to outsourcing and subcontracting of work, creating new tensions around employment security. The problem is particularly salient for the call centers, where advances in call distribution systems allow companies to invisibly switch call loads to locations across ever larger geographic areas. At a unionized AT&T center in Dallas, for example, the local union president began to notice a slow decline in call volumes in 1997. After three years, a fast decline began, and 200 service reps were fired in four months. By 2000, the workforce was down to 468, from 1,600. The experience was duplicated at five other centers across the country, with a resulting loss of 6,000 union jobs. AT&T had shifted the work to call centers run by subcontractors. At Verizon in New England in 2000, the CWA observed a similar pattern of centers losing call volume. However, subcontracting of work had been a strike issue in 1998, and the subsequent agreement prohibited subcontracting of work outside the region. In this case, the union mobilized members to collect information from online accounts, such as sales codes or 800 numbers that were not from New England. The sales reps also started getting phone calls from centers in the South, asking them questions about the accounts. The union presented its evidence to the company, and call volumes picked up shortly thereafter. The 2001 Verizon contract limits the company's ability to shift work from one region to another (from the former Bell Atlantic North to the South or to former GTE locations) to 0.7 percent of all work.

Overall, however, union workplaces continue to provide greater job security than nonunion ones, according to data from our 1998 national survey of telecommunications establishments. For example, in residential call centers, temporary workers averaged 1.2 percent of the workforce in union centers but 6.5 percent in nonunion centers. Reported layoffs as a percentage of the current workforce were 6 percent in union establishments but 34 percent in nonunion centers. Among technicians, temporary workers were 2 percent of the union workforce and 7 percent of the nonunion workforce.

Union Institutional Security

Management's intentions about its future relationship with the union are most readily conveyed by its willingness to negotiate union institutional security provisions. Since these provisions make it easier for the union to organize and gain representation rights, they reveal whether management wants a constructive long-term relationship with the union or prefers to restrict or possibly eliminate the union's representative role. Union institutional security arrangements are permissive subjects of bargaining, which cannot be brought to impasse, making them truly voluntary issues for management. Union institutional security agreements facilitate union organizing at large corporations, which have the capacity to choose their union status in today's legal environment (Kochan,

McKersie, and Chalykoff 1986). Basically these provisions recreate the framework for organizing that prevailed prior to Taft-Hartley (1947), when unions achieved their greatest organizing successes. Although each of the regional Bell companies and AT&T have created nonunion subsidiaries since divestiture, they have each granted some of these provisions, except for Qwest/US West. The CWA made "wall-to-wall" representation a goal shortly after divestiture and has worked to educate members to fight for organizing rights in their contracts. AT&T was the first to negotiate neutrality language in 1992, but the 1994 NYNEX agreement set the standard. Other companies have followed, with the unions pushing for stronger language in each successive contract, as exemplified in the case of SBC, discussed previously. Table 7 summarizes the union security provisions contained in collective bargaining agreements at the former Bell affiliates. The most prevalent provision is neutrality, where management agrees not to hire consultants or engage in a campaign to keep the union out of a nonunion workplace. Clearly, however, the ability of the union to win organizing campaigns based on neutrality and card check language depends on the character of union–management relations and the company's willingness to abide by the contract. As indicated previously, while the union has organized 11,000 workers at SBC's Cingular Wireless, it has been unable to gain representation rights at Verizon's wireless entity. Organizing success in the nonunion subsidiaries will be closely linked to the success of strategic partnership strategies.

Bargaining for Service and Sales Representatives

A very significant trend over the last decade has been the increasing salience of issues specific to the female-dominated service and sales workforce. In 1998, for the first time, the failure to resolve these issues contributed to strikes at Bell Atlantic, US West, and SNET. Historically, customer service employees were located in the business offices of telephone companies where they handled orders and billing and were the least unionized or militant occupational group. Since deregulation, however, the former Bell affiliates have turned "order-taking" jobs into sales-maximizing positions, an affront to workers trained to care about providing excellent service to the public. Most local service bureaus have been consolidated into large remote call centers, making possible the application of industrial engineering models to automate and standardize customer transactions. Automated call distribution systems control the pace of work, and constant electronic monitoring exposes

TABLE 7

Collectively Bargained Organizing Rights: Neutrality, Expedited Elections, Card Check, and Workplace Access for Organizers

Company	Neutrality	Expedited NLRB consent elections	Card check	Organizer access	Exceptions
AT&T	X	X	0	X	Third party can order card check
BellSouth	X	X	0	?	
Cingular Wireless (all SBC areas)	X	0	X	X	Except in BellSouth region
Lucent	X	X	0	0	Wholly-owned subsidiaries
Qwest (formerly US West)	0	0	0	0	Successorship
SBC (includes Ameritech, PacBell, SNET, SWB)	X	0	X	X	
Verizon	X	0	X	X	In former Bell Atlantic and NYNEX
Verizon Southwest	X	X	0	?	Card check in existing areas
Verizon Wireless	X	0	X	X	Area-Bell Atlantic Mobile Language in arbitration

Source: CWA.

employees to discipline based on a myriad of contradictory performance measures, including adherence to schedules, scripts, sales quotas, call-handling time, and tone and manner with customers. All parties agree that these have become the most stressful jobs in the industry, with intense pressure to be polite to customers, while maximizing sales within a 300-second time limit per call.

Ongoing contentious issues include commission pay, sales quotas, electronic monitoring, discipline for failure to meet performance standards, "adherence to schedules," and outsourcing and subcontracting. To respond to these issues, the union in 1990 began organizing annual "marketing conferences," which bring together 200 to 300 activists and local leaders from service and sales centers across the country. The conferences focus on developing coordinated mobilization strategies, bargaining agendas, and contract language regarding key workplace issues. For example, when the Bell companies began adopting tight restrictions on scheduling, including requirements that service reps "adhere" to their schedules (plugged into the computer and telephone lines) 90 percent of the day, the reps jointly developed mobilization campaigns to combat the pressure. The national union also has commissioned quantitative studies of health and safety, including ergonomics; carpel tunnel syndrome; and job-related stress, which members use in negotiations.

All companies have sought to introduce individual sales incentives and commission pay, and the union has fiercely debated its response. There are three categories of incentives. "Trash and trinkets" are prizes, trips, or other awards for winning sales competitions for particular products or time-limited campaigns. Cash incentive plans provide periodic bonuses by the piece or for meeting sales objectives (for example, 50 to 100 dollars per month over base pay). Commission pay plans put a portion of base pay at risk.

One approach is to "just say no," which the unions initially did. However, in some cases, companies have simply implemented a trash-and-trinkets or incentive plan, and the union has filed an unfair labor practice charge for failure to bargain or has arbitrated the case. However, this scenario is politically risky because many members like the extra money and prizes, and the union is portrayed as taking money away from members. Also, as an alternative to incentives, companies may simply institute sales quotas and discipline members, including termination, for failure to reach them. BellSouth, for example, has taken this approach, which has led to ongoing grievances and arbitrations. Beginning in the 1980s, the former Bell affiliates implemented trash-and-trinkets programs, either with or without union approval. The unions at SBC, Southwestern Bell Telephone (SWBT), and SNET have not bargained over sales incentives but have been able to influence management strategies through joint committees on sales objectives and performance standards.

A second approach is to negotiate over sales incentives but not commission pay. In general, the union attitude has shifted from "just say no" to a recognition that sales incentives are a reality and the union should negotiate over them based on a set of principles. In 1998, the CWA and Pacific Telepone negotiated what has become a model agreement on principles for sales incentive plans. The agreement states that sales shall be "a win for all stakeholders," providing customers with good service, employees with pay opportunities and employment security, and the company with higher revenues. It requires training for all employees on product knowledge and sales techniques, strict adherence to ethical sales practices, no wages at risk, no sales quotas, sales goals based on sales opportunities, no performance evaluation based solely on sales, no discipline for failure to meet sales goals, and joint union–management oversight. Other union principles include negotiated adjustments for time not worked and clauses that allow workers who do not want to sell or who are not making objectives to transfer to a nonsales environment (Verizon contract). The union also states that incentive plans should not undermine the union's ability to represent members. This is especially an issue with commission pay plans where stewards may lose pay because they are not fully compensated for time spent on union duties.

The CWA has negotiated commission pay at two companies: AT&T (1992) and US West (1995). The current AT&T plan, which covers several hundred employees providing inbound and outbound sales to business customers, provides for a guaranteed base of 80 percent of the full salary equivalent and a target of 20 percent for incentive pay. On average, the plan must pay out at least 90 percent of full salary equivalent. The plan is overseen by a joint union–management governance committee, and the union negotiated a series of protective measures, including a transition period for new hires, full pay for employees on leave, and an appeals process for commission calculation. Data from 1995 through 1997 indicate that on average employees earned between 105 percent and 160 percent of full equivalent salary. In 1995, CWA District 7 at US West negotiated commission pay on a voluntary basis, and 58 percent of employees volunteered. All new employees, however, are hired under the plan. The plan, which is considerably more complex than that of

AT&T, includes five different levels of base wages and at-risk pay targets (trainees, who have no pay at risk, plus four levels of pay at risk: 10, 20, 25, and 30 percent). Most employees have 20 percent at risk. Payouts are based on a complex formula for meeting individual and team targets for sales, service quality, and access (80 percent of calls answered within twenty seconds). Employees are paid the base wage for time off for training or union business, but savings plan, life insurance, and pension are calculated on the basis of average total monthly earnings. On average, sales consultants received about 23 percent higher wages in 1996, but the payouts were significantly lower in subsequent years. Even in 1996, about 40 percent of the workers on commission received wages that were lower than the base wage, and this percentage grew in subsequent years. By the late 1990s, less than half of sales reps were meeting their monthly objectives. As a result, the union challenged the plan in arbitration, insisting that the objectives were not reasonable. Other negative outcomes include high turnover rates (of over 50 percent) and the union's difficulty in getting a sufficient number of experienced union stewards to represent members at the sites.

While the companies have pushed for sales compensation plans, the unions have fought to reduce stress and onerous working conditions, improve safety and health, limit mandatory overtime, provide for time "off-line," and restrict electronic monitoring and performance-based discipline. Joint union–management committees designed to address stress, health and safety, or performance measures are functioning at Verizon, BellSouth, and the SBC companies of Southwestern Bell, Pacific Bell, Ameritech, and SNET. Forced overtime became a key issue in 1998 and 2001 bargaining, and the unions gained contract language restricting (but not eliminating) its use at Verizon, SBC, Ameritech, BellSouth, and GTE-Southwest. In 2001, the CWA also won "closed time" provisions at these companies, guaranteeing employees thirty minutes of time offline each day for work-related tasks, such as following up on customer orders or reading e-mail.

Model contract language on electronic monitoring effectively bans secret call sampling, restricts the number of times per month that employee calls can be sampled, limits sampling of calls to employees who are not meeting performance objectives, and pushes companies to use monitoring primarily for developmental rather than disciplinary purposes. The AT&T contract, for example, requires the company to give prior notice on the day the sampling occurs and to allow employees to choose whether they want remote or side-by-side monitoring. The contract also prohibits discipline as a result of individual sampling except for gross customer abuse, fraud, violation of privacy, or when development efforts have not been successful. Agreements with Qwest, BellSouth, and the SBC companies of Pacific Bell, Ameritech, SWBT, and SNET provide similar language. The Pacific Bell contract also limits monitoring to ten per month, no more than two days per month, and no more than one session per day, and requires feedback to employees within twenty-four hours (SNET and Verizon also have some of these limitations). The Ameritech agreement adds the clause that employees may request work time to review results. In 2001, Verizon-South agreed to a three-month trial moratorium on sampling of employees who meet performance requirements. The CWA has also negotiated language to limit unreasonable discipline based on monitoring, for example, for commonsense deviations from required scripts.

The data from our 1998 national survey of establishments suggest that overall, the unions have been successful in limiting cost-cutting strategies in the call centers. Wages and working conditions are significantly better in union establishments along many dimensions. For example, in centers serving residential customers, union wages were 20 percent higher than in nonunion centers; and benefits as a percentage of median pay were 32 percent in union centers but only 23 percent in nonunion centers. The average percentage of pay that is contingent (including profit sharing, gain sharing, and commission pay) was reported as 7.3 percent in unionized centers but 15.5 percent in nonunion centers. Moreover, union centers continue to invest more in the workforce, providing almost twice as much initial training (7.8 weeks versus 3.9 weeks) and ongoing training (2.8 weeks versus 1.9 weeks per year) compared to their nonunion counterparts. As a result, annual quit rates in union centers are less than half those in nonunion centers (8.5 percent versus 17.7 percent). Finally, the percentage of the workforce with more than ten years' service was 50 percent in the union centers but only 28 percent in nonunion establishments (see Batt, Colvin, Katz, and Keefe 2000).

Conclusion

Labor–management relations remain relatively stable in this industry despite very considerable restructuring. The Bell companies still dominate every aspect of the industry, including wireline access, wireless, long distance, and data sectors. The recent consolidation trend in this industry may strengthen the process of collective bargaining. The CWA and IBEW are seeking to extend their influence into the growing sectors of the industry, particularly wireless, through neutrality and card check agreements. During this period CWA has found and mobilized new power resources by lobbying, engaging in politics, developing media relations, and educating their members. Nonetheless, the growth in employment of managerial employees in their traditional strongholds of technical, sales, and service functions poses some unique challenges to the unions, given the constraints imposed by the NLRA.

The future of labor–management relations and employment in telecommunications remains uncertain. Further consolidation is likely as the industry recovers from the excesses of speculation and the Internet bubble. The most stable companies are BellSouth, Verizon, and SBC, where union representation is embedded and stronger now than ten years ago.

Notes

[1] Research for this chapter was funded in part by a generous grant from the Alfred P. Sloan Foundation.

[2] The Bell System monopoly consisted of AT&T, Western Electric, Bell Labs, and twenty-two local telephone companies. A court-ordered divestiture split the system into its component parts and reconfigured the local telephone companies into seven regional Bell operating companies (RBOCs).

[3] Communications Workers of America, or CWA, founded in 1947, is a direct descendant of the company unions established by AT&T in 1918 that were transformed by the NLRA. The CWA is America's largest communications union; it represents more than 740,000 men and women in both private and public sectors, including some 300,000 workers in telecommunications. The union includes some 1,200 chartered local unions across the United States, Canada, and Puerto Rico. CWA holds more than 2,000 collective bargaining agreements, which are under the control of the national union. The CWA views SBC (Southwest Bell, Ameritech, Pacific Bell, Southern New England Telephone, and Cingular) and Verizon as its two most important and strategic relationships in the industry. CWA members are employed in telecommunications, broadcasting, cable TV, journalism, publishing, electronics, and general manufacturing, as well as airline customer service, government service, health care, education, and other fields.

[4] The International Brotherhood of Electrical Workers, or IBEW, was founded in 1891 as an AF of L craft union to represent the emerging trade of electrical workers. IBEW represents more than 40,000 employees in the telecommunications industry, with more than 400 industrial-type collective bargaining agreements. For the most part, IBEW locals bargain their own contracts, but they may also come together to form a System's Council for the purpose of collective bargaining. In comparison with the CWA, IBEW locals retain much greater local autonomy than CWA locals. The IBEW also runs telecommunications apprenticeship programs through its 354 training centers in North America. These employees work under building trades agreements. Overall, the IBEW has approximately 750,000 members in the construction trades, electric utility industry, manufacturing, railroads, telecommunications, and government.

[5] For prior analyses of industry restructuring and union–management relations, see Keefe and Boroff (1994), Keefe and Batt (1997), and Batt and Keefe (1999). Keefe and Boroff (1994) analyze industry trends and restructuring in the 1980s and postdivestiture collective bargaining agreements (1986, 1989, 1992), demonstrating the continued existence of industrywide pattern bargaining led by AT&T. Keefe and Batt (1997) explore the competing influences and strategies of centralization and decentralization in the industry, between 1984 and 1996. For that period, they analyze changes in product markets, technology, and business strategy. They particularly focus on competing management strategies for the reorganization of work and internal labor markets in the core occupational groups: network technicians, customer service and sales workers, operators, and the managers of these groups. Batt and Keefe (1999) analyze the extent of variation in employment practices within firms (particularly within the former Bell companies) and across firms (with a review of trends in the union/nonunion wage gap). They analyze shifts in the occupational distribution of employment, from 1982 to 1995, by race and sex. They also update the analysis of postdivestiture markets, technologies, and business strategies through 1995 and update Keefe and Boroff's (1994) analysis of collective bargaining outcomes through 1995.

[6] Under the new North American Industrial Classification System (NAIC), SIC 481 is NAIC 5132 and SIC 484 is NAIC 5133.

[7] The sample is a stratified random sample drawn from the Dun and Bradstreet listing of establishments. Establishments were stratified by size (10 to 99 employees, 100-plus employees) and by SIC code (4812, cellular; 4813, wireline; 4841, cable), with establishments that have more than 100 employees oversampled to capture a larger percentage of the workforce. The sample was also stratified by state location, and all states are represented. Because Internet service providers (ISPs) are an important new part of the industry, but not systematically captured by SIC code, additional ISPs were identified through the Directory of National Dial-Up Providers and Area Codes of Operation. A university-based survey team administered the telephone survey in fall 1998. The telephone interview averaged fifty-two minutes and yielded a 54 percent response rate. To check for response bias, we estimated a logit model, with the dependent variable equal to 1 if the establishment participated in the survey. There were no statistically significant effects for whether the establishment was a branch or a single location, whether it was publicly or privately held, or whether a Bell company owned it. ISPs were somewhat less likely to respond so that they may be slightly underrepresented in this sample.

[8] Relations between CWA and IBEW in the region were strained. Prior to the 1989 Bell Atlantic talks, for example, CWA and IBEW leaders committed to keeping their respective members on strike until the company withdrew its demand for managed care. The IBEW leadership was angered when CWA leaders abruptly accepted management's proposal for managed care and returned to work after a three-week strike. In 1995, with the contract for both unions scheduled to expire in August, Bell Atlantic first bargained a new five-year contract with IBEW Local 827, which represents some 8,000 network employees in New Jersey. The IBEW obtained upgrades for all incumbent installation and repair technicians to top craft titles. However, in exchange for five years of job security, the union agreed to a two-tier wage agreement and the creation of a new unionized subsidiary, Bell Atlantic Communications

and Construction Systems Inc. (BACCSI). The new company would be allowed to perform traditional telephone installation and repair, but the new workforce would have fewer rights and benefits and top out at 50 percent of the pay of incumbent workers. The BACCSI agreement set wages and benefits at or below nonunion levels in the cable TV industry. In addition, the new contract required a 2 percent copay for retiree health insurance and provided only a 10 percent pension improvement and 8 percent in wage increases over the first three years of the agreement.

[9] Data for this analysis come from the merged annual earnings file of the CPS for the telecommunications services industry (SIC code 481) between 1983 and 1998 (prior years do not include union status). The data are from the monthly outgoing rotation group. The method used follows Katz and Murphy (1992). Our sample includes persons over sixteen years of age who were employed for at least thirty-five hours per week and who reported earnings above the minimum wage. The sample, therefore, excludes part-time workers, thereby providing a relatively conservative estimate of wage inequality. We identify two occupational groups: clerical/sales and technical. Clerical includes computer operators, secretaries, typists, telephone operators, and order clerks. We combine clerical and sales groups for purposes of analysis because the content of work in these two categories overlaps. "Customer service representatives," for example, often primarily do sales. Technical workers include computer programmers, electrical and electronic technicians, telephone installers and repairmen, linemen and splicers, electronic repairers, and other technicians. Wages are adjusted according to the CPI–U, where 1983 equals 99.6.

References

Batt, Rosemary. 2000. "Strategic Segmentation and Frontline Services: Matching Customers, Employees, and Human Resource Systems." *International Journal of Human Resource Management*, Vol. 11, no. 3, pp. 540–61.

Batt, Rosemary, Alex Colvin, Harry Katz, and Jeffrey Keefe. 2000. "Telecommunications 2000: Strategy, HR Practices, and Performance." CAHRS working paper series, ILR School, Cornell University.

Batt, Rosemary, and Jeffrey Keefe. 1999. "Human Resource and Employment Practices in Telecommunications Services." In Peter Cappelli, ed., *Employment Practices and Business Strategy*. Oxford: Oxford University Press.

Batt, Rosemary, and Paul Osterman. 1993. "Workplace Training Policy: Case Studies of State and Local Experiments." Economic Policy Institute Working Paper No. 105. January.

Clifton, Jean. 1999. "Restructuring the Employment Relationship: Implications for Firms, Unions, and Employees." Ph.D. thesis, ILR School, Cornell University.

Communications Workers of America (CWA). 1997. "CWA at Southwestern Bell: Five Years to Card Check." Washington, DC: CWA.

_____. 2001. "Bungling on Bundling at AT&T." Washington, DC: CWA.

Current Population Survey (CPS). 1999. Merged Outgoing Rotation Group.

Federal Communications Commission (FCC). 2001. *Long Distance Telecommunications Statistics of the Industry*. January. Washington, DC: Federal Communications Commission.

Freedman, David. 1999. *Telecommunications Untethered*. New York: Bear Stearns.

Katz, Lawrence, and Kevin Murphy. 1992. "Changes in Relative Wages, 1963–1987: Supply and Demand Factors." *Quarterly Journal of Economics,* Vol. 107, no. 1 (February), pp. 35–78.

Keefe, Jeffrey. 1998. *Monopoly.com: Will the WorldCom-MCI Merger Tangle the Internet?* Washington, DC: Economic Policy Institute.

_____. 1999. "The Future of Work and Labor Organization on Telecommunications Networks." *Proceedings of the Fifty-First Annual Meeting of the Industrial Relations Research Association,* Vol. 1, pp. 227–36.

Keefe, Jeffrey, and Rosemary Batt. 1997. "United States." In Harry Katz, ed., *Telecommunications: Restructuring Work and Employment Relations Worldwide.* Ithaca, NY: Cornell University Press.

Keefe, Jeffrey, and Karen Boroff. 1994. "Telecommunications Labor Management Relations After Divestiture." In Paula Voos, ed., *Contemporary Collective Bargaining in the Private Sector.* Madison, WI: Industrial Relations Research Association.

Kochan, Thomas, Robert McKersie, and John Chalykoff. 1986. "The Effects of Corporate Strategy and Workplace Innovations on Union Representation." *Industrial and Labor Relations Review,* Vol. 39, no. 4, pp. 487–501.

Rosenberg, Nathan. 1994. *Exploring the Black Box.* New York: Cambridge University Press.

Chapter 8

Trucking: Collective Bargaining Takes a Rocky Road

Michael H. Belzer

Wayne State University

At the core of the freight transportation sector in the United States is the trucking industry, which accounts for more than 80 percent of all the freight revenue. This share has been growing for decades as shippers increasingly demand rapid and timely delivery in response to lean production and short cycle times in both manufacturing and distribution. With the growth of international trade, both within North America and between the United States and other parts of the world, trucking has become the most critical transportation mode for the delivery of freight.

The Industry

The trucking industry is composed of the for-hire sector only (Trucking and Warehousing, SIC 42, and Trucking and Courier Services, SIC 421). Shippers desiring to engage a trucking company negotiate a price with the carrier or a discount on a posted tariff. Before deregulation and elimination of the Interstate Commerce Commission (ICC), common carriers posted their rates, which were reviewed and approved by rate bureaus and ICC auditors to ensure that they covered the full cost of the movement (rates had to be "fully compensatory"), including insurance. Contract carriers provided service for no more than eight shippers, generally were unregulated with respect to rates and services, and usually did not insure the value of the cargo. These rules no longer apply, as the industry now is governed by market relationships.

Today, rate bureaus have a very limited responsibility: to determine proper rates for transportation and advise carriers of the full cost. Each carrier, however, is free to discount freight to gain market share, and discounts commonly range from 50 percent to 70 percent, which makes the full rate nearly meaningless. This pricing flexibility leads to competitiveness in the industry and tends to drive rates and wages down. Since transportation services cannot be stockpiled and because carriers must pick up a return load after every outbound load, transportation providers tend to engage in cutthroat competition. The industry is divided broadly into two sectors: general and specialized commodities. General commodities is a catch-all for a wide variety of freight, ranging from textiles to computers and from heavy machinery to small parcels. General freight tends not to require special handling, although carriers that specialize in small parcels, such as United Parcel Service (UPS) and Federal Express (FedEx), require elaborate sorting facilities and automated conveyor systems to handle volume efficiently (see Belzer 2002).

General freight is divided broadly into three sectors: package delivery, less-than-truckload (LTL), and truckload (TL). The defining characteristic for each category is shipment size. Package shipments generally average about ten pounds and require an elaborate sort-and-segregate operation, as well as a very dense network of pickup and delivery units. LTL freight averages about 1,000 pounds per shipment, and TL shipments average more than 25,000 pounds. This distinction was created by ICC regulation, which defined LTL freight as less than 10,000 pounds (which would include UPS). Although regulation has been all but eliminated, most carriers define themselves as either one or the other. By weight, 20 percent of all general freight is in LTL shipments and the rest is in TL. Because LTL costs more to handle, however, 60 percent of all general freight revenue goes to these carriers. LTL freight requires a network of dock workers, as well as local and linehaul (intercity) drivers, whereas TL requires only a truck, a driver, and a telephone.

The distinction has become more important in today's competitive environment. Before deregulation, common carriers hauled both TL and LTL freight, but market forces have caused them to concentrate on physical and network efficiencies, including balanced flows of either TL or LTL freight, but not both. The industry segmentation into TL, LTL, and package carriers is a direct consequence of deregulation.

The specialized commodities portion of the trucking industry, which moves mostly in TL shipments, covers a wide range of goods that tend to need special handling. Bulk commodities, for example, require liquid or dry bulk tankers and special equipment for loading and unloading. Heavy machinery, such as tractors, earthmovers, and large stationary equipment such as turbines and presses, require specialized flat-bed or low-boy trailers and even customized equipment setups. Automobiles are moved on special trailers that require particular driver skills.

The intermodal container is a special variant on TL that can be moved by road, rail, or water. The containers may be truck trailers that piggyback on flatcars, but the fastest growing type is a box either twenty or forty feet long that fits on a trailer chassis to be hauled by truck. Removed from the chassis, it can be loaded onto a single- or double-stacked railcar or directly onto a barge or ship. Rail is used for relatively long-haul freight movements (generally more than 1,000 miles) that are somewhat time insensitive (other than unit trains purchased by carriers such as UPS, rail continues to be rather unreliable and slow). Container ships carry a growing share of international freight and are replacing break-bulk freighter haulage, and the continued shift to containers hauled by trucks to final delivery is anticipated.

Local cartage and drayage accounts for the remainder of the for-hire sector. Data are sparse on this portion of the industry. Cartage is the intrametropolitan hauling of freight from local shippers to consignees. This sector is composed of many small operators who run a variety of vehicles that range from full tractor-trailer combinations to small panel trucks. Drayage refers to intermodal freight and has been around a long time, ever since horse-drawn wagons were the final delivery mode for rail and water freight. Drayage carriers today haul piggyback trailers and containers to and from railheads and ports, and this may be the most competitive sector in trucking.

Number of Trucks and Drivers

The trucking function employs about three times as many drivers as does the trucking industry itself, although industry workers make up the majority of long-haul and "heavy" truck drivers. The trucking function may be performed by employees of for-hire motor carriers or of firms in other industries that deliver their own products. These firms choose to control this activity for various reasons. Many industries, such as grocery, have long maintained private fleets to haul freight from their warehouses and distribution centers to retail outlets, which allows them to retain control of a critical element in the supply chain. Although many of these drivers are Teamsters, most work outside SIC 42. Table 1 shows the fraction of all truck drivers working in the trucking industry. The combination of light and heavy categories, however, dramatically increases the number of covered drivers and biases the data heavily toward local drivers. LTL and package carriers have a substantial number of local drivers, and local package carriers operate light route trucks, but the trucking industry generally consists of tractor-trailer and straight-truck drivers either in local cartage or intercity operations.

TABLE 1

Truck Drivers, by Industry

Industry	Truck drivers, light and heavy Number	Percentage
Total, all industries	2,969,641	100.0
Motor freight transportation (SIC 42)	880,779	29.7
Self-employed, primary job	252,295	8.5
Wholesale trade (SICs 50, 51)	478,967	16.1
Manufacturing	286,375	9.6
Air transportation (SIC 45)	154,785	5.2
Transportation, except trucking and air	40,030	1.3
Construction (SICs 15–17)	135,827	4.6
Eating and drinking places (SIC 58)	87,409	2.9
Retail, except eating and drinking	265,087	8.9
Communication and utilities (SICs 48, 49)	33,114	1.1
Agriculture, forestry, and fishing	29,563	1.0
Mining	30,390	1.0
Finance, insurance, and real estate	4,290	0.1
Services	209,048	7.0
Government	65,837	2.2
Self-employed, secondary job	14,059	0.5
Unpaid family, secondary job agriculture	1,786	0.1

Source: U.S. Department of Labor (1998).

As of August 2001, 1.658 million people were employed in the trucking and courier industry (SIC 421) as inside workers (clerks, dispatchers, administrative personnel, and management) and outside workers (dock workers and foremen, and both local and long-haul truck drivers). (See Table 2.) Of these, according to the Current Employment Statistics (CES), 1.465 million were production workers—drivers, dock workers, clerical staff, and nonmanagement administrative personnel—earning an average of $597 weekly (U.S. Department of Labor 2001). For all industries, according to the Occupational Employment Statistics (OES) (U.S. Department of Labor 2001), there were 1.577 million heavy- and tractor-trailer truck drivers in 2000, who earned an average of $32,810 annually, and 1.033 million light-truck or delivery drivers, who earned $24,520 per year. SIC 421 accounted for 747,120 of the heavy- and tractor-trailer truck drivers and 133,180 of the light-truck drivers (that is, more than 47 percent of the first group and less than 13 percent of the second), which highlights the difference between the for-hire and not-for-hire sectors. The CES and OES exclude self-employed workers, so the approximately 252,000 owner–drivers who are considered self-employed are

TABLE 2

National Industry-Specific Occupational Employment
SIC 421—Trucking and Courier Services, Except Air, 2000

Occupational title	Total employees	Percentage total
Industry total	**1,646,310**	**100.0**
Management Occupations	**69,660**	**4.2**
Chief Executives	5,130	0.3
General and Operations Managers	31,470	1.9
Advertising and Promotions Managers	220	0.0
Marketing Managers	1,390	0.1
Sales Managers	3,750	0.2
Public Relations Managers	60	0.0
Administrative Services Managers	2,780	0.2
Computer and Information Systems Managers	1,060	0.1
Financial Managers	2,540	0.2
Human Resources Managers	2,070	0.1
Purchasing Managers	350	0.0
Transportation, Storage, and Distribution Managers	14,920	0.9
Engineering Managers	120	0.0
Business and Financial Operations Occupations	**14,590**	**0.9**
Purchasing Agents, except Wholesale, Retail, and Farm Products	1,040	0.1
Claims Adjusters, Examiners, and Investigators	120	0.0
Compliance Officers, except Agriculture, Construction, Health and Safety, and Transportation	170	0.0
Cost Estimators	920	0.1
Employment, Recruitment, and Placement Specialists	1,570	0.1
Compensation, Benefits, and Job Analysis Specialists	360	0.0
Training and Development Specialists	1,120	0.1
Management Analysts	100	0.0
Accountants and Auditors	6,340	0.4
Budget Analysts	170	0.0
Financial Analysts	140	0.0
Computer and Mathematical Occupations	**2,910**	**0.2**
Computer Programmers	1,260	0.1
Computer Support Specialists	420	0.0
Computer Systems Analysts	230	0.0
Database Administrators	260	0.0
Network and Computer Systems Administrators	360	0.0
Healthcare Practitioners and Technical Occupations	**530**	**0.0**
Occupational Health and Safety Specialists and Technicians	180	0.0

TABLE 2—(*Continued*)
National Industry-Specific Occupational Employment
SIC 421—Trucking and Courier Services, Except Air, 2000

Occupational title	Total employees	Percentage total
Sales and Related Occupations	**20,900**	**1.3**
Office and Administrative Support Occupations	**249,170**	**15.1**
First-Line Supervisors/Managers of Office and Administrative Support Workers	13,700	0.8
Switchboard Operators, Including Answering Service	2,660	0.2
Bill and Account Collectors	3,150	0.2
Billing and Posting Clerks and Machine Operators	18,720	1.1
Bookkeeping, Accounting, and Auditing Clerks	17,230	1.1
Payroll and Timekeeping Clerks	3,500	0.2
Procurement Clerks		0.0
Correspondence Clerks	780	0.1
Credit Authorizers, Checkers, and Clerks	270	0.0
Customer Service Representatives	17,020	1.0
File Clerks	1,600	0.1
Order Clerks	4,010	0.2
Human Resources Assistants, Except Payroll and Timekeeping	1,370	0.1
Receptionists and Information Clerks	5,760	0.4
Cargo and Freight Agents	3,830	0.2
Couriers and Messengers	43,650	2.7
Dispatchers, Except Police, Fire, and Ambulance	36,970	2.3
Production, Planning, and Expediting Clerks	1,110	0.1
Shipping, Receiving, and Traffic Clerks	8,110	0.5
Stock Clerks and Order Fillers	2,810	0.2
Weighers, Measurers, Checkers, and Samplers, Recordkeeping		0.0
Executive Secretaries and Administrative Assistants	7,400	0.5
Secretaries, Except Legal, Medical, and Executive	8,290	0.5
Computer Operators	1,200	0.1
Data Entry Keyers	2,020	0.1
Word Processors and Typists	490	0.0
Mail Clerks and Mail Machine Operators, Except Postal Service	340	0.0
Office Clerks, General	36,020	2.2
Office Machine Operators, Except Computer	160	0.0
Installation, Maintenance, and Repair Occupations	**89,720**	**5.5**
First-Line Supervisors/Managers of Mechanics, Installers, and Repairers	5,880	0.4
Automotive Body and Related Repairers	630	0.0
Automotive Service Technicians and Mechanics	5,210	0.3

TABLE 2—(*Continued*)
National Industry-Specific Occupational Employment
SIC 421—Trucking and Courier Services, Except Air, 2000

Occupational title	Total employees	Percentage total
Bus and Truck Mechanics and Diesel Engine Specialists	58,420	3.6
Mobile Heavy Equipment Mechanics, Except Engines	70	0.0
Tire Repairers and Changers	1,550	0.1
Maintenance and Repair Workers, General	10,740	0.7
Maintenance Workers, Machinery	590	0.0
Helpers—Installation, Maintenance, and Repair Workers	1,550	0.1
Transportation and Material Moving Occupations	**1,177,240**	**71.5**
Aircraft Cargo Handling Supervisors	970	0.1
First-Line Supervisors/Managers of Helpers, Laborers, and Material Movers, Hand	11,530	0.7
First-Line Supervisors/Managers of Transportation and Material-Moving Machine and Vehicle Operators	26,060	1.6
Driver/Sales Workers	13,210	0.8
Truck Drivers, Heavy and Tractor-Trailer	*747,120*	*45.4*
Truck Drivers, Light or Delivery Services	*133,180*	*8.1*
Taxi Drivers and Chauffeurs	840	0.1
Rail Yard Engineers, Dinkey Operators, and Hostlers	590	0.0
Service Station Attendants		0.0
Transportation Inspectors	860	0.1
Conveyor Operators and Tenders		0.0
Crane and Tower Operators	1,230	0.1
Excavating and Loading Machine and Dragline Operators	1,930	0.1
Industrial Truck and Tractor Operators	*37,160*	*2.3*
Cleaners of Vehicles and Equipment	3,250	0.2
Laborers and Freight, Stock, and Material Movers, Hand	*136,660*	*8.3*
Packers and Packagers, Hand	11,020	0.7
Refuse and Recyclable Material Collectors	32,300	2.0
All other occupations	**21,790**	**1.4**

Source: U.S. Department of Labor (2000).

not included, and most of them drive heavy trucks. Since all owner–drivers must be in the for-hire sector, they account for about 16 percent of all heavy-truck drivers but approximately 25 percent of all for-hire drivers.

Estimates vary by data set but not by a great deal. The March 2000 outgoing rotation of the Current Population Survey (CPS) estimates that

1.2 million employee truck drivers work in SIC 42 (Trucking and Ware-housing), a somewhat smaller estimate from a broader category, and that 255,336 owner–drivers work in this industry. The Vehicle Inventory and Use Survey (VIUS) shows that the average truck tractor runs 70,400 miles, and trucks that were used for forty-nine or more weeks ran 82,500 miles. Over-the-road trucking raises special issues, however. Although trucks that operate more than 200 miles from home base comprise only 30 percent of all trucks heavy enough to require a commercial drivers license (at least 26,000 pounds), they account for 57 percent of all such intercity miles. In addition, 75 percent of these are for hire, rather than private carriage, which means that about half of all drivers work for private carriers but mostly perform local work. Trucks in use all year that are larger than 26,000 pounds gross weight and operated more than 200 miles from home average 111,700 miles annually. This figure compares favorably to data from a survey by the University of Michigan Trucking Industry Program (UMTIP) in 1997 and 1998, which shows that the average road driver runs 110,000 miles. When the for-hire group is split from the private carriers, the survey shows that the average private carrier road driver runs 95,900 miles, compared to 117,100 miles for the average for-hire driver (U.S. Department of Commerce 1997; see also Belzer 2001a, Belzer 2001b).

A further comparison comes from the Motor Carrier Financial and Operating Statistics (F&OS) data available from the U.S. Department of Transportation's (DOT) Bureau of Transportation Statistics (BTS) (1997). The F&OS 1997 sample of 1,500 Class I and II carriers,[1] screening out firms that earn more than 30 percent of revenue from local cartage (to keep the focus on highway drivers), shows that the average over-the-road driver who is paid by the mile runs 98,826 miles per year (general freight drivers run 103,100 miles). This estimate is made by dividing the total miles for all these firms by the number of drivers employed (not trucks), but the average is remarkably close to the UMTIP measure.

Using the 117,100 mile figure from VIUS and assuming drivers maintain an average speed of forty-five miles per hour over the entire year (allowing for congestion, driving on rural two-lane roads through little towns, driving in cities to make pickups or deliveries, weather, and so on), I estimate road time of 2,600 hours annually per driver. Evidence from the UMTIP survey shows that 25 percent of the average driver's work time is spent loading, unloading, and waiting, which suggests that the average road driver actually works 3,250 hours per year (for calculations based on slightly different data, see Belzer 2000b). These long hours are a central issue in trucking industrial relations, as working conditions are widely characterized as "sweatshops." Most recently, Julie Cirillo, the Federal Motor Carrier Safety Administration's chief safety officer, said, "We have to come to grips with the fact that the people who carry the majority of the economy's freight are basically sweatshop workers" (Pyle 2001).

Key Influences and Pressures

Although the industry continues to be extremely competitive, there has been substantial concentration since deregulation. Some experts claim that 10,000 motor carriers are large enough to be required to file F&OS data, although the BTS says that 2,600 meet the filing criteria and 1,811 complied in 1998. The reporting threshold for a Class II motor carrier is $3 million in revenue, which represents approximately twenty-five trucks, and Class I carriers also are required to report (the compliance rate is at best 70 percent in this group). The lack of reliable data hampers estimates of industry concentration.

The LTL sector is the most concentrated, and package carriers lead the list. UPS and FedEx dominate in the United States, though they are challenged internationally by Deutsche Post, the German post office, which has used its monopoly handling German mail to leverage the purchase of more than 100 logistics firms over the past few years. UPS is suing Deutsche Post for unfair competition.

The rest of the LTL sector is somewhat concentrated, but this is changing rapidly. Intrastate deregulation in 1995 led to the dramatic expansion of relatively small and mainly nonunion regional carriers, which have challenged the "Big Four" who dominated the business until the late 1990s. ConWay, a spin-off of three regional carriers created by Consolidated Freightways, threw its "parent" out of the house, took all the assets, and is now a national carrier. FedEx bought out the failed Caliber (a spin-off from Roadway Express) and retained an efficient West Coast carrier, Viking. FedEx most recently purchased American Freightways, an aggressive and sophisticated regional carrier that successfully expanded from its Arkansas base to the entire area east of the Rocky Mountains and is creating a national LTL carrier subsidiary; both American and Viking are nonunion. Most recently, Roadway Express (a leading unionized LTL carrier) purchased Arnold Industries (without its logistics operations), owner of New Penn, which is one of the nation's most profitable carriers and a Teamster National Master Freight Agreement (NMFA) signatory. Other regional firms have expanded significantly in the past decade, and at least two are now transcontinental. All the aggressive new entrants are non-union and likely to remain so.

The TL sector remains extremely competitive. Tens of thousands of small carriers compete for business by cutting rates and driver pay, and many push drivers to work more than the legal limit. Data are inadequate since no agency has the authority or the funds to track down these carriers and require reporting and Class III carriers are not required to report in any case. The sector has experienced some concentration. The largest firm is Schneider National, which is the nation's fifth largest carrier (by revenue) and the largest privately-held carrier; its gross revenue is in excess of $3 billion, and it employs 14,000 tractors and 40,000 trailers. The second and third largest TL carriers are Swift and J.B. Hunt, both publicly held. Swift gained that ranking after it purchased MS Carriers; current revenue tops $2 billion per year, and more than 10,000 tractors are employed. J.B. Hunt has annual revenue of more than $2 billion and employs 11,000 tractors and 40,000 trailers. These three carriers employ approximately 30,000 drivers, but they still represent less than 5 percent of the TL sector.

The Future

The general trend in trucking is for continued competition. Companies are expanding aggressively, where possible, notably by purchasing Mexican carriers in anticipation of the North American Free Trade Agreement (NAFTA) implementation. Concentration and competition will continue to be conflicting tendencies, as carriers attempt to corner the market in their sector and battle against new entrants attempting to do the same.

Perhaps the greatest impetus for change will be NAFTA. If U.S. carriers are allowed to own and operate Mexican carriers, as NAFTA permits, those that are sufficiently large and sophisticated to operate internationally will have a great advantage. Even if only 5 percent of all freight moves from Mexico to destinations in the United States, the resulting downward pressure on rates likely will lead to similar and substantial pressure on the labor market, driving "sweatshop" earnings even lower for U.S. drivers. They eventually may be replaced by Mexican drivers, and carriers without strong Mexican operations may go out of business. It is unlikely that U.S. trucking companies will be able to pay U.S. wages to drivers in Mexican freight lanes, which could create a shortage as drivers exit the industry. Current rules affecting domestic cabotage are unclear because Immigration and Naturalization Service

(INS) and Customs regulations conflict (see U.S. Department of Transportation n.d.), but any further downward pressure on wages will make trucking careers even less attractive to U.S. workers than they are now. A driver shortage should cause wages to rise, but experience over the past two decades suggests otherwise. It is likely the trucking industry would lobby for the use of Mexican carriers in domestic cabotage, which would virtually eliminate U.S. drivers in TL. The only survivors would be trucking firms with Mexican subsidiaries that employ Mexican drivers, which might lead to substantial concentration even in the TL sector, along with internationalization of the industry.

The Parties

Major Employers

The trucking industry generally is decentralized, so no single employer or set of employers dominates. Companies have diverse interests and are unevenly organized into professional or industry associations. The American Trucking Association (ATA) is the largest group and claims to represent the entire industry, but it is an uneasy confederation of state trucking associations and groups representing specific industry sectors. ATA has conferences that represent truckers in LTL and distribution, agriculture, household moving, carhaul, liquid and dry bulk, and other industry segments. Historically it represented TL carriers as well, although the Truckload Carriers Association has now emerged. ATA also has conferences that represent functional activities, such as accounting and finance; safety, loss, and prevention; and maintenance. A major restructuring and downsizing of ATA is under way, to cut back on services in order to balance the books. Its primary function, as envisioned by the current leadership, is as a lobbying organization for the industry.

Two offshoots of ATA became important in the 1990s: the Truckload Carriers Association (TCA) and the Motor Freight Carriers Association (MFCA). After years of uneasy quasi-independence, TCA finally broke with ATA in 2000 because the latter insisted that carriers who belonged to each association pay dues to both. The TL sector is so competitive that carriers cannot afford to pay double dues. Some major TL carriers remain in ATA, but TCA has become a key organizational force.

The MFCA is another offshoot of ATA. From an industrial relations standpoint, it is an outgrowth of Trucking Management Incorporated (TMI), the association responsible for bargaining with Teamster NMFA carriers. Members of MFCA did not necessarily pull out of ATA, but the group is a powerful association of some of the largest LTL carriers. Development beyond the current base is not clear. In many ways, the MFCA speaks for the LTL industry, but it represents a narrow constituency. The MFCA includes the four largest national carriers, plus New Penn (soon to be owned by Roadway) and A-P-A, which are eastern regional firms.

A number of LTL carriers that were unionized at the time of deregulation remain so today. The largest carriers are Roadway Express, Yellow Freight System, Consolidated Freightways, and ABF (originally known as Arkansas Best Freightways). The fifth and sixth largest LTL carriers, Overnite and ConWay, are nonunion, as are transnational challengers Old Dominion and Watkins. The seventh largest national carrier is the combination of Viking and American Freightways, now owned by Federal Express (at this writing, it is hard to distinguish its size, as its data are commingled with those of FedEx). The Teamsters have tried to organize Overnite for decades and are involved in a prolonged strike for recognition (officially considered an unfair labor practice strike, given the numerous labor law violations committed by the carrier, which the NLRB and federal courts have ruled were orchestrated at the highest level). The remaining union firms are smaller, regional carriers and local cartage companies, the largest of which is Holland, a member of the U.S. Freightways system. With the exception of Overnite, the Teamsters have not organized any significant new carriers in several decades (and Overnite seems to be slipping through its fingers).

Most of the other companies in the industry are nonunion or operate under "white paper" agreements, signed between the Teamsters and individual carriers and often by individual locals. Almost all TL general freight carriers are nonunion, although a few retain representation that existed before deregulation. Among the specialized carriers, unionization remains strong in the carhaul industry, but fifty-five nonunion locations have opened in the past two years (Teamsters for a Democratic Union 2001). Unionization has declined in the tank industry (Chemical Lehman and Matlack, the two largest union carriers, have failed in recent years) and in household moving (representation is confined to isolated local franchise operators). It persists in the construction sector, where union density is greater.

Major Unions

Although several unions represent truck drivers, almost all who are union members belong to the Teamsters, which represents trucking employees in the for-hire sector. In the not-for-hire sector, there are many other unions, generally due to unionization of nontrucking firms that employ their own drivers. In the trucking industry itself, the Teamsters dominate.

A significant exception is New England Motor Freight, a large regional LTL carrier based in New Jersey, which broke away from the then mob-dominated Local 560 by taking a strike in 1984 when it operated with replacement employees and management personnel. In 1985, the company was organized by the International Association of Machinists, which now represents all terminals.

The Union of Transportation Employees (UTE) and the Chicago Truck Drivers Union (CTDU) are the only other significant trucking unions (for a brief description of those unions, see Belzer 1993:34–35). Both, however, were forced to merge with larger unions. The UTE voted to affiliate with the Oil, Atomic, and Chemical Workers Union in 1996 when its Texas trucking base collapsed with the failure of Merchants Fast Motor Lines, which was a direct consequence of intrastate deregulation in 1995. In December 2000, the CTDU joined Local 710 of the Teamsters, which brought nearly 5,000 mostly local drivers into a local union that represents mainly linehaul drivers and dock workers.

Regulation and Other Government Involvement

In 1977, the Interstate Commerce Commission (ICC) began relaxing the restrictions on market entry and pricing that had been in effect in the trucking industry for more than forty years. This deregulation represents a major event in the trucking industry. The introduction of markets to interstate trucking was confirmed by Congress with passage of the Motor Carrier Act in 1980. This institutionalized changes made by the ICC. No longer were there requirements to publish rates or make them fully compensatory;[2] restrictions on free entry by carriers into any market;[3] and regulations separating for-hire and not-for-hire, as well as common and contract carriers, among other changes. Many states, however, including some of the largest and most important (such as California, Texas, Michigan, and Pennsylvania) retained regulation for intrastate shipments. The resulting patchwork of regulation created incentives for firms to ship intrastate freight circuitously so that it crossed state lines and became "interstate." In 1995, Congress mandated removal of intrastate regulations and there was an explosion of new carriers (mainly nonunion) that moved aggressively into regional operations in an already very competitive industry.

This environment produced critical labor market problems. Wages of drivers and dock workers dropped nearly 30 percent in the following five years.[4] The great majority of union carriers disappeared and hundreds of thousands of trained workers lost their jobs. Some found work in the surviving unionized LTL sector,[5] but many more undoubtedly left the industry. Interviews ten years after deregulation with company recruiters, safety managers, and operations managers revealed a decline in hiring standards (experience, safety record) and the "character" of the driver pool (Belzer 1993:161–64 and unpublished research notes). With inadequate wage and benefit packages and more demanding and strenuous work loads to offer, carriers find it extremely difficult to recruit drivers.

The government's response primarily has been to tighten regulations affecting driver safety, mostly designed to exclude from the market those with alcohol and drug problems as well as accident and moving violations records. Before the commercial driver's license (CDL) was created, drivers often had multiple licenses from various states; when they accumulated too many points on one license or developed an unacceptable accident record, they obtained a license in another state. The CDL has not been perfect, and regulators have repeatedly tightened criteria governing it; but it definitely has reduced the use of multiple licenses and has discouraged applications from those who know they will not pass the drug screening.

The federal government has long been under pressure from safety groups to reduce truck crashes and fatalities, and to that end in the late 1980s Congress required the DOT to develop more effective hours-of-service regulations for truck drivers. This proved difficult, however, and when the new rules finally were announced in May 2000 there were protests from the industry, drivers, and the safety community that derailed the entire effort. The problem is that pay and safety are linked and economic competition in the industry keeps wages so low that carriers find it impossible to hire the human resources they need (see Belzer, Rodriguez, and Sedo 2001).

Workers and Labor Markets

Average Education and Skill Levels

Truck driving has not been considered a high-skill industry, but the ease of entry seems to conflict with the public's demand for safe and reliable drivers. The raw skills of truck drivers are not terribly high, and drivers are classified as semiskilled. The modal education level is a high school diploma, with some having less and some having more. It is not clear, however, that there is much of a link between education and driver quality, and driver quality can be measured at the most elementary level with the written and driving tests required for a CDL. Analyses of driver quality have not found a link between education and safety, for example (Belzer, Rodriguez, and Sedo 2001). The big issue is whether carriers would be well-advised to broaden their labor market to include youth and felons. The TCA has proposed that the industry hire nineteen-year-olds (currently persons must be twenty-one to qualify for a CDL) and convicted felons. Unfortunately, there is strong evidence that young people do not have the necessary judgment (though this is strongly contested by the TCA, for those brought in with careful selection, training, and supervision) and that convicted felons may not be good bets based on both their prior records and the fact that this may be their only choice for full-time employment.

Earnings

The CPS Establishment Survey indicates production workers in trucking (mostly drivers, but also dock workers in LTL as well as clerical workers) have experienced a 30 percent reduction in real pay since 1977, though most of the decline came between 1977 and 1984. Recent research suggests a somewhat smaller reduction, controlling for other factors, such as the general decline in blue collar wages (Belman and Monaco 2001). Regardless, real earnings are now at the same level they were in 1958 and are similar to the earnings of production workers in general manufacturing (Belzer 2000b:123–26).

Most important, bad jobs increasingly outnumber good jobs in the trucking industry. The union premium has risen to about 30 percent ceteris paribus, but union jobs are becoming scarce. Pay levels also vary by sector, in part due to union bargaining power in the package sector (UPS retains strong market share, and the Teamsters represent its production workers) and in LTL. The four largest national LTL carriers, as well as most of the regional carriers unionized before 1980, are still represented by the Teamsters. The current NMFA and UPS agreements provide for driver pay greater than twenty dollars per hour and full pay for both driving and nondriving time. Most Teamster road drivers, whether or not they are covered by the NMFA, are paid mileage for driving time and hourly for all nondriving labor time, whereas most UPS drivers are paid hourly for all work.

The average straight-time pay rate for nonunion over-the-road TL drivers has dropped to less than ten dollars per hour. Trucking employees of motor carriers engaged in interstate commerce are not covered by the overtime provision of the Fair Labor Standards Act (FLSA), and judicial interpretation of the FLSA allows employers to average paid and unpaid labor time when determining whether drivers earn the minimum wage equivalent. This means that pay compares with a rate of $8.17 per hour outside intercity trucking. More broadly, for all drivers in the for-hire trucking industry (both local and long distance), and controlling for firm size only, the CPS shows that the average driver earns $7.01 for all hours fewer than sixty (the legal limit) and $6.20 for all hours sixty and above (with no FLSA correction). Because drivers are paid on piecework rates, these calculations represent only a ratio of their weekly earnings divided by number of hours worked; overtime pay does not apply. In this sense, piecework rates obscure the driver's understanding of his or her true pay rate: TL drivers almost always are paid by the mile or by a percentage of freight revenue, and in 1998 the average mileage rate was $.0305 per mile. In addition, TL drivers are rarely paid for their nondriving time, which takes up about 25 percent of their working time.

The situation of the owner–driver is especially complex. Although the Teamsters were formed by owner–drivers and have represented them for more than seventy years, a court decision in the early 1970s ruled that they are independent businessmen. Today, more than 250,000 over-the-road drivers are subcontractors to motor carriers. Although they operate on the carriers' authority and are not free to work for anyone they wish (without terminating their lease), as independent contractors they are not allowed to retain union representation or to bargain, which leaves them defenseless in the market. Almost 40,000 intermodal drivers, who work out of the ports, are paid even less; data are not available, but anecdotal information suggests that they earn far less than the minimum wage.

Employment Stability

The trucking labor market has become unstable. Turnover tends to be low at unionized LTL carriers (rates of 3 percent are reported) but typically runs about 100 percent per annum at nonunion TL carriers. Unionized carriers always have Teamster pension plans, usually multi-employer plans with ten years to vest. These provide strong incentives for employees to stay with the company and the union plan, whereas nonunion carriers always have single-employer defined contribution plans. Very few drivers stay the five years legally required to vest, and survey evidence suggests that most nonunion drivers (and virtually all owner–drivers) never earn a pension. A UMTIP case study of fourteen LTL carriers further revealed that, although pay rates do not differ significantly across LTL carriers, benefits cost twice as much at unionized companies and turnover rates are twice as high at nonunion firms.

The Bargaining Context

Federal Court Intervention and Democratic Elections

In 1988 the Department of Justice filed a suit against the Teamsters under the Racketeer Influenced and Corrupt Organizations (RICO) amendments to the 1970 Organized Crime Control Act. In less than a year, the Teamsters general executive board signed a consent decree giving the federal courts indefinite oversight authority over the union. This was an admission that the union had become a corrupt enterprise dominated by the Mafia. The virtual trusteeship allowed the government to lower the standard of proof required to bar persons from office and from the union, and an investigations officer and an administrator were appointed to carry out reform by first removing hundreds of corrupt officials from the union (see Crowe 1993; Belzer and Hurd 1999).

Under court supervision, rules for union elections and conventions were changed, which forced the union to accept a plebiscite on national officers and spawned a democratic process within the Teamsters. There have been four national elections since the consent decree. The first took place in 1991, when the forces of Ron Carey (able to mount only a skeletal showing at the Teamsters convention) upset the incumbents (who had split into two contending camps).

In the 1996 general election, the "old guard" coalesced around James P. Hoffa, son of the legendary James R. Hoffa, and he was nominated at the summer convention in Philadelphia. Carey had made informal deals with local union leaders, who promised to support him; but at the convention they reneged, and an early test vote revealed that Carey did not have majority control. He made it through the weeklong convention with a series of stalling maneuvers, and in the fall 1996 election he eked out a very slim victory. An ensuing investigation found that his lieutenants had used union funds inappropriately in the election, and the result was overturned (based on a showing that, but for the violation, the challenger would have won).

Carey was removed from office in November 1997. He endorsed Ken Hall, a loyalist who had gained some visibility within the union during the recent UPS strike; but after six months Hall withdrew, unable to assemble a slate. Tom Leedham, international vice president, warehouse division director, and an officer in Portland Local 206, immediately announced his candidacy. After a brief campaign, begun late and under-funded, Leedham received nearly 40 percent of the vote in the 1998 rerun. Another candidate received 5 percent of the vote, which gave Jim Hoffa the victory with 55 percent. Carey was banned from the union for life. He was tried in federal court for perjury in summer 2001 and acquitted of all counts.[6] In 2000, Jim Hoffa was reelected as Teamsters Union president.

The unprecedented court trusteeship of the Teamsters Union in 1989 remains a fact of life at the dawn of the twenty-first century. The union's leadership continues to urge it be lifted, but recent serious charges by the Independent Review Board against prominent allies of current union officials make this unlikely.

Union Politics and Recent Bargaining History

The Teamsters have negotiated three contracts with most of the rep-resented carriers since the reform process began in 1989. This period has been marked by intraunion conflict that has disrupted traditional bargaining patterns. The election of Ron Carey in 1991 brought a surge of militancy to the Teamsters, along with a focus on organizing. The first contract Carey negotiated with UPS, in 1993, made no substantial changes, but his conflict with the company and its determination to raise the package weight limit from 50 to 150 pounds led to a national wildcat strike in February 1994.

UPS made the unilateral announcement about the weight limit early in 1994, and Carey called the wildcat on the presumption that it would be considered an unfair labor practice strike, prompted by a unilateral work rule change so soon after the contract had been negotiated. Response to the strike was uneven across the nation: Carey supporters honored the strike call, but many local and regional officials, loyal to Carey's opponents, refused to support it. The strike lasted only a few days, and its legality was never tested because the parties settled out of court some months later; but it allowed Carey's enemies to drive a wedge between themselves and the reformers.

During the same period Carey took another risk that he lost. He needed funds to increase organizing and generally finance the interna-tional union's activities,[7] but member approval was required before dues could be raised. Carey held a referendum on a dues increase and even offered to split it with the locals to garner their support. His opponents beat back the attempt to raise dues by a 2-to-1 margin.

Carey forces then moved to eliminate the regional conferences (Western, Southern, Central, and Eastern), which were bastions of the old guard and a way for double-dippers to hide their multiple salaries. The maneuvering distracted attention from a critical bargaining round for the NMFA, which was due to expire April 1. Although Carey ultimately eliminated the area conferences, he failed to shift organizational activity to the industry conferences, which could have created an alternative power base.

The NMFA posed special problems for the Carey people. Carey himself came out of an exclusively UPS local, and he fully understood the contract and bargaining issues in that sector. He had no experience in general freight and a poor understanding of the bargaining issues, as well as the complexity of multilateral national bargaining with strong local issues and local leaders. Few in the Carey team had that experience either. Due to the mistrust between the reformers and old guard forces, Carey was unable or unwilling to allow knowledgeable but untrustworthy union leaders to lead the bargaining for him. By the time the contract was set to expire, negotiations had not proceeded very far. The union was in disarray, and management, with its back to the wall because of intense economic competition, knew exactly what it wanted. After a twenty-one-day strike, the Teamsters agreed to go back to work on management's terms: the union lost the right to strike on deadlocked grievances (a major power lever), and management gained the right to divert up to 28 percent of freight volume to the rails. The Teamsters gained a raise of $1.30 over four years, along with higher health and welfare contributions.

The strike had severe consequences for the Teamsters. Its treasury was already dwindling due to Carey's spending on organizing, and $200 per week went to the nearly 100,000 union members who struck for three weeks (the strike benefits alone cost nearly $60 million). The Teamsters were forced to borrow $14 million from the AFL-CIO (a loan later forgiven) to pay strike benefits. The treasury was so depleted that the international union invoked a constitutional provision allowing it to impose a surcharge of one dollar per month on every member, which remains in effect today.

Carey's last hurrah was the successful campaign against UPS in 1997, which used newly perfected member-to-member organizing techniques. Through depth of organization, lengthy preparation, and masterful communications, the Teamsters won a three-week strike against the union's largest employer. The result was favorable to the members, but the opposition was now well organized and ready to close in on Carey and the reform movement the following year.

Extent of Unionization

Union density in trucking broadly is about 18 percent, a decline of about 25 percent since 1990, although statistics are complicated by a lack of information on owner–operators, virtually all of whom are nonunion. A UMTIP survey of road drivers in the upper Midwest in 1997 and 1998 found union density of about 9 percent, but the sample of approximately 1,000 is too small to be relied on. Density is much higher in LTL, although no recent survey is available on which to base a reliable estimate. In 1995 I estimated union density among Class I General Freight carriers as of 1990 at 47.6 percent, excluding UPS, and at 65.1 percent, including UPS. Since that time, the Bureau of the Census has shifted package carriers (including UPS) from SIC 421 to SIC 451 (Air Transportation, Scheduled, and Air Courier), even though the vast majority of UPS freight moves by truck. This misclassification strips trucking of nearly 200,000 union employees paid at a higher rate than average, which distorts comparability and introduces error for anyone who attempts to study trucking (see Belzer 2000b:220). In addition, intrastate deregulation in 1995 boosted newer nonunion regional carriers, whose growth has outstripped that of the older carriers and thus has reduced union density somewhat further in LTL.

Major Developments Since the 1980s

Unionized trucking may be at risk, and the actions of Teamster leaders during the next five years may determine whether they continue to represent employees in this industry. Owner–drivers became dissatisfied with poor representation in the 1960s and 1970s, and militant rank-and-file activity by such organizations as the Fraternal Association of Steelhaulers (FASH) led to a decertification effort. When FASH attempted to recertify itself as the bargaining representative of owner–operators, the court ruled that these drivers were business owners and thus ineligible.

As deregulation developed in the late 1970s and early 1980s, the Teamsters lacked a coherent political and organizational strategy. Consequently, TL drivers were vulnerable to de-unionization, starting with Schneider National's efforts in 1976 and culminating in the virtual collapse of unionized TL after the Motor Carrier Act of 1980. The Teamster approach to deregulation after 1980 was rather unimaginative. It abandoned TL freight and responded to carriers' resultant revenue pressures by reducing members' wages substantially to match those of nonunion drivers.

By the 1990s the TL general freight industry was almost entirely nonunion, as was much of the tank and other specialized carrier sectors. The Teamsters did not organize any significant new carriers, including failed attempts with the nation's largest nonunion LTL carrier in the early 1980s and with Overnite during the late 1990s.[8] The gap between union and nonunion wages seems to be closing, and bargaining leverage of the union appears to be declining. The latest major threat comes from the carhaul industry, as automobile manufacturers have awarded contracts to dozens of nonunion firms, which threatens to de-unionize the strongest single organized sector.

It is reasonable to believe that at some point union contracts will be untenable in trucking. Without a very imaginative and aggressive effort, unionization may disappear entirely from the industry.

Trends in Bargaining Outcomes

Bargaining has been difficult for the Teamsters because the environmental pressure is severe and is becoming more so. Although the union has retained bargaining power in the package sector because of the unionization of UPS, it must reckon with the growth of UPS' main competitor, Federal Express. As noted earlier, FedEx has purchased a number of carriers during the past five years. Its purchase of Caliber put FedEx squarely in the LTL trucking industry, as the most viable Caliber asset was Viking, a relatively well-run, nonunion western LTL carrier. In 2000, FedEx purchased American Freightways, allowing it to expand its presence in the LTL industry at the regional and national level.

The FedEx entry into LTL, in addition to the success of new regional entrants and newly-expanded regional, interregional, and transcontinental nonunion carriers, threatens LTL bargaining and the NMFA. LTL generally is less price competitive than TL, and while there may be no difference in wages between union and nonunion carriers in LTL, benefit costs and the cost of union work rules pressure the collective bargaining relationship.

The NAFTA Effect

NAFTA presents the most serious threat to both the union and nonunion sectors of the trucking industry. In 1995, under pressure from the Teamsters and safety advocates, President Clinton declined to implement the NAFTA provision that allowed U.S. firms to purchase

Mexican carriers and gave Mexican carriers and drivers full access to U.S. roads in border states. As a result, U.S. carriers are still restricted to 49 percent ownership, and Mexican drivers are confined to a border zone. Full NAFTA implementation was scheduled for 2001, when U.S. carriers could own 100 percent of Mexican carriers and Mexican drivers would have access to U.S. highways. In February 2001 a five-member panel of arbitrators ruled that the United States was in violation of NAFTA and susceptible to penalties invoked by the Mexicans. President Bush vowed to open the borders by early 2002, but Congress has balked due to widespread concern that Mexican trucks and drivers will not meet U.S. safety standards. Mexican truckers currently are not required to fill out driver logs, and Mexico has no limit on hours of work. Although the United States has such rules, the median driver violates them (Belzer 2000b), and NAFTA implementation would complicate the DOT plan to use electronic onboard recorders for enforcement purposes as well as new rules to reduce fatigue and improve highway safety.

NAFTA may have several unintended consequences. For example, Canadian drivers, who operate under U.S. Custom rules, are currently allowed to haul a load from Canada to any place in the United States and take a return load home. U.S. Customs rules permit one prearranged domestic move that is "incidental" to the international movement of goods, but INS regulations do not.[9] Although the more conservative INS policy applies for now to all foreign drivers, if competitive pressure created by NAFTA results in a driver shortage, it is likely that trucking companies will lobby for the U.S. Customs rules to be applied. It will likely be necessary to apply such a change to drivers from both Canada and Mexico.

The market forces unleashed by NAFTA could result in displacement of U.S. drivers by dramatically cheaper Mexican drivers in international freight lanes because freight could be hauled at much lower rates. According to the UMTIP survey, the current average wage rate is about 31 cents per mile for nonunion U.S. drivers, compared to 11.8 cents per mile for Mexican drivers (Schultz 2001b). It is by no means clear that FLSA minimum wage rates, which are required in interstate trucking but are practically unenforceable, would provide a wage floor (see Belzer et al. 2002; Belzer 1995; Belzer 2000b). Celadon, the nation's tenth largest TL carrier, reports fully loaded U.S. driver compensation at 38 to 39 cents per mile, compared with a Mexican figure of 12 cents (Bailey 2001). Due to downward pressure on freight rates and wages,

U.S. owner–drivers likely would exit the industry if Mexican drivers are allowed to operate on U.S. roads; already in dire financial straits, many would be pushed out of business. An intermodal effect from NAFTA also is likely. Lower freight rates would cause some rail container traffic to divert to trucking, which would increase the number of trucks on the road and intensify demand for low-paid drivers. The pressure on rail rates could mean reduced operations for already cash-poor railroads. If a driver shortage results in relaxed INS rules regarding domestic cabotage, similar to those of U.S. Customs, Mexican carriers would be allowed the incidental move described earlier. Almost any pattern could be considered incidental to an international haul between the United States and Mexico. In the most extreme example, a Mexican driver hauls a load from Mexico City to New York, picks up a load for San Francisco, where a load is available for the return trip to Mexico. The consequence would be rate cutting in purely domestic lanes. Assuming that U.S. drivers would not work for about 10 cents per mile (approximately $2.50 per hour), the domestic trucking industry would be in mortal danger. A national freight transportation crisis would likely occur.

While initially this might be considered simply an effectively functioning market, the trucking industry will exhaust its supply of experienced and trained Mexican drivers quickly and turn to new hires from the factories of northern Mexico and from the impoverished farms in central Mexico (farms already put out of business by their inability to compete with mechanized corn production in the United States). If these persons obtain the necessary Mexican driver's license, they will likely find jobs as drivers. This could have serious implications for safety on the highways.

Recent research suggests that a downward pay slide may have a substantial effect on safety. Conservatively, statistical analysis suggests that every 10 percent decline in pay increases truck crashes by 20 percent, and the problem would be exacerbated if more trucks are on the road (Belzer, Rodriguez, and Sedo 2001).

The NAFTA effect on collective bargaining could be staggering, as no unionized carrier could compete in the circumstances previously outlined. Repeated work stoppages, such as those by low-paid immigrant owner–drivers in U.S. ports over the past two or three years, would increase; but neither carriers nor shippers have any institution with which to negotiate. Under current labor and antitrust law, owner–drivers are prohibited from organizing and bargaining collectively.

The Future of Collective Bargaining

Potential Changes in Representation

It is increasingly difficult to find a voice that can speak for the growing number of unorganized workers in the trucking industry. With unionization below 20 percent nationally and perhaps below 10 percent among over-the-road freight drivers, the Teamsters Union now represents a narrow set of employee interests, mainly in LTL and the package sector, along with such specific areas as warehouse, food distribution, and local delivery. Furthermore, labor law remains hostile to union organizing. One solution may be the minority representation model long advocated by Clyde Summers, Charles Morris, and others. It calls for labor to organize outside the NLRA (i.e., representation of worker interests broadly but without the traditional stress of collective bargaining). The model is not accepted by unions generally, but it may prove useful. It is not proposed as a replacement for collective bargaining but as an alternative strategy.

An example is the Owner Operator Independent Drivers Association (OOIDA), the only grassroots organization among independents that has survived and grown. Founded during the wildcat strikes of 1974, it has 72,000 members, most of whom are owner–drivers and some of whom are employee ("company") drivers. It offers valuable services, including hard-to-get health and life insurance, truck insurance, and equipment discounts. Membership dues and revenues from various services support an extensive array of activities, such as an active force of lawyers who are class-action specialists and who use the court system to gain redress for drivers in cases involving taxation, truth in leasing, and other broad grievances.

The OOIDA is a representative for drivers who lack union representation, and in some respects it resembles the nineteenth-century Knights of Labor. In its ranks are small independents who own a truck and operate on their own authority, as well as owners of small fleets who lease to motor carriers. Others are owner–drivers of a single truck that is leased to a motor carrier and who operate under its authority and are dispatched in much the same way as employee drivers (the carrier obtains the freight and the driver provides the power). Some OOIDA members lease their truck from the motor carrier and function as owner–drivers (all too often, when the driver is close to paying off the truck, the freight revenue mysteriously disappears). Yet, others are employee drivers who join to receive the magazine and to support OOIDA's advocacy of trucker interests.[10]

The Teamsters might take a lesson from OOIDA's approach, which emphasizes public outreach. The views of OOIDA, like the Teamsters, are sought on regulation, legislation, and matters of importance to truckers. Unlike the Teamsters, OOIDA limits representation to broad issues that affect all drivers, especially those who own their own truck, and does not engage in collective bargaining. This is not necessarily the only model for nonunion representation, but it has proved effective for OOIDA.

Pressures on Managers

Trucking is extremely competitive, and managers struggle daily to move freight on time, undamaged, and safely at the lowest possible cost. To the shipper, service is very important, but transportation is a cost. Freight rates have declined in real terms over the past two decades, and only during the economic boom of the 1990s could firms sustain rate increases. Trucking firms have had to do more with less.

"Less" means lower pay and fewer resources. As workers leave for industries with higher pay and easier working conditions, drivers and dock workers with generally less desirable qualifications are hired (Belzer 1993). The most serious problem, however, may be the difficulty of attracting managers willing to work long and often unappealing schedules in a high-pressure environment. Dock management in LTL, for example, works in covered but exposed terminals during the heat of the summer and the bitter cold of winter, with most freight crossing the dock in the middle of the night. DOT data show that real earnings of all classes of employees, with the sole exception of firm officers, have declined during the past twenty years.

An important development over the past two decades is overnight service. In the regional sector, service standards have increased greatly, and competitive carriers must be able to pick up freight in the afternoon and deliver it the following morning more than 500 miles away. Tight schedules and time windows often are complicated by the requirement to notify the shipper or consignee of pickup or delivery times, the need to preschedule out-of-route appointments, or last-minute pickups. Line managers describe this as a daily battle to clear the dock both morning and evening.

Technology has given management more tools but has raised customer expectations. Computerized routing and scheduling has made it possible for carriers to deemphasize the dispatcher. In TL this takes the form of automatic dispatching software that determines the optimum driver load assignment, depending on available hours, deadhead miles, and time pressure on pickup and delivery. While this software is by no means foolproof and is costly, it does take the initial decision away from the dispatcher and reduces transaction time, and only leading technology carriers utilize it. Many LTL carriers now use computer-aided dispatching, especially in optimizing network structures.

Shippers and consignees expect to be able to track their freight from origin to destination (called "visibility") and want real-time and accurate answers to the perennial question: "Where's my freight?" In TL this is relatively easy since the shipment can be traced to a single truck. In LTL, however, a carrier needs bar coding and information systems to track freight from one trailer to another and from one dock terminal to another. It appears that nonunion carriers are ahead of unionized firms in this respect. The latter tend to pay higher wages, so employees are relatively well educated and likely to stay. For nonunion firms, turnover is substantially higher, which increases the need for foolproof tracking systems. This may give these carriers a long-term advantage (for the effect of technology on trucking industrial relations, see Belzer 2002).

Employee turnover may be the major daily challenge for managers. It is low in the unionized LTL sector, averaging much less than 10 percent, but greater among nonunion carriers, depending on occupation (see Table 3). The problem is most severe in TL, where wages are low and drivers are not paid for nondriving time. A turnover rate of 100 percent is common, although a driver who works for a company for six months or more has a low probability of quitting. J. B. Hunt, the second largest TL carrier in 1997, had a 96 percent turnover rate before raising wages 38 percent, which cut turnover by half. The UMTIP driver survey shows that the average job tenure of mileage-paid drivers is four years, which supports the contention that the turnover problem is greatest among new hires. Labor market churning is a major challenge for managers.

TABLE 3

Employee Turnover and Full-Time Employment in LTL, 1997–1998
(As a Percentage of Total Employees)

	Dock workers		Pickup-and-delivery drivers		Linehaul drivers	
	Union	Nonunion	Union	Nonunion	Union	Nonunion
Workers who quit	5.6	17.9	3.0	12.6°	2.0	16.5°
Workers who were fired	1.2	12.0°°	0.4	6.1°°	1.3	10.2
New workers hired	5.6	74.1°	15.0	22.5	15.3	23.0
Full-time workers	76.7	52.1°	92.1	94.0	97.5	98.2

Source: Belzer 2000a.
N = 14.
Mean differences: ° significant at .10, °° significant at .05, two-tailed tests.

Bargaining Issues on the Horizon

The cost of employee benefits is a growing concern for most businesses, and trucking is no exception. A study of fourteen LTL carriers that included large and small firms, half union and half nonunion firms, showed a statistically significant difference across them only in the cost of benefits (Belzer 1999).

The reason is twofold. First, union benefits are extensive. The health, dental, and optical coverage provided by most Teamster health and welfare plans is far superior to that available in the nonunion sector, even for management. Union pension programs also are better and come from defined-benefit plans. Second, the cost of benefits is high because unionized carriers contribute to many different funds. The largest and most well-known is the Central States fund, but many others cover union members in different regions and localities. Each has its own administration, which adds to the cost. Further, each fund is subject to the Taft-Hartley Act requirement of management and union trustees, all of whom are paid, and some handsomely.

Work rules would seem to be a major issue for union carriers, but interviews with managers suggest that most of the old restrictions are gone. The union contract provides parameters within which they can operate without major difficulty. Even nonunion carriers indicate that they have very similar rules and can manage within them. Although the latter can change the rules if they wish, employee expectations of procedural justice limit their discretion (Belzer 1999).

The Threat of Terrorism

A less contentious bargaining issue emerged from the terrorist attacks on September 11, 2001, which drew attention to the vulnerability of America's efficient logistics system. Approximately 800,000 hazardous materials shipments occur every day. Although very few involve immediate and dramatic danger (a full gasoline tanker contains more flammable material than most fully-loaded airliners), the security of these shipments is vitally important. The Teamsters and OOIDA have joined with major employers (both union and nonunion) and trade associations that represent all segments of the trucking industry to identify vulnerabilities and explore ways to prevent their exploitation. The clear challenge for trucking is to establish a framework for operating a highly competitive and decentralized industry in a safe, secure, and productive fashion.

Nonbargaining Issues

The question of re-regulation has arisen but was not taken seriously until September 11. Although the trucking industry broadly opposed deregulation in the 1970s, by the 1990s it had adapted to the new level of competition (in view of the widespread failure of firms in the 1980s, this adaptation may be, in part, a survivor phenomenon). A core industry problem, however, is that freight rates do not support adequate profits (that is, high enough to attract market capital) or sufficient wages to attract qualified labor.

Low wages and high turnover raise security concerns because people with dubious employment backgrounds, including released felons, may be hired (Schultz 2001a). Another example is drayage operations in the ports, where many illegal immigrants essentially buy themselves a job by purchasing a truck and becoming owner–operators. Their earnings are far below the mean and likely below minimum wage, and they have conducted periodic job actions throughout the 1980s and 1990s, to no avail. Furthermore, low pay has long presented a security risk because it can lead to theft, to which is now added a national security concern that intermodal containers might be used as weapons or for weapons smuggling.

It is too early to tell whether these concerns may prompt re-regulation, but Congress already has acted to require that all commercial driver's license holders with hazardous materials certification undergo a criminal and security background check. In months to come, policy makers may explore a broad array of measures designed to make transportation secure.

The terrorist attacks also may affect NAFTA, which is based on free trade and open borders. In the aftermath of September 11, border crossings (especially between the United States and Canada) have experienced extended delays. Differences between Canadian and U.S. privacy standards, for example, will complicate preclearance of Canadian trucks entering the United States. Expected new regulations, following up on the antiterrorism Patriot Act, will tighten standards for Canadian drivers in the United States and will make it much more difficult to implement an open border with Mexico in the near future.

The Future of the Teamsters

The union organizing drive at Overnite, the nation's fifth largest LTL carrier, has stalled and is not likely to be successful. The TL sector is almost completely nonunion, leaving the Teamsters in a difficult position. Although the union retains substantial bargaining power in some sectors, the lack of successful organizing has weakened union density in the trucking industry so much that it may be on the knife-edge. It may have reached a critical tipping point from which union bargaining power cannot recover.

The Teamsters face two immediate, major bargaining challenges. The first comes directly on the heels of the 2001 union election. The UPS contract expires during summer 2002. The Teamsters currently are developing a strategy for this contract, using member surveys to solicit input. Immediately following this negotiation, the union will shift into high gear to begin negotiating the NMFA, which is due to expire April 1, 2003. Both of the contracts produced in these negotiations will provide important signals of Teamster bargaining power, but much of the real contest may take place between the Teamsters and small carriers, particularly in cartage.

The trucking industry and the Teamsters have a local heritage. Before the 1980s the NMFA represented some 600 carriers, most of them local and regional. As competition drove out marginal carriers, it also made the centralized union contract untenable at the local level. The carriers that survived and remained unionized ordinarily did so by negotiating "white paper" contracts—contracts written for that carrier alone and customized to its needs and bargaining environment. The continued fractionalization of the industry has left these carriers and the local unions with which they have contracts on their own. The union can be expected to retain these agreements as long as the terms provide only a marginal advantage over nonunion competitors. This market pressure limits union bargaining power with these small carriers and with larger regional and national carriers as well. The sharpest pressure, however, is on the NMFA carriers, the employees of which enjoy the greatest union differential. The future of the Teamsters will be determined by the outcome of these negotiations.

Conclusion

Despite the challenges, the trucking industry will continue to grow. The nation relies on trucking to haul most of its finished goods. Trucking provides the cement for our economy and will remain the most important mode of transportation for the foreseeable future.

The future of union–management relations is not so bright. The Teamsters face a critical crossroads, and the direction the union takes will determine whether unionization remains a factor in trucking industrial relations. The Hoffa regime has virtually abandoned national organizing efforts and is focusing on local unions at the very time carriers are becoming national and international in scope. If the union fails to rebuild its strength in the next five years, trucking unionization may be "history." At least one union official has been quoted as saying that the next NMFA will be the last. Absent a major shift in union policy and strategy, the demise of unionized trucking may come sooner rather than later.

Acknowledgments

I thank George Fulton, Donald Grimes, Stanley Sedo, Stephen Burks, and expert Peter Swan for research contributions.

Notes

[1] All carriers with more than $3 million in annual revenue, which equates to about twenty-five trucks, are required to report, and about 15 percent comply.

[2] Rates continued to be filed with the ICC for another decade and a half, but they were masked both by removing the names of the shippers served and discounting the published rates by as much as 70 percent, which made the published figure meaningless.

[3] Carriers previously restricted to specific products and freight lanes now could compete anywhere and with anyone.

[4] Wages declined for dock workers the most, at least in nonunion firms, since they are considered general labor, whereas truck drivers, who must have a commercial driver's license and on whom the carriers depend to make service commitments, are not as easily replaced. The shortage of drivers since the early 1990s has underscored the need to maintain their wages even at the expense of dock workers if necessary and practical.

[5] Several national unionized carriers survived and have remained dominant, and some unionized regional carriers have hired additional drivers as they expanded. Many displaced workers, however, found jobs with nonunion carriers at lower wages and benefits or exited the industry. Those who went to the TL sector found the work intolerable and eventually left.

[6] Under the RICO Consent Decree, Justice Department actions require a relatively low standard of proof. In Carey's case, the government had to prove perjury beyond a reasonable doubt.

[7] Teamsters locals pay the lowest per capita tax of any major union, $3.90 per month per member, which is hardly enough to operate a national union today and is less than 15 percent of all dues collected.

[8] The organizing campaign at Overnite in the 1980s generally was unsuccessful (the largest unit organized was in Chicago, where Local 705 struck the carrier for

recognition, to no avail), but the 1990s campaign fared better: the union organized or won bargaining orders for sites representing approximately 40 percent of all employees. In the 1990s organizing drive (initiated under Carey and pursued by Hoffa, who is still trying to negotiate a first contract), Overnite committed widespread unfair labor practices, which resulted in an unfair labor practice strike that at this writing has not yielded any returns for the union.

[9] "Incidental" is defined as any loaded move from the inbound destination of the international trip to the origin point of a return load to the home country. For example, a Canadian truck can unload in New York and pick up a return load in St. Louis.

[10] Truck drivers, perhaps uniquely among workers, often pass seamlessly among these classifications throughout their working life. Opportunities abound to own their own truck, and many do so because they seek the independence and control as well as the opportunity to have their own piece of equipment that they can be proud of (for excellent accounts of truck driver culture, see Di Salvatore 1988a and 1988b, and Ouellet 1994). Most of them also return to being company drivers, though, as the failure rate among owner–drivers is high. One critical reason behind this high rate of failure is the fact that they are price takers and are not allowed to organize, and they lease on to carriers that are also price takers in a highly competitive business environment.

References

Bailey, Jeff. 2001. "Building a Business on Government Policies Has Its Hitches: Small Trucking Firm's Payoff from Open Mexican Border Is Delayed Again in Wake of Sept. 11." *The Wall Street Journal*, November 13, p. B2.

Belman, Dale L., and Kristen A. Monaco. 2001. "The Effects of Deregulation, De-Unionization, Technology, and Human Capital on the Work and Work Lives of Truckers." *Industrial and Labor Relations Review*, Vol. 54, no. 2A (March), pp. 502–24.

Belzer, Michael H. 1993. "Collective Bargaining in the Trucking Industry: The Effects of Institutional and Economic Restructuring." Ph.D. diss., Cornell University, Ithaca, NY.

_____. 1995. "Collective Bargaining in the Trucking Industry: Do the Teamsters Still Count?" *Industrial and Labor Relations Review*, Vol. 48, no. 4, pp. 636–655.

_____. 1999. "Hours of Service Impact Assessment." Report to U.S. Department of Transportation, Office of Motor Carriers (Contract No. DTFH61-96-C-00038; Engineering, Analytic and Research Support for Motor Carrier Safety Activities, with University of Michigan Transportation Research Institute). Report prepared with research contributions from Dale Ballou, Stephen Burks, Donald Grimes, George Fulton, Daniel Lass, and Kristen Monaco.

_____. 2000a. "Less-Than-Truckload Trucking Industry Case Study and Benchmarking Report." University of Michigan Trucking Industry Program (unpublished confidential report).

_____. 2000b. *Sweatshops on Wheels: Winners and Losers in Trucking Deregulation*. New York: Oxford University Press.

_____. 2001a. "Reply to Thomas Hubbard—American Trucking Associations Critique of University of Michigan Trucking Industry Program Driver Survey Data." Available from http://www.ilir.umich.edu/sweatshopsonwheels/.

_____. 2001b. "Life on the Road Captured in Accurate Surveys." *Transport Topics*, October 22, p. 9.

_____. 2002. "Technological Innovation and the Trucking Industry: Information Revolution and the Effect on the Work Process." *Journal of Labor Research*, Vol. 23, no. 3.

Belzer, Michael H., and Richard Hurd. 1999. "Government Oversight, Union Democracy, and Labor Racketeering: Lessons from the Teamsters Experience. *Journal of Labor Research*, Vol. 20, no. 3 (Summer), pp. 343–65.

Belzer, Michael H., Daniel Rodriguez, and Stanley Sedo. 2001. "Estimating the Safety Effects of Pay Level and Method, and Changes in Truck Driver Compensation Levels." Presented to Manitoba Truck Safety Symposium IV, University of Manitoba, Winnipeg, Manitoba, Canada (October 24).

Belzer, Michael H., George A. Fulton, Donald R. Grimes, Gregory M. Saltzman, Stanley Sedo, and Lucie G. Schmidt. 2002. "Proposed Changes in Motor Carrier Hours of Service Regulations: An Assessment." Draft report to the University of Michigan Transportation Research Institute, for submission to the Federal Motor Carrier Safety Administration, March 6, in fulfillment of Contract No. DTFH61-96-C-00038.

Crowe, Kenneth C. 1993. *Collision: How the Rank and File Took Back the Teamsters*. New York: Charles Scribner's Sons.

Di Salvatore, Bryan. "Large Cars." *The New Yorker*, September 12, 1988, pp. 39–77.

_____. "Large Cars." *The New Yorker*, September 19, 1988, pp. 63–84.

Ouellet, Lawrence J. 1994. *Pedal to the Metal: The Work Lives of Truckers*. Philadelphia: Temple University Press.

Pyle, Encarnacion. 2001. "Rolling Sweatshops: Low Pay, Long Hours and Difficult Conditions Are Driving Big Changes in the Trucking Industry." *The Columbus Dispatch*, November 18.

Schultz, John. 2001a. "'Crisis' Now: FMCSA's Cirillo Calls for National Dialogue to Upgrade Freight Infrastructure, Driver Pay." *Traffic World*, January 22, pp. 10–11.

_____. 2001b. "Open the Border, Already!" *Traffic World*, April 16, pp. 23–24.

Teamsters for a Democratic Union. 2001. *Convoy Dispatch* #196, September, p. 11.

U.S. Department of Labor, Bureau of Labor Statistics. 2001. "Current Employment Statistics." http://stats.bls.gov/ces/home.htm.

_____. 1998, 2000. "Occupational Employment Statistics." http://stats.bls.gov/oes/home.htm#overview.

U.S. Department of Commerce, Bureau of the Census. 1997. "Vehicle Inventory and Use Survey" http://www.census.gov/econ/www/viusmain.html.

U.S. Department of Transportation, Bureau of Transportation Statistics. 1997. "Motor Carrier Financial and Operating Statistics." http://www.bts.gov/ntda/mcs/.

U.S. Department of Transportation, Federal Motor Carrier Safety Administration. n.d. "Cabotage Rules for Canadian Drivers." http://www.fmcsa.dot.gov/rulesregs/fmcsrhome.htm.

CHAPTER 9

Practitioner Commentary

RICHARD BANK
AFL-CIO

The views expressed herein are the author's and do not necessarily
reflect the views of the AFL-CIO or its affiliated unions.

Introduction

The reports in this volume demonstrate that collective bargaining
relationships are shaped both by influences specific to particular industries and by general influences that cut across industrial lines. Perhaps
the most powerful general influence affecting collective bargaining in
the private sector is declining union density, which continues apace. For
example, in durable goods manufacturing, where unions have traditionally had a strong presence, membership density declined from 23.8 percent in 1984 (Hirsch and Macpherson 1984:87) to 15.2 percent in 2001
(Hirsch and Macpherson 2002:49).

It is axiomatic that all companies strive relentlessly to cut costs, including labor costs. Most employers, if given a chance, would escape their
unions to do so. Nevertheless, when a unionized labor force dominates a
market and labor costs are largely taken out of competition, unionized
employers have less incentive to drive hard bargains or to escape their
unions.

When density drops significantly, unionized employers are put at a
substantial labor cost disadvantage. They respond with intensified resistance to union demands, intensified resistance to organizing efforts at
their nonunion operations, attempts to de-unionize, and attempts to shift
union jobs to nonunion providers and venues. At the same time, declining density also intensifies resistance by nonunion employers to unionization of their operations.

Unless private-sector unions can find a way to build density in industries where they have a presence, bargaining and organizing will become
increasingly more difficult for them. I will review here some of the

forces that—from my perspective as a union negotiator—drive density loss by reinforcing or facilitating the already strong and innate motivation employers have to lower labor costs by shedding union jobs. I will then explain Bargaining to Grow, a union response to density decline that integrates bargaining and organizing strategies to rebuild and expand union density.

Forces That Contribute to Declining Union Density

The Pressure to Maximize Shareholder Value at All Costs

Wall Street has increasingly escalated pressure on businesses to maximize shareholder value to the exclusion of the interests of other stakeholders, including employees. In this atmosphere, the goal becomes more than just to make a reasonable profit. The goal becomes to extract every last cent of profit, even when profits are huge. Jack Welch, GE's former CEO and chairman of the board, is perhaps the best-known apostle of this creed, which he calls "squeezing the lemon" (Bernstein 1999:74). Of course, labor costs are part of the lemon.

How top corporate officials are compensated gives them a very personal incentive to "squeeze the lemon." Currently, many of these officials have much—sometimes most—of their compensation tied to bonuses dependent on short-term profits and to options whose value depends on the short-term appreciation of company stock. This compensation scheme provides a powerful motivation to maximize profits by any means—regardless of the effect on long-term shareholder value, workers, communities, or the national interest. These means obviously include squeezing worker wages and benefits, cutting union jobs, shifting work to nonunion venues and providers, and resisting unionization.

Tying management compensation to short-term profits and short-term appreciation of stock value fueled the recent Enron and Global Crossing fiascos, which utterly decimated shareholder value, not to mention the jobs and pensions of thousands of employees. Outrages committed at Enron and Global Crossing in the name of short-term gain have so inflamed public passions and political rhetoric that reform may actually be possible.

Deterring companies from granting outsized stock options to management would by no means be a panacea for the overall density dilemma unions face. However, it would help. A good first step would be to eliminate accounting and tax incentives that make stock options such an attractive form of compensation.

Companies currently have a double-barreled impetus to grant overly generous stock options. Stock options need not be reported as a business expense on a company's books, but they can be deducted from taxes as just such an expense. This anomaly, which applies to no other form of compensation, simultaneously increases a company's bottom line and lowers its tax liability. It should be rectified by requiring companies to treat stock options consistently on their financial returns and tax statements. If stock options are not reported as expenses on a financial statement, they should not be deductible for income tax purposes on a tax return. Legislation to enact this stricture has been introduced in the Senate.[1]

Globalization

U.S. workers in mobile industries such as auto parts, electronics, telecommunications, apparel, textiles, steel fabrication, and food processing are increasingly competing with workers from countries with far lower labor costs. This competition cripples organizing efforts, constrains bargaining demands, and results in massive job loss (Bronfenbrenner 2000:v).

In an industry subject to the perils of globalization, the scenarios for union density decline are straightforward. Foreign companies with low labor costs have a competitive advantage in U.S. and world markets. U.S. companies threaten to move jobs overseas unless workers bargain against third world standards by restraining their demands or making concessions. Union compliance may be effective for a while in slowing job erosion, but usually it is not enough. The labor cost gap is too great, and U.S. workers would have to utterly devastate their living standards to become truly competitive. In the end, U.S. companies suffer major market share loss. They downsize, or go out of business, or export U.S. jobs overseas to countries with low labor costs. Some companies exit production but market or assemble products produced by low cost foreign suppliers.[2]

Some employers are not content to export just their own jobs. They pressure suppliers to relocate their operations to countries with low labor costs. Employers who are prime customers of suppliers have the leverage to enforce such demands. For example, GE threatened in "supplier migration" conferences it held to shift business from suppliers unless they relocated manufacturing operations from the United States to Mexico (Bernstein 1999:74).

Even where employers have no intention of relocating, the mere threat to relocate is enough to convince unions to lower demands or make concessions. Likewise, the threat to relocate if workers unionize is a lethal weapon against organizing drives and efforts to reach first contracts (Bronfenbrenner 200:vi, 19).

Obviously, globalization presents daunting challenges for U.S. unions. They have no legal right to organize foreign workers. Moreover, as part of a program to maintain a labor cost advantage in international markets, the governments of some countries suppress labor and human rights. International treaties and accords that purport to protect the right of workers to organize and to protect workers from inhumane conditions of employment are woefully inadequate instruments for redressing these abuses, as are the provisions of domestic law that protect U.S. industries from unfair foreign competition.

Beneficent policies can also create labor cost differentials. Many industrialized countries subsidize health and pension benefits for active workers and retirees as societal obligations. This puts U.S. employers, who must fund their health and pension costs without direct governmental aid, at a substantial disadvantage.

Globalization in many respects recapitulates the historical flight of unionized industries to the misnamed "right-to-work" states, which boast low-cost labor markets, blatantly antiunion state and municipal governments, and prohibitions against union shops. This phenomenon is still alive and prospering, working in tandem with globalization to thin union density in industries where flight is feasible. It is no accident that Japanese and German automobile companies, which are heavily unionized in their home countries, almost uniformly choose to locate their transplants in "right-to-work" states in the South. There, they have been successful in fighting off all attempts by the United Auto Workers (UAW) to organize their U.S. workforces.

Tax, trade, and monetary policies reinforce employer financial incentives to export jobs. U.S. employers can defer taxes on profits earned in foreign countries, and they receive a credit for taxes paid to foreign governments. The Export-Import Bank subsidizes investment in foreign projects by U.S. firms. The Overseas Private Investment Corporation (OPIC) insures overseas investments of private U.S. corporations. The strong dollar puts U.S. exports at a competitive disadvantage.

Multinational employers, unless constrained by restrictions in collective bargaining contracts, can move jobs to a variety of overseas and domestic locations to achieve the most favorable combination of labor costs, tax benefits, exchange rates, subsidies, and so on. Jack Welch captured this concept succinctly when he said he wished he could put every

GE job "on a barge" so that production could be moved at will (CNN *Moneyline* 1998).

In the long run, there are policy changes that would help level the playing field for U.S. businesses and dampen the incentives to export jobs. Some of the most important are as follows:

- Require that International Labor Organization (ILO) core labor standards be included in all trade agreements.
- Strengthen the "import surge" provisions of Section 201 of the Trade Act of 1974.
- Require that subsidies granted to exporters by the Export-Import Bank and OPIC take account of their impact on domestic businesses and employment.
- Eliminate foreign profit tax deferral and foreign tax credits.
- Where companies have received domestic tax abatements and other subsidies on the promise that they will create jobs, require repayment when operations are relocated.
- Lower the value of the dollar.

The labor movement alone cannot bring about these reforms. However, there are solid reasons why other constituencies might support them.[3] Our huge and growing foreign debt makes us increasingly vulnerable to financial crisis. The most feasible way to reduce foreign debt is through exports, but we cannot export unless we preserve and expand domestic industries. Furthermore, the United States is now embroiled in a de facto state of war against terror. This war will be long and far-flung, and it will therefore require increased acquisition of weapons, ships, airplanes, computers, communications equipment, and other high-end products. With a shrinking industrial base, the United States would have to rely on foreign sources for production, a perilous plan that many would question.

Firm Restructuring and Disintegration of Businesses

Domestic and cross-border mergers, acquisitions, and asset sales provide many opportunities to shift unionized work to nonunion entities. So do creation of other business arrangements, including holding companies, subsidiaries, spin-offs, joint ventures, and partnerships. The increasing proclivity of employers to identify narrow "core competencies" and to outsource the rest of their operations provides similar opportunities (Katz, MacDuffie, and Pil 2002).

Technological Advances

Technology alters, eliminates, and creates jobs, processes, and lines of business. These attributes of technological advance provide opportunities for management to eliminate union jobs, reclassify union jobs as management or nonbargaining unit functions, and place new types of work outside the union's jurisdiction (Stanger 2002).

Deregulation

Where entry barriers are low, deregulation can devastate union density. Following deregulation, nonunion competitors flood markets, and union density declines dramatically. An evolving nonunion labor market creates labor cost disparities that make it difficult for unionized employers to compete. Density continues to decline as unionized businesses downsize or go out of business (Belzer 2002).

Unfair Labor Laws

In combating the effects of all these influences, unions and workers must organize and bargain under labor laws that are substantially and notoriously biased in favor of employers. A recent report by Human Rights Watch aptly summarized this deplorable situation under the National Labor Relations Act (NLRA), which governs the vast majority of workers in this country:

> The reality of NLRA enforcement falls far short of its goals. Many workers who try to form and join trade unions to bargain with their employers are spied on, harassed, pressured, threatened, suspended, fired, deported or otherwise victimized in reprisal for their exercise of the right to freedom of association. . . .
>
> In the United States, labor law enforcement efforts often fail to deter unlawful conduct. When the law is applied, enervating delays and weak remedies invite continued violations. Any employer intent on resisting workers' self organization can drag out legal proceedings for years, fearing little more than an order to post a written notice in the workplace promising not to repeat the unlawful conduct and grant back pay to a worker fired for organizing. . . . As a result, a culture of near-impunity has taken shape in much of U.S. labor law and practice (Human Rights Watch 2000:9).

The specific advantages accruing to employers under the NLRA are myriad. A few examples suffice to make the point:

Employers are not required to provide unions seeking to organize their employees with employee names and addresses until shortly before a certification election. (*Excelsior Underwear, Inc.* 1996). In contrast, from the beginning to the end of an organizing drive, the employer knows every employee's name, address, phone number, and work location.

Unions generally have no access rights to employer premises during organizing drives. Employers, on the other hand, have access to employees throughout the workday. During the workday, supervisors have boundless opportunities to proselytize against the union. Moreover, employers can force employees to attend "captive audience" meetings during paid work time. At these meetings, employees are subjected to intense doses of antiunion propaganda, and the union has no right to be present and reply.

As the Human Rights Watch report emphasizes, employers can, with virtual impunity, fire union supporters in attempts to kill organizing drives. With the delays and appeals the law allows, employers know that they can postpone reinstatement and compensation of wrongfully terminated pro-union workers for years, long after intimidation of the workforce has undermined union support and defeated an organizing drive. Eventually, having to compensate wrongfully terminated employees is no deterrent because such compensation is usually far cheaper and less troublesome than having to deal with a union.

Where unions do win elections, employers can delay bargaining for a first contract by filing postelection objections and, after they are resolved in favor of the union, by testing the union's certification in the courts. Even after employers exhaust their appeals and are forced to bargain, they can still stall to rid themselves of unions. Under the NLRA, there is a strong presumption that a union enjoys majority support within a bargaining unit for one year following certification (*Brooks v. NLRB* 1954; *NLRB v. Paper Manufacturers Co.* 1986). Employers wishing to rid themselves of unions drag out bargaining for a first contract until the certification year elapses, continue bargaining, and never reach agreement. This gives them plenty of time to dissipate the union's majority through workforce intimidation and the natural process of employee turnover. Then, they await—and sometimes promote—decertification of the union by disgruntled workers.

Dragging out bargaining with no real intention of reaching agreement is not difficult because it is hard to prove a failure to bargain in good faith under the NLRA. With good legal advice, employers can string out the negotiating process indefinitely. Employees can force the issue by exercising their legal right to strike to enforce their contractual demands. However, the NLRA gives employers the right to permanently replace employees who strike over economic demands, which violates worker rights under ILO core conventions Nos. 87 and 98 (International Labor Organization 2002) to freedom of association and to organize and bargain collectively. Employers can and do capitalize on their right to replace strikers by provoking strikes and supplanting their unionized workforces with nonunion personnel.

There is no question that to rebuild and expand density, the huge inequities in current labor law that hamstring unions in organizing and bargaining must be eliminated. The AFL-CIO and its affiliated unions have fought hard for labor law reform for many years without success. Labor law reform remains a top labor movement priority, and initiatives to make reform a reality will continue and escalate. In the meantime, unions must develop strategies and tactics that avoid a legal regime calculated to defeat them.

Bargaining to Grow As an Alternative to the NLRA

The forces driving density loss are powerful and cannot be overcome solely by union action in the labor relations arena. Nevertheless, smart organizing and bargaining are powerful weapons in the long-term fight to rebuild and expand union density. Bargaining to Grow (BTG) is an approach being developed and refined by the AFL-CIO and its affiliated unions that integrates organizing and bargaining strategies in the fight against density decline. An integrated approach is absolutely essential to success. Organizing puts workers under union jurisdiction. Good contracts with strong job security provisions keep them there. Organizing without negotiating job security is like trying to fill a bucket with a hole in it.

BTG's core is to bypass the NLRA by negotiating fair rules and procedures with employers that govern organizing and bargaining at their operations. BTG envisions a staged process in which organizing and bargaining interact progressively and synergistically in an ever-widening ambit:

Stage 1: The union negotiates private rules with a nonunion employer that govern organizing, gaining recognition, and bargaining first contracts at one or more operations.

Stage 2: The union organizes employees and gains recognition at employer operations governed by the negotiated rules.

Stage 3: The union negotiates a first contract.

Stage 4: Once a mature bargaining relationship has been established, the union negotiates with the employer to extend BTG principles governing organizing, recognition, and bargaining first contracts to all other similar nonunion operations of the employer. The union also negotiates with the employer to extend such provisions to similar nonunion operations of affiliated entities that the employer controls (e.g., subsidiaries, partnerships, spin-offs, joint ventures).

Stage 5: As the bargaining relationship evolves, the union negotiates collective bargaining contracts with the employer that protect union jobs and jurisdiction. The union also negotiates provisions that automatically apply the union's contracts with the employer to any similar nonunion operations of the employer, where the union subsequently gains recognition.

Stage 6: The cycle begins anew and expands. Under the rules and procedures negotiated with the employer, the union organizes and establishes good contracts at other nonunion operations of the employer and its affiliates.

Negotiated Rules for Organizing, Recognition, and First Contracts

Optimum BTG rules governing organizing, recognition, and first contracts nullify the advantages the NLRA confers upon employers. Many unions—notably the Hotel Employees and Restaurant Employees International Union (HERE), Communications Workers of America (CWA), Service Employees International Union (SEIU), UAW and United Steelworkers of America (USWA)—have been successful in negotiating some or all of them:

- Recognition—the employer recognizes the union upon a showing that a majority of the bargaining unit has signed cards designating the union as its bargaining representative[4]

- Employer neutrality—the employer takes no position on unionization, holds no captive meetings, and hires no union busters to combat organizing drives

- Agreement on the appropriate bargaining unit or on binding procedures for determining the appropriate bargaining unit

- Union access to employees on the employer's property during organizing drives

- Accurate lists of employees in the bargaining unit, with home addresses, work locations, and phone numbers, which are provided on request and updated regularly

- Expedited and binding arbitration of all disputes arising out of organizing drives and the recognition process
- Procedures for negotiating and reaching first contracts, including time limits within which parties must conduct negotiations and attempt to reach agreement, and provisions for a neutral party to decide the terms of the first contract if no agreement is reached

Automatic Application of Existing Collective Bargaining Agreements

To apply the terms of an existing collective bargaining agreement with an employer to similar nonunion operations of the employer, unions try to negotiate two types of provisions. Each pertains to a different context.

Accretion clauses are legally limited to very narrow circumstances and accomplish recognition and contract application in one stroke. Accretion clauses provide that a small, nonunion operation will be absorbed into a significantly larger nearby unionized bargaining unit if both operations perform substantially similar work and if employees at both operations have a "community of interest." Once accreted, the smaller unit is automatically covered by the larger unionized unit's contract.

To cover situations where accretion is inappropriate, unions negotiate clauses providing that, after they gain recognition or certification at an employer's nonunion operation, the union's existing contract with the employer will apply at that operation. The key for unions in these clauses is to have BTG principles (card check, neutrality, etc.) govern recognition.

Maintaining Density—Job Security Provisions

By using BTG to establish union labor costs throughout a complex of affiliated entities, a union diminishes incentives and opportunities to transfer work and jobs from unionized to nonunion operations within the complex. However, given the many opportunities employers have to bleed union jobs, this prophylactic effect is insufficient to maintain density and must be supplemented with strong collectively bargained job security provisions that protect against density loss from the following:

- job exportation to nonunion venues and sources—by banning or strictly limiting subcontracting, outsourcing, closing operations, relocating operations, and laying off workers
- cyclical downturns—by giving workers extended recall rights, income and health care benefits maintenance, rights to transfer to other employer locations, and training that prepares them for other jobs with the employer

- technological change—by granting lifetime job security for incumbents when new technology is introduced and by providing skills training to qualify workers for jobs that technology will create
- changes in work—by granting unions the broadest possible initial jurisdiction over work, by negating unilateral employer reclassification of jobs, and by automatically bringing new job classifications and lines of work under union jurisdiction
- sale or other disposition of union operations—by requiring successors to honor union contracts at operations they acquire

These provisions are difficult to negotiate. Some are fraught with legal complexities. However, there are precedents for union success in negotiating all of them.

Comprehensive Campaigns

Few employers, even where they have good relationships with their unions, will volunteer to agree to BTG principles that divest them of the significant advantages they enjoy under current law when confronting unions in organizing drives or at the bargaining table. In building leverage to enforce BTG demands, traditional collective bargaining strategies are of limited use to unions. First, some BTG campaigns occur entirely outside of a collective bargaining context. They involve union attempts to obtain employer agreement to BTG principles governing organizing and recognition before the union represents any of the employer's employees. Second, even where a union represents an employer's employees and BTG demands are made within a collective bargaining context, the law prohibits unions from forcing employers to negotiate about some BTG issues or striking over them.

To persuade employers to agree to BTG principles, unions often mount comprehensive campaigns, which are also a potent supplement to traditional sources of union power in regular collective bargaining.[5] The basic elements of a comprehensive campaign are the same, regardless of the campaign's context:

- Educating workers to understand the importance of the union's demands and committing workers to fight for them
- Mobilizing workers in activities that forcefully portray to the employer their commitment to the union's demands
- Educating and mobilizing union allies in support of the union's demands

- Exposing employer legal, regulatory, political, and public opinion vulnerabilities
- Offering positive inducements to employers to agree to union demands

When BTG demands are made in the course of negotiations for a collective bargaining agreement, worker education and commitment are especially crucial. In such negotiations, many issues of immediate and grave importance to workers and their families—like wages, pensions, and health benefits—are in play. Employers may threaten never to reach an agreement on a contract improving wages and benefits if the union pursues BTG demands. As an endgame, employers may offer improvements in wages and benefits if the union will drop BTG demands. Keeping workers committed to BTG demands requires that workers see such an exchange as what it is, an offer to buy their futures cheaply.

In industries where employers are growing their businesses away from unions, it is also important to beware of false compromises. An employer may be willing to trade agreement to BTG principles in a dying line of business where a union has high density in return for agreement by the union not to organize workers in a new and growing line of business. When faced with such an offer, unionized workers must understand that their future lies with the new business and that opportunities there depend on the union's ability to organize it under BTG principles.

Unions employ a variety of tactics to build alliances with community groups, religious groups, politicians, and others. Unions make their case by emphasizing aspects of their demands that appeal to fairness, justice, and the particular interests of these constituencies. Unions also offer to support allies in their own battles with the employer. The potency of unions at the ballot box is a powerful source of leverage in persuading politicians who need the labor vote to advocate for workers' interests in organizing drives or bargaining disputes, and to mediate or to intercede in the union's behalf. Unions sometimes have the leverage to convince others with influence over the employer to mediate or intercede, too.

In its 2000 negotiations with Los Angeles contractors who provide janitorial services in Los Angeles County commercial buildings, SEIU mounted a successful comprehensive campaign that encompassed many of these tactics. SEIU effectively characterized its fight for a fair contract as a civil rights crusade, one that pitted poor immigrant workers in a David versus Goliath battle against rich landlords and contractors. This characterization captured public and media sympathy for the underdog janitors, galvanized support for their cause, and encouraged high-powered clergy and politicians to advocate in their behalf. Los Angeles's Cardinal Mahoney and Mayor Richard Riordan went further and at several points intervened to bring the parties back to the bargaining table when negotiations broke down. SEIU created a public opinion climate in which the landlords were held responsible for the welfare of janitors who worked in their buildings. This moral pressure enabled SEIU to persuade one of the most powerful landlords to try to broker a deal between the union and the contractors, and to threaten to make his own deal with the unions if the contractors failed to meet the union's final demands.

The labor movement was also heavily involved. Scores of unions supported the strikers by honoring picket lines, staffing food banks, and raising money.

The agreement produced by this campaign encompassed significant improvements in wages and health care benefits. SEIU capitalized on the momentum from the Los Angeles County negotiations and the highly favorable publicity they generated to obtain positive outcomes in closely timed subsequent negotiations for janitors across the country. Lining up the expiration dates of janitors' contracts across the country was part of a long-range plan that had taken years to execute.

In some cases, unions have something valuable to offer employers in exchange for agreement to BTG principles. These positive inducements can supplement, or substitute for, confrontation. For example, the USWA has a history of cooperating with the basic steel industry on legislative and regulatory matters. However, in its bargaining goals, the USWA states unequivocally that employer agreement to neutrality, card check, and other BTG principles is the price of partnership: "On these issues there can be no compromise. No company which opposes, in any way, shape or form, our efforts to represent all of its workers should ever enjoy a stable or constructive relationship with this Union" (United Steelworkers of America 1998).

CWA used positive inducements as part of its successful strategy to win BTG rights at Southwestern Bell's subsidiaries during the 1990s. The company wanted continued CWA support on legislative and regulatory matters. CWA premised continuation of such support upon agreement to its demands for card check. CWA explained to SBC that support was "a two-way street: SBC couldn't expect CWA to support growing the company if in turn the company used the profits to establish antiunion subsidiaries" (CWA 1997:19).

Labor movement solidarity is a primary component of most comprehensive campaigns. Solidarity can be expressed as structural labor movement support for individual unions and as cooperation and coordination
among unions facing common employers.

To raise public awareness of the problems workers face when they try
to organize, the AFL-CIO promotes Voice@Work, a program in which
grassroots labor activists across the country support organizing efforts and
highlight the tactics employers use to thwart organizing rights. These
activists contact community groups, the clergy, and politicians in their
areas to build support for workers in particular campaigns and to build
support for labor law reform. Top AFL-CIO officers, including AFL-CIO
President John Sweeney, Secretary-Treasurer Richard Trumka, and Executive Vice President Linda Chavez-Thompson participate in these efforts
and address rallies across the country in support of Voice@Work activities.

The AFL-CIO has fortified its efforts to promote labor movement
solidarity in bargaining through its Strategic Approaches Committee.
The Strategic Approaches Committee has a twofold mission. First, it
mobilizes and coordinates labor movement assistance to unions involved
in critical collective bargaining struggles. Second, it supports unions
involved in such struggles with the AFL-CIO's unique resources: its
nationwide infrastructure, its national and international political reach,
its national and international media access, and its relations with the
worldwide labor movement.

The 2000 negotiations between Boeing and the Society of Professional Engineering Employees in Aerospace/International Federation of
Professional and Technical Engineers (SPEEA/IFPTE), which represents
Boeing's aerospace engineers and technicians, exemplify these twin
themes. The union struck after the parties failed to reach agreement on a
new contract. SPEEA/IFPTE represented more than 21,000 employees
at the time, and this was the largest white collar strike in U.S. history.
SPEEA/IFPTE immediately requested and received AFL-CIO assistance
through the auspices of the Strategic Approaches Committee.

The AFL-CIO's state federation in Washington and its Seattle area
labor council mobilized the local labor movement and its allies to support
the strike financially, on the picket line, in the media, and in the community. The AFL-CIO and its affiliated international unions also made major
financial contributions to support the strike. The Strategic Approaches
Committee assisted SPEEA/IFPTE in designing and executing its strike
and negotiating strategies. The AFL-CIO facilitated SPEEA/IFPTE's
access to the Federal Aviation Administration, Congress, and national

media. This bolstered the union's efforts to warn the government and the public that the safety of airplanes manufactured during the strike was suspect because of the absence of a normal complement of union engineers and technicians.

Massive labor movement support combined with the militancy of the striking engineers and technicians to generate a settlement in which SPEEA/IFPTE achieved substantial contractual improvements and won the right to a vote by bargaining unit members on whether union security provisions should be implemented. Capitalizing on the momentum of its success in negotiations, SPEEA/IFPTE won the union security vote handily.

In addition, following negotiations, SPEEA/IFPTE substantially increased its density within Boeing and the aerospace industry. With assistance from the AFL-CIO, the union organized 4,000 Boeing engineers in Wichita in the biggest NLRB election in 2000 and then negotiated a first contract for them.

Labor solidarity is increasingly international in scope as unions confront common multinational employers across the globe. There are many recent examples of cross-border cooperation, a few of which follow.

Offshore Mariners United (OMU)—a federation of the Seafarers, Marine Engineers' Beneficial Association; Masters, Mates & Pilots; and American Maritime Officers—is attempting to organize offshore mariners employed by Trico Marine. The AFL-CIO and numerous foreign labor organizations are vigorously supporting this effort. Foreign unions have petitioned Trico to allow its U.S. employees to organize without interference and have visited Trico's U.S. operations to monitor and publicize alleged worker intimidation, firings, and harassment. Representatives of foreign unions have attended the company's annual meeting to endorse the workers' efforts to organize and have undertaken solidarity activities in their own countries. The Norwegian Oil and Petrochemical Workers Union (NOPEF) has brought suit in Norway to establish its right to boycott Trico-related work unless the company pledges to give its U.S. workers a fair opportunity to decide whether they wish to be unionized.

The Air Line Pilots Association (ALPA) has established an entity to advise and assist overseas pilots' unions in negotiations with their employers. This activity increases solidarity among unions whose members are increasingly linked by corporate global alliances. In the long run, it also helps protect ALPA's density. To the extent ALPA can buttress the wages and benefits of foreign pilots, it decreases the incentive to shift pilots' jobs to foreign domiciles as airlines in global alliances consolidate their structural relationships and financial interests.

Through the auspices of the International Federation of Chemical, Energy, and Mine Workers (ICEM), leaders from twenty-one unions in eleven countries on five continents recently established a global union network at International Paper Company, the largest paper company in the world. Participating unions will share information about wages and working conditions, take common action at International Paper in support of each other, and seek to establish labor standards at all company operations.

Conclusion

There are no easy answers to density loss in the private sector. The causes of density loss are multiple and complex. They involve powerful forces, many of which unions cannot adequately confront or resolve within organizing or collective bargaining contexts. While the labor movement and its allies combat the causes of density loss in public policy, political, international, and legal arenas, unions must build density within current constraints. BTG—because it bypasses employer-biased labor laws and integrates organizing and bargaining activities in a long-range strategic plan—shows promise as an approach toward achieving this very difficult goal.

Notes

[1] Statement of Senator Carl Levin before the Committee on Finance hearing on corporate governance and executive compensation, April 18, 2002.

[2] The pressure to export jobs is expanding to more industries, and the opportunities to export jobs are also expanding. For example, the global s infrastructure allows call center jobs to be exported to low-wage, English-speaking countries where workers who identify themselves with American names answer consumer questions for less than one-third the wage rate paid to U.S. workers (Iritani 2002). Even high-end computer programming and engineering jobs are being shipped overseas (Gertzen 2002).

[3] The National Association of Manufacturers (NAM), no friend of unions, supports lowering the value of the dollar. Jerry Jasinowski, NAM president, recently testified before Congress that "[The high dollar] is decimating U.S. manufactured-goods exports, artificially stimulating imports and putting hundreds of thousands of American workers out of work" (Phillips 2002).

[4] If the union cannot obtain agreement to card check, an alternative is an expedited non-NLRA election, subject to the same final and binding arbitration provisions that govern card check disputes.

[5] Comprehensive campaigns take on special importance in first contract campaigns (Hickey 2002:71–91).

References

Belzer, Michael H. 2002. "Trucking: Collective Bargaining Takes a Rocky Road." In Paul F. Clark, John T. Delaney, and Ann C. Frost, eds., *Collective Bargaining in the Private Sector*. Champaign, IL: Industrial Relations Research Association, pp. 311–342.

Bernstein, Aaron. 1999. "Welch's March to the South." *Business Week*, December 6, p. 74.

Bronfenbrenner, Kate. 2002. "Uneasy Terrain: The Impact of Capital Mobility on Workers, Wages, and Union Organizing." U.S. Trade Deficit Review Commission, September 6. <http://www.ilr.cornell.edu/extension/files/finaldraftreport0908.doc>

Brooks v. NLRB. 1954. 348 U.S. 96.

CNN *Moneyline*. 1998. December 8, 1998.

Communications Workers of America. 1997. "CWA at Southwestern Bell: Five Years to Card Check." Washington, DC. Training Materials. July.

Excelsior Underwear, Inc. 1996. 156 NLRB 1236, 61 LRRM 1217.

Gertzen, Jason. 2002. "Samyog Teams with Programmers in India." *Milwaukee Journal Sentinel*, March 3, p.   .

Hickey, Rob. 2002. "Strategic Contract Campaigns at Multinational Corporations." *Labor Studies Journal*, Vol. 27, no. 1 (Spring), pp. 71–91.

Hirsch, Barry T., and David A. Macpherson. 1984. *Union Membership and Earnings Data Book 1984*. Washington, DC: Bureau of National Affairs.

_____. 2002. *Union Membership and Earnings Data Book 2002*. Washington, DC: Bureau of National Affairs.

Human Rights Watch. 2000. *Unfair Advantage: Workers' Freedom of Association in the United States Under International Human Rights Standards*. Washington, DC: Human Rights Watch.

International Labor Organization. 2002. Global Report Highlights. *ILO News*.

Iritani, Evelyn. 2002. "High Paid Jobs Latest U.S. Export." *Los Angeles Times*, April 2, p. A1.

Katz, Harry C., John Paul MacDuffie, and Frits K. Pil. 2002. "Autos: Continuity and Change in Collective Bargaining." In Paul F. Clark, John T. Delaney, and Ann C. Frost, eds., *Collective Bargaining in the Private Sector*. Champaign, IL: Industrial Relations Research Association, pp. 55-90.

NLRB v. Paper Manufacturers Co. 1986. 786 F. 2d 163 (CA 3).

Phillips, Michael M. 2002. "Industry Execs Seek Relief; Senate Hearing Turns Combative." *The Wall Street Journal*, May 2, online edition.

Stanger, Howard R. 2002 "Newspapers: Collective Bargaining Decline Amidst Technological Change." In Paul F. Clark, John T. Delaney, and Ann C. Frost, eds., *Collective Bargaining in the Private Sector*. Champaign, IL: Industrial Relations Research Association, pp. 179–215.

United Steelworkers of America. 1998. Statement of the International Wage Policy Committee, June 16.

CHAPTER 10

Practitioner Commentary

PETER WARRIAN

University of Toronto

Introduction

The outlook for the future of collective bargaining has been likened to a game of snakes and ladders. The snakes are the downsides of globalization and the New Economy. The ladders are areas of opportunity for trade union organizing, new bargaining strategies, and political coalitions (Crouch 2000).

This paper examines the issues emerging from this changing landscape of contemporary collective bargaining and draws on my experiences in the steel industry to shed light on some potential future paths. In section one, there is a brief personal reflection on my experiences in the steel industry and the evolution of bargaining in that industry. Section two looks to the future and suggests a perspective on changing dynamics in collective bargaining from the perspective of negotiations theory. Section three reviews research on some of the key drivers of union bargaining agendas: the changing social values of union members and activists and how they will likely affect bargaining strategies in the future. Section four makes some suggestions about future directions in collective bargaining and the context of negotiations in the steel industry.

A Biographical Perspective on Steel Bargaining

Twenty-five years ago I joined the research department in the Canadian National Office of the United Steelworkers of America. In the mid-1970s, the union was still engaged in the last great days of distributional battles over wages, COLAs, and pensions. This was adversarial bargaining as good as it got, though a sea change was already on the horizon with the introduction of the Experimental Negotiating Agreement (ENA) in the U.S. industry and the rising challenge of Japanese steel imports. The ENA included a no-strike provision for extended periods and for the first time included language that we would later recognize as an industry partnership.

In the 1980s, the global crisis of overcapacity, among other things, hit the steel industry, cutting the union's membership almost in half. Faced with an unprecedented challenge, the United Steelworkers of America (USWA) in Canada, under the leadership of Gerard Docquier, initiated a dialogue with the industry that led to an entirely new labor–management organization, the Canadian Steel Trade and Employment Congress (CSTEC). I was involved with the setting up of CSTEC and later served as its executive director.

The somewhat awkward name of the organization accurately reflected the nature of this union–management coalition. The steel companies' core issue was the steel trade issue, particularly the need for action on surging imports and the challenges posed to Canadian steel makers by restrictions under President Reagan's steel import control program. The Canadian steel companies, though longtime members of the American Iron and Steel Institute (AISI), had been abandoned by their erstwhile colleagues in favor of American exclusionism. Therefore, the Canadian companies needed the assistance of the Canadian section of the USWA in lobbying for relief with the U.S. Congress and with the USWA in Pittsburgh.

The union's core issue was the provision of services and subsidies for the thousands of laid-off steelworkers, who needed massive retraining and job search assistance. Eventually some 14,000 steelworkers were successfully retrained and re-employed at equal or higher wages through the CSTEC program. Because of differences in political culture and a different attitude in American management, the same sort of industrywide, labor–management–government innovation could not be negotiated in the United States.

However, the steelworkers in the United States, under the leadership of then-president Canadian Lynn Williams, embarked on an innovative bargaining program to deal with the crisis on a company-by-company basis. The union made wage concessions but changed the matrix of managerial control through stock ownership and the establishment of joint committees at the plant and departmental levels to deal with technological change, contracting out, training, and work processes. Necessity is said to be the mother of invention, and the USWA was faced with a compelling crisis that drove its efforts. Nevertheless, the content of the new bargaining program was truly remarkable. It is true to say that the union in Canada was not able to achieve the same sort of qualitatively different collective bargaining outcomes. However, by the end of the 1980s, the union in Canada did produce a dramatically different policy direction in its Empowering Workers document, to which I made some contribution. The policy articulated a strategy for strategic negotiation of labor–management power sharing at the plant level, union input to investment and technology decisions, as well as the formulation of a joint industry–union agenda for government policy.

In the 1990s I served as chief economist of the social democratic New Democratic Party government of the Province of Ontario. Among the issues we had to deal with was the bankruptcy and eventual bailout of Algoma Steel, the number three steel producer in Canada. It was a seismic event for the union and the community of Sault Ste. Marie, Ontario, a very large, virtually single-industry town. A turnaround was made with Algoma, with the union members buying a majority of the shares of the company, introducing new joint management to the board of directors and onto the shop-floor levels. Many of the innovations the USWA had made in the United States in terms of union involvement in firm governance were introduced into the Algoma contract and put into practice in the mill. However, the turnaround could not and would not have happened without the financial and regulatory backstop of a social democratic government that was willing to underwrite the restructured company's debt and encourage the full set of labor–management innovations.

Meanwhile in the United States, the Steelworkers were continuing to innovate in the bargaining arena. The union, under President George Becker, continued to improve bargaining, based on the precedents of the Williams administration, on a range of issues that would have been literally inconceivable when I first started working in the research department. This included negotiating the ratios of productive (shop-floor) to nonproductive (office) labor, USWA bids for work being contracted out, investment programs, new equipment purchases, and so on. A consistent theme, in my experience, has been that the union negotiates more successfully at the macroeconomic level in Canada and more successfully at the microeconomic level in the United States.

The year 2002 still has me working on and in the steel industry (some people never learn!). The subject of my current academic research is on innovation in the steel industry. How do steel companies learn? The union's private view is that they never do. However, the technical literature on innovation systems proposes that a key factor in sustainable economic success is local clusters of technology, institutions, skills, and social networks. The modern steel industry is part of a social network, not an island unto itself. This raises the intriguing issue of the union as learning agent, a far cry from the norm of "Obey now, grieve later" that was adhered to when I came into the industry twenty-five years ago. At the same time, Algoma Steel is back into bankruptcy again.

We also have the phenomenon in 2002 of the new U.S. steel trade cases announced by President Bush. This is full of ironies. The USWA has emerged in this context, at least, as a surprisingly successful player at the macroeconomic level, a direct player in steel trade policy of an unprecedented kind. This has been accomplished under the leadership of another innovative Canadian leader, the current international president of the USWA, Leo Gerard. At the same time, one of the underlying objectives of the trade cases is to facilitate a consolidation in the industry. The banks have said that they will not finance the restructuring of the industry unless the industry is able to off-load its legacy of health and pension costs, which run into the billions of dollars. Ironically these are exactly the same benefits that were at the forefront of the bargaining agenda when I came into the union in the 1970s. All of this leads to the conclusion that union bargaining has had to make quite a stretch in configuring to the dynamics of the New Economy.

Bargaining Strategies and Negotiations Theory in the New Economy

To understand the impact of the New Economy on unions, it is best to think of the economy in terms of a two-sector model: the traded sector (manufacturing and resources and traded services, for example, the steel and auto industries) and the nontraded sector (public-sector and private-sector services and small business, for example, the health care and newspaper industries).

The Old Economy/New Economy divide is rooted in the impact that information technology (IT) has had on the structure of the economy (sectors, new enterprises, new occupations) and the accompanying new human resource management practices usually associated with technological innovation. Traditional low-skill, manual occupations that were very much the heart of industrial trade unionism in the mass production industries have witnessed the heaviest losses in union membership. The surviving steelworkers in the new steel industry are highly skilled—half the shop-floor workers at the newest mills have a college education—high wage earners. They also expect, and in fact receive, regular production planning and consultation meetings with management, a far cry from the old command-and-control norm in the mills.

Though not limited to the traded sector, the Old Economy/New Economy divide is most evident in that sector. Meanwhile, life in the nontraded sector goes on much as it did before the radical transformations brought about by information technology. Where change has occurred, it has been driven by market-oriented policies such as deregulation or privatization, not by the accelerated adoption of IT or new models of human resource management. These distinctions have direct relevance for trade union organizing and representation. As suggested below, the tension between the Canadian Auto Workers (CAW) and the USWA, though not confined to them, is largely about the relative value of new versus old bargaining strategies in the traded sector. On the other hand, public-sector unionists of the nontraded sector are well over half the membership of the Canadian Labor Congress (CLC). Unionists there are grappling with a different set of issues concerning the new market dynamics in the nontraded sector.

The Old Economy/New Economy divide hides a more important division in the labor market—that between good jobs and lousy jobs. Lousy jobs were always a feature of the Old Economy. They are also a feature of some sectors of the New Economy, such as call centers. To grind an old axe, a strategic problem for the labor movement and its bargaining strategy continues to be that the Wagner Act model is predicated on large, static workplaces. Those outside the scope of this model get left out, whether they are in the Old Economy or the New Economy. The real schizophrenia in the labor movement is not about the political ideology of the autoworkers versus the steelworkers union. It is that rhetorically the movement as a whole wishes to think of itself as organizing and representing the low paid, when the reality of our labor relations model is that trade unions are effectively confined to representing those who are moderately well paid and more or less securely employed.

The Wagner Act model of union representation will have to be fundamentally rethought if it is to be relevant to a broad spectrum of the workforce and firms of the New Economy. Otherwise, trade unions doing the same old, same old will become marginalized and represent permanently declining memberships.

At root, unions are what they bargain. Workplace-based union bargaining strategies in the New Economy can be placed into a two-by-two matrix of old and new unionism in the Old Economy and the New Economy (see Chart 1). Taking from the literature on strategic negotiations, the content of the matrix can be filled out by the key terms: distributive versus integrative bargaining and compliance versus commitment relationships (Walton, Cutcher-Gershenfeld, and McKersie 2001).

Distributive bargaining has the function of resolving pure conflicts of interest. It serves to allocate fixed sums of resources ("dividing the pie") and hence often has a win–lose quality. It is usually associated with a forcing strategy in negotiations. In contrast, integrative bargaining has the function of finding common or complementary interests and solving problems confronting both partners. It serves to optimize the potential for joint gains ("expanding the pie") and hence often has a win–win quality. It is usually associated with a fostering strategy in negotiations.

Under mutual compliance, the parties merely agree to comply with certain set terms of employment ("armed truce"). It is an employment relationship captured by the classic phrase "It ain't my job, Jack." In contrast, under mutual commitment, employees become more broadly committed to the enterprise, and management becomes more broadly committed to the well-being of employees ("mutual gains").

CHART 1
Bargaining Strategies in the Old and New Economy

Old unionism/Old economy	Old unionism/New economy
Solidarity Forever Everyone knows what to do	CAW Buzzing Along
Distributive bargaining Compliance relationships	Distributive bargaining Commitment and cooperation relationships
New unionism/Old economy	**New unionism/New economy**
USWA: Dancing with Leo	Members.net: Members service themselves
Relationship bargaining Compliance relationships	Relationship bargaining Commitment and cooperation relationships

Old/Old: Solidarity Forever

Under the Old Unionism–Old Economy regime, everyone knew what to do, and this was generally to take it out on the other guy. Bargaining was inherently a distributive, zero-sum game: what is won by me is lost by the other party, and what is won by the other party is lost by me.

Workers were expected to park their brains at the gate and follow the strict dictates of management. The labor law norm of "Obey now, grieve later" became "Work now, think later." Each side of the bargaining table knew the other's speech.

Old/New: CAW Buzzing Along

Applying the old paradigm to the New Economy has best been symbolized by the position of Buzz Hargrove, president of the Canadian Autoworkers, and the CAW's mantra of "No Surrender." Straight-up distributive bargaining has been pursued while keeping clear lines demarcated between the union and management. Meanwhile we see car commercials on television extolling the virtues of employee engagement in the workplace. In the real world, local labor–management relations and flexibility agreements outside of the Master Agreements in Auto are in fact more nuanced and pragmatic than the national union's rhetoric. However, the official line from CAW headquarters has real importance in the politics of bargaining and public perceptions of the negotiations process. In fact, for its core bargaining units in the assembly plants, at least, the CAW has been delivering the goods on their agenda throughout the 1990s. In the next five years this bargaining philosophy will probably continue to deliver in visible ways on its agenda. Therefore, the CAW position will tend to become the fallback position for most trade union members faced with diminishing returns in the globalized economy.

New/Old: USWA—Dancing with Leo

The third, more future-oriented, bargaining policy is summarized in the Empowering Workers agenda of the Steelworkers under the leadership of Leo Gerard. This strategy is not limited to the USWA; it has its parallel in the Communications, Energy, and Paperworkers Union (CEP), the Power Workers Union (PWU) and the United Food and Commercial Workers (UFCW), among others. It seeks more than anything to negotiate a new set of relationships in the workplace not only at the official union–management level but also at the shop floor in retraining and work reorganization and at the industry level in sector councils such as CSTEC. The basic problems facing this strategy are the shortage of consistent dancing partners on the management side and finding specific deliverables for the members. The returns from the Empowering Workers agenda to individual steelworkers have been less evident than the evident gains for autoworkers from the CAW's more traditional strategy. The spectacular success at Algoma Steel was, among other things, only possible through the agency of a sitting New Democratic Party government. The challenge for the Empowering Workers agenda is that if it doesn't show more results for the members in the coming five years, then worker preferences will tilt toward the CAW position.

New/New: Members.net

Bargaining strategy for a new unionism in the New Economy quadrant will be characterized by integrative bargaining and commitment-based employment relationships. For unions this means that the members will largely service and represent themselves. The challenge to the union leadership will be to manage and enhance the network. There will be bargaining, but it will be relationship based. The key leverage will be the union's capacity to orchestrate the commitment and skills of its members in the workplace.

Dilemma: Can't Get There from Here

The key dilemma for a union workplace strategy for the New Economy is that you can't get there from here—you can't just leapfrog from the upper-left quadrant to the lower-right quadrant. The literature on strategic negotiations is quite clear and sobering. It actually takes a combination of forcing and fostering tactics to get to the New/New quadrant. In the typical case, parties have only found the means to move to a different relationship after a bitter strike and the realization that they had to find a better way to do business together. An example would be the bitter strike at Inco in 1979–80, followed by a remarkable turnaround in union–management attitudes. But, at the same time, both the Old/New and New/Old cells of the matrix are inherently unstable. The first is vulnerable to disinvestment, such as is currently happening to the CAW in auto assembly plants in Ontario. The second is vulnerable to membership revolt, such as the recent rollbacks to the innovative labor contract at the Saturn plant in Tennessee.

Does Individualization in Members Pose a Bigger Threat to Unions Than Globalization?

Trade unionists' concerns that trade liberalization not lead to a race to the bottom in social, environmental, and living standards are not misplaced. Rapid, dramatic shifts in trade patterns and the business environment can overwhelm the most enlightened efforts of union and management negotiators. Post–Seattle, these issues have been placed on the trade policy agenda. The problem in the future is going to be exactly how to implement them. For instance, there is already a draft agreement on trade and labor standards. Discussions on linking the International Labor Organization (ILO) to the World Trade Organization (WTO) are well advanced. But, by contrast, there is no international organization for environmental issues.

Labor groups spent the last decade condemning the Free Trade Agreement (FTA), the North American Free Trade Agreement (NAFTA), and the WTO. They are going to spend the next ten years falling in love with them. The much-abused dispute mechanism in the WTO, for example, is going to become a meaningful enforcement mechanism for labor rights–labor standards and collective bargaining rights that will exceed anything that traditional labor relations tribunals could offer in the way of enforcement powers.

The most troubling and problematic issue about globalization for trade unionists and social democrats is that enthusiasts of globalization have overloaded the trade regime. Trade unionists and social democrats have a vital interest in supporting a sensible international trade regime. The problem is that, instead of dealing with the "border issues" of tariff and non-tariff barriers, as in the General Agreement on Tariffs and Trade, the ideologues of the "Washington Consensus" are seeking to apply the trading regime to a completely different and inappropriate domain—the boundaries between the public and private sector. The trading regime is about boundaries and rules among trading nations, not about the boundaries and rules for our public space. Trade unionists and social democrats have an important role to play in the next decade in rebalancing that system.

Notwithstanding the concerns about globalization, as symbolized by the WTO, the greater challenge the trade union movement will face in the coming years is not the external threat, nor will it be the domestic ideology of privatization and contracting out. The greatest challenge will be the processes of individuation/individualization in everyday life among union members. How well they deal with these issues will be the test for unions bridging to represent members in the New Economy.

For this reason, it is important to understand that Tony Blair and the Third Way are not simply about ideological shifts to the Right (Giddens 2000). Whatever the merits and demerits of the specifics of the Third Way political program, it in fact springs from a profound reflection on the changing nature of the working class experience and what is referred to in the academic literature as the "politics of risk society" (Franklin 1998).

What does this have to do with trade unionism? Actually, a lot. Postwar trade unionism and the Keynesian welfare state were a system for the social management of economic risk. In the New Economy and with social marketing in the Internet era, where n = 1, social solidarity will become a voluntary act, not a categorical imperative. Unions will have to persuade their members, not "speak" for them. The task of the union will be to assist the members in representing and servicing themselves.

Changing Social Values of Local Union Leaders

Pivotal to understanding unions, now and in the past, is understanding what is going on with local union leaders, shop stewards, and activists. This is critical not only for understanding the changing sociology and politics of unions, but also as a factor in how innovation will happen in the economy. Labor market institutions, industrial relations, and work organization are all understood as crucial factors in the innovation systems of the New Economy. The last two decades in North America have seen a marked decline in the role of national bargaining structures, for instance, in the steel industry. For this reason, growing weight has been given to the role of local union leadership and workplace relations at the local level.

Recent studies of European trade unionists emphasize that the role of trade unions in modern society is challenged partly by external factors but primarily by changes from within the organizations themselves. It has been found that the processes of individualization and an increasing differentiation of the workforce undermine unions' traditional forms of interest representation because different groups and generations express differing relationships to the union movement. Data for blue collar workers indicate that the older generation shares the ideology and mission of its unions, while the younger generation expresses more instrumental union attitudes (Alvin and Sverke 2000).

Theorists such as Beck (1992) and Giddens (2000), who provide the theoretical underpinnings for the Third Way for Blair and Schroeder, suggest that the collective frames of reference that once served as the basis of individual identity and the foundation of working class solidarity are losing significance and are gradually being replaced by multitudes of different sources of identification—a belief in the efficacy of the self, more autonomous attitudes toward institutions, and a declining preparedness to participate in collective movements.

The following data have been gathered on psychographic profiles of local union leaders across Canada. The trends in Canadian social values, as measured by the fifteen-year annual Environics 3SC survey of 2,700 households, indicate a consistent movement away from outward-directed and traditional values and toward more individualistic, self-satisfaction indices, as measured by a set of eighty-four variables.[1] As Chart 2 shows, there has been a movement from the upper-left quadrant of the 3SC "map" toward the bottom-right quadrant.

CHART 2

Psychographic Profiles of Local Union Leaders

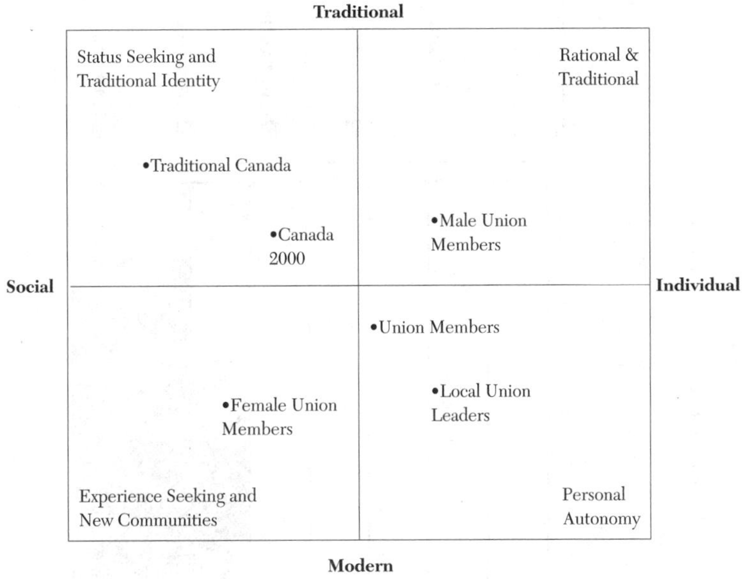

Traditional

Status Seeking and Traditional Identity	Rational & Traditional

• Traditional Canada

• Canada 2000   • Male Union Members

Social ——————————————— **Individual**

• Union Members

• Female Union Members   • Local Union Leaders

Experience Seeking and New Communities	Personal Autonomy

Modern

A special survey was conducted to analyze the trends among local union leaders and compare them with trends in the Canadian population, as a whole. The local union leadership survey indicates that not only have union leaders and members followed this trend, but by the latest data, they are well out in front of it (Figure 1). For instance, in regard to distrust of authority, while the general Canadian population has an index rating of 100, local union leaders have a distrust index of 340! Similarly for a set of other key indices—priority of personal happiness over duty, need for autonomy, connectivity, and adaptive navigation—local union leaders rate considerably higher than the average Canadian. The data indicate a major shift away from the set of social values that inspired the original union song "Solidarity Forever."

FIGURE 1
Social Values of Local Union Leaders

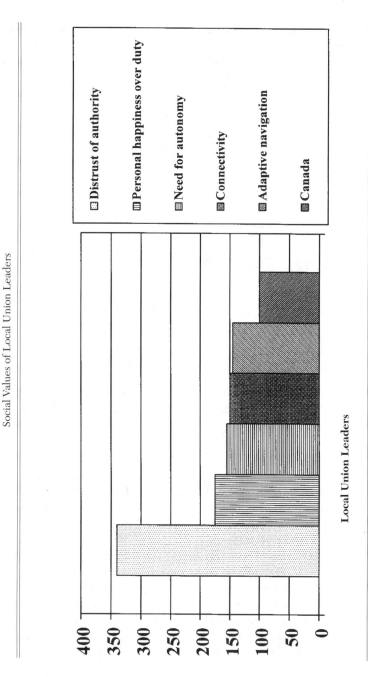

The survey also pursued a number of workplace, human resource, and union policy issues. These also produced a set of problematic messages for unions. There are indications that union leaders' trust of management is conditional and selective. There are definite issues concerning directions for workplace restructuring and employment relations preferences. The local leadership also views the national and international levels of the union as not being particularly effective, while areas within local jurisdiction are valued more highly. Does this mean the end of the union song? No. It indicates that change efforts by the union will have to be very focused and build on the motivations of the local union leadership. The union will have to prove itself in regard to local site relevance, it will have to achieve direct and immediate workplace gains for members, and it will have to be radically decentralized.

Future Challenges and Context

The USWA today speaks as a voice on behalf of 1.2 million steelworkers, the same number as when I first joined the union. The difference is that the actual number of active steelworkers is half that total; the others are former, mostly retired members. In the past, the union acted as an island unto itself, dominated by the dynamics of large steel mill locals with 10,000 to 20,000 members each. It is now an organization composed of small local organizations. It consciously and rightly positions itself as a "partner" in the future of the steel industry and has become an astute practitioner of coalition politics.

In conclusion, we come back to the challenge of snakes and ladders. The snakes (downside) are pretty obvious: the decline of manufacturing and public-sector employment, abandonment of Keynesian demand management, and the rise of nonstandard jobs and part-time employment, all of which are related directly and indirectly to globalization and the New Economy.

The ladders, or upside opportunities, for labor get less attention. They exist but they require significant strategic shifts on the part of unions, trade union leaders, and social democratic parties. I shall mention only two of the upside opportunities.

First, the trade union movement, particularly but not exclusively in the public sector, has the opportunity to play a major part as a direct player in the restructuring and reinvigoration of health care. It has a little-acknowledged but as important role to play in health care in Canada as the German trade union movement has and does play in the German pension and income maintenance system. To play that role, however, will require public-sector unions debating and endorsing a social partnership role and changing their traditional bargaining and workplace strategies. Public-sector Wagnerism is over.

Second, the trade union movement, particularly in the private sector, will have to engage in issues of part-time employment and nonstandard jobs in Canada the way the Dutch trade union movement has done in the Netherlands. This will have to include constructive engagement in labor market regulatory change that is different from the one-size-fits-all prescriptions of the past.

Finally, the measure of success for trade unions and social democratic parties is the improvement of living standards over time. This is the fundamental negotiating challenge. The appropriate metric is not the applause meter for the latest passing parade of demonstrators. Improving living standards in the New Economy is a profoundly difficult and complicated challenge. Unions have not backed off from that challenge in the past . . . neither should they now.

Note

[1] For details on the methodology, see http://3sc.environics.net.

References

Alvin, M., and M. Sverke. 2000. "Do New Generations Imply the End of Solidarity? Swedish Unionism in the Era of Individualization." *Economic and Industrial Democracy*, Vol. 21, pp. 71–95.

Beck, Ulrich. 1992. *Risk Society: Towards a New Modernity*. Thousand Oaks, CA: Sage.

Crouch, Colin. 2000. "The Snakes and Ladders of Twenty-First Century Unionism." *Oxford Review of Economic Policy*, Vol. 16, no. 1, pp. 70–83.

Franklin, Jane. 1998. *The Politics of Risk Society*. Oxford: Blackwell.

Giddens, Anthony. 2000. *The Third Way and Its Critics*. Oxford: Blackwell.

Walton, Richard E., Joel Cutcher-Gershenfeld, and Robert B. McKersie. 2001. *Strategic Negotiations*. Ithaca, NY: ILR Press.

ABOUT THE CONTRIBUTORS

Richard Bank is director of the AFL-CIO's Center for Collective Bargaining. He has served as special counsel to the president of the Teamsters and as executive assistant to the president of the United Mine Workers. He received his law degree from the University of Pennsylvania.

Rosemary Batt is associate professor of human resource studies at the New York State School of Industrial and Labor Relations, Cornell University. She received her Ph.D. from the Sloan School of Management, Massachusetts Institute of Technology. Her research interests include service sector productivity and competitiveness, strategic human resource management, work design and technology use, and white collar careers. She has also authored or coauthored numerous scholarly publications on the telecommunications and information services industry. She is coauthor of *The New American Workplace: Transforming Work Systems in the United States*, Cornell University Press.

Michael H. Belzer is associate professor of industrial relations at Wayne State University and co-associate director of the Sloan Foundation's Trucking Industry Program. He received his Ph.D. from the New York State School of Industrial and Labor Relations, Cornell University. Belzer has written widely on industrial relations in the trucking industry and is the author of *Sweatshops on Wheels: Winners and Losers in Trucking Deregulation*.

Paul F. Clark is professor of labor studies and industrial relations at Pennsylvania State University. He received his M.S. from the New York State School of Industrial and Labor Relations, Cornell University and his Ph.D. from the University of Pittsburgh. Much of his research has focused on union structure, government, and administration and on collective bargaining in the coal and steel industries. Over the past few years, his work has increasingly focused on labor–management relations in health care. He is the author of *Building More Effective Unions*, published by Cornell ILR Press in 2001.

John T. Delaney is professor and associate dean for M.B.A. programs at the Broad College of Business, Michigan State University. He holds master's and Ph.D degrees from the Institute of Labor and Industrial Relations at the University of Illinois and has published widely on a number of industrial relations topics, including workplace cooperation, union effectiveness and innovation, and labor and politics.

James B. Dworkin has served as professor and associate dean at the Krannert School of Management, Purdue University. He is currently chancellor of Purdue's North Central Campus. He received his M.A. from the University of Cincinnati and his Ph.D. from the University of Minnesota. Dworkin's book, *Owners Versus Players: Baseball and Collective Bargaining*, was one of the earliest scholarly efforts to look at collective bargaining in professional sports. In addition to professional sports, Dworkin's research has focused on representation and decertification elections and the transformation of industrial relations.

Vincent H. Eade is the Claudine Williams Distinguished Professor and assistant dean at the Harrah College of Hotel Administration, University of Nevada, Las Vegas. He has held numerous executive management positions in the gaming and hospitality industry and has authored, coauthored, and contributed chapters to three books on the subject.

Ann C. Frost is assistant professor of organizational behaviour and dean's faculty fellow at the Richard Ivey School of Business, University of Western Ontario. She received an M.Sc. from the University of British Columbia and a Ph.D in industrial relations from the Massachusetts Institute of Technology. Her research and publications have focused on the role of local unions in workplace restructuring, restructuring in the steel and health care industries, and changes in low-wage work and careers.

Nancy Brown Johnson is associate professor of management at the Carol Martin Gatton College of Business and Economics, University of Kentucky. She received her M.B.A. and Ph.D. from the University of Kansas. Her research on the airline industry has appeared in numerous scholarly publications.

Harry C. Katz is Sheinkman Professor of collective bargaining at the New York State School of Industrial and Labor Relations, Cornell University. He received his Ph.D. from the University of California at Berkeley and previously taught at the Massachusetts Institute of Technology. Katz is a highly respected and widely published scholar whose interests include the transformation of American industrial relations, high-performance work systems, worker participation, worker training, and work restructuring. Much of his work has focused on the auto and telecommunications industries.

Jeffrey Keefe is associate professor of labor and employment relations at the School of Management and Labor Relations, Rutgers University. He received his M.A. from the New School for Social Research and his Ph.D. from the New York State School of Industrial and Labor Relations, Cornell University. He has published extensively on the restructuring of the telecommunications and information services industry.

John Paul MacDuffie is associate professor of management, Wharton School, University of Pennsylvania. He received his Ph.D. from the Massachusetts Institute of Technology (MIT). MacDuffie has focused much of his research on change in the worldwide auto industry and is currently codirector of MIT's International Motor Vehicle Program.

Frits K. Pil is an assistant professor at the Katz School of Business, University of Pittsburgh. He received his master's and Ph.D. from the Wharton School, University of Pennsylvania. In conjunction with the International Motor Vehicle Program, he has undertaken extensive survey research of automobile assembly plants around the world. His research has resulted in a series of academic publications, and he has been cited widely by the business press, including *Automotive News*, *Business Week*, *Fortune*, and *The Wall Street Journal*.

Richard A. Posthuma earned his master's degree in labor and industrial relations from Michigan State University in 1977; his J.D., cum laude, from the Thomas M. Cooley Law School in 1992; and his Ph.D. in organizational behavior and human resource management from Purdue University in 1999. He has published several articles on labor relations issues in top journals, including *Industrial Relations and Personnel Psychology*. He teaches and conducts research related to negotiations and employee selection in cross-cultural, cross-border, and international settings at the University of Texas, El Paso.

Howard R. Stanger is associate professor of management/marketing at Canisius College. He received his M.A. in labor studies from Rutgers University and his Ph.D. in labor and human resources from The Ohio State University. His research has focused on industrial relations in the newspaper industry, from both a historical and contemporary perspective.

C. Jeffrey Waddoups is an associate professor of economics at the University of Nevada, Las Vegas. He received his Ph.D. in economics from the University of Utah. His latest research has explored the role of labor unions in regional economies that contain high proportions of service sector and, more specifically, hotel/casino employment. His publications on this issue have appeared in several scholarly journals.

Peter Warrian is senior research fellow at the Centre for Industrial Relations at the University of Toronto. He received his Ph.D. from the University of Waterloo and has served as the assistant deputy minister of finance and chief economist for the Province of Ontario and as executive director of the Canadian Steel Trade and Employment Congress.

IRRA Organizational Memberships

The IRRA provides a unique forum where representatives of all stakeholders in the employment relationship and their views are welcome.

We invite your organization to become a member of our prestigious, vibrant association. The Industrial Relations Research Association (IRRA) is the professional membership association and learned society of persons interested in the field of industrial relations. Formed more than fifty years ago, the IRRA brings together representatives of labor, management, government, academics, advocates, and neutrals to share ideas and learn about new developments, issues, and practices in the field. Members share their knowledge and insights through IRRA publications, meetings, and IRRA listservs. In addition, the IRRA provides a network of 60-plus chapters where professionals meet locally to discuss issues and share information.

The purpose of the IRRA is to encourage research and to foster discussion of issues affecting today's workplace and workers. To that end, the IRRA publishes an array of information, including research papers and commentary presented at Association meetings; the acclaimed practitioner-oriented magazine, *Perspectives on Work*; a printed membership directory; quarterly newsletters; and an annual research volume. Recent research volumes include *Collective Bargaining in the Private Sector*, Paul F. Clark, John T. Delaney, and Ann C. Frost, editors; *The Future of the Safety Net: Social Insurance and Employee Benefits*, Sheldon Friedman and David Jacobs, editors; *Nonstandard Work: The Nature and Challenges of Changing Employment Arrangements*, Françoise Carré, Marianne A. Ferber, Lonnie Golden, and Stephen A Herzenberg, editors; and *Employment Dispute Resolution and Worker Rights*, Adrienne E. Eaton and Jeffrey Keefe, editors. Other member publications and services include online IR/HR degree programs listings, an online member directory, job announcements, calls and announcements, competitions and awards for students and practicing professionals, and much more.

IRRA is a non-profit, 501(c)(3) organization governed by an elected Executive Board comprised of representatives of the various constituencies within the Association.

Organizational memberships are available on an annual or sustaining basis and include individual memberships for organization designees, a wealth of IRRA research and information, and numerous professional opportunities. Organizational members receive all IRRA publications and services. Your support and participation will help the Association continue its vital mission of shaping the workplace of the future. For more information, contact the IRRA National Office, 504 East Armory Ave, Room 121, Champaign, IL 61820, www.irra.uiuc.edu.

Sustaining Members
One-time contribution of $5,000 to $10,000

AFL-CIO
The Alliance for Growth and Development
Boeing Quality Through Training Program
Ford Motor Company
General Electric
National Association of Manufacturers
National Education Association
UAW-Ford National Education, Training and Development Center
United Steelworkers of America

Annual Organizational Members 2002*

Albert Shanker Institute
American Federation of Teachers
Bechtel Nevada Corporation
Chapman University
Communication Workers of America
Cornell University-School of Industrial and Labor Relations
Georgia State University, Beebe Institute
Las Vegas Metropolitan Police Department
Massachusetts Institute of Technology-Sloan School of Management
Michigan State University - School of Labor & Industrial Relations
New York Nurses Association
Rutgers University-School of Management and Labor Relations
Society for Human Resource Management
St. Joseph's-Erivan K. Haub School of Business
University of Illinois at Urbana-Champaign-Institute of Labor & Industrial Relations
University of Michigan-Institute of Labor and Industrial Relations
University of Minnesota-Twin Cities, Industrial Relations Center
University of Notre Dame-Higgins Labor Research Center

Annual organizational memberships are available at the following levels:
Benefactor, *$5,000 or more*   *6 employee members*
Supporter, *$1,000 to $4,999*   *6 employee members*
Annual or Major University, *$500*   *2 employee members*
Educational or Non-Profit, *$250*   *2 employee members*